Torts II
Workbook

A Behavioral Approach to Learning

Nelson P. Miller

Torts II Workbook–

A Behavioral Approach to Learning

Nelson P. Miller

Publisher:
Crown Management LLC – June 2018
1527 Pineridge Drive
Grand Haven, MI 49417
USA

ISBN-13: 978-1-7322387-3-2

All Rights Reserved
© 2018 Nelson P. Miller
c/o 111 Commerce Avenue S.W.
Grand Rapids, MI 49503
(616) 560-0632

Table of Contents

Introduction   1

Whole-Course Outlines   3
    Bullet-Point Outline. Paragraph-Format Outline.

Week 1:   **Negligence Defenses (continued)**   20
    Bullet Outline. Paragraph Outline. Fluency Cards. Definitions Worksheet. Issue-Spotting Worksheet. Comprehensiveness Worksheet. Discrimination Exercise. Problem-Solving Exercise. Drafting Exercise.

Week 2:   **Products Liability**   36
    Bullet Outline. Paragraph Outline. Fluency Cards. Definitions Worksheet. Issue-Spotting Worksheet. Comprehensiveness Worksheet. Framework Exercise. Examples/Non-Examples Exercise. Problem-Solving Exercise. Drafing Exercise. Review Exercise.

Week 3:   **Products Liability (continued)**   56
    Bullet Outline. Paragraph Outline. Fluency Cards. Definitions Worksheet. Issue-Spotting Worksheet. Comprehensiveness Worksheet. Factors-Practice Exercise. Sameness Exercise. Attributes-Analysis Worksheet. Problem-Solving Exercise. Review Exercise.

Week 4:   **Strict Liability**   71
    Bullet Outline. Paragraph Outline. Fluency Cards. Definitions Worksheet. Issue-Spotting Worksheet. Comprehensiveness Worksheet. Factors-Practice Exercise. Sameness Exercise. Drafting Exercise.

Week 5:   **Misrepresentation**   83
    Bullet Outline. Paragraph Outline. Fluency Cards. Definitions Worksheet. Issue-Spotting Worksheet. Comprehensiveness Worksheet. Scenario-Generating Worksheet. Drafting Exercise. Review Exercise. Problem-Solving Exercise.

Week 6:   **Defamation (Common Law)**   98
    Bullet Outline. Paragraph Outline. Fluency Cards. Definitions Worksheet. Issue-Spotting Worksheet. Comprehensiveness Worksheet. Scenario-Generating Worksheet. Sameness Exercise. Drafting Exercise. Review Exercise. Problem-Solving Exercise.

Week 7: **Defamation (Constitutional Protection & Privileges)**   **116**
Bullet Outline. Paragraph Outline. Fluency Cards. Definitions Worksheet. Issue-Spotting Worksheet. Comprehensiveness Worksheet. Sameness Exercise. Scenario-Generating Worksheet.

Week 8: **Invasion of Privacy**   **129**
Bullet Outline. Paragraph Outline. Fluency Cards. Definitions Worksheet. Issue-Spotting Worksheet. Comprehensiveness Worksheet. Discrimination Exercise. Sameness Exercise. Review Exercise. Drafting Exercise.

Week 9: **Damages**   **146**
Bullet Outline. Paragraph Outline. Fluency Cards. Definitions Worksheet. Issue-Spotting Worksheet. Comprehensiveness Worksheet. Examples/Non-Examples Exercise. Skills Exercise. Review Exercise.

Week 10: **Multiple Parties**   **161**
Bullet Outline. Paragraph Outline. Fluency Cards. Definitions Worksheet. Issue-Spotting Worksheet. Comprehensiveness Worksheet. Discrimination Exercise. Role-Play Exercise. Review Exercise.

Week 11: **No-Fault Systems**   **177**
Bullet Outline. Paragraph Outline. Fluency Cards. Definitions Worksheet. Issue-Spotting Worksheet. Comprehensiveness Worksheet. Examples/Non-Examples Exercise. Skills Exercise. Review Exercise. Problem-Solving Exercise.

Week 12: **Misuse of Legal Procedure**   **192**
Bullet Outline. Paragraph Outline. Fluency Cards. Definitions Worksheet. Issue-Spotting Worksheet. Comprehensiveness Worksheet. Discrimination Exercise. Role-Play Exercise. Review Exercise.

Week 13: **Business Torts**   **205**
Bullet Outline. Paragraph Outline. Fluency Cards. Definitions Worksheet. Issue-Spotting Worksheet. Sameness Exercise. Examples/Non-Examples Exercise. Problem-Solving Exercise. Role-Play Exercise.

Practice Assessments   **219**

Introduction

This workbook is for a three-credit course Torts II, comprised of thirteen weeks of new studies, identified as Week 1, Week 2, etc., followed by a Review Week and a Final Exam Week. The workbook's topics follow the order of the casebook *The Practice of Tort Law (3rd ed.)* by Nelson Miller, Paul Sorensen, Monica Nuckolls, and Karen Chadwick.

The exercises in this workbook provide the most benefit when you complete them with other students, in pairs or small groups. The exercises' value is not only in thinking and writing but also talking and listening. The more that you can see and hear, and that others can see and hear you, the better these exercises are likely to serve you.

This workbook provide answers to its exercises, questions, and problems, generally on the back of the page from which you work. Immediate feedback enables you to confirm or correct your thought and expression. To use the answers for their best effect, try to complete the exercise first before referring to the answer. The value is in part in striving.

The exercises vary somewhat from week to week to increase your interest and so that you learn in different ways and practice different skills. The exercises help you start with discrete knowledge components that you gradually build into complex sequences involving applying law and solving problems. The exercises generally build from one to another, as follows:

1. The opening bullet-point outline, paragraph-format outline, and diagrams are presenting stimuli, giving you the knowledge components and their framework of relationships;

2. Fluency cards enable you to practice recall, from a brief law stimulus, the core concepts, building your fluent recall for verbal expression, although only in discrete parts;

3. Definitions worksheets enable you to practice recall, from a law-question prompt, of the discrete knowledge components, to assemble in more-complete, written sentences;

4. Framework worksheets enable you to practice recall, from abbreviated stimuli, of the assembled knowledge framework showing concept relationships;

5. Comprehensiveness worksheets enable you to examine incomplete law statements to supply the missing components, testing and confirming your recall of law detail;

6. Discrimination worksheets enable you to practice distinguishing law statements that over-generalize, under-generalize, or misconceive of the correct law;

7. Scenario-generating worksheets enable you to practice articulating illustrative scenarios of law statements, demonstrating your understanding and improving advocacy;

8. Issue-spotting worksheets enable you to practice associations, from a fact-pattern prompt, of the discrete knowledge components with fact scenarios implicating them;

9. Sameness worksheets enable you to practice associating law concepts with multiple fact scenarios, confirming critical attributes of the law and its application to facts;

10. Example/non-example worksheets enable you to practice distinguishing fact scenarios that illustrate or do not illustrate given law statements, confirming your knowledge;

11. Attributes-analysis worksheets enable you to study closely complex law statements to practice discerning their critical and variable parts, as applied to fact scenarios;

12. Factors worksheets enable you to practice recalling, choosing, and analyzing factors of law tests as you apply those factors to multiple changing fact scenarios;

13. Problem-solving worksheets enable you to practice generating new, unusual, and novel rules from fact patterns and procedural context in think-aloud problem-solving method;

14. Review worksheets enable you to recall and apply law from earlier in your studies to move knowledge from short-term to long-term memory;

15. Drafting worksheets enable you to place your law knowledge and skills in their practice context while honing your writing and drafting skills;

16. Role-play exercises enable you to place your law knowledge and skills in their practice setting while honing your interpersonal and advocacy skills;

17. Multiple-choice questions enable you to practice applying your law knowledge and skills to multiple fact patterns, one for each concept that you are learning; and

18. Essay questions enable you to practice applying your law knowledge and skills to fact patterns, while expressing your reasoning in organized and coherent written form.

The full outlines at the beginning of the book and partial outlines at the beginning of each week's exercises have superscript numbers before the law that they state. The superscript numbers correlate with the multiple-choice questions, so that you have one multiple-choice question for each bit of law that you learn.

Use this workbook to push yourself deeper into grasping, recalling, and applying the fundamental concepts of tort law. The more active that your studies are, and the more that you strive at the boundaries of your capabilities, the better you should acquire tort knowledge and skills for their practical use and benefit, to you, clients, and others. Best wishes for good studies.

Bullet-Point Outline

WEEK 1   NEGLIGENCE DEFENSES *(continued from Torts I—recall comparative negligence and assumption of risk)*
[1] **Statutes of limitation** bar actions within different periods after claim accrues
- periods could be as short as 90 days or as long as 10 years but are usually 2 to 3 years
- [2] discovery rule tolls the limitations period until plaintiff should have known and filed
- [3] notice-of-claim statutes bar certain claims if no notice of claim w/i 90 or 120 days
- [4] filing suit tolls the limitations period
- Statutes toll limitations periods for minority, insanity, military service, fraud

[5] **Statutes of repose** bar future claims a certain number of years after the service or activity ceased
- for architects, engineers, maybe physicians, often drugs, products, buildings

Immunity
- [6] Intra-family immunity between spouses or parents and children
    - inter-spousal immunity abolished in most states
    - parent/child immunity preserved in most states
    - [7] watch exceptions for insurance, motor vehicle accidents, changes in the family relationship
- [8] Charitable immunity (abolished or limited in most states)
- [9] Governmental immunity (abolished in some states)
    - states tend to follow the Federal Torts Claims Act (FTCA) abolishing immunity w/ big exceptions
    - [10] liability for proprietary (non-governmental) functions & ministerial (non-discretionary) acts
    - immunity waivers are also common for vehicles, buildings, highway and sidewalk defects
    - government-contractor defense is a bit like immunity, where government specifies product

WEEKS 2 & 3 PRODUCTS LIABILITY
[11] **Three forms:** negligence, warranty and strict products liability (SPL) *(always analyze all three)*
- [28] merchants in distribution chain share warranty and SPL
    - so do suppliers of defective component parts
    - [29] but not one-time resellers of used products
    - [38] no products liability for mixed product sale/service if service predominates
    - [39] Human tissue and writings not considered products
        - rules vary on whether animals are products
- [30] Entities in the chain of distribution indemnify one another
    - loss shifts upstream to the responsible party, usually the manufacturer

Negligence (applies best to known careless acts)
- analyze duty (reasonable care), breach (fault), causation (but-for and proximate), and damages (DBCD)
- use violation of law, regulation, or standard for presumption or inference of breach

[12] **Warranty** (applies best to communications and relationships)
- express warranty (EW)
- [13] implied warranty of merchantability (IWM)
    - defined as fitness for ordinary purpose (FFOP)
- implied warranty of fitness for particular purpose (FFPP)
    - hardware store warranty
- [14] merchants may disclaim some warranties but not merchantability or for personal injury
- [15] economic-loss doctrine limits recovery of economic losses where there is no physical impact

[16] **Strict products liability**
- **2nd Rest.:** merchants selling products in a defective condition unreasonably dangerous (DCUD)

- must also be in the business (IB) and no modification (NM) of product
- defectiveness depends on one of two tests, risk-utility or consumer expectation
- [17]risk-utility test (RU) determines unreasonable danger
    - seven factors (RUSEAAP) include product utility, product risk, whether substitute products exist, whether the user was aware of the risk, and whether the user could avoid the risk, and the price or cost of alternative safer designs
- [18]consumer-expectation (CE) test asks what the consumer would have expected
- [19]3rd **Rest.** classifies defects as manufacturing, design, or warning (MD, DD, WD)
    - [20]manufacturing defect = product departs from its design
    - [21]design defect requires risk-utility or consumer-expectation test
        - [22]may require showing an alternative feasible design
        - [31]subsequent remedial changes inadmissible except to prove disputed feasibility
    - [23]failure to warn requires that omitting warning made the product unreasonably dangerous
        - [24]need be no warning as to obvious risks
            - courts recognize an open-and-obvious defense.
        - [25]warnings must be adequate, describing the hazard, risk, and means of avoiding
        - [26]law may presume the user would have read and heeded a warning
        - [27]consider the user's sophistication and learned intermediaries

Defenses
- [32]comparative negligence
- [33]assumption of risk
- [34]statute of limitations and statute of repose
- [35]exclusive-remedy provision of worker's compensation act as to employer and co-workers only
- [36]product misuse, but manufacturers may have to anticipate foreseeable misuse
- [37]federal preemption

Week 4   STRICT LIABILITY

Definition: liability without fault (even with all due care) for activities or conditions on land
- [45]applies to conditions on land, not manufacture of products
- [47]the harm must be that which makes the activity abnormally dangerous
    - otherwise, the courts may find no causation
- [46]Assumption of risk and comparative negligence are defenses

Two kinds: (1) abnormally dangerous activities and (2) animals
- **animals** (three main kinds of strict liability for animals)
    - [42]wild animals
    - [41]livestock depending on fence-in or fence-out rules
    - [43]dog bites
        - statutory strict liability with provocation exception
        - common law only with abnormally dangerous propensities
- [40]**abnormally dangerous activities** (dam or explosives are examples)
    - 2nd Rest.: unable to eliminate high risk of harm from uncommon activity of uncertain value
        - apply 6-factor test (HARVUL): harm, abnormal, risk, value, uncommon, location
    - [44]strict liability for environmental harm
        - by statute but also as an abnormally dangerous activity under the common law

Week 5   MISREPRESENTATION

Definition (elements): [48]false representation knowingly made to induce reliance causing loss (FRK MRCL)
- goes by fraud, misrepresentation, fraudulent misrepresentation, fraud in the inducement, etc.
    - [54]seller must know of falsity for it to be actionable
        - requires intent, desire, or purpose (scienter or guilty mind)
    - Some states recognize [50]negligent misrepresentation for careless false statement
        - a few even recognize innocent misrepresentation
            - [55]if no intent to defraud, then law may limit recovery to restitution

- [58]professionals who carelessly misrepresent facts to third-parties are liable only when they know of third-party reliance and take action supporting reliance
  - [51]the misrepresentation must be verifiably false when made
    - not merely conjecture, salesperson puffing, or opinion
    - honest statements of prediction or intent are not actionable
  - the misrepresentation must ordinarily be affirmative
    - [52]bare nondisclosure without duty to disclose is not actionable
      - [49]silent fraud is knowing refusal to disclose where disclosure expected
    - [53]fraudulent concealment, when active, can constitute misrepresentation
  - [56]claimant must actually and justifiably rely on the misrepresentation
    - [57]misrepresenting law is not actionable unless falsely implying underlying facts
    - we are presumed to know the law and cannot rely on its misrepresentation
  - [59]claimants must prove fraud by clear and convincing evidence, not merely a preponderance
  - [60]measure fraud damages by the lost benefit of the bargain
    - some states limit fraud damages to out-of-pocket loss

Weeks 6 & 7   DEFAMATION

Three-part analysis: (1) common law, (2) constitution, (3) privileges *(always analyze all three)*
- the tort's gist is its gossip-like false sting lowering a person's reputation
- analyze all three parts whether or not you think they apply

Common law (False Word POEMS)
- Forms: [62]libel (written) and slander (oral)
  - [71]slander claims require special damages
  - exceptions for loathsome disease, incompetence in trade or profession, sexual misconduct, or crimes of moral turpitude (DISC)
  - [72]libel claims do not require proof of special damages
- Definition (elements): [61]false words published of and concerning another that with extrinsic facts carries a defamatory (reputation-lowering) meaning, with special damages except where presumed
  - [63]false words means verifiably (objectively) false, not opinions
  - [64]publication means false words must reach and be understood by another
    - [65]primary publishers (originators) must reasonably anticipate republication
    - secondary publishers (media who publish and distribute) bear same liability
      - [66]internet service providers have statutory immunity unless creating the content
    - [67]some courts recognize compelled self-publication
    - [68]single-publication rule triggers the statute of limitation once at first publication
  - [69]of-and-concerning element means the publication must identify the claimant
    - not necessary by name if circumstances reveal identity
    - [70]individual claim for defaming groups of smaller number
  - defamatory meaning element means publication has sting lowering reputation
    - must lower reputation among at least a respectable minority of persons
  - [73]special damages are pecuniary loss (lost job, income, medical expense)

Constitution (First Amendment free-speech and free-press protection)
- [74]public officials and public figures must prove actual malice (AM)
  - [77]public official includes public employees whose qualifications the public would want to know
    - interest-beyond-the-general-interest (IBGI) test
  - [78]universal public figure has general fame, prominence, and influence
  - limited public figure voluntarily injected self into public issue and has media access
    - may also be involuntary public figures
- [75]actual malice is knowledge or recklessness regard of falsity (KRD)
  - [76]also includes high degree of awareness of falsity (HAD), subjective serious doubt as to truth (SSD), purposeful avoidance of truth (PAT), and materially changing meaning in quote (MCM)

- [79]private figure on public issue proves fault for liability & malice for presumed or punitive damages
  - [80]private figure on public issue must also retain burden of proof on falsity
- [81]private-figure/private issue cases are unaffected by the constitutional standards
  - just prove common law elements

Common-law privileges
- absolute (privileged even if actual malice or bad faith)
  - [82]judicial privilege protects lawyers, judges, and others for relevant statements in court
  - [83]legislative privilege protects speakers in legislative proceedings on any matter
  - [84]executive privilege protects within scope of official duties
- [85]qualified privileges (privileged only if without actual malice or bad faith)
  - self interest, common interests, or interest of others
  - [86]fair reporting (accurate summary) and fair comment

[87]**Defamation remedies**
- nominal damages
- presumed damages
  - not available for slander unless fits DISC exception (see above)
  - not available for public officials, public figures, or public issue without actual malice
- compensatory damages for economic and non-economic losses
- punitive damages
  - some states require unmet demand for retraction

Week 8   INVASION OF PRIVACY

[88]**Four forms:** appropriation, intrusion, public disclosure, and false light
- [89]appropriation is use of another's persona for commercial or other advantage without permission
  - misuse can be of name, likeness, image, or anything associated with person
  - often involves the famous but not always
  - often involves commercial (called commercial exploitation) use but not always
    - can involve political or public-interest uses
  - damages and injunction for forms of relief
- [90]intrusion form arises on highly offensive intrusion into reasonably expected privacy
  - is often into a physical place but can also be into confidential records or information
- [91]public disclosure of private facts arises on highly offensive publication to more than a few persons
  - again, privacy expectation must be reasonable
  - [92]must overcome constitutional protection to publish matters of public interest
- [93]false light arises highly offensive false public depiction

[94]**First Amendment** protects right to intentionally inflict emotional distress if by parody or for public expression

Week 9   DAMAGES

Categories: [95]economic (special) and non-economic (general)
- [96]economic loss begins with medical expense and wage loss
  - [103]claimants may recover for aggravation of pre-existing conditions
    - defendants pay all if parties are unable to distinguish old from new injury
  - [98]spouse of an injured tort victim also has claim for loss of consortium
    - includes lost services, support, love, society, companionship
- [97]non-economic loss is pain and suffering
  - may also include humiliation, shock, fright, mortification, scarring, disfigurement, disability, lost enjoyment of life, etc.
  - avoid duplicating damages

Procedures
- [108]motion in limine asks court to bar inflammatory damages evidence
- [99]motion for remittitur asks court to reduce excessive damages resulting from passion and prejudice

- [100]collateral-source rule bars evidence of health or other insurance, gratuitous payments
  - [101]insurers who pay for loss may have right of subrogation
- [102]defendants may plead plaintiff's failure to mitigate damages
  - plaintiffs must take reasonable action to reduce their loss
- [104]damages caps limit personal-injury plaintiffs' recoveries in many states
  - some states have held caps unconstitutional
- [105]Recoveries on account of physical injury are not taxed
  - recoveries where there is no physical injury are taxed
  - [106]claimants may also structure settlements without tax on the investments' earnings
- [107]contingency fees must be reasonable

Wrongful death action (a procedural device only, not another underlying tort theory)
- [109]allows tort recovery even after death
  - claimants must still have an underlying tort theory such as negligence
- [110]usually brought in the name of the decedent's estate
  - controlled by the estate's personal representative
- [111]spouses and dependent children are typical beneficiaries
  - some states also recognize parents, siblings, and lineal descendants
- [112]acts differ as to the measure of loss
  - some limit to pecuniary loss
  - others allow non-economic loss to beneficiaries
  - some allow loss to the estate

[113]**Survival actions** permit estate to recover for losses the decedent suffered before death

Property damage
- [114]usual measure is market value of property at time of loss
  - [115]personal value to owner only for special items like family heirlooms
- [116]temporary deprivation measured by rental value
- partial destruction measured by reduction in market value

Punitive damages
- [117]where allowed, to punish defendant rather than compensate plaintiff
  - allowed only for more-reprehensible wrongs like willful and wanton misconduct
- [118]Constitution prohibits excessive punitive damages
  - consider ratio to actual damages, reprehensibility, and other available remedies (RRR)

Week 10   MULTIPLE PARTIES

Satisfaction and release
- [119]release—plaintiff signs agreement releasing defendant from further liability
  - [124]be sure to release only those persons whom the parties intend to release
    - preserve rights against non-settling defendants
      - old rule was release one, release all
      - avoided in some states by convenant not to sue
      - modern rule is look to intent of parties signing release agreement
  - [121]courts set aside release only for fraud, duress, undue influence, or mutual mistake
- [120]satisfaction—defendant pays money judgment after trial
  - [122]single-satisfaction rule—plaintiffs are entitled to only a single satisfaction of damages
    - even when multiple parties are jointly and severally liable for those damages.
  - [123]partial-satisfaction rule—non-settling defendants get credit for settlements paid by others

Joint-and-several liability
- [125]traditional rule: plaintiff collects all or a portion of the damages from any defendant
  - joint liability means that all defendants share in paying the loss
  - several liability means that any one defendant must pay for all of the loss
- forms
  - [126]concerted action of two or more tortfeasors working together, causing loss
  - [127]independent actors causing indivisible injury (e.g., MV accident with two at-fault drivers)
  - [128]failures in a common duty (e.g., landlord and property manager both owing duty to repair)

- [129]most jurisdictions abolish joint-and-several liability
  - factfinder must apportion fault and judge apportion damages among liable defendants

Vicarious liability
- [130]Vicarious liability holds one party liable for the torts of another.
- forms
  - [131]respondeat superior (employer vicarious liability)
    - for negligence of employees within course of employment
    - [132]Commuting to and from work is not within course of employment
    - personal errands are not within the course of employment
      - employer errands are within course of employment
    - [133]no vicarious liability for intentional torts
      - unless the act furthered employer's mission or
      - employer authorized or ratified the act
    - [134]employers may have direct liability for negligent hiring or entrustment
  - [135]no vicarious liability for independent contractors except where
    - the one hiring the contractor retains control
    - the one hiring the contractor has nondelegable duties
    - the work involves inherently dangerous activities or
    - the contractor has apparent authority to act for the one hiring the contractor
  - [136]joint enterprises meaning common purpose, agreement, interest ($), and direction (PAID)
  - [137]no vicarious liability for bailments except where
    - owner-consent statutes exist for loaned motor vehicles
    - family-purpose doctrine for loaned motor vehicles
    - also watch for direct liability for negligent entrustment

Contribution and indemnity
- [138]contribution requires a defendant to pay a fair share of the damage for which the defendant is liable
  - [140]defendants who settle in good faith are not subject to contribution
    - courts give wide latitude to parties to agree on what is a good-faith settlement
  - [141]contribution actions are not necessary where law apportions liability among defendants
    - no contribution where the law abolishes joint-and-several liability
- [139]indemnity reimburses a defendant who pays the liability of another
  - [142]common-law indemnity where defendant seeking indemnity has only vicarious liability
  - [143]contractual indemnity allocates liability by advance agreement (e.g., insurance)

Successive injuries
- [144]plaintiff suffering successive injuries from separately liable defendants apportions damages
  - [145]if parties cannot separate injuries, then defendant causing successive injury pays all

WEEK 11   NO-FAULT SCHEMES
Motor-vehicle no-fault
- [146]motor-vehicle insurance has statutory-minimum liability limits ($20k/$40k in Michigan)
  - [152]insurance often includes uninsured- and underinsured-motorists coverage
- [147]12 states have motor-vehicle no-fault acts (Michigan, New York, and Florida included)
  - [148]those suffering loss first look to their own motor-vehicle insurers for first-party benefits
    - [150]issues of coverage, exclusions, priority, benefits, setoffs, and valuation
    - [151]benefits typically include medical expense, work loss, and replacement service
  - all no-fault states retain some negligence liability
    - [149]bar negligence claims for vehicle damage and minor injuries
  - vehicle owners pay for their own collision coverage
    - allows negligence claims only for a threshold injury
  - serious impairment, permanent serious disfigurement, or death

Worker's compensation
- [153]provides injured employees with limited benefits without respect to fault
  - [154]injury must be incident to employment
  - [155]injury must be accidental

- progressive conditions not compensated except for occupational disease
- [156]benefits include medical expense and work loss
- [157]benefits are employee's exclusive remedy for employer negligence
  - intentional-tort claims not barred
- [158]resolved through an administrative system
  - contingency-fee lawyers represent injured employees

WEEK 12   MISUSE OF LEGAL PROCEDURE
Malicious prosecution
- [159]plaintiff must show defendant maliciously caused criminal charges to issue without probable cause
  - charges must resolve in plaintiff's favor before trial
- [160]malice element requires that defendant caused charges to issue for ulterior purpose
- [161]damages are presumed
  - plaintiff may prove compensatory damages for mental distress, lost reputation and income
  - punitive damages may also be available
- [162]some jurisdictions recognize malicious civil prosecution
  - may have to prove special damages in those cases

Abuse of process
- [163]plaintiff must show defendant used legal process for ulterior purposes

WEEK 13   BUSINESS TORTS
- [164]protects against harm to commercial interests in three forms
  - **injurious falsehood** (2 kinds)
    - [165]slander of title, meaning a false statement calculated to harm plaintiff's pecuniary interest by publication with malice causing special damage
    - [166]trade disparagement, meaning a false statement calculated to harm plaintiff's trade or business, with knowledge or reckless disregard of falsity, causing special damage
  - **interference with business relations**
    - [167]intentional harmful interference with contract or business expectancy by improper means
    - [168]interfering need not be illegal but must violate accepted business standards
  - **unfair competition**

Paragraph Outline

I. NEGLIGENCE DEFENSES

In Torts I, you studied contributory or comparative negligence and express or implied assumption of risk as defenses to claims of negligence. (Remember that there are also defenses for intentional torts, like consent, self defense, defense of others, defense and recovery of property, and public and private necessity.) Here are some additional defenses.

[1]Different statutes of limitation bar different tort actions within different defined periods after the claims accrue. You may find statutes in different states barring defamation claims after one year, intentional torts after a one or two-year period, negligence after two, three, or four years, and other tort claims after four, five, or six years. You will learn these specific periods when you decide what state in which to seek a law license. [2]A discovery rule may toll the limitations period until the plaintiff should have known of the injury and its connection to the defendant's conduct. What that means is that if the plaintiff does not know nor should have known of the claim, then the statute of limitations may not run against the plaintiff. [3]Special notice-of-claim statutes may bar certain claims if the injured person does not notify the responsible agency within a period shorter than the statute of limitations. These notice of claim statutes in effect work like limitations periods barring the plaintiff's claim unless the plaintiff has given timely notice of the claim. [4]Filing suit tolls the limitations period, meaning that the plaintiff need no longer be concerned about the statute of limitations running out as to those defendants against whom the plaintiff filed the complaint. Statutes may also toll limitations periods for minority, insanity, military service, and fraudulent concealment, meaning for instance that a child would have no need for concern that the limitations period would bar the child's claim until the child turned adult.

[5]Statutes of repose bar potential future claims a certain number of years after the service or activity that created the risk. Statutes of repose are like limitations periods in that they will have certain periods for certain kinds of service or activity, such as designing or constructing a building, or providing a medical service. Statutes of repose are different from limitations periods in that they do not ask when a claim accrued. They instead ask when the service or activity ended, whether or not anyone then had a claim. Once the period ends, the statute of repose bars all claims whether or not they have accrued.

Immunity is another tort defense. There are several types of immunity. [6]Many states grant intra-family tort immunity between spouses or between parents and children. [7]States recognizing intra-family tort immunity may have exceptions for insurance, motor vehicle accidents, and changes in the family relationship on which the immunity is based, meaning (for instance) the divorce of spouses or emancipation of children. [8]A few states continue to recognize tort immunity for charitable organizations, although most states have abolished charitable immunity. [9]State and federal law may also recognize governmental immunity to tort claims, either broadly or in defined circumstances as under the Federal Tort Claims Act. Depending on the jurisdiction, there are many variations of and exceptions to governmental immunity, often for government operation of motor vehicles and construction and maintenance of highways and buildings. In some states, statute or case law distinguish cases where there will be governmental liability from cases where there will be no immunity based on the type of action or function in which the government engages. For example, [10]governmental immunity may be waived for proprietary rather than governmental functions and for ministerial rather than discretionary actions.

II. PRODUCTS LIABILITY

Products liability is a broad category of tort claims. It can help to understand products liability as a type of negligence claim (the reasonableness of the defendant's actions remains an explicit or implicit consideration in most cases) but with theories that significantly alter or go well beyond the typical negligence requirements. In some cases involving injury or damage from a product, a simple negligence theory with the usual elements of duty, breach, causation, and damage may still make the most sense.

[11]Products liability includes not only negligence claims but also claims based on warranty and strict products liability. [12]Manufacturers and retailers may expressly warrant a product's fitness for particular purposes. [13]Manufacturers, distributors, and retailers also impliedly warrant a product's merchantability, meaning its fitness for its intended purpose. You should consider breach of express or implied warranty whenever you evaluate a claim involving injury by a product. [14]Merchants may disclaim some warranties but not the warranty of merchantability or warranties protecting against personal injury. [15]The economic-loss doctrine may also limit recovery of economic losses where there is no physical impact or injury from the defective product.

Strict products liability is a third products-liability theory after negligence and breach of warranty. [16]Strict products liability provides that merchants who sell products in a defective condition unreasonably dangerous to users are liable for resultant injury. The significant issue is what constitutes an unreasonably dangerous and defective condition. In many cases, [17]a risk-utility test will determine what is unreasonably dangerous for purposes of strict products liability. Risk-utility tests include factors such as the utility of the design, the risks it creates, the severity of the likely harm, whether it could have been avoided by alternative designs, and whether the user would know of and be able to avoid the risk, with or without a warning. [18]Strict products liability also includes a consumer-expectation test that basically asks how the consumer would have expected the product to perform. Some cases make sense for one test, and others for the other test. [19]The Third Restatement's approach is to classify defects as either design, manufacturing, or warning. Practitioners commonly begin from the standpoint of whether the case is one for defective design, defects in manufacture, or failure to warn. [20]A manufacturing defect exists when at the time of manufacture the product departs from its design. [21]Design-defect claims depend on showing that the product is not reasonably safe as designed and are likely determined by risk-utility and consumer-expectation tests. [22]Design-defect claims may require showing an alternative feasible design at the time of manufacture.

[23]Failure-to-warn claims depend on showing that the omission of a warning made the product unreasonably dangerous. [24]There generally need be no warning as to obvious risks. Courts will recognize an open-and-obvious defense. [25]Warnings must be adequate, generally meaning that they should describe the hazard, injury risk, and means of avoiding the risk. [26]As to causation in failure-to-warn cases, most jurisdictions will presume that the injured user would have read and heeded a warning. [27]In failure-to-warn cases, courts will also consider the user's sophistication and whether there were any learned intermediaries who should have given warnings.

[28] All merchants within the chain of distribution bear the same liability to the injured user as the manufacturer, as do suppliers of defective component parts. [29] Strict products liability generally does not extend to one-time resellers of used products. [30] Entities in the chain of distribution typically indemnify one another, shifting products liability to the responsible party. [31] Subsequent remedial changes in design defects are generally inadmissible except to prove disputed feasibility.

[32] Comparative negligence is an available defense to products-liability claims in a majority of jurisdictions. [33] Assumption of risk is another products-liability defense available in some jurisdictions. [34] The statute of limitations and statute of repose are also common products-liability defenses. [35] Exclusive-remedy provisions of worker's compensation acts may bar claims against involved employers but not manufacturers of the injury causing product. There are several additional defenses to products liability claims, beyond other negligence defenses. [36] Product misuse is another common defense, although manufacturers may have to anticipate foreseeable misuses. [37] Federal preemption is yet another possible defense, where state tort law would contradict federal statute or regulation.

[38] There is generally no products liability for services which do not involve products as their essential activity. [39] Human tissue and writings are generally not considered to be products, and there are varying rules on whether animals are products.

III. STRICT LIABILITY

There are other forms of strict liability in addition to strict products liability, which is more like a negligence claim than strict liability. [40] Strict liability exists for abnormally dangerous activities, defined in the Second Restatement by the inability to eliminate a high risk of harm from uncommon activities of uncertain value. Making a dam for a waterway or storing explosives are two common examples. When injury or property damage result from an abnormally dangerous activity, liability exists without respect to fault.

The other common form of strict liability has to do with injury or property damage caused by animals. For example, [41] there may be strict liability for property damage by livestock, depending on the fence-in, fence-out, or other rules of the jurisdiction. [42] There may also be strict liability for property damage or injury from wild animals. [43] There may also be strict liability under statute for dog bites and under the common law for injury from a pet's abnormally vicious propensities.

[44] Strict liability for environmental harm is typically a subject for statute but may also exist as an abnormally dangerous activity under the common law. [45] Strict liability for abnormally dangerous activities generally applies to conditions on land, not the manufacture of products. [46] Assumption of risk and comparative negligence may be defenses to strict liability. [47] For there to be strict liability, the harm must ordinarily be that which makes the activity abnormally dangerous; otherwise, the courts may find no causation.

III. MISREPRESENTATION

Misrepresentation, also commonly known as fraud, is another tort cause of action. Misrepresentation claims are often pled in combination with breach of contract and other business tort claims, and sometimes with defamation and other torts affecting personal interests.

[48]Misrepresentation is a knowing false material statement made with the purpose and effect of inducing justifiable reliance to the hearer's detriment. [49]Silent fraud or fraudulent concealment involves the knowing refusal to disclose under circumstances where disclosure is reasonably expected. Notice that misrepresentation requires intent, desire, or purpose, or what might in the criminal law be thought of as scienter or a guilty mind. Some states do recognize a different form of misrepresentation that does not depend on desire or purpose. [50]Negligent misrepresentation involves not a knowing but a careless false statement of fact, whereas innocent misrepresentation involves a false statement made despite care, both torts being recognized in some jurisdictions.

Each element of a misrepresentation claim can raise its own issues, giving rise to special rules, definitions, or conditions. For example, [51]to be actionable, the "misrepresentation" must be verifiably false, not merely conjecture, salesperson puffing, or opinion. [52]Bare nondisclosure, without a duty to disclose arising out of the relationship or circumstances, is not actionable. [53]Active concealment of a condition about which a buyer would want to know can constitute a misrepresentation. [54]The seller must know of the statement's falsity for it to be actionable. Honest statements of prediction or intent are not actionable when the predicted event does not occur. [55]Where recognized, negligent-misrepresentation claims may be limited to recovery of out-of-pocket losses rather than benefit-of-the-bargain damages. [56]The fraud claimant must show that the claimant's reliance on the misrepresentation was justifiable. [57]Misrepresentations of law are generally not actionable unless falsely implying underlying facts. [58]Professionals who misrepresent facts are liable to third-parties only when they know of their reliance and take some overt action in support of it. [59]Claimants must prove fraud by clear and convincing evidence, not merely a preponderance. [60]A majority of jurisdictions measure fraud damages by the lost benefit of the bargain, although some limit damages to out-of-pocket loss.

IV. DEFAMATION

Defamation is the next new tort theory you learn in Torts II. [61]Defamation involves false communication published of and concerning another that, together with extrinsic facts, harms the reputation of that other, with special damages except where damages are presumed. [62]Defamation in written form is libel, whereas defamation in oral form is slander, with some differences in elements as to each. [63]Although it is often said that truth is a defense to defamation claims, more accurately, the defamation claimant has the burden to prove falsity.

As in the case of misrepresentation and other tort claims, defamation has common-law elements that give rise to special issues requiring special rules, definitions, and conditions. For example, [64]to satisfy the publication element of a defamation claim, the false statement must reach and be understood by another. It can help to think of defamation as a strict liability tort. [65]Primary publishers must reasonably anticipate republication and pay for resulting damage from defamatory statements. [66]Internet service providers have statutory immunity from defamation liability when they are not the information content provider. [67]Some courts recognize defamation claims in which circumstances compelled the claimant to self-publish the false statements. [68]Under a single-publication rule, most jurisdictions treat the original publication date as the date the cause of action arose, rather than treating subsequent printings as additional accrual dates, for purposes of the statute of limitations.

[69]Defamation's of-and-concerning element requires that the publication identify the claimant, although not necessarily by name if the circumstances make it sufficiently clear to whom the publication refers. [70]A publication can defame an individual by referring to a group of which the

individual was a member, so long as the reasonable person would identify the individual in that manner (for reasonably small groups). [71]Slander claims ordinarily require proof of special damages except where the slander is as to loathsome disease, incompetence in one's trade or profession, sex, or crimes of moral turpitude. [72]Libel claims, based on writings or their equivalent, do not require proof of special damages. [73]Special damages are shown by proof of pecuniary loss from third persons believing and acting on the defamatory statement.

Once you understand defamation's common-law elements, you must then appreciate how the First Amendment changes those elements in many cases. [74]The First Amendment requires public officials and public figures to prove actual malice in defamation claims. [75]Actual malice means knowledge of or recklessness with regard to the falsity of the defamatory statement. [76]Actual malice may also include a high degree of awareness of falsity, subjective serious doubt as to truth, purposeful avoidance of truth, and deliberate misquotes materially changing meaning. [77]A public official includes any public employee whose qualifications the public would want to know, beyond the general interest in the qualifications of all public employees. [78]A universal public figure has prominence and influence, whereas a limited public figure has media access and engaged in conduct from which one would expect public interest. [79]If the publication concerns a private figure but is on a public issue, then the private figure must show fault for liability and actual malice for presumed and punitive damages. [80]If the publication concerns a private figure but is on a public issue, then the private figure must retain the burden of proof to prove the statement false. [81]Only private-figure/private issue cases are unaffected by the constitutional standards.

Defamation claims require a third consideration beyond the common-law elements and constitutional considerations. Common-law privileges may provide additional protection against defamation claims. [82]An absolute judicial privilege protects lawyers, judges, and others from defamation claims based on relevant publications made in court proceedings. [83]An absolute legislative privilege protects speakers in legislative proceedings against defamation claims made based on any (not just relevant) matters. [84]An absolute executive privilege, protecting statements made within the scope of official duties, extends to all administrative-branch officials at the federal level but in most states only as to higher officials at the state level. [85]Qualified privileges allow one to protect one's own interests, common interests, or the interests of others, without being subject to defamation claim. [86]There are also qualified common-law privileges of fair reporting and comment, to make accurate summary of an official proceeding containing defamatory publications and to comment on them.

[87]Defamation remedies may include nominal damages, compensatory damages for economic and non-economic losses, and punitive damages, although some states first require demand for retraction.

V. INVASION OF PRIVACY

[88]The invasion-of-privacy tort takes one of four forms, either appropriation, intrusion, disclosure, or false light. [89]Invasion of privacy's appropriation form involves use of persona for commercial or other advantage without the person's permission, with injunctions and damages for relief. [90]Invasion of privacy's intrusion form arises when there is an unauthorized intrusion into a private place that would be highly offensive to the reasonable person. [91]Invasion of privacy's disclosure form arises when there is publication without legitimate interest to more than a few persons of private facts that would be offensive to the reasonable person. [92]The disclosure form of invasion of privacy must overcome constitutional protection to publish matters of public

interest. [93]Invasion of privacy's false light form arises when a person publicly depicts another in a false manner that would be highly offensive to the reasonable person. [94]The First Amendment protects the right of media to intentionally inflict emotional distress if also done for purposes of destroying a person's reputation by parody.

VI. DAMAGES

[95]There are two main categories of personal injury damages, economic and non-economic, sometimes called special and general. [96]Economic loss typically begins with medical expense and wage loss. [97]Non-economic loss is usually thought of as pain and suffering but may include humiliation, shock, fright, mortification, scarring, disfigurement, disability, and loss of enjoyment of life.

Beyond those two basic categories and their various components or divisions, tort-damages law involves many other special substantive and procedural considerations. For example, [98]the spouse of an injured tort victim may have a claim for loss of consortium, meaning loss of services, love, society, and companionship. [99]On motion for remittitur, the court will reduce or set aside excessive damages verdicts which are the result of passion and prejudice or not supported by the evidence. [100]Where still recognized, the collateral-source rule bars evidence of health or other insurance, gratuitous payments, and other reimbursement for the tort claimant's losses. [101]Insurers who pay for the plaintiff's loss may have the contract right to reimbursement out of the plaintiff's tort recovery or to seek that recovery if the plaintiff has not pursued it.

[102]Tort claimants have the duty to mitigate their damages, meaning to take reasonable action to reduce their loss. [103]Tort claimants may recover for aggravation of pre-existing conditions and hold defendant liable for all disability if the parties are unable to distinguish the old condition from new injury. [104]Damages caps limit personal-injury plaintiffs' recoveries in many states, although some states have held caps unconstitutional. [105]Recoveries on account of physical injury are not taxed, but recoveries where there is no physical injury are taxed. [106]The tax code permits tort claimants to have a third party structure their settlements without tax on the investments' earnings. [107]Contingency fees must be reasonable. [108]Parties may challenge the admissibility of inflammatory damages evidence with a motion in limine heard before trial.

The death of an individual due to a tort creates other special issues. [109]Wrongful-death acts in all 50 states allow tort recoveries for death, but the claimants must still have an underlying tort theory such as negligence. In other words, do not mistake wrongful death as a substantive cause of action. It is really a procedural device for addressing the special considerations the law must address when the tort victim died as a result of the tort. [110]Wrongful-death actions are usually brought in the name of the decedent's estate and controlled by the estate's personal representative. [111]Spouses and children are typical beneficiaries under wrongful-death acts, as may be parents and possibly siblings and other lineal descendants. [112]Wrongful-death acts differ as to the measure of loss, some limited to pecuniary loss while others allow non-economic loss to beneficiaries and some even loss to the estate. [113]Survival actions permit the estate to recover for losses the decedent suffered before death.

Property damage has its own rules different from the rules for personal injury and wrongful death damages. [114]The usual measure of damages for property loss is the market value of the property at the time of loss. [115]Personal value to the owner is not usually considered unless the loss involved an item having the history of a family heirloom. [116]Damages for temporary deprivation may be measured by rental value, whereas damages for partial destruction may be measured by reduction in market value.

Punitive damages are another category of damages, in addition to the broad category of compensatory damages, that some states allow, but with constitutional (due process) limitations. [117]Some jurisdictions allow punitive damages in some cases where there is a more culpable wrong, to punish the defendant rather than compensate the plaintiff. [118]The Constitution prohibits states from awarding excessive punitive damages, measured against the actual damages, the reprehensibility of the tortious conduct, and the nature of other available civil and criminal penalties.

VII. MULTIPLE PARTIES

Many tort claims involve more than one party on each side, creating related procedural issues. [119]When parties settle a tort claim, the plaintiff signs an agreement releasing the defendant from further liability, while attempting to preserve rights against non-settling defendants. [120]When parties are unable to voluntarily settle a claim and a money judgment is instead entered after trial, the liability is extinguished when the defendant satisfies the judgment. [121]The courts will set aside a release only for fraud, duress, undue influence, or mutual mistake. [122]Plaintiffs are entitled to only a single satisfaction of their damages even when multiple parties are jointly and severally liable for those damages. [123]Non-settling defendants who are jointly and severally liable get credit for amounts paid by settling defendants. [124]Releases must be carefully considered and crafted to release only those parties and their agents whom the parties intend to release. [125]The traditional rule of joint-and-several liability means that the plaintiff may collect all or a portion of the damages from any defendant. [126]Joint-and-several liability may arise from the concerted action of two or more tortfeasors. [127]Joint-and-several liability may also arise from two independent actors causing an indivisible injury. [128]Joint-and-several liability may also arise from failures in a common duty. [129]Most jurisdictions alter joint-and-several liability to require the factfinder to apportion fault and the judge to apportion damages among liable defendants.

[130]Vicarious liability holds one party liable for the torts of another. [131]A first form of vicarious liability is the respondeat-superior liability of an employer for the negligent acts of employees within the course of employment. [132]Commuting to and from work, and running personal errands, are not within the course of employment, but running employer errands is. [133]There is generally no vicarious liability for intentional torts unless the act was in furtherance of the employer's mission or the employer authorized or ratified the act. [134]Employers may also have direct liability for negligent hiring or entrustment. [135]There may also be vicarious liability for the acts of independent contractors, where the one hiring the contractor retains control or has nondelegable duties or inherently dangerous activities, or the contractor has apparent authority. [136]Another form of vicarious liability arises around joint enterprises, defined by a common purpose, agreement, and pecuniary interest, and shared direction or control. [137]Bailors are not generally liable to third parties who suffer damage from the bailees use of the personal property, but owner-consent statutes commonly change that rule as to vehicles.

[138]Contribution is the claim of a defendant that another party pay a fair share of the damage for which the defendant is liable. [139]Indemnity is the right of a defendant to reimbursement from the party whose fault created the defendant's liability. [140]A defendant who settles liability in good faith is no longer subject to contribution from other parties. [141]Contribution actions are not necessary or allowed where tort law apportions liability among the liable defendants. [142]Common-law indemnity applies where the defendant seeking indemnity has only vicarious liability. [143]Contractual indemnity allocates the liability for fault by advance agreement among the responsible defendants. [144]When the plaintiff has suffered successive injuries from

separately liable defendants, then damages are apportioned to each defendant. [145]When plaintiff is unable to prove which defendant caused which successive injury, the defendants may have the burden of proof to separate the injuries.

VIII. NO-FAULT SCHEMES

There are two areas in which states may alter the tort system in no-fault schemes: motor vehicle accidents and worker's compensation. [146]States require motor-vehicle insurance with varying liability limits. [147]About 12 states have motor-vehicle no-fault acts of varying kind, but all retain some negligence liability in certain situations. [148]In no-fault states, those suffering damage from motor-vehicle accidents first look to their own motor-vehicle insurers for first-party benefits. [149]No-fault acts typically bar liability claims for vehicle damage and minor injuries, allowing negligence claims only for a threshold injury such as serious impairment, permanent serious disfigurement, or death. [150]First-party claims against one's own motor-vehicle insurer involve issues of coverage, exclusions, priority, benefits, setoffs, and valuation. [151]First-party no-fault benefits typically include coordinated medical-expense coverage and limited work-loss and replacement-service-expense benefits. [152]Motor-vehicle insurance often includes uninsured- and underinsured-motorists coverage for liability claims where there is insufficient insurance.

[153]Worker's compensation acts in all 50 states provide injured employees with limited benefits without respect to fault. [154]Worker's compensation benefits depend on showing an employee's injury incident to employment. [155]Only accidental injuries are compensated, meaning that progressive conditions generally are not, except for occupational disease. [156]Worker's compensation benefits typically include coordinated medical expense and limited work-loss benefits. [157]Worker's compensation acts are an employee's exclusive remedy for injuries caused by employer negligence, although intentional-tort claims are not barred. [158]Worker's compensation claims are resolved through an administrative system in which lawyers working on contingency-fee basis represent the injured employees.

IX. MISUSE OF LEGAL PROCEDURES

Two torts address liability when an individual misuses legal procedures. [159]The tort of malicious prosecution requires plaintiff to show that defendant maliciously caused criminal charges to issue without probable cause, with the charges resolved in the plaintiff's favor. [160]The malice element of malicious prosecution requires plaintiff to show that defendant caused the charges to be issued for a purpose other than to bring plaintiff to justice. [161]Tort law presumes malicious-prosecution damages, although plaintiff may also prove compensatory damages for mental distress and loss of reputation and income, and punitive damages may also be available. [162]Some jurisdictions recognize a malicious prosecution claim for initiating a groundless civil action, but those jurisdictions tend to require proof of special damages in those cases. [163]The tort of abuse of process requires plaintiff to show that defendant used legal process for ulterior purposes. [164]Tort liability extends to protect against harm to commercial interests, either for injurious falsehood, interference with business relations, or unfair competition.

X. BUSINESS TORTS

Tort law also recognizes forms of business tort. [165]Injurious falsehood includes slander of title, meaning a false statement calculated to harm plaintiff's pecuniary interest by publication with malice causing special damage. [166]Injurious falsehood also includes trade disparagement, meaning a false statement calculated to harm plaintiff's trade or business, with knowledge or reckless disregard of falsity, causing special damage. [167]Interference with business relations is established by proof of intentional harmful interference with a contract or business expectancy by improper or wrongful means. [168]The interfering conduct need not be illegal so long as it violates generally accepted business standards.

Week 1

Negligence Defenses (Time & Immunities)

BULLET OUTLINE FOR WEEK 1:
NEGLIGENCE DEFENSES (continued)
[1] **Statutes of limitation** bar actions within different periods after claim accrues
- periods could be as short as 90 days or as long as 10 years but are usually 2 to 3 years
- [2] discovery rule tolls the limitations period until plaintiff should have known and filed
- [3] notice-of-claim statutes bar certain claims if no notice of claim w/i 90 or 120 days
- [4] filing suit tolls the limitations period
- Statutes toll limitations periods for minority, insanity, military service, fraud

[5] **Statutes of repose** bar future claims a certain number of years after the service or activity ceased
- for architects, engineers, maybe physicians, often drugs, products, buildings

Immunity
- [6] Intra-family immunity between spouses or parents and children
  - inter-spousal immunity abolished in most states
  - parent/child immunity preserved in most states
  - [7] watch exceptions for insurance, motor vehicle accidents, changes in the family relationship
- [8] Charitable immunity (abolished or limited in most states)
- [9] Governmental immunity (abolished in some states)
  - states tend to follow the Federal Torts Claims Act (FTCA) abolishing immunity w/ big exceptions
  - [10] liability for proprietary (non-governmental) functions & ministerial (non-discretionary) acts
  - immunity waivers are also common for vehicles, buildings, highway and sidewalk defects
  - government-contractor defense is a bit like immunity, where government specifies product

PARAGRAPH OUTLINE FOR WEEK 1:
NEGLIGENCE DEFENSES (continued)

In Torts I, you studied contributory or comparative negligence and express or implied assumption of risk as defenses to claims of negligence. (Remember that there are also defenses for intentional torts, like consent, self defense, defense of others, defense and recovery of property, and public and private necessity.) Here are some additional defenses.

[1] Different statutes of limitation bar different tort actions within different defined periods after the claims accrue. You may find statutes in different states barring defamation claims after one year, intentional torts after a one or two-year period, negligence after two, three, or four years, and other tort claims after four, five, or six years. You will learn these specific periods when you decide what state in which to seek a law license. [2] A discovery rule may toll the limitations period until the plaintiff should have known of the injury and its connection to the defendant's conduct. What that means is that if the plaintiff does not know nor should have known of the claim, then the statute of limitations may not run against the plaintiff. [3] Special notice-of-claim statutes may bar certain claims if the injured person does not notify the responsible agency within a period shorter than the statute of limitations. These notice of claim statutes in effect work like limitations periods barring the plaintiff's claim unless the plaintiff has given timely notice of the claim. [4] Filing suit tolls the limitations period, meaning that the plaintiff need no longer be concerned about the statute of limitations running out as to those defendants against

whom the plaintiff filed the complaint. Statutes may also toll limitations periods for minority, insanity, military service, and fraudulent concealment, meaning for instance that a child would have no need for concern that the limitations period would bar the child's claim until the child turned adult.

[5]Statutes of repose bar potential future claims a certain number of years after the service or activity that created the risk. Statutes of repose are like limitations periods in that they will have certain periods for certain kinds of service or activity, such as designing or constructing a building, or providing a medical service. Statutes of repose are different from limitations periods in that they do not ask when a claim accrued. They instead ask when the service or activity ended, whether or not anyone then had a claim. Once the period ends, the statute of repose bars all claims whether or not they have accrued.

Immunity is another tort defense. There are several types of immunity. [6]Many states grant intra-family tort immunity between spouses or between parents and children. [7]States recognizing intra-family tort immunity may have exceptions for insurance, motor vehicle accidents, and changes in the family relationship on which the immunity is based, meaning (for instance) the divorce of spouses or emancipation of children. [8]A few states continue to recognize tort immunity for charitable organizations, although most states have abolished charitable immunity. [9]State and federal law may also recognize governmental immunity to tort claims, either broadly or in defined circumstances as under the Federal Tort Claims Act. Depending on the jurisdiction, there are many variations of and exceptions to governmental immunity, often for government operation of motor vehicles and construction and maintenance of highways and buildings. In some states, statute or case law distinguish cases where there will be governmental liability from cases where there will be no immunity based on the type of action or function in which the government engages. For example, [10]governmental immunity may be waived for proprietary rather than governmental functions and for ministerial rather than discretionary actions.

Fluency Cards for Week 1

Cover and uncover the response to each prompt until you fluently recall the exact response.

Limitations Period	**Tolling**
Bar actions a certain period after each claim accrues (when all elements are present).	For minority, insanity, military service, discovery, or fraudulent concealment.

Notice-of-Claim Statutes

Bars claim unless claimant gives agency notice in short period (highway or sidewalk defects).

Statutes of Repose

Bars certain building-defect, drug-defect, or medical-treatment claims certain years after last activity.

Intra-Family Immunity

Varies but often between parent/child, less often spouses.

Common Exceptions

Motor-vehicle accidents, available insurance, emancipation / divorce, intentional torts.

Charitable Immunity

Some states recognize especially as to volunteers or cap liability at insurance limits.

Governmental Immunity

Where exists, bars claims against government, especially for discretionary functions.

Categorical Approach

Some permit claim for vehicle accident, building/highway defect, or gross negligence.

Definitions Worksheet for Week 1

1. [Review:] Define and contrast contributory negligence and comparative negligence.

2. [Review:] Define assumption of risk, and then contrast express from implied assumption.

3. What is a statute of limitations? What are typical statutory periods?

4. What stops a statute of limitation from running against the plaintiff's claim?

5. What is a statute of repose? Compare and contrast it to a statute of limitation.

6. What are common immunity defenses?

Answer Key

1. **[Review:]** *Define and contrast contributory negligence and comparative negligence.* Contributory negligence bars claims by the plaintiff at fault in part in the plaintiff's own harm. Comparative negligence reduces plaintiff's damages by plaintiff's percentage fault, the pure form from 1 to 99% but modified forms up to 50% then barring the claim.

2. **[Review:]** *Define assumption of risk, and then contrast express from implied assumption.* Assumption of risk bars plaintiff's claim if plaintiff voluntarily encountered and accepted hazards of a known risk. Express assumption of risk involves statements or writings accepting a disclosed risk unless barred as adhesion contracts, by unequal power, or by public policy. Implied assumption of risk arises from circumstances showing the plaintiff's voluntary acceptance of a known risk.

3. *What is a statute of limitations? What are typical statutory periods?* Different statutes of limitation bar different tort actions within different defined periods after the claims accrue. You may find statutes in different states barring defamation claims after one year, intentional torts after a one or two-year period, negligence after two, three, or four years, and other tort claims after four, five, or six years.

4. *What stops a statute of limitation from running against the plaintiff's claim?* Filing the lawsuit tolls the limitation period. Statutes may also toll the period for minority, insanity, military service, and other statuses. A discovery rule may toll the limitations period until the plaintiff should have known of the injury and its connection to the defendant.

5. *What is a statute of repose? Contrast it to a statute of limitation.* Statutes of repose bar potential future claims a certain number of years after the service or activity that created the risk. Statutes of repose are like limitations periods in that they have certain periods for certain kinds of service or activity, such as designing or constructing a building, or providing a medical service. Statutes of repose are different from limitations periods in that they do not ask when a claim accrued. They instead ask when the service or activity ended, whether anyone then had a claim. Once the period ends, the statute of repose bars all claims whether they have accrued.

6. *What are common immunity defenses?* Many states grant intra-family tort immunity between spouses or between parents and children, although many states have exceptions for insurance, motor-vehicle accidents, and changes in the family relationship (divorce of spouses or emancipation of children). A few states recognize immunity for charitable organizations. State and federal law may also recognize governmental immunity, particularly for discretionary functions. Exceptions to governmental immunity often include negligent operation of motor vehicles, defective highways, sidewalks, and buildings, and proprietary functions.

Issue-Spotting Worksheet for Week 1

State the law each scenario raises. No analysis. Just spot the issue and state the law.

1. You meet with a new client who begins by describing an incident that occurred "about three years ago." You ask the exact date, and the client gives a date the three-year anniversary of which is tomorrow.

2. Your client, who just turned 21 and recently joined the military, describes an injury that put the client in a coma for an extended period. It then took the client many more months to figure out who was responsible for the client's injury.

3. Your client finally gets down to explaining that a heavy ceiling tile fell on the client's head when the client attended a college- and military-recruiting event at an old and decrepit (not to mention unsafe) conference center.

4. Your client further explains that the city owns the conference center, although private entities designed and constructed it.

5. Later the same day, you meet with a husband and wife, potential new clients, who describe a motor-vehicle accident in which the wife was driving and the husband and one of their children both got seriously hurt.

Answer Key for Issue-Spotting Worksheet

1. ***This scenario implicates the statute of limitations.*** Different statutes of limitation bar different tort actions within different defined periods after the claims accrue. Statutes in different states bar defamation claims after one year, intentional torts after a one or two-year period, negligence after two, three, or four years, and other tort claims after four, five, or six years.

2. ***This scenario implicates tolling of limitations periods.*** Filing suit tolls the limitations period. Federal law tolls limitations periods for active-duty servicemembers. State laws may also toll limitations periods for things like minority (young age), insanity, and fraudulent concealment. In some states, a discovery rule tolls the limitations period until the plaintiff should have known of the injury and its connection to defendant.

3. ***This scenario implicates statutes of repose.*** Statutes of repose bar future claims a certain number of years after the service or activity that created the risk. Statutes of repose are like limitations periods in that they will have certain periods for certain kinds of service or activity, such as designing or constructing a building, or providing a medical service. Statutes of repose are different from limitations periods in that they do not ask when a claim accrued. They instead ask when the service or activity ended, whether anyone then had a claim.

4. ***This scenario implicates governmental immunity.*** State and federal law may also recognize governmental immunity to tort claims, either broadly or in defined circumstances as under the Federal Tort Claims Act. Functional tests may grant immunity for discretionary but not ministerial functions, and for governmental but not proprietary functions, or permit suit for gross negligence. Categorical tests may permit suits for negligent operation of motor vehicles and construction and maintenance of defective highways, sidewalks, and buildings.

5. ***This scenario implicates intra-family immunity.*** Intra-family immunity is another tort defense, many states granting it between parents and children, and some states also between spouses. States recognizing intra-family tort immunity may have exceptions for insurance, motor vehicle accidents, and changes in the family relationship on which the immunity is based, meaning (for instance) the divorce of spouses or emancipation of children.

TORTS WORKBOOK

Comprehensiveness Exercise for Week 1

Insert words at the ^ mark that would make for a more-accurate or more-detailed law statement.
Follow the italicized hints for help. Suggested answers are on the next page.

1. ^ Comparative negligence and express or implied assumption of risk are common negligence defenses available in many jurisdictions. ^ Comparative negligence comes in pure and modified forms, the modified forms in not-greater-than or less-than forms. *[Another form besides comparative? Define that other form?]*

2. Express assumption of risk involves written or spoken acknowledgment ^ accepting known risks ^ . Implied assumption of risk involves voluntarily encountering a ^ risk when the circumstances suggest acceptance. *[What about accepting risks under duress? Any exceptions to enforcement? What about unknown risks?]*

3. State limitation periods require claimants to file ^ within specific time for specific torts, ^ although state laws may toll the limitations period for minority or insanity ^ . *[File what? Time within when? Other tolling provisions?]*

4. Immunity may provide a negligence defense. Common immunities include intra-family immunities, ^ governmental immunity, worker's compensation immunity, and motor-vehicle no-fault immunity. *[One more immunity?]*

5. Many states recognize parent-child immunity in some form, although many states waive the immunity after emancipation ^ . Many states have eliminated inter-spousal immunity, while the few retaining it may recognize exceptions ^ . *[Other exceptions beyond emancipation? Examples of inter-spousal immunity exceptions?]*

6. State laws may recognize governmental immunity. Some states follow a functional test granting immunity to government officials and agencies for discretionary but not ministerial functions ^ . Other states follow a categorical test waiving immunity for things like vehicle accidents, building defects, highway defects, and sidewalk defects. *[Any other distinctions or tests?]*

Answer Key for Comprehensiveness Exercise

1. ***Contributory or*** comparative negligence and express or implied assumption of risk are common negligence defenses available in many jurisdictions. ***Contributory negligence bars a plaintiff's claim for any fault on plaintiff's part, while comparative negligence reduces the plaintiff's claim by the percentage of the plaintiff's fault.*** Comparative negligence comes in pure and modified forms, the modified forms in not-greater-than or less-than forms.

2. Express assumption of risk involves written or spoken acknowledgment ***voluntarily*** accepting known risks, ***as long as the agreement is not coercive or against public policy***. Implied assumption of risk involves voluntarily encountering a ***known*** risk when the circumstances suggest acceptance.

3. State limitation periods require claimants to file ***the complaint*** within specific time for specific torts, ***after the cause of action arises, meaning when all elements are present***, although state laws may toll the limitations period for minority or insanity ***and fraudulent concealment, and federal law for active-duty military service***.

4. Immunity may provide a negligence defense. Common immunities include intra-family immunities, ***charitable immunity,*** governmental immunity, worker's compensation immunity, and motor-vehicle no-fault immunity.

5. Many states recognize parent-child immunity in some form, although many states waive the immunity after emancipation ***or for insurance, motor-vehicle accidents, or intentional torts***. Many states have eliminated inter-spousal immunity, while the few retaining it may recognize exceptions ***for divorce, domestic violence, and other intentional torts***.

6. State laws may recognize governmental immunity. Some states follow a functional test granting immunity to government officials and agencies for discretionary but not ministerial functions***, or for governmental but not proprietary activities, or for gross negligence***. Other states follow a categorical test waiving immunity for things like vehicle accidents, building defects, highway defects, and sidewalk defects.

Discrimination Exercise for Week 1

Indicate whether each statement *overgeneralizes*, *undergeneralizes*, or *misconceives* the rule, explaining why. *Overgeneralizing* states the rule too broadly, capturing circumstances to which it does not apply. *Undergeneralizing* states the rule too narrowly, omitting circumstances to which it applies. *Misconceiving* states the rule incorrectly.

1. Statutes of limitation bar tort actions within a single defined period after any claims accrue, which is when the defendant last acts.
____OVER/____UNDER/____MISS/ Why? _____
_____

2. Filing a lawsuit within the defined limitations period is the plaintiff's only way of tolling (satisfying) the limitations period.
____OVER/____UNDER/____MISS/ Why? _____
_____

3. Statutes of repose for all claims bar potential future claims a certain number of years after the service or activity that created the risk.
____OVER/____UNDER/____MISS/ Why? _____
_____

4. States grant intra-family tort immunity between spouses and between parents and their children.
____OVER/____UNDER/____MISS/ Why? _____
_____

5. A few states recognize immunity for religious organizations and their employees and members acting in the scope of religious activities.
____OVER/____UNDER/____MISS/ Why? _____
_____

6. State and federal law may also recognize governmental immunity, except for discretionary functions.
____OVER/____UNDER/____MISS/ Why? _____
_____

7. Exceptions to governmental immunity often include defective highways, sidewalks, and buildings.
____OVER/____UNDER/____MISS/ Why? _____
_____

Answer Key For Discrimination Exercise

1. The statement **MISconceives** the rule. Statutes of limitation bar *different tort actions* within *different* defined periods after the claims accrue, which is when *all elements are present*, not when defendant last acts (which instead involves a statute of repose). Statutes in different states may bar defamation claims after one year, intentional torts after one or two years, malpractice after two years, negligence after three years, and other claims after other periods.

2. The statement **UNDERgeneralizes** the rule. While filing a timely lawsuit tolls or satisfies the limitations period, *statutes may also toll the period for minority, insanity, military service, and other statuses*. *A discovery rule may also toll the limitations period* until the plaintiff should have known of the injury and its connection to the defendant.

3. The statement **OVERgeneralizes** the rule. While statutes of repose bar potential future claims a certain number of years after the service or activity that created the risk, *they apply only to certain classes of cases* like designing or constructing buildings, manufacturing defective drugs, or providing medical service, *not to all claims*. Once the period ends, the statute of repose bars all claims whether they have accrued.

4. The statement **OVERgeneralizes** the rule. While many states grant some intra-family tort immunity between spouses or between parents and children, *some states have abolished the immunity*, and *many other states have exceptions* for insurance, motor-vehicle accidents, and changes in the family relationship (divorce of spouses or emancipation of children).

5. The statement **UNDERgeneralizes** the rule. While a few states recognize immunity for religious organizations, including for employees and members acting in the organization's scope of activities, *charitable immunity in those states typically also extends to other charitable organizations like hospitals, private schools, and social services*.

6. The statement **MISconceives** the rule. While state and federal law may also recognize certain governmental immunity, those laws *especially do so for discretionary functions*. The governmental-immunity laws tend *not* to recognize governmental immunity for non-discretionary (otherwise known as *ministerial*) functions.

7. The statement **UNDERgeneralizes** the rule. While exceptions to governmental immunity often include defective highways, sidewalks, and buildings, exceptions also commonly include proprietary (business-like or profitmaking) functions and negligent operation of motor vehicles.

Problem-Solving Exercise Week 1 (Problem 1)

Think-aloud problem solving (TAPS) is a proven method of using vocalization to become a more creative and better problem solver. Professionals are effective problem solvers when they speak aloud to another, speaking aloud to themselves, or let their mental operations taking the silent form of words, concepts, principles, and strategies to reach partial solutions and then chain partial solutions toward final novel solution. Read the following example (EX) and non-example (NE) of an unknown new rule (RU), one that the judges writing their opinions and orders have not expressly stated but that you must instead discern and record as your problem solution. Vocalize each mental operation taken toward a partial solution, until you reach and record the final novel rule. Check your answer against the model answer at the bottom of the next page when the professor says to do so.

EX   OPINION AND ORDER: In this case, the plaintiff minor child alleges through the child's conservator appointed in this case that the child's defendant parent negligently supervised the child, causing the child serious injury, when the parent permitted the child to swing on a rope tied to a tree limb along the bank of a pond, and instead of swinging out over the water to drop into the pond, the child let go of the rope too soon, landing on the bank and fracturing the child's shoulder. Defendant through counsel assigned by defendant's insurer has moved to dismiss. The Court grants defendant's motion, dismissing plaintiff's case with prejudice.

NE   OPINION AND ORDER: In this negligence case, the plaintiff minor child alleges through the child's next friend that the child's defendant parent carelessly caused the child injury when the parent loaded the child's canoe with a wood paddle plainly weakened by rot and shoved the child's canoe into a swift waterway, following which the child's paddle broke as the child navigated the waters, the canoe capsized, and the child suffered a broken leg striking submerged boulders. Defendant has moved to dismiss. The Court denies defendant's motion, setting plaintiff's claim for jury trial.

RU   _____

_____

_____

_____

Answer to problem on next page: While the state recognizes immunity for functions that a governmental officer or agency performs involving the exercise of discretion, governmental immunity does not extend to *proprietary functions*, meaning commercial activities in which government engages in competition with private for-profit entities.

Problem-Solving Exercise Week 1 (Problem 2)

Think-aloud problem solving (TAPS) is a proven method of using vocalization to become a more creative and better problem solver. Professionals are effective problem solvers when they speak aloud to another, speaking aloud to themselves, or let their mental operations taking the silent form of words, concepts, principles, and strategies to reach partial solutions and then chain partial solutions toward final novel solution. Read the following example (EX) and non-example (NE) of an unknown new rule (RU), one that the judges writing their opinions and orders have not expressly stated but that you must instead discern and record as your problem solution. Vocalize each mental operation taken toward a partial solution, until you reach and record the final novel rule. Check your answer against the model answer at the bottom of the next page when the professor says to do so.

EX   OPINION AND ORDER: In this negligence case, the plaintiff office-park owner complains against the defendant county corrections department alleging that in the course of a work-release program that the county operates providing lawn services in competition with private vendors, inmate program participants carelessly operated ride-along mower equipment, destroying sprinkler systems, lawn, and vegetation, at a loss of $95,000. Plaintiff seeks recovery in that amount. Defendant has moved to dismiss. The Court denies defendant's motion, bringing this case on for jury trial as to defendant's negligence and the amount of resulting damages.

NE   OPINION AND ORDER: In this negligence case, the plaintiff industrial-plant owner complains against the defendant township fire department alleging that department personnel carelessly operated a township fire truck onto and across plaintiff's property, striking and destroying expensive industrial equipment and machinery, in the course of responding to a fire false alarm. Plaintiff seeks recovery of the $100,000 value of the destroyed equipment and machinery. Defendant has moved to dismiss. The Court grants defendant's motion and dismisses plaintiff's case with prejudice.

RU   _____

_____

_____

_____

Answer to problem on prior page: Although the state has rejected parent/child immunity, a parent remains immune from a minor child's claim that the parent *negligently supervised* the child because short of abuse and neglect, the state will not interfere with parental decisions on how to raise a child.

Drafting Exercise for Week 1: Affirmative Defenses

Draft the affirmative defenses at the end of this answer in a motor-vehicle negligence case in which the plaintiff Mrs. Wolf alleges that your client defendant Mr. Wolf negligently operated their vehicle in which she was a passenger, causing her serious injuries. Mr. and Mrs. Wolf were married at the time but are now separated with a pending divorce. Mr. Wolf was driving his personal motor vehicle to a conference of state officials in his employment with the state's Department of Consumer Services. Mrs. Wolf was accompanying him as his guest. A model answer follows.

[Caption omitted.]

Answer

Defendant Bartram K. Wolf answers the complaint of plaintiff Miriam O. Wolf by like headings and numbered paragraphs as follows:

PARTIES, JURISDICTION, AND VENUE

1. No contest as to Mrs. Wolf's residence.
2. Admitted as to Mr. Wolf's residence in Wayfair, Glen County, Michigan.
3. No contest that the complaint alleges a case within this Court's jurisdictional minimum, but Mr. Wolf denies that he is liable to Mrs. Wolf in any amount.
4. No contest as to the location of the vehicle collision for purposes of establishing venue in this Court, but Mr. Wolf denies that Mrs. Wolf has this cause of action against him.
5. No contest as to this Court's jurisdiction over the parties in this case.
6. No contest that this Court is a proper and convenient venue for this case.

FACT ALLEGATIONS

7. Admitted that the motor-vehicle collision occurred, but denied as untrue that the collision occurred as Mrs. Wolf's complaint alleges. Mr. Wolf denies that he was negligent and affirmatively avers that Mrs. Wolf was comparatively negligent and the sole cause of any injury or damage.
8. Admitted that the collision occurred, but denied as untrue that the collision occurred as Mrs. Wolf's complaint alleges. Mr. Wolf denies that he was negligent and affirmatively avers that Mrs. Wolf was comparatively negligent and the sole cause of any injury or damage.
9. No contest as to the time and date of the collision at or about 8:26 p.m. on June 14, 2014.
10. Admitted that Mr. Wolf was driving a Toyota Corolla motor vehicle that Mr. and Mrs. Wolf together owned.
12. Admitted only that Mr. Wolf's vehicle was eastbound on Beacon Boulevard. Mr. Wolf affirmatively avers that he entered the intersection prudently and lawfully, was not negligent, and was not a cause of the collision.
13. Denied as untrue in the manner and form alleged that Mr. Wolf received and acknowledged traffic citations for causing the collision. Citations are inadmissible as evidence of fault. While Mr. Wolf received unwarranted citation, he did not acknowledge and instead denied and disputed that any violation occurred.
14. Admitted only that the collision damaged both vehicles and temporarily disabled Mr. Wolf's vehicle. Mr. Wolf denies any further allegation in this paragraph, leaving Mrs. Wolf to her proofs.
15. No knowledge as to the full and detailed extent of Mrs. Wolf's injuries, leaving Mrs. Wolf to her proofs, but Mr. Wolf affirmatively avers that he was not at fault and is not liable for any of Mrs. Wolf's injury, loss, or damage.
16. No knowledge as to the full and detailed extent of Mrs. Wolf's injuries, leaving Mrs. Wolf to her proofs, but Mr. Wolf affirmatively avers that he was not at fault and is not liable for any of Mrs. Wolf's injury, loss, or damage.
17. No knowledge as to Mrs. Wolf's work history and alleged disability, leaving Mrs. Wolf to her proofs, but Mr. Wolf affirmatively avers that he was not at fault and is not liable for any of Mrs. Wolf's injury, loss, or damage.

18. No knowledge as to the full and detailed extent of Mr. Wolf's losses, leaving Mrs. Wolf to her proofs, but Mr. Wolf affirmatively avers that he was not at fault and is not liable for any of Mr. Wolf's losses.

COUNT I: MOTOR-VEHICLE NEGLIGENCE, MCL §500.3135

[Answers omitted.]

Affirmative Defenses

For his affirmative defenses, defendant Bartram K. Wolf states as follows:

A. _____

B. _____

C. _____

D. _____

E. _____

F. _____

G. _____

H. _____

I. _____

J. _____

ON THESE DEFENSES, defendant Bartram K. Wolf prays for judgment in his favor and that the Court dismiss the complaint of plaintiff Miriam O. Wolf with prejudice, together with costs and attorney's fees most wrongfully sustained.

[Signature block omitted.]

Model answer: A. Plaintiff Mrs. Wolf has failed to state a claim against Mr. Wolf in that Mr. Wolf was not negligent and did not cause any injury to Mrs. Wolf. B. Mr. and Mrs. Wolf were married at the time of Mrs. Wolf's alleged injury, and interspousal immunity bars her claim. C. Mrs. Wolf may have failed to file her complaint within the three-year limitations period provided for under MCL §600.5805(10), in which instance her claim would be barred. D. Mr. Wolf was operating his motor-vehicle in the course and scope of his duties as a governmental official, and thus Mrs. Wolf's negligence claim against him may be barred in whole or in part by governmental immunity, notwithstanding the state's waiver of governmental immunity for motor-vehicle accidents as to the state itself. E. Mrs. Wolf was comparatively negligent in failing to wear her seat belt and in other ways, and her comparative negligence was greater than any negligence on the part of Mr. Wolf (of which there was none), such that the applicable law bars her damages in whole or in part. F. Mrs. Wolf's comparative negligence was the sole factual and legal or proximate cause of her injuries. G. Mr. Wolf leaves to the Court whether Mrs. Wolf's alleged injuries meet Michigan's statutory tort threshold of serious impairment of body function with respect to No-Fault Act immunity. MCL §500.3135. H. Mrs. Wolf has received and is entitled to receive No-Fault Act work-loss, allowable-expense, and replacement-service-expense benefits, such that the No-Fault Act bars her claim for economic loss other than excess economic loss. MCL §500.3135. I. If the proofs show that Mrs. Wolf failed to mitigate her damages, then the applicable law will bar those damages in whole or in part. J. Mr. Wolf reserves defenses pending discovery.

Week 2
Products Liability

BULLET OUTLINE FOR WEEK 2:
PRODUCTS LIABILITY
[11]**Three forms:** negligence, warranty and strict products liability (SPL) *(always analyze all three)*
- [28]merchants in distribution chain share warranty and SPL
  - so do suppliers of defective component parts
  - [29]but not one-time resellers of used products
  - [38]no products liability for mixed product sale/service if service predominates
  - [39]Human tissue and writings not considered products
    - rules vary on whether animals are products
- [30]Entities in the chain of distribution indemnify one another
  - loss shifts upstream to the responsible party, usually the manufacturer

Negligence (applies best to known careless acts)
- analyze duty (reasonable care), breach (fault), causation (but-for and proximate), and damages (DBCD)
- use violation of law, regulation, or standard for presumption or inference of breach

[12]**Warranty** (applies best to communications and relationships)
- express warranty (EW)
- [13]implied warranty of merchantability (IWM)
  - defined as fitness for ordinary purpose (FFOP)
- implied warranty of fitness for particular purpose (FFPP)
  - hardware store warranty
- [14]merchants may disclaim some warranties but not merchantability or for personal injury
- [15]economic-loss doctrine limits recovery of economic losses where there is no physical impact

[16]**Strict products liability**
- 2nd **Rest.:** merchants selling products in a defective condition unreasonably dangerous (DCUD)
  - must also be in the business (IB) and no modification (NM) of product
  - defectiveness depends on one of two tests, risk-utility or consumer expectation
  - [17]risk-utility test (RU) determines unreasonable danger
    - seven factors (RUSEAAP) include product utility, product risk, whether substitute products exist, whether the user was aware of the risk, and whether the user could avoid the risk, and the price or cost of alternative safer designs
  - [18]consumer-expectation (CE) test asks what the consumer would have expected
- [19]3rd **Rest.** classifies defects as manufacturing, design, or warning (MD, DD, WD)
  - [20]manufacturing defect = product departs from its design
  - [21]design defect requires risk-utility or consumer-expectation test
    - [22]may require showing an alternative feasible design
    - [31]subsequent remedial changes inadmissible except to prove disputed feasibility

PARAGRAPH OUTLINE FOR WEEK 2:
PRODUCTS LIABILITY
Products liability is a broad category of tort claims. It can help to understand products liability as a type of negligence claim (the reasonableness of the defendant's actions remains an explicit or implicit consideration in most cases) but with theories that significantly alter or go well

beyond the typical negligence requirements. In some cases involving injury or damage from a product, a simple negligence theory with the usual elements of duty, breach, causation, and damage may still make the most sense.

[11]Products liability includes not only negligence claims but also claims based on warranty and strict products liability. [12]Manufacturers and retailers may expressly warrant a product's fitness for particular purposes. [13]Manufacturers, distributors, and retailers also impliedly warrant a product's merchantability, meaning its fitness for its intended purpose. You should consider breach of express or implied warranty whenever you evaluate a claim involving injury by a product. [14]Merchants may disclaim some warranties but not the warranty of merchantability or warranties protecting against personal injury. [15]The economic-loss doctrine may also limit recovery of economic losses where there is no physical impact or injury from the defective product.

Strict products liability is a third products-liability theory after negligence and breach of warranty. [16]Strict products liability provides that merchants who sell products in a defective condition unreasonably dangerous to users are liable for resultant injury. The significant issue is what constitutes an unreasonably dangerous and defective condition. In many cases, [17]a risk-utility test will determine what is unreasonably dangerous for purposes of strict products liability. Risk-utility tests include factors such as the utility of the design, the risks it creates, the severity of the likely harm, whether it could have been avoided by alternative designs, and whether the user would know of and be able to avoid the risk, with or without a warning. [18]Strict products liability also includes a consumer-expectation test that basically asks how the consumer would have expected the product to perform. Some cases make sense for one test, and others for the other test. [19]The Third Restatement's approach is to classify defects as either design, manufacturing, or warning. Practitioners commonly begin from the standpoint of whether the case is one for defective design, defects in manufacture, or failure to warn. [20]A manufacturing defect exists when at the time of manufacture the product departs from its design. [21]Design-defect claims depend on showing that the product is not reasonably safe as designed and are likely determined by risk-utility and consumer-expectation tests. [22]Design-defect claims may require showing an alternative feasible design at the time of manufacture.

Fluency Cards for Weeks 2 & 3

Cover and uncover the response to each prompt until you fluently recall the exact response.

Products Theories	**Products Defendants**
Negligence, warranty, and strict products liability.	Manufacturers, distributors, and retailers, with indemnity up the chain.

Warranty Theories

Express, implied merchantability (fit for ordinary purpose), and implied fitness for particular purpose.

Strict Products Liability Conditions

In the business, no material modification, and defective condition unreasonably dangerous.

Strict Products Liability Tests

Risk-utility (risk, utility, substitute, eliminate, avoid, aware, price) or consumer-expectation.

Types of Defect

Manufacturing defect (departs from design), design defect, or failure to warn.

Defenses

Comparative, open and obvious, sophisticated user, learned intermediary, federal preemption, repose statute.

Definitions Worksheet for Week 2

1. What three different products-liability theories do many jurisdictions recognize?

___

___

2. When is negligence a preferred products-liability theory? Give a core example.

___

___

3. How do express warranties arise for breach of warranty in products-liability cases?

___

___

4. Define each implied warranty, also stating how or where each arises.

___

___

5. What three conditions does strict products liability have under the Second Restatement?

___

___

6. How under the Second Restatement do you determine whether a product is defective?

___

___

Answer Key for Definitions Worksheet

1. *What three different products-liability theories do many jurisdictions recognize?* Many states recognize negligence, breach of warranty, and strict products liability as separate theories in products-liability cases. Some combine the theories.

2. *When is negligence a preferred products-liability theory? Give a core example.* Negligence is best when you have evidence of what the defendant did wrong rather than simply have a dangerous product. You may then prove a standard of care and its breach. A manufacturer failing to test a product or a distributor breaking it in shipment are examples.

3. *How do express warranties arise for breach of warranty in products-liability cases?* Express warranties arise when the defendant describes, pictures, or advertises the product for certain uses, or instructs in its use as in a manual. Words or pictures representing product safety or other qualities form the basis of express warranties.

4. *Define each implied warranty, also stating how or where each arises.* The Uniform Commercial Code recognizes an implied warranty of merchantability, requiring that the product be fit for ordinary purpose, in all product sales by merchants and an implied warranty of fitness for particular purpose when the customer specifies the use and the seller supplies the product to meet the specification.

5. *What three conditions does strict products liability have under the Second Restatement?* The defendant must be in the business relating to the product, no one may have materially modified the product in an unforeseeable manner, and the product must be in a defective condition unreasonably dangerous to the user.

6. *How under the Second Restatement do you determine whether a product is defective?* The Second Restatement determines defectiveness under the seven-factor risk-utility test or consumer-expectation test. The consumer-expectation test simply asks what the consumer would have expected of the product's safe performance. The risk-utility test weighs risk, utility, whether a substitute product was available, whether the maker could have eliminated the danger, whether the user was aware of the danger, whether the user was able to avoid the danger, and how a safer product would have affected pricing.

TORTS WORKBOOK

Issue-Spotting Worksheet for Week 2

State the law each scenario raises. No analysis. Just spot the issue and state the law.

1. You just met with your law firm's managing partner and a new client who suffered a serious injury using a new snow blower for the first time. The client described the injury and its mechanism in detail, signed a fee agreement, and then left you and your managing partner to discuss theories.

2. The client already had some information about the new snow blower because after the injury the service person from the shop that sold it came out to look at it and said that it looked like it was missing a guard and clamp that they always have on them when they come from the manufacturer and that someone, probably back at the manufacturing plant, obviously carelessly left them off.

3. The client further described how he had read the snow blower's manual and thought that he had followed the instructions when he got injured. He even had a picture from the manual that showed a user doing just what he did when he got hurt.

4. The client had explained that he just wanted the snow blower to do what snow blowers are supposed to do, although he had also spent some real time at the sales counter explaining the snow depths and driveway length so that the shop could sell him just the right one.

5. After you had briefly reminded the managing partner about the three theories of products liability, the managing partner wanted to know more about the one having to do with product defects and whether that theory would apply to the snow blower's manufacturer.

6. Finally, the managing partner wanted to know what an engineering expert would have to discern to make out a case against the snow blower's manufacturer. You had a good idea of the kind of things that the expert would need to address.

Answer Key for Issue-Spotting Worksheet

1. ***This scenario implicates the three products-liability theories.*** Many states recognize negligence, breach of warranty, and strict products liability as separate theories in products-liability cases. Some combine the theories.

2. ***This scenario implicates negligence as a products-liability theory.*** Negligence can be the best products-liability theory when you have evidence of what the defendant did wrong rather than simply have a dangerous product. You may then prove a standard of care and its breach. A manufacturer failing to test a product or a distributor breaking it in shipment are examples.

3. ***This scenario implicates the express-warranty theory of products liability.*** Express warranties arise when the defendant describes, pictures, or advertises the product for certain uses, or instructs in its use as in a manual. Words or pictures representing product safety or other qualities form the basis of express warranties.

4. ***This scenario implicates the implied-warranty theories of products liability.*** The Uniform Commercial Code recognizes an implied warranty of merchantability, requiring that the product be fit for ordinary purpose, in all product sales by merchants, and an implied warranty of fitness for particular purpose when the customer specifies the use and the seller supplies the product to meet the specification.

5. ***This scenario implicates the three conditions for products liability.*** To have products liability under the Second Restatement, the defendant must be in the business relating to the product, no one may have materially modified the product in an unforeseeable manner, and the product must be in a defective condition unreasonably dangerous to the user.

6. ***This scenario implicates the Second Restatement's definition of a defect.*** The Second Restatement determines defectiveness under the seven-factor risk-utility test or consumer-expectation test. The consumer-expectation test simply asks what the consumer would have expected of the product's safe performance. The risk-utility test weighs risk, utility, whether a substitute product was available, whether the maker could have eliminated the danger, whether the user was aware of the danger, whether the user was able to avoid the danger, and how a safer product would have affected pricing.

TORTS WORKBOOK

Comprehensiveness Exercise for Week 2

Insert words at the ^ mark that would make for a more-accurate or more-detailed law statement. Follow the italicized hints for help. Suggested answers are on the next page.

1. Products-liability theories include negligence ^ and strict products liability. Analyze negligence claims in products liability as you would for other negligence claims using the elements of duty, breach, and causation. *[One more theory. And one more negligence element.]*

2. Products liability's warranty theories under the UCC include ^ express warranty and ^ implied warranty. Express warranties can arise from any representation such as product instructions. *[Warranting is not the claim. And not only instructions but several other things.]*

3. Implied warranty theories include ^ the implied warranty of merchantability and ^ the implied warranty of fitness for particular purpose. The merchantability warranty, imposed as to every product ^, means the product is fit for its ordinary purpose. *[Again, warranty is not the theory. And every product sold by anyone?]*

4. Under the Second Restatement, the defendant must be in the business, the product must not have been modified, and the product must be in a ^ condition unreasonably dangerous. *[In what business? Any modification? And any condition?]*

5. The Second Restatement's Section 402A determines defectiveness under a ^ test including risk, and ^ whether ^ the maker could have eliminated the risk and the user was aware of the risk ^. *[What does law call the test? What's the second main factor? What are the other two missing factors?]*

6. The Third Restatement also requires proof of an unreasonably unsafe product but divides the claims into manufacturing defects ^ and design defects, determined under the seven-factor risk-utility test ^. *[Can you define manufacturing defect? And what's the third type of defect and how one proves it?]*

47

Answers to Comprehensiveness Exercise

1. Products-liability theories include negligence, **breach of warranty**, and strict products liability. Analyze negligence claims in products liability as you would for other negligence claims using the elements of duty, breach, and causation**, and damages**.

2. Products liability's warranty theories include **breach of** express warranty and **breach of** implied warranty. Express warranties can arise from any representation such as product instructions, **specifications, descriptions, illustrations, and advertising**.

3. Implied warranty theories include the **breach of the** implied warranty of merchantability and **breach of** the implied warranty of fitness for particular purpose. The merchantability warranty, imposed as to every product **sold by a merchant in the business of selling that product**, means the product is fit for its ordinary purpose.

4. Under the Second Restatement, the defendant must be in the business **of selling that product**, the product must not have been modified **materially and unforeseeably**, and the product must be in a **defective** condition unreasonably dangerous.

5. The Second Restatement's Section 402A determines defectiveness under a **seven-factor risk-utility** test including risk, **utility,** whether **a safer substitute is available**, the maker could have eliminated the risk, and the user was aware of the risk**, and the cost or pricing of making the product safer**.

6. The Third Restatement also requires proof of an unreasonably unsafe product but divides claims into manufacturing defects, **meaning a departure from design**, and design defects, determined under the seven-factor risk-utility test**, and warning defects or failure to warn, also evaluated under a risk-utility test**.

TORTS WORKBOOK

Framework Exercise for Week 2

PL **N** **D B C D**

W EW — express warranty
IWM — implied warranty of merchantability
IWFFP — implied warranty of fitness for particular purpose

SPL 2ⁿᵈ
    IB (in the business)   NM (no modification)   DCUD (defective condition unreasonably dangerous)

3ʳᵈ
    MD (manufacturing defect)   DD (design defect)   WD (warning defect)

D
CCN — contributory or comparative neg.
AR — assumption of risk
SL — statute of limitation
SR — statute of repose
SU — sophisticated user
LI — learned intermediary
FP — federal preemption
GC — government contractor

- -

Hide the above to reproduce below from memory the above framework's abbreviations.

PL **N** __ __ __ __ __

W __
    __
    __

SPL 2ⁿᵈ __ __ __
      3ʳᵈ __ __ __

D __ __ __ __ __ __ __ __

After checking your answer to be sure it is accurate and complete, try again on the next page.

49

Reproduce the framework again, this time with fewer tips.

PL   N
      W

      SPL

D

- -

Reproduce the framework again, this time with no tips.

PL

Check your answer to be sure it is accurate and complete

TORTS WORKBOOK

Examples/Non-Examples Exercise for Week 2

Identify whether each fact pattern is an example (E) or non-example (NE) of the **highlighted concept**. Answers follow. In the blanks, generate an additional example and non-example.

1. Many states recognize negligence, breach of warranty, and strict products liability as separate theories in ***products-liability cases***. Some combine the theories.
   ___ The paddle broke as soon as he first used it, causing him serious injury getting the canoe back to shore.
   ___ The airbag suddenly exploded without any vehicle impact, causing the car to crash injuring the driver.
   ___ The walkway on which the resident fell was sheer black ice that the manager missed when salting.

   E: _____

   N: _____

2. ***Negligence is the best products-liability theory*** when you have evidence of what the defendant did wrong rather than simply have a dangerous, injury-causing product.
   ___ The fire destroyed the electric heater, leaving no evidence of what, if anything, had gone wrong with it.
   ___ Investigation showed the assembler had used the wrong bolt and nut that failed at the device's first use.
   ___ The elevator admitted that it had mistakenly mixed arsenic into the grain it sold the farmer for cow feed.

   E: _____

   N: _____

3. ***Express warranties*** arise when the defendant describes, pictures, or advertises the product for certain uses, or instructs in its use as in a manual.
   ___ The packaging clearly showed children using the mixer the same way that the injured child had used it.
   ___ The rancher had purchased the old augur secondhand without any information about it before it failed.
   ___ Instructions inside the drill's box referred to using grinding wheels of the type that had exploded in it.

   E: _____

   N: _____

4. An ***implied warranty of merchantability*** in product sales by merchants requires that the product be fit for its ordinary purpose.
   ___ The appliance store sold the meat grinder to the hunter whose venison sausage it filled with bits of metal.
   ___ The homeowner bought the old lawnmower used from a neighbor who said nothing of its oil leak.
   ___ The defective tanning bed badly burned the young man even though he had only used it for two minutes.

   E: _____

   N: _____

5. An ***implied warranty of fitness for particular purpose*** arises when the customer specifies the use and the seller supplies the product to meet the specification.
   ___ The fabricator bought the metal sheets online from a wholesale supplier without disclosing his uses.
   ___ The lumber yard did all calculations on its own for the defective trusses it sold the homebuilder.

Torts Workbook

The contractor used the recommended adhesive exactly as the manufacturer told him, but it still failed.

E: _____

N: _____

6. For strict products liability to apply, the defendant must be *in the business relating to the product's manufacture, distribution, or sale*.

___ The retailer had sold the defective fireworks that exploded, in its regular July 4th sales bonanza.
___ The vehicle's failed suspension was in the first line that the manufacturer had introduced.
___ The finance company had repossessed and resold the defective vehicle without knowing of any problem.

E: _____

N: _____

7. For strict liability to apply, others must not have *materially modified the product* in an unforeseeable manner after its manufacture and sale.

___ Investigation revealed that the table saw was missing the guard that the maker had sold installed on it.
___ Comparison to exemplars and design drawings show the same design problem as the failed supports.
___ The microscope photographs showed that someone had filed the gun's trigger mechanism after sale.

E: _____

N: _____

8. One test for strict products liability asks whether the product is in a *defective condition unreasonably dangerous*, under a seven-factor risk-utility test.

___ Records showed no injury reports relating to the seatback's design in thousands of vehicle accidents.
___ The lawnmower's design let it run on, blade spinning, for seconds after release of the shut-off handle.
___ The snowmobile's unguarded track had a small area where a foot or hand could get caught in the gears.

E: _____

N: _____

9. Another test for strict products liability asks whether the product *fails to meet consumer expectations*, in a way that injured the consumer.

___ The inflatable emergency raft turned out to be so small that it couldn't float and carry even a single user.
___ Test showed the tanning lotion had lye that burned the skin rather than helping the sun tan it.
___ The engineers had made the complex control system to integrate into the manufacturer's design.

E: _____

N: _____

Answers: 1 EEN; 2 NEE; 3 ENE; 4 ENE; 5 NEE; 6 EEN; 7 ENE; 8 NEE; 9 EEN

TORTS WORKBOOK

Problem-Solving Exercise Week 2 (Problem 1)

Think-aloud problem solving (TAPS) is a proven method of using vocalization to become a more creative and better problem solver. Professionals are effective problem solvers when they speak aloud to another, speaking aloud to themselves, or let their mental operations taking the silent form of words, concepts, principles, and strategies to reach partial solutions and then chain partial solutions toward final novel solution. Read the following example (EX) and non-example (NE) of an unknown new rule (RU), one that the judges writing their opinions and orders have not expressly stated but that you must instead discern and record as your problem solution. Vocalize each mental operation taken toward a partial solution, until you reach and record the final novel rule. Check your answer against the model answer at the bottom of the next page when the professor says to do so.

EX OPINION AND ORDER: In this products-liability case, the plaintiff police officer alleges that the defendant ammunition maker designed, manufactured, and sold armor-piercing ammunition that through the chain of commerce reached a criminal suspect who intentionally shot the plaintiff using the ammunition, the bullet piercing plaintiff's protective vest that would have prevented serious injury from a non-armor-piercing bullet, causing plaintiff serious injury. Defendant through counsel assigned by defendant's insurer has moved to dismiss, arguing that ammunition is an inherently dangerous product. The Court grants defendant's motion for failure to state a claim, dismissing plaintiff's case with prejudice.

NE OPINION AND ORDER: In this products-liability case, the plaintiff minor child, twelve years old at the time of the incident and acting here through his parent conservators, alleges that the defendant toy maker designed, manufactured, and sold a "Davy Crockett" air rifle specifically to a minor-child target market, supplying significantly greater pneumatic force to a significantly larger projectile having a mass and shape significantly more likely to cause physical harm, that did in fact cause the plaintiff to suffer serious facial injury when loaning his Dave Crockett gun to an eleven-year-old friend who accidentally shot him in the face. Defendant has moved to dismiss, arguing that guns are inherently dangerous products. The Court denies defendant's motion, bringing on plaintiff's claim for jury trial.

RU _____

_____

_____

_____

Answer to problem on next page: While a manufacturer owes a duty of reasonable care including a duty not to design, manufacture, and sell an unreasonably dangerous product, manufacturers need only exercise reasonable care, not adopt state-of-the-art designs, materials, or technology.

Problem-Solving Exercise Week 2 (Problem 2)

Think-aloud problem solving (TAPS) is a proven method of using vocalization to become a more creative and better problem solver. Professionals are effective problem solvers when they speak aloud to another, speaking aloud to themselves, or let their mental operations taking the silent form of words, concepts, principles, and strategies to reach partial solutions and then chain partial solutions toward final novel solution. Read the following example (EX) and non-example (NE) of an unknown new rule (RU), one that the judges writing their opinions and orders have not expressly stated but that you must instead discern and record as your problem solution. Vocalize each mental operation taken toward a partial solution, until you reach and record the final novel rule. Check your answer against the model answer at the bottom of the next page when the professor says to do so.

EX OPINION AND ORDER: In this products-liability case, the plaintiff scuba diver alleges that the defendant manufacturer designed a scuba-diving-tank system, specified its materials, and adopted technologies that differed in material respects from systems marketed by its primary competitor, in ways that substantially and unreasonably increased the system's risk of failure at depths within the reasonable range of the system's ordinary use, resulting in system failure, lack of oxygen to plaintiff using the system, and plaintiff's serious brain injury. Defendant has moved to dismiss. The Court denies defendant's motion, bringing this case on for jury trial.

NE OPINION AND ORDER: In this products-liability case, the plaintiff sky diver alleges that the defendant manufacturer designed an air-tank system, specified its materials, and adopted technologies that, while in general use in the relevant industry, were less reliable and safe than experimental designs, materials, and technologies that, while not yet adopted in the industry, were known or should have been known, and were reasonably available to, defendant whose failure to adopt those innovations caused plaintiff's system to fail catastrophically, resulting in oxygen loss, unconsciousness, and serious brain injury and other injuries. Defendant has moved to dismiss. The Court grants defendant's motion and dismisses plaintiff's case with prejudice.

RU _____

_____

_____

Answer to problem on prior page: While the sale of an inherently dangerous product is not alone grounds for a products-liability claim, marketing the product to a target population for which the product is not merely inherently dangerous but also *unreasonably* dangerous may establish such grounds.

Drafting Exercise for Week 2: Jury Instructions

Lawyers draw proposed civil jury instructions from model instructions adopted in the jurisdiction. They also draft proposed special instructions. The trial judge then decides which instructions to adopt or modify to read to the jury. Choose which of the following Michigan model civil jury instructions you would propose for your client plaintiff in a products liability case in which the plastic receptacle of a common motorized kitchen mixer unexpectedly shattered in operation, sending plastic chips into your client's face. Mark up and modify the instructions to fit your client's case. Draft any other proposed special instructions.

M Civ JI 25.11 Express Warranty—Definition
   An express warranty is a representation or statement, made in writing, orally or by any other means, by a [manufacturer / seller], that his or her product has certain characteristics or will meet certain standards.
   *(An expression of opinion which cannot reasonably be believed or relied upon is sales talk or trade puffing and is not a representation or statement of an express warranty.)

M Civ JI 25.12 Express Warranty—Burden of Proof
   The plaintiff has the burden of proving each of the following:
   (a)   that the defendant expressly warranted the product in one or more of the ways claimed by the plaintiff
   (b)   that the [plaintiff / plaintiff's decedent] [relied upon / or / was protected by] the warranty
   (c)   that the product [description of alleged failure to meet express warranty]
   (d)   that the product [description of alleged failure to meet express warranty] at the time it left defendant's control
   (e)   that the [plaintiff / plaintiff's decedent] [was injured / sustained damage]
   (f)   that the [description of alleged failure to meet express warranty] was a proximate cause of the [injuries / damages] to [plaintiff / plaintiff's decedent].
   Your verdict will be for the plaintiff if you decide that all of these have been proved.
   Your verdict will be for the defendant if you decide that any one of these has not been proved.

M Civ JI 25.21 Implied Warranty—Definition
   When I use the words "implied warranty," I mean a duty imposed by law which requires that the manufacturer's product be reasonably fit for the [purpose / purposes] and [use / uses] intended or reasonably foreseeable by the manufacturer.

M Civ JI 25.22 Implied Warranty—Burden of Proof
   The plaintiff has the burden of proof on each of the following:
   (a)   that the [name of product] was not reasonably fit for the [use / uses] or [purpose / purposes] anticipated or reasonably foreseeable by the defendant, in one or more of the ways claimed by the plaintiff
   (b)   that the [name of product] was not reasonably fit for the [use / uses] or [purpose / purposes] anticipated or reasonably foreseeable by the defendant at the time it left the defendant's control
   (c)   that [plaintiff / plaintiff's decedent] [was injured / sustained damage]

(d) that the [description of claimed defect] was a proximate cause of the [injuries / damages] to [plaintiff / plaintiff's decedent].

*(Your verdict will be for the plaintiff if you decide that all of these have been proved.)

*(Your verdict will be for the defendant if you decide that any one of these has not been proved.)

M Civ JI 25.31 Negligent Production—Definition

The defendant had a duty to use reasonable care at the time of [production*] of the [product / [name of product]] so as to eliminate unreasonable risks of harm or injury that were reasonably foreseeable.

Reasonable care means that degree of care that a reasonably prudent manufacturer would exercise under the circumstances that you find existed in this case. It is for you to decide, based on the evidence, what a reasonably prudent manufacturer would do or would not do under those circumstances.

A failure to fulfill the duty to use reasonable care is negligence.

However, the defendant had no duty to _____* a [product / [name of product]] to eliminate reasonable risks of harm or injury or risks that were not reasonably foreseeable.

M Civ JI 25.32 Negligent Production—Burden of Proof

The plaintiff has the burden of proof on the following propositions:

(a) that the defendant was negligent in one or more of the ways claimed by the plaintiff *(as stated to you in these instructions);

(b) that the plaintiff [was injured / sustained damage];

(c) that the negligence of the defendant was a proximate cause of the [injuries / damages] to the plaintiff;

(d) that the product was not reasonably safe at the time it left the defendant's control;

**(e) that, according to generally accepted production practices at the time the specific unit of the product left the control of the defendant, a practical and technically feasible alternative production practice was available that would have prevented the harm without significantly impairing the usefulness or desirability of the product to users and without creating equal or greater risk of harm to others. An alternative production practice is practical and feasible only if the technical, medical, or scientific knowledge relating to production of the product, at the time the specific unit of the product left the control of the defendant, was developed, available, and capable of use in the production of the product and was economically feasible for use by the manufacturer. Technical, medical, or scientific knowledge is not economically feasible for use by the manufacturer if use of that knowledge in production of the product would significantly compromise the product's usefulness or desirability.

***Your verdict will be for the plaintiff if you decide that all of these have been proved.

***Your verdict will be for the defendant if you decide that any one of these has not been proved.

Special instructions:

_____

_____

Review Exercise for Week 2
Match these facts with the law on the next page that they trigger.

Wow, what a day it had been. ____ 1. First, he'd barely gotten the day started when his old juicer exploded as he fixed his morning smoothie, damaging his expensive new kitchen countertop and cabinets. ____ 2. Then, when he stopped at the American Red Cross to donate blood for disaster relief on his way to work, he slipped and fell hard on some plasma on the clinic floor. ____ 3. And then, right after he signed the donation form, the phlebotomist damaged his elbow's tendon while trying to draw his blood. ____ 4. When he tried going on to work anyway, a police vehicle ran a red light, clipping the front of and spinning his vehicle, causing him to strike and badly cut his ear on the door post. ____ 5. He may have been entering the intersection on a late yellow while going a little over the speed limit, but hey, he had the right of way, didn't he?! ____ 6. Well, true, the police vehicle did have its warning lights and siren on, but he'd been distracted by a text message on his cell phone. ____ 7. At work, a process server had left a summons and complaint with him over a many-years-old business dispute that he thought was over and in the past. ____ 8. He'd had a falling-out with a business partner when the National Guard had called the partner up on active duty, leaving him with all of the work. ____ 9. And then, to top it all off, after work, he'd carelessly struck his teenage son while mowing with the lawn tractor, breaking his son's foot and ankle.

Review Exercise for Week 2
Match this law with the facts on the prior page that the facts trigger.

___A. Comparative negligence reduces plaintiff's damages by plaintiff's percentage fault.

___B. The pure form of comparative negligence applies no matter how much at fault plaintiff is, but modified forms bar plaintiff's claim at 50% or 51%.

___C. Assumption of risk bars plaintiff's claim if plaintiff voluntarily encountered hazards of a known risk.

___D. Statutes of limitation bar tort actions within different defined periods after the claims accrue.

___E. Statutes or other law may toll the limitations period for minority, insanity, military service, or discovery.

___F. Statutes of repose bar potential future claims a certain number of years after the service or activity that created the risk.

___G. States may grant intra-family tort immunity between spouses or between parents and children, although many states have exceptions.

___H. A few states recognize immunity for charitable organizations.

___I. State and federal law may also recognize governmental immunity, particularly for discretionary functions.

Answer key: 1F, 2H, 3C, 4I, 5A, 6B, 7D, 8E, 9G

Week 3

Products Liability (continued)

BULLET OUTLINE FOR WEEK 3:
Strict products liability (continued)
- o [23]failure to warn requires that omitting warning made the product unreasonably dangerous
  - [24]need be no warning as to obvious risks
    - courts recognize an open-and-obvious defense.
  - [25]warnings must be adequate, describing the hazard, risk, and means of avoiding
  - [26]law may presume the user would have read and heeded a warning
  - [27]consider the user's sophistication and learned intermediaries

Defenses
- [32]comparative negligence
- [33]assumption of risk
- [34]statute of limitations and statute of repose
- [35]exclusive-remedy provision of worker's compensation act as to employer and co-workers only
- [36]product misuse, but manufacturers may have to anticipate foreseeable misuse
- [37]federal preemption

PARAGRAPH OUTLINE FOR WEEK 3:
PRODUCTS LIABILITY (continued)

[23]Failure-to-warn claims depend on showing that the omission of a warning made the product unreasonably dangerous. [24]There generally need be no warning as to obvious risks. Courts will recognize an open-and-obvious defense. [25]Warnings must be adequate, generally meaning that they should describe the hazard, injury risk, and means of avoiding the risk. [26]As to causation in failure-to-warn cases, most jurisdictions will presume that the injured user would have read and heeded a warning. [27]In failure-to-warn cases, courts will also consider the user's sophistication and whether there were any learned intermediaries who should have given warnings.

[28]All merchants within the chain of distribution bear the same liability to the injured user as the manufacturer, as do suppliers of defective component parts. [29]Strict products liability generally does not extend to one-time resellers of used products. [30]Entities in the chain of distribution typically indemnify one another, shifting products liability to the responsible party. [31]Subsequent remedial changes in design defects are generally inadmissible except to prove disputed feasibility.

[32]Comparative negligence is an available defense to products-liability claims in a majority of jurisdictions. [33]Assumption of risk is another products-liability defense available in some jurisdictions. [34]The statute of limitations and statute of repose are also common products-liability defenses. [35]Exclusive-remedy provisions of worker's compensation acts may bar claims against involved employers but not manufacturers of the injury causing product. There are several additional defenses to products liability claims, beyond other negligence defenses. [36]Product misuse is another common defense, although manufacturers may have to anticipate foreseeable misuses. [37]Federal preemption is yet another possible defense, where state tort law would contradict federal statute or regulation.

[38]There is generally no products liability for services which do not involve products as their essential activity. [39]Human tissue and writings are generally not considered to be products, and there are varying rules on whether animals are products.

Definitions Worksheet for Week 3

1. [Review:] Distinguish Third Restatement products liability from Second Restatement.

2. How does a claimant establish a failure-to-warn claim? Explain.

3. How does law treat the relative liability of entities within the chain of distribution?

4. List common products-liability defenses.

5. What test separates products liability from service, such as doctors implanting devices?

6. [Extra credit:] What of design change after injury? What if the injury happens at work?

Answer Key for Definitions Worksheet

1. *[Review:] Distinguish Third Restatement products liability from the Second Restatement.* While the Second Restatement requires proof of a defective condition unreasonably dangerous under risk-utility or consumer-expectation tests, Third Restatement theories are manufacturing defect, design defect, and failure to warn. Manufacturing defects depart from design, but one still applies the risk-utility or consumer-expectation tests for the other theories.

2. *How does a claimant establish a failure-to-warn claim? Explain.* Failure-to-warn claims depend on omission of a warning making the product unreasonably dangerous. Warnings must be adequate, describing the hazard, injury risk, and means of avoiding, but obvious risks need no warning. Most jurisdictions presume that the injured user would have read and heeded a warning. Also, consider the user's sophistication and whether learned intermediaries should have warned.

3. *How does law treat the relative products liability of entities within the chain of distribution?* All merchants within the chain of distribution bear the same liability to the injured user as the manufacturer, as do suppliers of defective component parts. Strict products liability generally does not extend to one-time resellers of used products. Entities in the chain of distribution typically indemnify one another, shifting products liability to the responsible party.

4. *List common products-liability defenses.* Comparative negligence is an available defense to products-liability claims in a majority of jurisdictions. Assumption of risk is another products-liability defense available in some jurisdictions. The statute of limitations and statute of repose are also common products-liability defenses. Product misuse is another common defense, although manufacturers may have to anticipate foreseeable misuses. Federal preemption is yet another possible defense, where state tort law would contradict federal statute or regulation.

5. *What test separates products liability from service, such as doctors implanting devices?* Ask whether services or products predominate. Law offers no products liability for services that do not involve products as their essential activity. Human tissue and writings are generally not considered to be products, and rules vary on whether animals are products.

6. *[Extra credit:] What of design change after injury? What if the injury happens at work?* Subsequent remedial changes in design defects are generally inadmissible except to prove disputed feasibility. Exclusive-remedy provisions of worker's compensation acts may bar claims against involved employers but not manufacturers of the injury causing product.

Issue-Spotting Worksheet for Week 3

State the law each scenario raises. No analysis. Just spot the issue and state the law.

1. Your law firm's managing partner calls you back in with some questions and ideas about the snow-blower case with which you dealt last week. Your partner wants to focus on the snow blower not being like the other snow blowers that the retailer sold and only use other theories as a fallback, like whether the manufacturer should have had a different way of making the snow blower.

_____

_____

2. Then your managing partner had a thought, asking again about the manual that the client had left with you and whether the manual should have had other instructions. Maybe, too, the snow blower should have had other markings, the managing partner queried.

_____

_____

3. The managing partner told you to go draft a complaint. As you were leaving, you asked whom to name as defendants. The managing partner said she didn't know but wanted to hear your thoughts.

_____

_____

4. Coincidentally, the associate down the hall popped into your office with a few questions about a products-liability case that the firm had just assigned her to handle. Her case, though, was a defense case, and she wanted your thoughts on what to plead in the answer.

_____

_____

5. As you worked on your own case, the plaintiff's case involving the snow blower, the thought crossed your mind again about the service desk at the retailer and whether your client might have any theory based on the advice and service.

_____

_____

Answer Key for Issue-Spotting Worksheet

1. ***This scenario implicates the Third Restatement forms of products liability.*** While the Second Restatement requires proof of a defective condition unreasonably dangerous under risk-utility or consumer-expectation tests, Third Restatement theories are manufacturing defect, design defect, and failure to warn. Manufacturing defects depart from design, but one still applies the risk-utility or consumer-expectation tests for the other theories.

2. ***This scenario implicates the failure-to-warn theory of products liability.*** Failure-to-warn claims depend on omission of a warning making the product unreasonably dangerous. Warnings must be adequate, describing the hazard, injury risk, and means of avoiding, but obvious risks need no warning. Most jurisdictions presume that the injured user would have read and heeded a warning. Also, consider the user's sophistication and whether learned intermediaries should have warned.

3. ***This scenario implicates the liability of entities in the distribution chain.*** All merchants within the chain of distribution bear the same liability to the injured user as the manufacturer, as do suppliers of defective component parts. Strict products liability generally does not extend to one-time resellers of used products. Entities in the chain of distribution typically indemnify one another, shifting products liability to the responsible party.

4. ***This scenario implicates products-liability defenses.*** Comparative negligence is an available defense to products-liability claims in most jurisdictions. Assumption of risk is another products-liability defense available in some jurisdictions. The statute of limitations and statute of repose are also common products-liability defenses. Product misuse is another common defense, although manufacturers may have to anticipate foreseeable misuses. Federal preemption is yet another possible defense, where state tort law would contradict federal statute or regulation.

5. ***This scenario implicates the distinction between products liability and negligence in service.*** Ask whether services or products predominate. Law offers no products liability for services that do not involve products as their essential activity. Human tissue and writings are generally not considered to be products, and rules vary on whether animals are products.

TORTS WORKBOOK

Comprehensiveness Exercise for Week 3

Insert words at the ^ mark that would make for a more-accurate or more-detailed law statement. Follow the italicized hints for help. Suggested answers are on the next page.

1. Third Restatement products-liability theories are manufacturing defect ^ and failure to warn. Manufacturing defects depart from design, but one applies the consumer-expectation test ^ for ^ failure to warn. *[What's the third type of defect? And what's the other test and the other type of defect to which it applies?]*

2. Warnings must be adequate, ^ describing the type and seriousness of injury and means of avoiding it. Most jurisdictions presume that the injured user would have read ^ a warning. Also, consider whether ^ intermediaries should have warned. *[But first, a warning must do what? Just read the warning? What kind of intermediaries?]*

3. Retailers ^ bear the same liability to the injured user as the manufacturer ^. Liability generally does not extend to one-time resellers of used products. Entities in the distribution chain typically indemnify one another, shifting liability to the responsible party ^. *[Just retailers? And what about beyond the manufacturer? Also, what kind of indemnity?]*

4. ^ Comparative negligence, assumption of risk, and the statute of limitations ^ are common products-liability defenses. Product misuse ^ ^ ^ and federal preemption are other possible defenses. *[Just comparative, or another form, too? Another kind of time limitation? Other defenses?]*

5. Subsequent remedial changes in design, correcting a dangerous design after the product has already injured the claimant, are inadmissible as evidence in the claimant's products-liability action ^. *[But you can get the evidence in for two other purposes.]*

6. Exclusive-remedy provisions of worker's compensation acts bar an employee's products-liability claims against the employer ^ but not against ^ installers of the injury causing product. *[Bars claims against certain others, too. And doesn't bar claims against another important party relating to products.]*

65

Answers to Comprehensiveness Exercise

1. Third Restatement products-liability theories are manufacturing defect, **design defect,** and failure to warn. Manufacturing defects depart from design, but one applies the consumer-expectation test **or risk-utility test** for **design defect and** failure to warn.

2. Warnings must be adequate, **alerting the user to a hazard and** describing the type, **frequency,** and seriousness of injury and means of avoiding it. Most jurisdictions presume that the injured user would have read **and heeded** a warning. Also, consider whether **learned** intermediaries should have warned.

3. Retailers **and distributors** chain bear the same liability to the injured user as the manufacturer, **as do suppliers of defective component parts**. Products liability generally does not extend to one-time resellers of used products. Entities in the chain of distribution typically indemnify one another, shifting liability to the responsible party **either by contract or common law**.

4. **Contributory or** comparative negligence, assumption of risk, and the statute of limitations **or repose** are common products-liability defenses. Product misuse, **open and obvious, sophisticated user, government contract,** and federal preemption are other possible defenses.

5. Subsequent remedial changes in design, correcting a dangerous design after the product has already injured the claimant, are inadmissible as evidence in the claimant's products-liability action **other than to prove feasibility or control**.

6. Exclusive-remedy provisions of worker's compensation acts bar an employee's products-liability claims against the employer **and co-workers** but not against **manufacturers and** installers of the injury-causing product.

Torts Workbook

Factors-Practice Exercise for Week 3

The Second Restatement's *seven-factor risk-utility test* asks whether a product is in defective condition unreasonably dangerous so that a merchant in the business of its sale has strict products liability for injury. For each scenario, choose which one of the factors (1) risk, (2) utility, (3) substitute product, (4) eliminate danger, (5) avoid danger, (6) aware of danger, and (7) pricing would weigh most heavily in favor of one party or the other and analyze that factor by filling in the blanks.

1. Complaints of serious injury flooded the company as soon as it put the saw's-all on the market.
   The [_choose a factor_] favors the [_choose a party_] when [_state relevant facts_] because [_explain your reasoning_].

2. The defibrillator sometimes shocked the technician or a bystander but saved many lives.
   The [_choose a factor_] favors the [_choose a party_] when [_state relevant facts_] because [_explain your reasoning_].

3. The electric griddle occasionally burned heedless users who foolishly touched its hot surface.
   The [_choose a factor_] favors the [_choose a party_] when [_state relevant facts_] because [_explain your reasoning_].

4. The maker overlooked that a simple lock mechanism would have prevented the hitch's undoing.
   The [_choose a factor_] favors the [_choose a party_] when [_state relevant facts_] because [_explain your reasoning_].

5. The engineer admitted that the cement mixer's alternative safer design would have cost nothing.
   The [_choose a factor_] favors the [_choose a party_] when [_state relevant facts_] because [_explain your reasoning_].

6. The fast-food chain had in the past sold lots of kids' meals with toys without the choking hazard.
   The [_choose a factor_] favors the [_choose a party_] when [_state relevant facts_] because [_explain your reasoning_].

Sameness Exercise for Week 3

Sort the fact patterns into the best product-defect form: manufacturing (M); design (D); failure to warn (W).

1. The new high-speed cut-off saw was unfortunately missing the shield to the cutting wheel.
2. The welding machine's trigger had no guard so that an inadvertent bump could cause it to arc.
3. The manual told of how to avoid carbon monoxide, but nothing was on the generator itself.
4. The miter saw ran on dangerously after the trigger's release, exposing users to hand injury.
5. The pressure washer was so strong that any contact with bare skin could cause serious injury.
6. The carbon-fiber bike frames failed under stress because a supplier had sent the wrong epoxy.
7. The ladder that collapsed under them said nothing about being able to hold only 250 pounds.
8. Open rear windows would suck in dangerous fumes from the vehicle's side-mounted exhaust.
9. The table shot the wood back at the user because assemblers had misaligned the stock fence.
10. Without an auto shut-off handle, the untended floor-cleaning machine ran into the customer.
11. The contractor hadn't known that the base coat could ruin the new exterior-finish material.
12. The scaffolding began to shake and then collapsed for lack of any stabilizing cross-member.
13. The multi-tool snapped off right at where its missing weld would have been, gashing his hand.
14. The woman hadn't been able to tell from the packaging that the medicine was for animal use.
15. The company hadn't anticipated that the lift's bevel gears might rock and slip under vibration.
16. Engineers hadn't expected the new wooden props to swell in humidity, causing their failure.
17. The compressor's maker had failed to install its pressure-release valve, causing a hose to burst.
18. The owner's manual said nothing about fume buildup if the exhaust got plugged with algae.
19. The combine's engine cowl would get so hot that anyone touching it could get a serious burn.
20. The wheel, though fancy in looks, couldn't bear the vehicle's weight in high-speed cornering.
21. Weak without hardening, the grinder's wheel shattered, sending shards into the mechanic.
22. The excavator had a nasty tendency to tip dangerously with its arm fully loaded and extended.
23. Although it said nothing, the maker designed the car seat only for children over thirty inches.
24. The augur had a pin sticking prominently out just where it might catch a worker's clothing.
25. The soccer player cut his leg badly when he accidentally kicked the goal's razor-sharp corner.

Answers: 1M 2D 3W 4D 5W 6M 7W 8D 9M 10D 11W 12D 13M 14W 15D 16D 17M 18W 19W 20D 21M 22D 23W 24D 25D

Attributes-Analysis Worksheet for Week 3

Read the rule for the critical attributes and variable attributes listed below the rule. Then read each scenario to determine the single attribute that the scenario assesses, matching one scenario to each listed attribute. Finally, write your own scenario assessing the remaining attribute to which you have not yet matched a scenario.

While the Second Restatement requires proof of a defective condition unreasonably dangerous under risk-utility or consumer-expectation tests, the Third Restatement articulates three different strict-products-liability theories: (1) manufacturing defect; (2) design defect; and (3) failure to warn. Manufacturing defects depart from the maker's intended design. Design-defect claims require showing that omission of a reasonable alternative design left the product unreasonably dangerous. Failure-to-warn claims require showing that omission of a reasonable alternative warning left the product unreasonably dangerous. Warnings must be adequate, describing the hazard, injury risk, and means of avoiding, although obvious risks need no warning.

Critical Attributes:
1. Manufacturing-defect claims must show that the product departed from design.
2. Design-defect claims use reasonable alternative design to prove an unreasonably dangerous product.
3. Warning claims use reasonable alternative warnings to prove an unreasonably dangerous product.
4. Adequate warnings must describe the hazard.
5. Adequate warnings must describe the injury risk.
6. Adequate warnings must describe the means of avoiding injury.

Scenarios

I   A homeowner suffered serious hand injury using an electric hedge trimmer. Investigation proved the trimmer to be identical in condition to other trimmers of the same model and make. Yet the trimmer lacked a hand shield that some trimmers made by other manufacturers included. *What attribute does the scenario trigger?* ____

II   A homemaker suffered an eye injury when she stuck a wooden spoon in a kitchen mixer to push down the sauce that the mixer was churning. The kitchen mixer that injured the homemaker had a clear warning on its lid stating to keep utensils away when churning. *What attribute does the scenario trigger?* ____

III   A mechanic suffered serious knee injury when a truck spring on which the mechanic was working suddenly released with great force from its assembly. The assembly had a warning on it stating that the spring was under pressure and to avoid sudden forceful release. *What attribute does the scenario trigger?* ____

IV   A painter suffered serious back injury when the small work platform onto which he was stepping suddenly collapsed. Inspection proved that the collapse occurred because the particular platform the painter was using was missing the metal collar that the platform maker had designed but failed to provide to keep the platform legs locked in place. *What attribute does the scenario trigger?* ____

V   An electrician suffered serious hand wound when a threaded ceramic light fixture shattered as the electrician used vise grips to tighten the fixture into place. The fixture bore no warnings. A safety expert opined that the fixture and its packaging could readily have borne at virtually no additional cost a small, clear warning that serious injury could result from ceramic fracture when using a tool to over-tighten the fixture, and to only hand tighten. *What attribute does the scenario trigger?* ____

VI   *Write a scenario illustrating the last attribute that the prior scenarios do not assess:*

_____
_____
_____
_____
_____

Variable Attribute:
A   Obvious risks require no warning.

Scenarios
I   *Write a scenario illustrating the attribute:* _____

_____
_____
_____
_____
_____
_____

Problem-Solving Exercise Week 3 (Problem 1)

Think-aloud problem solving (TAPS) is a proven method of using vocalization to become a more creative and better problem solver. Professionals are effective problem solvers when they speak aloud to another, speaking aloud to themselves, or let their mental operations taking the silent form of words, concepts, principles, and strategies to reach partial solutions and then chain partial solutions toward final novel solution. Read the following example (EX) and non-example (NE) of an unknown new rule (RU), one that the judges writing their opinions and orders have not expressly stated but that you must instead discern and record as your problem solution. Vocalize each mental operation taken toward a partial solution, until you reach and record the final novel rule. Check your answer against the model answer at the bottom of the next page when the professor says to do so.

EX   OPINION AND ORDER: In this products-liability case, plaintiff metalworker alleges that she purchased a grinding-wheel product from defendant distributor that distributor had stored beyond its marked shelf life and thereafter sold in a dried-out and defective condition, causing the wheel to shatter on first use, resulting in the metalworker's serious injury. Distributor filed a third-party complaint against manufacturer, alleging that manufacturer owed distributor common-law indemnity because manufacturer made the grinding wheel. Manufacturer through counsel assigned by insurer has moved to dismiss, arguing that manufacturer does not owe common-law indemnity to distributor. The Court grants manufacturer's motion for failure to state a claim, dismissing distributor's case with prejudice.

NE   OPINION AND ORDER: In this products-liability case, plaintiff consumer sues defendant appliance manufacturer, alleging extensive smoke and fire damage from an oven fire due to a defective electrical control. Manufacturer filed a third-party complaint against component-parts supplier, alleging that supplier designed, manufactured, and sold the allegedly defective electrical control for manufacturer to incorporate into manufacturer's oven product, and that supplier therefore owes manufacturer common-law indemnity. Supplier has moved to dismiss, arguing that it does not owe manufacturer common-law indemnity. The Court denies supplier's motion, bringing this matter on for jury trial.

RU   _____

_____

_____

_____

Answer to problem on next page: While parties may contract for indemnity, and the court will enforce indemnity according to the contract terms, the court must construe the contract according to the parties' intent, which in the absence of a contrary express term, is to assign the indemnity obligation to the party whose fault gave rise to the obligation.

Problem-Solving Exercise Week 3 (Problem 2)

Think-aloud problem solving (TAPS) is a proven method of using vocalization to become a more creative and better problem solver. Professionals are effective problem solvers when they speak aloud to another, speaking aloud to themselves, or let their mental operations taking the silent form of words, concepts, principles, and strategies to reach partial solutions and then chain partial solutions toward final novel solution. Read the following example (EX) and non-example (NE) of an unknown new rule (RU), one that the judges writing their opinions and orders have not expressly stated but that you must instead discern and record as your problem solution. Vocalize each mental operation taken toward a partial solution, until you reach and record the final novel rule. Check your answer against the model answer at the bottom of the next page when the professor says to do so.

EX   OPINION AND ORDER: In this products-liability case, plaintiff metalworker alleges that she purchased a grinding-wheel product from defendant distributor that distributor had stored beyond its marked shelf life and thereafter sold in a dried-out and defective condition, causing the wheel to shatter on first use, resulting in the metalworker's serious injury. Distributor filed a third-party complaint against manufacturer, alleging that manufacturer owed distributor contractual indemnity under an express indemnity term stating only that "manufacturer shall indemnify distributor for liability caused by product failure." Manufacturer has moved to dismiss, arguing that manufacturer does not owe contractual indemnity to distributor. The Court grants manufacturer's motion for failure to state a claim, dismissing distributor's case with prejudice.

NE   OPINION AND ORDER: In this products-liability case, plaintiff consumer sues defendant appliance manufacturer, alleging extensive smoke and fire damage from an oven fire due to a defective electrical control. Manufacturer filed a third-party complaint against component-parts supplier, alleging that supplier designed, manufactured, and sold the allegedly defective electrical control for manufacturer to incorporate into manufacturer's oven product, under a supply contract stating only that "supplier and manufacturer shall each indemnify the other for liability caused by product failure." Supplier has moved to dismiss, arguing that it does not owe manufacturer contractual indemnity. The Court denies supplier's motion, bringing this matter on for jury trial.

RU _____

_____

_____

_____

> *Answer to problem on prior page:* A defendant party in the chain of commerce owes common-law indemnity to an upstream party in a products-liability case only if the defect arose upstream rather than in the hands of a downstream party. The defendant may trace indemnity as far upstream as the defect arose.

TORTS WORKBOOK

Review Exercise for Week 3
Match these facts with the law on the reverse side that they trigger.

She certainly hadn't expected the year to start like it had. ____ 1. First, her teenage son had developed a severe reaction to a medication that her son hadn't taken since he was an infant. ____ 2. Her son had a little trouble taking the medication when he was an infant but hadn't had anything like so severe a reaction until recently. ____ 3. Her son's doctor told her that a lot more children were developing the reactions and that the pharmaceutical company may be pulling the drug off the market soon. ____ 4. She felt that action would be too bad, in a way, because the drug has sure helped her son and probably a lot of other infants, but then, if it was causing too many severe reactions, she guessed that pulling the drug made sense. ____ 5. The drug pretty much did what the drug should have done, she knew that. ____ 6. In fact, she remembered that the drug had come with tear-open packaging that specifically recommended the drug for exactly the condition that her son had back when her son was an infant. ____ 7. She also remembered that the state government had either made the drug or at least sold it through a special state program. ____ 8. She was just really worried that she had somehow badly harmed her son by not being more careful about the whole thing back then, also wondering what her son's litigious father might do about it.

Review Exercise for Week 3

Match this law with the facts on the prior page that the facts trigger.

___A. A discovery rule may toll the limitations period until the plaintiff should have known of the injury and its connection to the defendant.^{Week 1}

___B. Statutes of repose bar potential future claims a certain number of years after the service or activity that created the risk.^{Week 1}

___C. States may grant intra-family tort immunity between spouses or between parents and children, although many states have exceptions.^{Week 1}

___D. Exceptions to governmental immunity often include discretionary functions or proprietary functions.^{Week 1}

___E. Express warranties arise when a manufacturer describes or advertises a product for certain uses, or instructs in its use in a manual.^{Week 2}

___F. The UCC imposes an implied warranty of merchantability, requiring that a product be fit for ordinary purpose, in sales by merchants.^{Week 2}

___G. A manufacturer has liability for a product that it makes in a defective condition unreasonably dangerous to the user.^{Week 2}

___H. One often determines defect under the Second Restatement's seven-factor risk-utility test or consumer-expectation test.^{Week 2}

Answer key: 1B, 2A, 3G, 4H, 5F, 6E, 7D, 8C

Week 4
Strict Liability

BULLET OUTLINE FOR WEEK 4:
STRICT LIABILITY
Definition: liability without fault (even with all due care) for activities or conditions on land
- [45]applies to conditions on land, not manufacture of products
- [47]the harm must be that which makes the activity abnormally dangerous
  - otherwise, the courts may find no causation
- [46]Assumption of risk and comparative negligence are defenses

Two kinds: (1) abnormally dangerous activities and (2) animals
- **animals** (three main kinds of strict liability for animals)
  - [42]wild animals
  - [41]livestock depending on fence-in or fence-out rules
  - [43]dog bites
    - statutory strict liability with provocation exception
    - common law only with abnormally dangerous propensities
- [40]**abnormally dangerous activities** (dam or explosives are examples)
  - 2nd Rest.: unable to eliminate high risk of harm from uncommon activity of uncertain value
    - apply 6-factor test (HARVUL): harm, abnormal, risk, value, uncommon, location
  - [44]strict liability for environmental harm
    - by statute but also as an abnormally dangerous activity under the common law

PARAGRAPH OUTLINE FOR WEEK 4:
STRICT LIABILITY

There are other forms of strict liability in addition to strict products liability, which is more like a negligence claim than strict liability. [40]Strict liability exists for abnormally dangerous activities, defined in the Second Restatement by the inability to eliminate a high risk of harm from uncommon activities of uncertain value. Making a dam for a waterway or storing explosives are two common examples. When injury or property damage result from an abnormally dangerous activity, liability exists without respect to fault.

The other common form of strict liability has to do with injury or property damage caused by animals. For example, [41]there may be strict liability for property damage by livestock, depending on the fence-in, fence-out, or other rules of the jurisdiction. [42]There may also be strict liability for property damage or injury from wild animals. [43]There may also be strict liability under statute for dog bites and under the common law for injury from a pet's abnormally dangerous propensities.

[44]Strict liability for environmental harm is typically a subject for statute but may also exist as an abnormally dangerous activity under the common law. [45]Strict liability for abnormally dangerous activities generally applies to conditions on land, not the manufacture of products. [46]Assumption of risk and comparative negligence may be defenses to strict liability. [47]For there to be strict liability, the harm must ordinarily be that which makes the activity abnormally dangerous; otherwise, the courts may find no causation.

Fluency Cards for Week 4

Cover and uncover the response to each prompt until you fluently recall the exact response.

Strict Liability	**Animal Liability**
Animals and abnormally dangerous activities.	Wild, known abnormally vicious propensities, dog-bite statutes, and roaming.

Abnormally Dangerous Activities	**Examples**
Factors are harm, ability to prevent, risk, value, uncommonness, location.	Blasting, storage or transport of explosives, or storage or transport of toxic waste.

Harm-of-Kind Rule

For causation, harm must be of kind that makes activity dangerous.

Definitions Worksheet for Week 4

1. Distinguish strict liability from strict *products* liability. Where would you use each?

2. What are the two main forms of strict liability?

3. Give two examples of the form of strict liability having to do with artificial conditions on land.

4. How does strict liability differ from negligence theories like malpractice, premises liability, and even strict products liability?

5. What is the test for the form of strict liability addressing artificial conditions on land?

6. Name as many rules for animal strict liability as you can recall.

7. Name two strict-liability defenses.

8. What peculiar causation issue can arise under strict liability?

Answer Key for Definitions Worksheet

1. *Distinguish strict liability from strict products liability. Where would you use each?* Strict liability has mainly to do with artificial conditions *on land*, while strict *products* liability has to do with unreasonable dangers from defects in products. Use strict liability when something on land injures another. Use strict products liability when a product injures another.

2. *What are the two main forms of strict liability?* One main form of strict liability has to do with liability for animals that one owns and controls on land. The other main form of strict liability has to do with liability for conditions that one creates and controls on land.

3. *Give two examples of the form of strict liability having to do with artificial conditions on land.* Making a dam for a waterway is one traditional example, from the *Rylands* case that started strict liability in England. Storing, transporting, or using explosives is a second example. Storing toxic waste, using toxic chemicals, digging deep pits, making large unstable material piles, or building unusual structures such as high towers could be other examples.

4. *What is the difference between strict liability and fault theories like negligence, malpractice, premises liability, and even strict products liability?* Strict liability exists without respect to fault, even in the exercise of all due care in fulfillment of every duty of reasonable care. Negligence theories all involve some degree of departure from the standard of care, even (arguably) in the proof of an unreasonably dangerous product.

5. *What is the test for the form of strict liability addressing artificial conditions on land?* Under the popular Second Restatement definition, strict liability exists for **abnormally dangerous activities** (ultrahazardous actitivites under the First Restatement). The Second Restatement Section 520 defines abnormally dangerous activities under a five-factor test including the inability to eliminate a high risk of harm from uncommon activities of uncertain value.

6. *Name as many rules for animal strict liability as you can recall.* Strict liability exists for property damage or injury from wild animals. Strict liability may exist for property damage by roaming livestock, depending on the fence-in, fence-out, or other rules of the jurisdiction. Strict liability may exist under statute for dog bites and under the common law for injury from the vicious propensities abnormal to its class as to a pet or other domesticated animal.

7. *Name two strict-liability defenses.* Assumption of risk and comparative negligence may be defenses to strict liability.

8. *What peculiar causation issues can arise under strict liability?* For strict liability, the harm must ordinarily be that which makes the activity abnormally dangerous. Otherwise, the courts may find no causation.

Issue-Spotting Worksheet for Week 4

State the law each scenario raises. No analysis. Just spot the issue and state the law.

1. Your managing partner calls you into her office to tell you about a new client whom she is thinking of representing in what she calls a *strict liability* claim involving a dangerous condition on land. The partner asks if you know anything about that kind of *strict liability* and if so whether you can give a few examples of it.

_____
_____
_____

2. So you've given the partner some strict-liability examples. The partner begins to talk about how the firm would prove the defendant's carelessness in causing the harm, asking if you think those proofs would make a good strict-liability claim.

_____
_____
_____

3. Your interjection impresses the partner who stops talking, hands you the file, and tells you to get working on a complaint. Your review of the file convinces you that indeed, the client has a strong strict-liability case. You decide to start drafting the complaint by writing out the allegations that address your jurisdiction's test for strict liability.

_____
_____
_____

4. Your administrative assistant interrupts your drafting of the strict-liability complaint with a message that a new client is on the phone asking to speak with you about a serious injury caused by a circus animal.

_____
_____
_____

Answer Key for Issue-Spotting Worksheet

1. ***This scenario implicates the common forms (examples) of strict liability.*** Making a dam for a waterway is one traditional example, from the *Rylands* case that started strict liability in England. Storing, transporting, or using explosives is a second example. Storing toxic waste, using toxic chemicals, digging deep pits, making large unstable material piles, or building unusual structures such as high towers could be other examples.

2. ***The scenario implicates the difference between strict liability and fault claims.*** Strict liability exists without respect to fault, even in the exercise of all due care in fulfillment of every duty of reasonable care. Negligence theories all involve some degree of departure from the standard of care, even (arguably) in the proof of an unreasonably dangerous product.

3. ***The scenario implicates the tests or standards for strict liability.*** Under the popular Second Restatement definition, strict liability exists for abnormally dangerous activities (ultrahazardous activities under the First Restatement). The Second Restatement defines abnormally dangerous activities under a five-factor test including the inability to eliminate a high risk of harm from uncommon activities of uncertain value.

4. ***The scenario implicates animal strict-liability laws.*** Strict liability exists for property damage or injury from wild animals. Strict liability may exist for property damage by roaming livestock, depending on the fence-in, fence-out, or other rules of the jurisdiction. Strict liability may exist under statute for dog bites and under the common law for injury from the vicious propensities abnormal to its class as to a pet or other domesticated animal.

Comprehensiveness Exercise for Week 4

Insert words at the ^ mark that would make for a more-accurate or more-detailed law statement. Follow the italicized hints for help. Suggested answers are on the next page.

1. Strict liability has to do with ^ activities on land, while strict products liability has to do with ^ dangers from ^ products. *[Any conditions on land? What kind of dangers? What part of products?]*

2. Strict liability is for ^ activities that one conducts on land ^ . *[What kind of activities? And what's the other category of strict liability?]*

3. Damming water ^ is a traditional example of an abnormally dangerous activity. Storing toxic waste ^ or building unusual structures such as high towers are other examples. *[Another traditional example? Other specific examples?]*

4. Strict liability exists without respect to fault ^ . Negligence theories require a ^ standard of care, while strict liability does not. *[What does without fault mean? Just a standard of care, or something more?]*

5. Strict liability exists for ^ dangerous activities. The Second Restatement defines dangerous activities under a test including inability to eliminate ^ harm from ^ activities of uncertain value. *[What degree of dangerous activities? How frequent harm? What kind of activities?]*

6. Strict liability exists for property damage or injury from wild animals, roaming livestock ^ , dog bites ^ , and vicious propensities ^ for other domesticated animals. *[Any specific roaming-livestock rules? What laws affect dog-bite liability? Normal vicious propensities?]*

7. Assumption of risk and ^ negligence may be defenses to strict liability. *[What two kinds of negligence?]*

Answers to Comprehensiveness Exercise

1. Strict liability has to do with ***abnormally dangerous*** activities on land, while strict products liability has to do with ***unreasonable*** dangers from ***defective conditions in*** products.

2. Strict liability has to do with liability for ***abnormally dangerous*** activities that one conducts on land ***and for injuries from animals***.

3. Damming water ***and storing or using explosives*** are traditional examples of an abnormally dangerous activity. Storing toxic waste, ***using toxic chemicals, digging deep pits, making large unstable material piles***, or building unusual structures such as high towers are other examples.

4. Strict liability exists without respect to fault ***even in the exercise of all due care***. Negligence theories require a ***violation of a*** standard of care, while strict liability does not.

5. Strict liability exists for ***abnormally*** dangerous activities. The Second Restatement defines dangerous activities under a test including inability to eliminate ***high risk of*** harm from ***uncommon*** activities of uncertain value.

6. Strict liability exists for property damage or injury from wild animals, roaming livestock ***depending on fence-in or fence-out rules***, dog bites ***depending on statute***, and vicious propensities ***abnormal to the class*** for other domesticated animals.

7. Assumption of risk and ***contributory or comparative*** negligence may be defenses to strict liability.

Factors-Practice Exercise for Week 4

Many states follow the Second Restatement's *six-factor test* for whether a condition on land is abnormally dangerous for strict-liability for injury or loss. For each of the following scenarios, choose which one of the factors (1) risk, (2) harm, (3) ability to prevent, (4) uncommonness, (5) location, and (6) value, would most weigh in favor of one or the other party and analyze the factor by filling in the blanks.

1. The demolition company hadn't expected the downtown building to topple left rather than right.
The [_choose a factor_] favors the [_choose a party_] when [_state relevant facts_] because [_explain your reasoning_].

2. The uranium waste, though hard to safely contain, was a necessary byproduct to national defense.
The [_choose a factor_] favors the [_choose a party_] when [_state relevant facts_] because [_explain your reasoning_].

3. The dynamiting inevitably produced stray rock projectiles that, though rare, caused damage.
The [_choose a factor_] favors the [_choose a party_] when [_state relevant facts_] because [_explain your reasoning_].

4. The company's waste lagoon somehow seeped into groundwater, causing deadly cancer.
The [_choose a factor_] favors the [_choose a party_] when [_state relevant facts_] because [_explain your reasoning_].

5. The hog farm sent an annoying stench toward the subdivision residences with every east wind.
The [_choose a factor_] favors the [_choose a party_] when [_state relevant facts_] because [_explain your reasoning_].

6. The mining district often shook with underground blasts, finally cracking a distiller's tanks.
The [_choose a factor_] favors the [_choose a party_] when [_state relevant facts_] because [_explain your reasoning_].

TORTS WORKBOOK

Sameness Exercise for Week 4

**Sort the fact patterns into *yes* animal strict liability (Y) or *no* animal strict liability (N).
Answers are at the bottom.**

1. _____ In a jurisdiction with a typical dog-bite statute, a non-vicious dog bit a young girl who ran past it.

2. _____ In a common-law jurisdiction, a non-vicious dog bit a young boy who rode a bike past it.

3. _____ In a fence-out jurisdiction, cattle broke through a farmer's gate to eat his cash-crop broccoli.

4. _____ In a fence-in jurisdiction, vandals let a bull out of its pen late one night, causing a car carsh.

5. _____ In a common-law jurisdiction, a dog bit a third child, even though the owner had restrained it.

6. _____ In a common-law jurisdiction, a notorious bronco bucked off a trail rider at a public stable.

7. _____ In a common-law jurisdiction, a pet-store parrot nipped the lip of a fourth patron, causing scarring.

8. _____ In a common-law jurisdiction, a friendly dog bit the leg of a mom who accidentally stepped on it.

9. _____ In a common-law jurisdiction, a mean house cat scratched a guest after escaping from its cage.

10. _____ In a traditional jurisdiction, a neighbor's goats ate a homeowner's laundry out on a line to dry.

11. _____ In a jurisdiction with a typical dog-bite statute, a caged dog bit the finger of a boy poking at it.

12. _____ In a traditional jurisdiction, a feral dog wandered onto a homeowner's land where it bit a child.

13. _____ In a jurisdiction with a typical dog-bite statute, a dog bit a trespasser who ignored a warning sign.

14. _____ In a traditional jurisdiction, a pet tiger cub scratched the eye of an adult playing quietly with it.

15. _____ In a traditional jurisdiction, sheep escaping from their owner's pen ate a grower's flower crop.

16. _____ In a traditional jurisdiction, a neighbor's cat kept sleeping on the homeowner's porch.

17. _____ In a jurisdiction with a typical dog-bite statute, owner warned a guest whom the dog bit anyway.

18. _____ In a traditional jurisdiction, a circus elephant stampeded from parade into furniture and vehicles.

19. _____ In a traditional jurisdiction, a pet alligator bit the finger off a visitor feeding it as owner invited.

20. _____ In a common-law jurisdiction, a horse stumbled, pitching its rider down a canyon.

21. _____ At a zoo, a gorilla broke the arm of a teen who climbed over a fence, slid down, and swam a moat.

22. _____ In a traditional jurisdiction, a pet boa in its outdoor pen strangled a neighbor's prize cat.

23. _____ In a jurisdiction with a typical dog-bite statute, a napping dog bit a child who mistakenly scared it.

24. _____ In a traditional jurisdiction, a runner tripped over a sleeping dog, breaking the runner's leg.

25. _____ In a common-law jurisdiction, an aggressive dog broke its chain and killed a neighbor's dog.

Answers for reverse side: 1Y 2N 3Y 4N 5Y 6Y 7Y 8N 9Y 10Y 11N 12N 13N 14Y 15Y 16N 17Y 18Y 19Y 20N 21N 22Y 23Y 24N 25Y

TORTS WORKBOOK

Drafting Exercise for Week 4: Demand Letter

A demand letter communicates to the wrongdoer or the wrongdoer's insurer the basis for the client's tort claim against the wrongdoer. The demand letter's goal is to promote a settlement of the claim before filing a lawsuit, by providing the information and analysis necessary for the wrongdoer and insurer to agree on liability and damages. Demand letters are typical before suit but not required except in medical-malpractice cases in certain states like Michigan and Florida. Demand letters often lead to further exchange of information and some negotiation, and occasionally even settlement, before suit. Working with a seatmate, **dictate a demand letter for a dog-bite incident in which the insured neighbor's four-year-old Siberian Husky dog bit and lacerated the face of your client homeowner's seven-year-old daughter**, consistent with the tone, form, and content of the following example.

LAW OFFICES

FAJEN AND MILLER, P.L.L.C.

JAMES A. FAJEN
RICHARD B. BAILEY
OF COUNSEL
NELSON P. MILLER

1527 PINERIDGE DRIVE
GRAND HAVEN, MICHIGAN 49417

(616) 846-9187
FAX (616) 846-9187

ANN ARBOR OFFICE:
2950 SOUTH STATE ST., #280
ANN ARBOR, MICHIGAN 48104
(734) 995-0181
FAX (734) 995-0184

February 15, 2012

Tyler Durgan, Claim Representative
State Farm Insurance Co.
1234 Meridian Road
Okemos, MI 48988

Re: Insured: ABC Trucking Co.
       Claimants: William R. Smith and Carlena J. Smith
       Claim No.:   14356789-00
       Loss Date: 02/01/2011

Dear Mr. Durgan:

This correspondence constitutes the demand and offer of William R. Smith and his spouse Carlena J. Smith to resolve their claims against your insureds ABC Trucking Co. and its driver/president Justin Doe, for third-party motor-vehicle no-fault losses arising out of the motor-vehicle accident at the intersection of Main Street and Michigan Avenue in Flint, Michigan, on February 1, 2011. This demand does not address or offer to release Mr. and Mrs. Smith's first-party rights and benefits.

Mr. and Mrs. Smith offer to resolve their third-party liability claims against your insureds ABC and Mr. Doe for the policy-limits amount of $100,000, provided that those policy limit amounts are all of the insurance coverage ABC and Mr. Doe have relating to the claims of Mr. and Mrs. Smith. If, instead, ABC or Mr. Doe has other coverage, including excess or umbrella coverage, then this offer is null and void. We will require that Mr. Doe execute on his own behalf and for ABC an affidavit reflecting that they have no other available insurance. We will also require a recital in the settlement agreement that the parties will set aside the agreement at no cost to Mr. and Mrs. Smith if other coverage becomes available.

The basis for this demand and offer includes the following. All records to which this analysis refers are already in your possession. The UD-10 accident report confirms that your insured ABC's truck driven by your additional insured Mr. Doe struck Mr. Smith while Mr. Smith was crossing the street within a crosswalk, under circumstances where police properly ticketed Mr. Doe for violating state law. Your insureds cannot genuinely dispute, and will instead likely admit, liability. The factfinder is unlikely to ascribe any comparative negligence to Mr. Smith.

Mr. Smith suffered three broken ribs, a broken right forearm, broken right clavicle, fractures to the right wrist, and associated injuries. Mr. Smith also suffered injuries to his neck, back, and nerves in the right shoulder, arm, and wrist. The mechanism of these injuries was the crushing force of ABC's truck striking Mr. Smith at a speed fast enough to throw Mr. Smith suddenly forward and to the ground. Ambulance removed Mr. Smith from the scene to the hospital where he remained for a period of approximately 10 days for immobilization of the rib and clavicle fractures and open-reduction surgical treatment of the broken right forearm and wrist.

On Mr. Smith's release from the hospital, physicians' orders confined Mr. Smith to bed rest at home in a hospital bed in his living room for a period of approximately 10 weeks. Mr. Smith simultaneously wore a hard cast to the right arm, wrist, and hand, exposing only the right-hand fingers. He also wore bandages fixing his right arm to his torso to stabilize the clavicle fractures, or at times, sling for the same purpose. His rib and clavicle injuries meant that he was unable to move or ambulate except with exceeding care and severe pain. Physicians medicated Mr. Smith heavily for pain during this period and afterward.

It has been approximately one year since the incident. Mr. Smith has yet to return to work because of lasting and likely permanent injuries to his neck, shoulder, arm, and wrist. The injuries are neurological in nature as confirmed by treating neurosurgeon Dr. Robert Ritter. Medical records and report indicate that the right shoulder, arm, and wrist injuries severely traumatized, stretched, or severed nerves controlling Mr. Smith's right wrist, hand, and fingers. Nerves regenerate slowly over a period of one to two years. Mr. Smith's continuing numbness, loss of sensation, and loss of control to the right wrist, hand, and fingers after one year indicate a substantial probability of permanent injury.

Mr. Smith's neck, back, arm, wrist, and hand pain has been so severe that he continues to treat under physician orders, indeed pain specialists, with strong pain-killing medication. That medication interferes with his ability to drive, think, concentrate, and focus for anything more than brief periods. As a natural and probable result, Mr. Smith has been unable to continue his work as an attorney in general practice. He has not worked since the incident and does not anticipate resuming work at any foreseeable time. Mr. Smith also no longer jogs, swims, lifts weights, and does yard and household work as he was doing before the incident. His injuries have understandably affected his relationship with Mrs. Smith.

This case is certainly a policy-limits case. Litigation will only add to the expense of this matter without changing these facts. I look forward to your response and acceptance. I have enclosed a summons and complaint but am extending the time for answer until two weeks from the date that I have your response. Thank you for your consideration.

Sincerely,

Nelson P. Miller

cc: William R. and Carlena A. Smith
Enclosure (summons and complaint)

TORTS WORKBOOK

Week 5
Misrepresentation

BULLET OUTLINE FOR WEEK 5:
MISREPRESENTATION
Definition (elements): [48]false representation knowingly made to induce reliance causing loss (FRK MRCL)
- goes by fraud, misrepresentation, fraudulent misrepresentation, fraud in the inducement, etc.
  - [54]seller must know of falsity for it to be actionable
    - requires intent, desire, or purpose (scienter or guilty mind)
    - Some states recognize [50]negligent misrepresentation for careless false statement
      - a few even recognize innocent misrepresentation
      - [55]if no intent to defraud, then law may limit recovery to restitution
      - [58]professionals who carelessly misrepresent facts to third-parties are liable only when they know of third-party reliance and take action supporting reliance
  - [51]the misrepresentation must be verifiably false when made
    - not merely conjecture, salesperson puffing, or opinion
    - honest statements of prediction or intent are not actionable
  - the misrepresentation must ordinarily be affirmative
    - [52]bare nondisclosure without duty to disclose is not actionable
      - [49]silent fraud is knowing refusal to disclose where disclosure expected
    - [53]fraudulent concealment, when active, can constitute misrepresentation
  - [56]claimant must actually and justifiably rely on the misrepresentation
    - [57]misrepresenting law is not actionable unless falsely implying underlying facts
    - we are presumed to know the law and cannot rely on its misrepresentation
  - [59]claimants must prove fraud by clear and convincing evidence, not merely a preponderance
  - [60]measure fraud damages by the lost benefit of the bargain
    - some states limit fraud damages to out-of-pocket loss

PARAGRAPH OUTLINE FOR WEEK 5:
MISREPRESENTATION

Misrepresentation, also commonly known as fraud, is another tort cause of action. Misrepresentation claims are often pled in combination with breach of contract and other business tort claims, and sometimes with defamation and other torts affecting personal interests. [48]Misrepresentation is a knowing false material statement made with the purpose and effect of inducing justifiable reliance to the hearer's detriment. [49]Silent fraud or fraudulent concealment involves the knowing refusal to disclose under circumstances where disclosure is reasonably expected. Notice that misrepresentation requires intent, desire, or purpose, or what might in the criminal law be thought of as scienter or a guilty mind. Some states do recognize a different form of misrepresentation that does not depend on desire or purpose. [50]Negligent misrepresentation involves not a knowing but a careless false statement of fact, whereas innocent misrepresentation involves a false statement made despite care, both torts being recognized in some jurisdictions.

Each element of a misrepresentation claim can raise its own issues, giving rise to special rules, definitions, or conditions. For example, [51]to be actionable, the "misrepresentation" must be verifiably false, not merely conjecture, salesperson puffing, or opinion. [52]Bare nondisclosure, without a duty to disclose arising out of the relationship or circumstances, is not actionable.

[53]Active concealment of a condition about which a buyer would want to know can constitute a misrepresentation. [54]The seller must know of the statement's falsity for it to be actionable. Honest statements of prediction or intent are not actionable when the predicted event does not occur. [55]Where recognized, negligent-misrepresentation claims may be limited to recovery of out-of-pocket losses rather than benefit-of-the-bargain damages. [56]The fraud claimant must show that the claimant's reliance on the misrepresentation was justifiable. [57]Misrepresentations of law are generally not actionable unless falsely implying underlying facts. [58]Professionals who misrepresent facts are liable to third-parties only when they know of their reliance and take some overt action in support of it. [59]Claimants must prove fraud by clear and convincing evidence, not merely a preponderance. [60]A majority of jurisdictions measure fraud damages by the lost benefit of the bargain, although some limit damages to out-of-pocket loss.

Fluency Cards for Week 5

Cover and uncover the response to each prompt until you fluently recall the exact response.

Misrepresentation

False representation knowingly made to induce reliance causing loss.

Falsity

Affirmative verifiably false statement of fact, not puffing or opinion.

Omissions

No liability (buyer beware) unless duty to disclose, special relationship, or active concealment.

Negligent Misrepresentation

Some states recognize negligent or innocent misrepresentation, limiting recovery to wrongdoer gain.

Proof Burden

Clear and convincing evidence rather than preponderance.

Professionals

Liable to third parties for careless false statements only when overt action induces reliance.

Definitions Worksheet for Week 5

1. What is the intuitive sense of misrepresentation (fraud)? What is its definition (elements)?

2. How does fraud by affirmative false statement differ from silent fraud (fraud in the omission)?

3. Is fraudulent concealment any different from silent fraud (fraud in the omission)?

4. How does fraud or misrepresentation differ from *negligent* or *innocent* misrepresentation?

5. What kinds of false statements can form the basis for a misrepresentation claim?

6. What about the victim of the alleged fraud? What kind of reliance must the victim prove?

7. When is a professional liable for misrepresentation relating to a client matter?

8. What is the burden of proof in fraud claims? Why does it change?

TORTS WORKBOOK
Answer Key for Definitions Worksheet

1. *What is the intuitive sense of misrepresentation (fraud)? What is its definition (elements)?* The public would know misrepresentation or fraud as a scheme, scam, or swindle, like someone fooling or cheating another in a transaction. Law defines misrepresentation as a knowing false material statement made with the purpose and effect of inducing justifiable reliance to the hearer's loss.

2. *How does fraud by affirmative false statement differ from silent fraud (fraud in the omission)?* While fraud ordinarily requires an affirmative false statement, certain circumstances support a claim for silent fraud or fraud in the omission, where the wrongdoer had a *duty to disclose* but purposely didn't do so. But *buyer beware* remains a basic rule. Bare nondisclosure, without a duty to disclose arising out of the relationship or circumstances, is not actionable.

3. *Is fraudulent concealment any different from silent fraud (fraud in the omission)?* Yes. While silent fraud involves a mere omission to disclose, fraudulent concealment involves actively hiding or covering up the material information, leaving a false impression. Jurisdictions are more likely to recognize fraudulent concealment than silent fraud in more cases. Active concealment of a condition about which a buyer would want to know can constitute a misrepresentation.

4. *How does fraud or misrepresentation differ from negligent or innocent misrepresentation?* Misrepresentation requires intent, desire, or purpose, meaning a guilty mind. By contrast, negligent misrepresentation, if recognized in the jurisdiction, involves not a knowing but *careless* false statement of fact. Innocent misrepresentation would involve a false statement made despite care.

5. *What kinds of false statements can form the basis for a misrepresentation claim?* To be actionable, the "misrepresentation" must be verifiably false, not merely conjecture, salesperson puffing, or opinion. The seller must also know of the statement's falsity for it to be actionable. Honest statements of prediction or intent are not actionable when the predicted event does not occur.

6. *What about the victim of the alleged fraud? What kind of reliance must the victim prove?* The fraud claimant must show that the claimant's reliance on the misrepresentation was *justifiable*. The victim's failure to do due diligence, or having done due diligence and knowing the true facts, can be significant factors in judging fraud claims.

7. *When is a professional liable for misrepresentation relating to a client matter?* Professionals who misrepresent facts are generally liable to third-parties only when they know of the third party's reliance and take some overt action in support of it.

8. *What is the burden of proof in fraud claims? Why does it change?* Claimants must prove fraud by clear and convincing evidence, not merely a preponderance. Fraud is thought too easy to allege, with claimants just making it up.

Issue-Spotting Worksheet for Week 5
Identify the law that each of the following fact patterns raise.

1. The client describes a long scenario involving the sale of the client's business, the buyer's failure to pay, the client's demand for payment, and the buyer's allegation of fraud. The client wants to know whether the client is in trouble or will ever get paid for the business.

_____

_____

2. The client asserts that the client made no disclosures about the business at all during the course of negotiations over its sale. The client asserts that the buyer should have done the buyer's own due diligence. The client wants to know whether the client can get in trouble simply for saying nothing.

_____

_____

3. In further discussion, the client soon admits that the buyer may have seen some rough worksheets on the business's income that did not include depreciation or litigation expense. The worksheets did indicate more profit than the business took in.

_____

_____

4. When you ask how the buyer got the worksheets, the client explains that the client hadn't intended that the buyer see them but that they were mistakenly among some equipment lists that the client supplied to the buyer.

_____

_____

5. Your client argues that the worksheets were just estimates, rough figures that the client had sketched out to get a sense of where the business was going.

_____

_____

6. The client next discloses that the buyer did have an accountant look over things, the client is pretty sure. At least, the buyer made some reference to an accountant's review.

_____

_____

Answer Key for Issue-Spotting Worksheet

1. ***This question implicates the elements or definition of fraud.*** Fraud is a false representation knowingly made to induce reliance causing loss. The false representation must be provably, verifiably false. The defendant must know of the falsity and intend reliance. The plaintiff must in fact have relied and that reliance must have been justifiable under all the circumstances.

2. ***This question implicates fraudulent omission or silent fraud.*** While fraud ordinarily requires an affirmative false statement, certain circumstances support a claim for silent fraud or fraud in the omission, where the wrongdoer had a *duty to disclose* but purposely didn't do so. But *buyer beware* remains a basic rule. Bare nondisclosure, without a duty to disclose arising out of the relationship or circumstances, is not actionable.

3. ***The question implicates fraudulent concealment.*** While silent fraud involves a mere omission to disclose, fraudulent concealment involves actively hiding or covering up the material information, leaving a false impression. Jurisdictions are more likely to recognize fraudulent concealment than silent fraud in more cases. Active concealment of a condition about which a buyer would want to know can constitute a misrepresentation.

4. ***The question implicates negligent or innocent misrepresentation.*** Misrepresentation requires intent, desire, or purpose, meaning a guilty mind. By contrast, negligent misrepresentation, if recognized in the jurisdiction, involves not a knowing but *careless* false statement of fact. Innocent misrepresentation would involve a false statement made despite care.

5. ***The question implicates the kinds of statements that can form the basis for a misrepresentation claim.*** To be actionable, the "misrepresentation" must be verifiably false, not merely conjecture, salesperson puffing, or opinion. The seller must also know of the statement's falsity for it to be actionable. Honest statements of prediction or intent are not actionable when the predicted event does not occur.

6. ***The question implicates the reliance element of a misrepresentation claim.*** The fraud claimant must show that the claimant's reliance on the misrepresentation was *justifiable*. The victim's failure to do due diligence, or having done due diligence and knowing the true facts, can be significant factors in judging fraud claims.

Comprehensiveness Exercise for Week 5

Insert words at the ^ mark that would make for a more-accurate or more-detailed law statement. Follow the italicized hints for help. Suggested answers are on the next page.

1. The public would know misrepresentation or fraud as a swindle, ^ but law defines misrepresentation as a ^ false ^ statement inducing ^ reliance to the hearer's loss. *[Other common names for fraud? What does the defrauder have to know? Any false statement? What kind of reliance?]*

2. Fraud ordinarily requires an affirmative false statement, but a claim for silent fraud or fraud in the omission may be possible where the wrongdoer failed to disclose ^ . *[Any failure to disclose?]*

3. Fraudulent concealment involves ^ missing ^ information, leaving a false impression. *[Just missing information? And what kind of missing information?]*

4. Misrepresentation requires a guilty mind. By contrast, negligent misrepresentation involves an unknowing ^ false statement of ^ fact. *[Just an unknowing false statement? And any fact?]*

5. To be actionable, a misrepresentation must be ^ false, not merely ^ conjecture. *[False to whom? Anything other than conjecture?]*

6. The fraud claimant must show that the claimant ^ relied on the misrepresentation. *[Any reliance?]*

7. Professionals who misrepresent facts are generally liable to third-parties only when they know of the third party's reliance. *[Knowledge alone is enough?]*

Answer Key for Comprehensiveness Exercise

1. The public would know misrepresentation or fraud as a swindle, **scheme, or scam,** but law defines misrepresentation as a **knowing** false **material fact** statement inducing **justifiable** reliance to the hearer's loss.

2. Fraud ordinarily requires an affirmative false statement, but a claim for silent fraud or fraud in the omission may be possible where the wrongdoer failed to disclose **when having a duty to disclose and for the purpose of causing loss**.

3. Fraudulent concealment involves **active, affirmative concealment of** missing **material** information, leaving a false impression.

4. Misrepresentation requires a guilty mind. By contrast, negligent misrepresentation involves an unknowing **careless** false statement of **material** fact.

5. To be actionable, a misrepresentation must be **provably and verifiably** false, not merely **opinion, prediction, estimate, or** conjecture.

6. The fraud claimant must show that the claimant **justifiably** relied on the misrepresentation.

7. Professionals who misrepresent facts are generally liable to third-parties only when they know of the third party's reliance **and take overt action toward that third party.**

Scenario-Generating Worksheet for Week 5
Generate a scenario demonstrating each of the following rules.

1. Fraud is a false representation knowingly made to induce reliance causing loss. The false representation must be provably, verifiably false. The defendant must know of the falsity and intend reliance. The plaintiff must in fact have relied and that reliance must have been justifiable under all the circumstances.

___

2. While fraud ordinarily requires an affirmative false statement, certain circumstances support a claim for silent fraud or fraud in the omission, where the wrongdoer had a duty to disclose but purposely didn't do so. But buyer beware remains a basic rule. Bare nondisclosure, without a duty to disclose arising out of the relationship or circumstances, is not actionable.

___

3. While silent fraud involves a mere omission to disclose, fraudulent concealment involves actively hiding or covering up the material information, leaving a false impression. Jurisdictions are more likely to recognize fraudulent concealment than silent fraud in more cases. Active concealment of a condition about which a buyer would want to know can constitute a misrepresentation.

___

4. Misrepresentation requires intent, desire, or purpose, meaning a guilty mind. By contrast, negligent misrepresentation, if recognized in the jurisdiction, involves not a knowing but careless false statement of fact. Innocent misrepresentation would involve a false statement made despite care.

___

5. The fraud claimant must show that the claimant's reliance on the misrepresentation was justifiable. The victim's failure to do due diligence, or having done due diligence and knowing the true facts, can be significant factors in judging fraud claims.

___

Examples for Scenario-Generating Worksheet

1. ***This scenario implicates the elements or definition of fraud.*** A schemer secured a post-office box and began to email elderly persons with urgent requests for charitable help with any fake need that the schemer could dream up, plying any person who responded with further fabricated stories to try to get them to send money to the post-office box.

2. ***This scenario implicates fraudulent omission or silent fraud.*** A real estate agent who had a representation agreement with the buyer, not the seller, decided not to tell the buyer about the home's foundation crack that the seller had disclosed to the agent, hoping that the buyer wouldn't notice and that the deal would go through so that the agent could earn the commission.

3. ***The scenario implicates fraudulent concealment.*** The owner of a leaky boat had the marina lift it out of the water and store it in dry dock during the height of the boating season so that the owner could represent that the boat was seaworthy, so that the owner could sell it for a better price and quickly leave town with the money.

4. ***The scenario implicates negligent or innocent misrepresentation.*** A small-business owner, who had only a general sense of the business's revenue, profit, and debt, wrote good-faith estimates on the back of one of the bar's napkins for a potential buyer to consider. The owner carelessly misstated the figures in ways that made the business look more valuable.

5. ***The scenario implicates the reliance element of a misrepresentation claim.*** A commercial building's seller misstated to a buyer the age of the building's roof and how recent were the building's last renovations in ways that made the building sound more valuable than it was, but the seller also inserted a no-representations clause in the sale agreement along with an inspection contingency. The buyer had an inspector look at parts of the building but not all of it, and received and reviewed the partial report.

Drafting Exercise for Week 5: Caption

Draft the caption of a fraud claim. A tort claimant's lawyer will typically make a written demand on the wrongdoer whose insurer will reply. If the claimant and insurer do not resolve the claim, then the claimant's lawyer may start a lawsuit by filing a complaint. Every complaint must have a caption providing the court and parties with certain information. The requirements differ a little from state to state and between the federal and state courts. This exercise follows rules common to Michigan state courts. Following the guide below, draft the caption of the following complaint.

1. You must choose the court in which to file the complaint, usually for businesses or commercial cases like this one the court of the county in which the defendant does business. Your client, a corporation headquartered in Kent County, suffered financial loss when fraudulently induced to invest in a business located in Ionia County.

2. You must state your client's legal name, which is Invest America, Inc.

3. You must state the defendant's legal name, which is Cooperative Ventures, Inc.

4. You must put the last two digits of the year when you file the complaint as the first part of the case number.

5. You must leave a blank for the court to assign the case number.

6. You must choose the correct two-letter case code. Contract disputes bear the CK case code. Business claims bear the CB case code. General civil cases bear the CZ case code.

7. You must leave a blank for the court to randomly assign the case judge.

8. You must list your name, bar number, address, telephone, and party whom you represent.

9. Every court paper must bear an appropriate title.

10. Every court paper would begin with a basic statement of its form including the party filing the paper and the party against whom the filing party seeks relief.

Torts Workbook
STATE OF MICHIGAN

IN THE [1]_____ COUNTY CIRCUIT COURT

_____
)
[2]_____,)   No. [4]____--[5]_____--[6]____
            Plaintiff,   )
        v   )   Hon.
[7]_____)
)
)
[3]_____,)
            Defendant.   )
_____)

[8]_____ (P_____)
_____
_____
_____
_____
Attorneys for _____
_____

                [9]_____

    Plaintiff _____ complains against defendant _____ stating:

PARTIES, VENUE, AND JURISDICTION
[Numbered paragraphs alleging the claim follow.]

ALLEGATIONS OF FACT
[Numbered paragraphs alleging the claim follow.]

COUNT I
[Numbered paragraphs alleging the claim follow.]

Review Exercise for Week 5
Match these facts with the law on the next page that they trigger.

Her life lately had been like a bad dream. ____ 1. First, she had borrowed a friend's snow blower only to seriously injure her ankle when the thing unexpectedly jumped back at her when she pulled on the start rope. ____ 2. She and her friend later looked it over including reviewing the manual, and they couldn't find caution about it doing that. ____ 3. She'd talked to a local sales person who told her that *yeah, they'd stopped making them like that anymore.* ____ 4. She'd hardly gotten over the shock of the whole incident when the neighbor's dog had bitten and lacerated her leg as she rode her bicycle out her driveway one morning. ____ 5. She'd limped over to the neighbor's house to complain only to find that she'd walked through poison oak and poison ivy that her neighbor later explained, after she'd broken out in severe rashes, that he was cultivating for their supposed medicinal effects. ____ 6. She'd argued with him that he was nuts and stupid for bringing that poisonous stuff into the neighborhood, but he'd argued right back that the stuff really was medicinal. ____ 7. The pharmacist had then sold her an expensive but ultimately useless remedy advertised for sunburn but that the pharmacist said worked great for poisonous-plant rashes. ____ 8. Then, her old shed out back of her house, one her dad had bought probably twenty years ago, had collapsed on her when she opened its rickety old door. ____ 9. When her dad inspected the collapsed shed for her, he showed her that her ex-husband's haphazard modifications to the shed's structure were probably the cause of its collapse. *Bad dream, indeed*, she thought.

Review Exercise for Week 5
Match this law with the facts on the prior page that the facts trigger.

___A. Statutes of repose bar potential future claims a certain number of years after the service or activity that created the risk.^(Week 1)

___B. States may grant immunity between spouses or between parents and children, although many have exceptions for insurance, motor-vehicle accidents, and change in the family relationship.^(Week 1)

___C. Law implies a warranty of fitness for particular purpose when a buyer specifies the use and a seller supplies the product for the use.^(Week 2)

___D. The Second Restatement's consumer-expectation test asks what the consumer would have expected of the product's safe performance.^(Week 2)

___E. Third Restatement theories are manufacturing defect, design defect, and failure to warn.^(Week 3)

___F. Subsequent remedial changes in design are inadmissible to prove defect but admissible to prove disputed feasibility.^(Week 3)

___G. Strict liability may exist under statute for dog bites and under the common law for injury from vicious propensities abnormal to the animal's class.^(Week 4)

___H. Under the Second Restatement, strict liability also exists for abnormally dangerous activities.^(Week 4)

___I. An abnormally dangerous activity depends on inability to eliminate a high risk of harm from uncommon activities of uncertain value.^(Week 4)

Answer key: 1D, 2E, 3F, 4G, 5H, 6I, 7C, 8A, 9B

TORTS WORKBOOK

Problem-Solving Exercise Week 5

Working with a seatmate, read the following example (EX) and non-example (NE) of an unknown new rule (RU), one that the judge writing the opinions and orders has not expressly stated but that you must instead discern and record as your problem solution. To solve the problem, one student vocalize each mental operation taken toward a partial solution, while the other student actively listens, confirming, shaping, correcting, and guiding the other student's vocalizations, until both of you reach and record the final novel rule. Check your answer against the model answer at the bottom after the professor says to do so.

EX OPINION AND ORDER: In this misrepresentation case, plaintiff alleges that he bought from defendant a used motor vehicle that defendant knowingly and falsely misrepresented as having no frame, floorboard, or panel rust, when to the contrary, all had substantial rust requiring extensive and expensive repair. Plaintiff signed an as-is disclaimer after completing the transaction and on the alleged oral assurances of the vehicle's condition, in which he expressly accepted the risk that the vehicle was in a condition other than as orally represented. Defendant has moved to dismiss, arguing that plaintiff cannot show justifiable reliance. The Court denies defendant's motion, bringing this matter on for jury trial.

NE OPINION AND ORDER: In this misrepresentation case, plaintiff alleges that she bought from defendant a used motor vehicle that defendant knowingly and falsely misrepresented as never having been in an accident, when to the contrary, accident had twisted the vehicle's frame and caused other substantial damage. Plaintiff signed an as-is disclaimer before completing the transaction and before the alleged oral statements of the vehicle's condition, in which she expressly accepted the risk that the vehicle was in a condition other than as orally represented. Defendant through counsel has moved to dismiss, arguing that plaintiff cannot show justifiable reliance. The Court grants defendant's motion, dismissing plaintiff's case with prejudice.

RU _____

_____

_____

_____

_____

Answer: While ordinarily, when a buyer signs a disclaimer for an as-is sale, the buyer cannot justifiably rely on oral statements of the item's condition, when instead the seller fraudulently induces the disclaimer signature, then the buyer may ignore the disclaimer, to proceed with a misrepresentation claim.

Week 6

Defamation (Common Law)

BULLET OUTLINE FOR WEEK 6:
DEFAMATION
Three-part analysis: (1) common law, (2) constitution, (3) privileges *(always analyze all three)*
- the tort's gist is its gossip-like false sting lowering a person's reputation
- analyze all three parts whether or not you think they apply

Common law (False Word POEMS)
- Forms: [62]libel (written) and slander (oral)
  - [71]slander claims require special damages
  - exceptions for loathsome disease, incompetence in trade or profession, sexual misconduct, or crimes of moral turpitude (DISC)
  - [72]libel claims do not require proof of special damages
- Definition (elements): [61]false words published of and concerning another that with extrinsic facts carries a defamatory (reputation-lowering) meaning, with special damages except where presumed
  - [63]false words means verifiably (objectively) false, not opinions
  - [64]publication means false words must reach and be understood by another
    - [65]primary publishers (originators) must reasonably anticipate republication
    - secondary publishers (media who publish and distribute) bear same liability
      - [66]internet service providers have statutory immunity unless creating the content
    - [67]some courts recognize compelled self-publication
    - [68]single-publication rule triggers the statute of limitation once at first publication
  - [69]of-and-concerning element means the publication must identify the claimant
    - not necessary by name if circumstances reveal identity
    - [70]individual claim for defaming groups of smaller number
  - defamatory meaning element means publication has sting lowering reputation
    - must lower reputation among at least a respectable minority of persons
  - [73]special damages are pecuniary loss (lost job, income, medical expense)

PARAGRAPH OUTLINE FOR WEEK 6:
DEFAMATION
Common Law. Defamation is the next new tort theory you learn in Torts II. [61]Defamation involves false communication published of and concerning another that, together with extrinsic facts, harms the reputation of that other, with special damages except where damages are presumed. [62]Defamation in written form is libel, whereas defamation in oral form is slander, with some differences in elements as to each. [63]Although it is often said that truth is a defense to defamation claims, more accurately, the defamation claimant has the burden to prove falsity.

As in the case of misrepresentation and other tort claims, defamation has common-law elements that give rise to special issues requiring special rules, definitions, and conditions. For example, [64]to satisfy the publication element of a defamation claim, the false statement must reach and be understood by another. It can help to think of defamation as a strict liability tort. [65]Primary publishers must reasonably anticipate republication and pay for resulting damage from defamatory statements. [66]Internet service providers have statutory immunity from defamation liability when they are not the information content provider. [67]Some courts recognize defamation claims in which circumstances compelled the claimant to self-publish the false statements. [68]Under a single-publication rule, most jurisdictions treat the original publication date as the date the cause of action arose, rather than treating subsequent printings as additional accrual dates, for purposes of the statute of limitations.

[69]Defamation's of-and-concerning element requires that the publication identify the claimant, although not necessarily by name if the circumstances make it sufficiently clear to whom the publication refers. [70]A publication can defame an individual by referring to a group of which the individual was a member, so long as the reasonable person would identify the individual in that manner (for reasonably small groups). [71]Slander claims ordinarily require proof of special damages except where the slander is as to loathsome disease, incompetence in one's trade or profession, sex, or crimes of moral turpitude. [72]Libel claims, based on writings or their equivalent, do not require proof of special damages. [73]Special damages are shown by proof of pecuniary loss from third persons believing and acting on the defamatory statement.

Fluency Cards for Week 6

Cover and uncover the response to each prompt until you fluently recall the exact response.

Defamation	**Sting**
False words published of another that with extrinsic facts lowers reputation, causing special damages.	Must lower reputation within at least a respectable minority community.

Falsity

Must be verifiably false, not subjective opinion.

Special Damages

Monetary loss, not required for libel (written), only for slander (oral), unless disease, incompetence, sex, or crime.

Publication

Must purposefully reach a third person who understands.

Publishers

Primary (originators) and secondary (republishers) both liable, but not conduits.

Group Defamation

Group must be small enough or victim prominent enough for individual to sue.

Definitions Worksheet for Week 6

1. What is the intuitive sense of defamation? What is its definition (elements)?

2. What are defamation's two forms? What defines each form? What test applies in a close call?

3. How do the elements change for each of the two forms of defamation?

4. What defines defamation's *publication* element? Must the publication be intentional?

5. Distinguish the defamation liability of primary publishers, secondary publishers, and conduits.

6. Must a statement use the person's name, to meet the of-and-concerning element? Explain.

7. What if the defamatory statement refers to a group rather than an individual?

Answer Key for Definitions Worksheet

1. *What is the intuitive sense of defamation? What is its definition (elements)?* The public would think of defamation as gossip, rumor, innuendo, or maybe *slander*, which is actually one of the two legal forms of defamation. Defamation involves false communication published of and concerning another that, together with extrinsic facts, harms the reputation of that other, with special damages except where law presumes damages.

2. *What are defamation's two forms? What defines each form? What test applies in a close call?* **Libel** and **slander** are defamation's two forms. Defamation in written form is libel, whereas defamation in oral form is slander, with some differences in elements as to each. In close calls such as radio or television read from a script, consider the impact that the defamation has (greater impact, then libel, but lesser impact, then slander), but also look for statutes in the media area.

3. *How do the elements change for each of the two forms of defamation?* Slander claims ordinarily require proof of special damages except where the slander is as to loathsome disease, incompetence in one's trade or profession, sex, or crimes of moral turpitude. Libel claims, based on writings or their equivalent, do not require proof of special damages. Special damages mean pecuniary loss from third persons believing and acting on the defamatory statement.

4. *What defines defamation's publication element? Must the publication be intentional?* To satisfy the publication element of a defamation claim, the false statement must reach and be understood by another. The publication must ordinarily be intentional, although in some cases negligence may be enough, such as mailing a publication to an address where others would open it.

5. *Distinguish the defamation liability of primary publishers, secondary publishers, and conduits.* Primary publishers are the ones who first originate the defamation, like a reporter writing a false story. Secondary publishers pass along the defamation, like the newspaper or media outlet that picks up the story. Both primary and secondary publishers have defamation liability. Conduits, having *no* defamation liability, simply transmit information without creating or even evaluating the content, an internet service provider, which have statutory immunity in any case.

6. *Must a statement use the person's name, to meet the of-and-concerning element? Explain.* Defamation's of-and-concerning element requires that the statement identify the claimant, although not necessarily by name if the circumstances make it sufficiently clear to whom the publication refers. If someone who knows the person would recognize the defamatory statement as referring to that person, then the statement satisfies the publication element.

7. *What if the defamatory statement refers to a group rather than an individual?* A publication can defame an individual by referring to a group of which the individual is a member, as long as the reasonable person would identify the individual in that manner.

Issue-Spotting Worksheet for Week 6
Identify the law that each of the following fact patterns raise.

1. Your client, a restaurant owner, describes a long scenario involving a former frequent customer of the restaurant with whom the owner had a dispute. The former customer is now spreading vicious rumors of all kinds about the restaurant and owner on social media. The owner is worried both about declining restaurant revenue and the owner's own reputational harm. The owner keeps saying that she wants to sue for *slander* but wants to know more about the law.

_____

_____

2. So you've told the client that what the client describes isn't exactly *slander*. The client wants to know *what is it?* The client looks suspicious about your theory of this thing *defamation*.

_____

_____

3. The client is now irked at what she calls your *lawyer talk*. She simply wants to know what difference *libel* or *slander* make and then have you get on with suing the former customer.

_____

_____

4. The client shares one other concern that he had only heard about the former customer's Facebook post but hadn't actually seen it and couldn't find it on the internet even through her own Facebook account.

_____

_____

5. The client is so concerned over losing her restaurant that she also wants to know whether Facebook, a review/ratings website, or an internet service provider like Charter (Spectrum) can also be liable.

_____

_____

Answer Key for Issue-Spotting Worksheet

1. ***This scenario implicates the elements or definition of defamation.*** The public would think of defamation as gossip, rumor, innuendo, or *slander*, which is actually one of the two legal forms of defamation. From the law's standpoint, defamation involves false communication published of and concerning another that, together with extrinsic facts, harms the reputation of that other, with special damages except where law presumes damages.

2. ***This scenario implicates the difference between libel and slander.*** *Libel* and *slander* are defamation's two forms. Defamation in written form is libel, whereas defamation in oral form is slander, with some differences in elements as to each. In close calls such as radio or television read from a script, the law consider the impact that the defamation has (greater impact, then libel, but lesser impact, then slander), but also look for statutes in the media area.

3. ***This scenario implicates the additional "special damages" requirement for slander.*** Slander claims ordinarily require proof of special damages. Special damages mean pecuniary loss from third persons believing and acting on the defamatory statement. Exceptions are where the slander is as to loathsome disease, incompetence in one's trade or profession, sexual misconduct, or crimes of moral turpitude. Libel claims, based on writings or their equivalent, do not require proof of special damages.

4. ***This scenario implicates the "publication" element.*** To satisfy the publication element of a defamation claim, the false statement must reach and be understood by another. The publication must ordinarily be intentional, although in some cases negligence may be enough, such as mailing a publication to an address where others would open it.

5. ***This scenario implicates primary and secondary publishers.*** Primary publishers are the ones who first originate the defamation, like a reporter writing a false story. Secondary publishers pass along the defamation, like the newspaper or media outlet that picks up the story. Both primary and secondary publishers have defamation liability. Conduits, having *no* defamation liability, simply transmit information without creating or even evaluating the content, like an internet service provider, which has statutory immunity in any case.

Comprehensiveness Exercise for Week 6

Insert words at the ^ mark that would make for a more-accurate or more-detailed law statement. Follow the italicized hints for help. Suggested answers are on the next page.

1. The public would know defamation as gossip or slander, but law defines defamation as false words ^ of and concerning someone that ^ lowers reputation ^ . *[Missing an important element. May need context. One last element in some cases.]*

2. Slander claims ordinarily require proof of special damages except where the slander is as to ^ disease, incompetence ^, ^ or crimes ^. *[What kind of disease, incompetence, and crime? Also, one more type.]*

3. To satisfy the publication element of a defamation claim, the false statement must reach ^ another. *[Just reach?]*

4. Primary publishers originate the defamation, like a reporter writing a false story. Secondary publishers pass along the defamation ^ . Conduits ^ simply transmit information ^ . *[Have an example? Why a conduits category? Have an example?]*

5. To satisfy the *false words* requirement, the statement must be provably ^ false ^ . *[What does provably mean? State a contrast.]*

6. A publication can defame an individual by referring to a group of which the individual is a member ^ . *[Need a limitation.]*

7. Defamation's of-and-concerning element requires that the statement identify the claimant ^ . *[You mean by name?]*

Answer Key for Comprehensiveness Exercise

1. The public would know defamation as gossip or slander, but law defines defamation as false words **published** of and concerning someone that **together with extrinsic facts** lowers reputation **causing special damages unless excepted**.

2. Slander claims ordinarily require proof of special damages except where the slander is as to **loathsome** disease, incompetence **in trade or profession**, **sexual misconduct,** or crimes **of moral turpitude**.

3. To satisfy the publication element of a defamation claim, the false statement must reach **and be understood by** another.

4. Primary publishers originate the defamation, like a reporter writing a false story. Secondary publishers pass along the defamation, **like a newspaper or media outlet that picks up the story**. Conduits, **having no liability,** simply transmit information, **like an internet service provider, which also has statutory immunity**.

5. To satisfy the *false words* requirement, the statement must be provably **verifiably, objectively false** false, **not subjective statements of evaluation or opinion**.

6. A publication can defame an individual by referring to a group of which the individual is a member, **if the reasonable person would identify the individual in that manner**.

7. Defamation's of-and-concerning element requires that the statement identify the claimant, **although not by name if the circumstances identify the individual to whom the publication refers**.

TORTS WORKBOOK

Scenario-Generating Worksheet for Week 6
Generate a scenario demonstrating each of the following rules.

1. The public would think of defamation as gossip, rumor, innuendo, or maybe *slander*, which is actually one of the two legal forms of defamation. Defamation involves false communication published of and concerning another that, together with extrinsic facts, harms the reputation of that other, with special damages except where law presumes damages.

_____

_____

2. *Libel* and *slander* are defamation's two forms. Defamation in written form is libel, whereas defamation in oral form is slander, with some differences in elements as to each.

_____

_____

3. Slander claims ordinarily require proof of special damages except where the slander is as to loathsome disease, incompetence in one's trade or profession, sex, or crimes of moral turpitude. Libel claims, based on writings or their equivalent, do not require proof of special damages. Special damages mean pecuniary loss from third persons believing and acting on the defamatory statement.

_____

_____

4. To satisfy the publication element of a defamation claim, the false statement must reach and be understood by another. The publication must ordinarily be intentional, although in some cases negligence may be enough, such as mailing a publication to an address where others would open it.

_____

_____

5. Primary publishers are the ones who first originate the defamation, like a reporter writing a false story. Secondary publishers pass along the defamation, like the newspaper or media outlet that picks up the story. Both primary and secondary publishers have defamation liability.

_____

_____

6. Defamation's of-and-concerning element requires that the statement identify the claimant, although not necessarily by name if the circumstances make it sufficiently clear to whom the publication refers. If someone who knows the person would recognize the defamatory statement as referring to that person, then the statement satisfies the publication element.

_____

_____

Example Scenarios

1. ***These rules call for a core example of defamation.*** A woman's angry ex-boyfriend spread vicious rumors about the woman's character, hoping that no one would ever trust her again.

2. ***These rules call for core examples of libel and slander.*** A stringer, hoping to help his reporter make a scoop, told the reporter about rumors that the mayor was frequenting a local dive bar to buy and snort cocaine. The reporter ran with it, writing a story repeating the rumors that the reporter's media service posted online.

3. ***These rules call for an example of special damages from slander.*** The physician couldn't explain why her patient load had fallen off so dramatically, costing her salary reductions and loss of bonuses and benefits, until she a longtime patient told her of the rumors that a competing physician was spreading saying she was incompetent.

4. ***These rules call for examples addressing defamation's publication element.*** For therapeutic release over dorm-room tension, a college student typed furious entries in her daily journal imagining horrible things that her roommate had done. The student accidentally left her laptop computer in the library where another student read her journal and posted it online.

5. ***These rules call for examples of primary and secondary publishers.*** A supervisor wrote up a report attributing to a subordinate employee several instances of serious misconduct that the employee had not done, and then forwarded the report to the company's management for action against the employee.

6. ***These rules call for an example of defamation's identification element.*** A blogger writing serial fiction, who got a lot of her craziest character ideas from watching her friends, hoped that her friends wouldn't recognize themselves but also hoped that they would recognize others.

TORTS WORKBOOK

Sameness Exercise for Week 6

Deductive legal reasoning applies a rule to a fact pattern to state determine the outcome. Analogic legal reasoning (reasoning by analogy) compares a hypothetical scenario to the real scenario to suggest an outcome. A policy argument construes a larger public interest from the recommended outcome of a private dispute. Working with a seatmate, sort the following fact patterns into deductive (D) or analogic (A) reasoning, or a policy (P) argument. Answers are on the next page.

____: Because the defendant read on radio the defamatory statement from a written script, and *libel* involves written defamation, the defendant committed libel rather than slander.

____: Because the defendant read on recorded, memorialized radio the defamatory statement, and memorialized writings are libel, the defendant committed libel rather than slander.

____: Because libel liability (without special damages) discourages defamation, and law should discourage radio defamation, defendant's radio defamation was libel rather than slander.

____: The employer *published* the fired employee's negative evaluation because the employer placed it in a shared drive where others read it, so that third parties read and understood it.

____: The court should rule the negative evaluation *published* because libel liability here will discourage other employers from further needlessly harming employees whom they fire.

____: The court should rule the negative evaluation *published* because placing it in a shared file is just like tacking it to a bulletin board or distributing it on printed flyers.

____: Using a pseudonym should still satisfy the *identification* element here, because persons who know the plaintiff would understand the false pseudonymous story to be about plaintiff.

____: Using a pseudonym satisfies the *identification* element because the pseudonym was in this circumstance no different than using the role or title, or a description, as to recognition.

____: Using a pseudonym should satisfy the *identification* element because the harm to a plaintiff from the inferred identification is just as bad, and defamation law should discourage that harm.

____: The false implication of a *charge* is clearly reputation lowering because pretty much like suggesting that plaintiff probably committed a crime or the police and prosecutor thought so.

____: The false implication of a *charge* satisfies the reputation-lowering element because carrying a sting damaging to reputation, making respectable others think less of plaintiff.

____: The plaintiff's loss of clients satisfies the *special damages* requirement for slander because client loss involves pecuniary or financial loss, as the law defines special damages.

____: The plaintiff's loss of clients satisfies the *special damages* requirement for slander because client loss is like a lost job or even like medical expense, insofar as it involves money lost.

Answer Key for Sameness Exercise

Deductive legal reasoning applies a rule to a fact pattern to determine the outcome. Analogic legal reasoning (reasoning by analogy) compares a hypothetical scenario to the real scenario to suggest an outcome. A policy argument construes a larger public interest from the recommended outcome of a private dispute. Below are examples of deductive (D) and analogic (A) reasoning, and policy (P) arguments.

D: Because the defendant read on radio the defamatory statement from a written script, and *libel* involves written defamation, the defendant committed libel rather than slander.

A: Because the defendant read on recorded, memorialized radio the defamatory statement, and memorialized writings are libel, the defendant committed libel rather than slander.

P: Because libel liability (without special damages) discourages defamation, and law should discourage radio defamation, defendant's radio defamation was libel rather than slander.

D: The employer *published* the fired employee's negative evaluation because the employer placed it in a shared drive where others read it, so that third parties read and understood it.

P: The court should rule the negative evaluation *published* because libel liability here will discourage other employers from further needlessly harming employees whom they fire.

A: The court should rule the negative evaluation *published* because placing it in a shared file is just like tacking it to a bulletin board or distributing it on printed flyers.

D: Using a pseudonym should still satisfy the *identification* element here, because persons who know the plaintiff would understand the false pseudonymous story to be about plaintiff.

A: Using a pseudonym satisfies the *identification* element because the pseudonym was in this circumstance no different than using the role or title, or a description, as to recognition.

P: Using a pseudonym should satisfy the *identification* element because the harm to a plaintiff from the inferred identification is just as bad, and defamation law should discourage that harm.

A: The false implication of a *charge* is clearly reputation lowering because pretty much like suggesting that plaintiff probably committed a crime or the police and prosecutor thought so.

D: The false implication of a *charge* satisfies the reputation-lowering element because carrying a sting damaging to reputation, making respectable others think less of plaintiff.

D: The plaintiff's loss of clients satisfies the *special damages* requirement for slander because client loss involves pecuniary or financial loss, as the law defines special damages.

A: The plaintiff's loss of clients satisfies the *special damages* requirement for slander because client loss is like a lost job or even like medical expense, insofar as it involves money lost.

TORTS WORKBOOK

Drafting Exercise for Week 6: Fact Allegations

Draft the fact allegations of a defamation complaint. Fact allegations are short and plain statements alerting the defendant to the events giving rise to the liability the following counts plead. In this case, your client intake established that a local newspaper The Pontiac Herald published that your client Jamie Baker, the treasurer for the private school Excellence Academy, had misappropriated and mishandled school funds, requiring the school to cut arts and sports programs. You made a demand for retraction that the newspaper ignored, and now your client has instructed you to sue.

[Caption omitted.]

Complaint

Plaintiff Jamie L. Baker complains against defendant The Pontiac Herald saying:

PARTIES, JURISDICTION, AND VENUE

1. Ms. Baker resides in Rockville, Glen County, Michigan.

2. The Herald is a Michigan corporation doing business in Glen County, Michigan.

3. This cause of action arose in Pontiac, Glen County, Michigan.

4. This case is for damages in excess of $25,000 exclusive of interest and costs.

5. This Court has jurisdiction over the parties in this case.

6. This Court is a proper venue and the only convenient venue for this case.

FACT ALLEGATIONS

7.

8.

9.

10.

11.

12.

13.

14.

COUNT I: DEFAMATION

15. This reference incorporates the above paragraphs into this count.

16. The Herald owed duties to Ms. Baker to publish only those statements about her that it knew to be true and not to publish false statements that lower her reputation, cause her lost income in her accounting practice and other loss and expense, and cause her embarrassment, humiliation, and other mental and emotional distress.

17. The Herald breached those duties and defamed Ms. Baker in that The Herald published the above false statements, knowing those statements to be false and acting in reckless disregard of their truth or falsity, causing Ms. Baker the above loss and damage as an actual and proximate result.

18. The Herald is thus liable to Ms. Baker in defamation for all resulting loss, expense, and damage, both economic and non-economic, now and in the future.

19. Ms. Baker made a retraction demand and otherwise has satisfied all law and rule with respect to her claim against The Herald.

ON THESE GROUNDS, plaintiff Jamie L. Baker prays for judgment in her favor and against defendant The Pontiac Herald for all amounts to which the Court finds her entitled, together with costs and attorney's fees most wrongfully sustained.

[Jury demand and signature block omitted.]

Model answer: 7. Ms. Baker is an accountant in private practice who before the wrongs that this complaint recites had a high reputation for honesty, integrity, and competence in her accounting field. 8. Ms. Baker was further the volunteer board treasurer for the Excellence Academy, responsible to ensure the integrity of the Academy's financial operations. 9. On January 24, 2018, The Herald falsely published on the front page of its evening edition, as shown in Exhibit A to this complaint incorporated here, that Ms. Baker had misappropriated and mishandled Academy funds requiring the Academy to cut arts and sports programs. 10. Those statements were false when made, remain false, and had the purpose and effect of lowering Ms. Baker's reputation for honesty, integrity, and competence in her accounting profession. 11. The Herald knew those statements to be false and acted in reckless disregard of their truth or falsity and yet published them to its thousands of readers. 12. As a direct result, Ms. Baker lost substantial accounting income due to clients terminating their relationship with her and new clients refusing to do business with her, loss and damage that will continue into the future. 13. As a further direct result, Ms. Baker suffered embarrassment, humiliation, and other mental and emotional distress for which Ms. Baker sought treatment during which she incurred medical and other expense, which will continue into the future. 14. Ms. Baker made a retraction demand through her attorneys on January 26, 2018, but The Herald ignored that demand and did not retract.

Review Exercise for Week 6
Match these facts with the law on the next page that they trigger.

His life lately had been like a roller-coaster ride, and more roll than coast. ____ 1. First, he had nearly cut off his finger when trying to use his new exercise equipment for the first time. ____ 2. He had gotten it online from a distributor who had advertised it as Swiss design, although labels on it said "Made in China." ____ 3. If he'd known that he could catch his finger in the cable under the seat, then he'd never have put his hand down there. ____ 4. When he later looked through the manual to see what if anything he'd done wrong to get cut so badly, he noticed the statement in all caps, "NOT LIABLE FOR PERSONAL INJURY FROM USE." ____ 5. Then, when he'd gotten home from the hospital with his finger all stitched and wrapped up, he had noticed his neighbor's goats in his garden, decimating his vegetable crop. ____ 6. To top it off, he had discovered at his business a set of old books showing that the business that he'd bought a few years earlier had been tanking. ____ 7. When he had bought the business, the owner had said it had been going so good. ____ 8. He had finally determined to go see a lawyer, who had only seemed concerned with how long ago he'd bought the business. ____ 9. He couldn't quite remember whether it was three or four years ago but could only recall that his military call-up had promptly made a mess of his taking over the business.

Review Exercise for Week 6
Match this law with the facts on the prior page that the facts trigger.

___A. A discovery rule may toll the limitations period until the plaintiff should have known of the injury and its connection to the defendant's conduct.^{Week 1}

___B. Statutes may toll limitations periods for minority, insanity, military service, and fraudulent concealment.^{Week 1}

___C. Merchants may disclaim some warranties but not the warranty of merchantability or warranties protecting against personal injury.^{Week 2}

___D. Strict products liability provides that merchants who sell products in a defective condition unreasonably dangerous to users are liable for resultant injury.^{Week 2}

___E. Failure-to-warn claims depend on showing that the omission of a warning made the product unreasonably dangerous.^{Week 3}

___F. All merchants within the chain of distribution bear the same liability to the injured user as the manufacturer, as do suppliers of defective component parts.^{Week 3}

___G. Strict liability exists for property damage by livestock, depending on the fence-in, fence-out, or other rules of the jurisdiction.^{Week 4}

___H. Misrepresentation is a knowing false material statement made to induce justifiable reliance causing the hearer's loss.^{Week 5}

___I. Bare nondisclosure, without a duty to disclose arising out of the relationship or circumstances, is not actionable.^{Week 5}

Answer key: 1D, 2F, 3E, 4C, 5G, 6I, 7H, 8A, 9B

Problem-Solving Exercise Week 6

Working with a seatmate, read the following example (EX) and non-example (NE) of an unknown new rule (RU), one that the judge writing the opinions and orders has not expressly stated but that you must instead discern and record as your problem solution. To solve the problem, one student vocalize each mental operation taken toward a partial solution, while the other student actively listens, confirming, shaping, correcting, and guiding the other student's vocalizations, until both of you reach and record the final novel rule. Check your answer against the model answer at the bottom after the professor says to do so.

EX   OPINION AND ORDER: In this defamation case, the plaintiff stockbroker alleges that his employer, the defendant brokerage firm, told plaintiff that it was firing plaintiff for embezzling customer funds, requiring plaintiff to make a public disclosure of the false and defamatory statement, in regulatory documents required by law. Defendant through counsel has moved to dismiss, arguing that plaintiff has no evidence that defendant published the defamatory statement to anyone other than plaintiff. The Court denies defendant's motion, bringing this matter on for jury trial.

NE   OPINION AND ORDER: In this defamation case, the plaintiff tradesman alleges that the defendant homeowner told plaintiff that she was firing plaintiff from her home-renovation job for shoddy work and for using false affidavits to obtain construction-loan draws, following which plaintiff shared the allegations with other customers and suppliers. Defendant through counsel has moved to dismiss, arguing that plaintiff has no evidence that defendant published the defamatory statements to anyone other than plaintiff. The Court grants defendant's motion, dismissing plaintiff's case with prejudice.

RU   _____

_____

_____

_____

_____

Answer: While plaintiff in a defamation case must produce evidence that defendant published the defamatory statement, plaintiff's self-publication satisfies the publication element where defendant knew at the time of defendant's false statement to plaintiff that plaintiff would have to disclose the statement to others.

Week 7
Defamation (Constitution & Privileges)

BULLET OUTLINE FOR WEEK 7:
DEFAMATION (continued)
Constitution (First Amendment free-speech and free-press protection)
- [74]public officials and public figures must prove actual malice (AM)
  - [77]public official includes public employees whose qualifications the public would want to know
    - interest-beyond-the-general-interest (IBGI) test
  - [78]universal public figure has general fame, prominence, and influence
  - limited public figure voluntarily injected self into public issue and has media access
    - may also be involuntary public figures
- [75]actual malice is knowledge or recklessness regard of falsity (KRD)
  - [76]also includes high degree of awareness of falsity (HAD), subjective serious doubt as to truth (SSD), purposeful avoidance of truth (PAT), and materially changing meaning in quote (MCM)
- [79]private figure on public issue proves fault for liability & malice for presumed or punitive damages
  - [80]private figure on public issue must also retain burden of proof on falsity
- [81]private-figure/private issue cases are unaffected by the constitutional standards
  - just prove common law elements

Common-law privileges
- absolute (privileged even if actual malice or bad faith)
  - [82]judicial privilege protects lawyers, judges, and others for relevant statements in court
  - [83]legislative privilege protects speakers in legislative proceedings on any matter
  - [84]executive privilege protects within scope of official duties
- [85]qualified privileges (privileged only if without actual malice or bad faith)
  - self interest, common interests, or interest of others
  - [86]fair reporting (accurate summary) and fair comment

[87]Defamation remedies
- nominal damages
- presumed damages
  - not available for slander unless fits DISC exception (see above)
  - not available for public officials, public figures, or public issue without actual malice
- compensatory damages for economic and non-economic losses
- punitive damages
  - some states require unmet demand for retraction

PARAGRAPH OUTLINE FOR WEEK 7:
DEFAMATION
Constitutional Protections. Once you understand defamation's common-law elements, you must then appreciate how the First Amendment changes those elements in many cases. [74]The First Amendment requires public officials and public figures to prove actual malice in defamation claims. [75]Actual malice means knowledge of or recklessness with regard to the falsity of the defamatory statement. [76]Actual malice may also include a high degree of

awareness of falsity, subjective serious doubt as to truth, purposeful avoidance of truth, and deliberate misquotes materially changing meaning. [77]A public official includes any public employee whose qualifications the public would want to know, beyond the general interest in the qualifications of all public employees. [78]A universal public figure has prominence and influence, whereas a limited public figure has media access and engaged in conduct from which one would expect public interest. [79]If the publication concerns a private figure but is on a public issue, then the private figure must show fault for liability and actual malice for presumed and punitive damages. [80]If the publication concerns a private figure but is on a public issue, then the private figure must retain the burden of proof to prove the statement false. [81]Only private-figure/private issue cases are unaffected by the constitutional standards.

Privileges. Defamation claims require a third consideration beyond the common-law elements and constitutional considerations. Common-law privileges may provide additional protection against defamation claims. [82]An absolute judicial privilege protects lawyers, judges, and others from defamation claims based on relevant publications made in court proceedings. [83]An absolute legislative privilege protects speakers in legislative proceedings against defamation claims made based on any (not just relevant) matters. [84]An absolute executive privilege, protecting statements made within the scope of official duties, extends to all administrative-branch officials at the federal level but in most states only as to higher officials at the state level. [85]Qualified privileges allow one to protect one's own interests, common interests, or the interests of others, without being subject to defamation claim. [86]There are also qualified common-law privileges of fair reporting and comment, to make accurate summary of an official proceeding containing defamatory publications and to comment on them.

Fluency Cards for Week 7

Cover and uncover the response to each prompt until you fluently recall the exact response.

First Amendment	**Actual Malice**
Public officials and public figures claiming defamation must prove actual malice.	Knowing or reckless disregard of the truth (also PAT, SSD, HDA, MCM).

Public Official

Controls government, in whom the public has an interest beyond general interest.

Public Figure

Universal fame or voluntarily injects self into public issue with media access.

Private Figure / Public Issue

Fault for liability and actual malice for presumed or punitive damages.

Absolute Privilege

Judicial, legislative, and executive, even in bad faith.

Qualified Privilege

Interest of self or others, and fair comment or reporting. Must be in good faith.

Defamation Damages

Nominal, compensatory, or punitive damages, but statute may require demand to retract.

Definitions Worksheet for Week 7

1. What does the First Amendment require of public officials or figures who claim defamation?

   _____

   _____

2. How does the law define *actual malice*?

   _____

   _____

3. How does the law define a *public official* and a *public figure*?

   _____

   _____

4. How does the First Amendment affect defamation claims by private figures?

   _____

   _____

5. Name and describe the three absolute privileges.

   _____

   _____

6. Name and describe the qualified privileges.

   _____

   _____

7. What remedies does the law offer for defamation?

   _____

   _____

Answer Key for Definitions Worksheet

1. *What does the First Amendment require of public officials or figures who claim defamation?* The First Amendment requires public officials and public figures to prove actual malice in defamation claims.

2. *How does the law define **actual malice**?* Actual malice means knowledge of or recklessness with regard to the falsity of the defamatory statement. Actual malice may also include a high degree of awareness of falsity, subjective serious doubt as to truth, purposeful avoidance of truth, and deliberate misquotes materially changing meaning.

3. *How does the law define a public official and a public figure?* A public official includes any public employee whose qualifications the public would want to know, beyond the general interest in the qualifications of all public employees. A universal public figure has prominence and influence, whereas a limited public figure has media access and engaged in conduct from which one would expect public interest.

4. *How does the First Amendment affect defamation claims by private figures?* If the publication concerns a private figure but is on a public issue, then the private figure must show fault for liability and actual malice for presumed and punitive damages, and must retain the burden of proof to prove the statement false. Only private-figure/private issue cases are unaffected by constitutional standards.

5. *Name and describe the three absolute privileges.* An absolute judicial privilege protects lawyers, judges, and others from defamation claims based on relevant publications made in court proceedings. An absolute legislative privilege protects speakers in legislative proceedings against defamation claims made based on any (not just relevant) matters. An absolute executive privilege, protecting statements made within the scope of official duties, extends to all administrative-branch officials at the federal level but in most states only as to higher officials at the state level. Absolute privileges protect whether the defendant made the statement in good faith or not.

6. *Name and describe the qualified privileges.* Qualified privileges allow one to protect one's own interests, common interests, or the interests of others, when making the statement without actual malice or in good faith. Qualified common-law privileges of fair reporting and comment allow one to make accurate summary of an official proceeding containing defamatory publications and to comment on them.

7. *What remedies does the law offer for defamation?* Defamation remedies may include nominal damages, compensatory damages for economic and non-economic losses, and punitive damages, although some states first require demand for retraction.

Issue-Spotting Worksheet for Week 7

State the law each scenario raises. No analysis. Just spot the issue and state the law.

1. Your client, a physician running for city council, is upset that the local newspaper has run an editorial suggesting that the physician is not qualified to run. The physician sputters something to you about wanting to sue for defamation. You first explain the common-law elements of defamation, wondering aloud whether the physician has a common-law claim. The unimpressed physician presses you to sue for the media's evident bias.

2. So you've told the client more about defamation law that you felt the client needed to know. The client wants to know what you meant when you mentioned *actual malice*.

3. The client scoffs that a city council member doesn't really have any power anyway, so why would anyone get to freely attack a council member more so than a private citizen.

4. The client insists that the client is still only a physician, not yet a council member, and wants to know what the client might do if the client loses or withdraws, and the paper continues its attack, affecting the client's medical practice.

5. Somewhat mollified with your thoughtful explanations, the client gets down to asking whether, if the client sues, or speaks out against the newspaper in a council meeting, or gets the mayor to do so, the newspaper might counterclaim for defamation.

6. The client also wants to know if the client would have any protection for asking friends about the effect of the newspaper's story on the client's reputation or the reputation of others who supported the client's campaign.

Answer Key

1. ***This scenario implicates First Amendment protection of defamation.*** The First Amendment requires public officials and public figures to prove actual malice in defamation claims.

2. ***This scenario implicates the definition of actual malice.*** Actual malice means knowledge of or recklessness with regard to the falsity of the defamatory statement. Actual malice may also include a high degree of awareness of falsity, subjective serious doubt as to truth, purposeful avoidance of truth, and deliberate misquotes materially changing meaning.

3. ***This scenario implicates the definitions of public official and public figure.*** A public official includes any public employee whose qualifications the public would want to know, beyond the general interest in the qualifications of all public employees. A universal public figure has prominence and influence, whereas a limited public figure has media access and engaged in conduct from which one would expect public interest.

4. ***This scenario implicates the First Amendment's effect on a private figure's defamation claim.*** If the publication concerns a private figure but is on a public issue, then the private figure must show fault for liability and actual malice for presumed and punitive damages, and must retain the burden of proof to prove the statement false. Only private-figure/private issue cases are unaffected by constitutional standards.

5. ***This scenario implicates the common-law absolute privileges.*** An absolute judicial privilege protects lawyers, judges, and others from defamation claims based on relevant publications made in court proceedings. An absolute legislative privilege protects speakers in legislative proceedings against defamation claims made based on any (not just relevant) matters. An absolute executive privilege, protecting statements made within the scope of official duties, extends to all administrative-branch officials at the federal level but in most states only as to higher officials at the state level. Absolute privileges protect whether or not the defendant made the statement in good faith.

6. ***This scenario implicates the common-law qualified privileges.*** Qualified privileges allow one to protect one's own interests, common interests, or the interests of others, when making the statement without actual malice or in good faith. Qualified common-law privileges of fair reporting and comment allow one to make accurate summary of an official proceeding containing defamatory publications and to comment on them.

Comprehensiveness Exercise for Week 7

Insert words at the ^ mark that would make for a more-accurate or more-detailed law statement. Follow the italicized hints for help. Suggested answers are on the next page.

1. The First Amendment requires public officials ^ to prove ^ malice in defamation claims. *[Who else? What kind of malice?]*

2. Actual malice means knowledge ^ of the defamatory statement's falsity. ^ ^ ^ ^ *[Knowledge or what else? Can you list other definitions?]*

3. A limited public figure ^ injected him or herself into a public issue from which one would expect public interest ^ . *[Injected how? And what else defines a limited public figure?]*

4. If the publication concerns a private figure but on a public issue, then the private figure must show fault ^ and actual malice for presumed ^ damages ^ . *[Fault for what? Presumed or what? And what other rule must the plaintiff satisfy?]*

5. Absolute privileges, protecting the publisher ^ , include the judicial and legislative ^ privileges. *[What does law mean by absolute? And law offers a third forum, too.]*

6. Qualified privileges allow one to protect one's own interests ^ when making the statement ^ . *[Just one's own interests? And what's the qualified limitation?]*

7. Qualified common-law privilege of fair reporting ^ allows one to make accurate summary of an official proceeding ^ . *[Just reporting or a little more? A summary or a little more?]*

Answer Key for Comprehensiveness Exercise

1. The First Amendment requires public officials **and public figures** to prove **actual** malice in defamation claims.

2. Actual malice means knowledge **or reckless disregard** of the defamatory statement's falsity. **Actual malice also includes a high degree of awareness of falsity, subjective serious doubt as to truth, purposeful avoidance of truth, and misquotes materially changing meaning.**

3. A limited public figure **voluntarily** injected him or herself into a public issue from which one would expect public interest **and has media access**.

4. If the publication concerns a private figure but on a public issue, then the private figure must show fault **for liability** and actual malice for presumed **or punitive** damages, **and must retain the burden of proof**.

5. The absolute privileges, protecting the publisher **even when speaking in bad faith**, include the judicial privilege and the legislative privilege **and executive privilege**.

6. Qualified privileges allow one to protect one's own interests**, common interests, or the interests of others,** when making the statement **in good faith, without actual malice**.

7. Qualified common-law privilege of fair reporting **and fair comment** allows one to make accurate summary of an official proceeding **and to comment on them**.

TORTS WORKBOOK

Sameness Exercise Week 7 (Problem 1)

The First Amendment protects defamers of public officials and public figures against liability unless the defamer acted with actual malice. A public official is an employee who controls government, in whose qualifications the public has an interest beyond the general interest. A public figure is either a universal public figure whom the media will grant access on any subject because of widespread fame or a limited public figure who, while not famous, voluntarily injected himself or herself into a public issue and has media access. Working with a seatmate, sort the following fact patterns into ones where the defamation victim is a **public official (PO), universal public figure (UPF), limited public figure (LPF),** or **none (N)** (private figure). Answers are at the bottom of the page.

1. _____ The mayor was aghast that the newspaper printed the false story of his assault conviction as a teen.
2. _____ The Las Vegas entertainer hadn't expected the tabloid to so grossly exaggerate his illness.
3. _____ The tradesperson lost every job he'd lined up after the credit bureau falsely reported him bankrupt.
4. _____ The agency director responsible for enforcement efforts consulted a lawyer about suing the media.
5. _____ The teacher hadn't gotten along with the parent but was shocked to see the false allegations online.
6. _____ The builder seeking the variance for the downtown tower had people tell him to sue the radio station.
7. _____ The shopper's friends told her to watch the late news to see if they re-ran the false shoplifting story.
8. _____ The false allegations of food poisoning caused the restaurant's revenue to fall by two thirds.
9. _____ The parent lied repeatedly at the public-agenda part of the meeting, about the board member.
10. _____ The comments falsely vilified the musician's competence, beneath her instructional videos.
11. _____ The online review site falsely suggested that the plaintiff's lawyer was an unlicensed fraud.
12. _____ The television documentary falsely trashed the best-selling author whose books became film hits.
13. _____ The police officer hadn't expected the motorist journalist to publish a false story of the traffic arrest.
14. _____ The congresswoman hadn't done any of the dishonest things about which the website accused her.
15. _____ The neighbor's false allegations of drug dealing shocked the homeowner into consulting a lawyer.
16. _____ The false newspaper story about property-tax fraud angered the homeowners' association chair.
17. _____ The talk-show host defamed the perennial all-star basketball star with the huge endorsement deals.
18. _____ The city manager hadn't expected the permit applicant to falsely accuse her before the board.
19. _____ The farmer spread vicious rumors around the district about the allegedly trespassing hunter.

Answers: 1PO 2UPF 3N 4PO 5N 6LPF 7N 8LPF 9PO 10LPF 11N 12UPF 13N 14PO 15N 16LPF 17UPF 18PO 19N

Torts II Sameness Exercise Week 7 (Problem 2)

The U.S. Supreme Court defines *actual malice* as **knowing or reckless disregard (KRD)** of the defaming statement's falsity. The Supreme Court has further defined knowing or reckless disregard as **purposeful avoidance of the truth (PAT), subjective serious doubt (SSD), high degree of awareness of falsity (HDA),** or **material change in meaning in a misquote (MCM)**. Working with a seatmate, sort the following fact patterns into the best one of the five above forms of actual malice, or mark the answer as **none (N)**. Answers are at the bottom of the reverse side, upside down so that you can flip the bottom of the page up to check your answers.

1. _____ The reporter deleted the interview's audio recording without listening to it before publishing the story.
2. _____ The commentator had reservations about what he was saying but was sure it would get good ratings.
3. _____ The test results clearly indicated otherwise, but the story was too good not to report the other way.
4. _____ The editor deleted the word "not" before "drunk" when publishing the politician's statement.
5. _____ While the report said she had a conviction, the journalist knew otherwise but went with it anyway.
6. _____ The blogger had no idea that the horrific account of the matter that she shared was false.
7. _____ The detective had read every report and so must have known but still made the announcement.
8. _____ One check of online court records would have shown otherwise, but the service refused to check.
9. _____ The reporter checked her usual sources, all of whom mistakenly verified the false account.
10. _____ The writer decided to shorten the quotes and, in doing so, to slant them the other way.
11. _____ The executive could have picked up the phone and asked the accountant but didn't want correction.
12. _____ The bookkeeper had examined the account statements and knew better but still made the accusation.
13. _____ The manager was wrong about who did it but had good reason to believe having been right.
14. _____ The editor knew that another reporter had the full story but discouraged any consult before publishing.
15. _____ The candidate had heard the source's reputation as unreliable but felt the opportunity too big to miss.
16. _____ The bureau relied on the same outlet that was right in the last six cases even though wrong here.
17. _____ When posting the witness's statement, the website removed several modifiers to juice the account.

Answers: 1PAT 2SSD 3HDA 4MCM 5SSD 6N 7HDA 8PAT 9N 10MCM 11PAT 12SSD 13N 14PAT 15SSD 16N 17MCM

Scenario-Generating Worksheet for Week 7
Generate a scenario demonstrating each of the following rules.

1. The First Amendment requires public officials and public figures to prove actual malice in defamation claims. Actual malice means knowledge of or recklessness with regard to the falsity of the defamatory statement.

_____

_____

_____

2. A public official includes any public employee whose qualifications the public would want to know, beyond the general interest in the qualifications of all public employees.

_____

_____

3. A universal public figure has prominence and influence, whereas a limited public figure has media access and engaged in conduct from which one would expect public interest.

_____

_____

_____

4. If the publication concerns a private figure but is on a public issue, then the private figure must show fault for liability and actual malice for presumed and punitive damages.

_____

_____

_____

5. If the publication concerns a private figure but is on a public issue, then the private figure must retain the burden of proof to prove the statement false.

_____

_____

6. Only private-figure/private issue cases are unaffected by the constitutional standards.

_____

_____

_____

Example Scenarios for Scenario-Generating Worksheet

1. ***This scenario implicates the First Amendment's protection of defamation.*** A candidate for public office thought that she was speaking the truth about the opposing candidate's conviction years earlier for fraud, based on press accounts, but her public statements turned out to be false and cause her opponent to lose the election.

2. ***This scenario implicates the definition of a public official.*** A parent falsely accused a school superintendent of misrepresenting enrollment figures to close the neighborhood school and of financial chicanery. The superintendent was an elected official who had the authority to open and close schools, and supervise district finances.

3. ***The scenario implicates the distinction between universal and limited public figures.*** A highly sought film star publicly disparaged a small-studio film producer with false allegations of sexual harassment and sex discrimination in the casting of roles and offers of production jobs, while the producer made false accusations back about the film star's private life.

4. ***The scenario implicates the treatment of a private-figure plaintiff defamed on a public issue.*** A hospital association's publicist defamed a private-practitioner nurse who was publicly advocating for the rights of hospital patients. The publicist manufactured the false allegations without source just to diminish the nurse's reputation for advocacy.

5. ***The scenario implicates the constitutional requirement that a private-figure plaintiff retain the burden of proof on public-issue defamation.*** The nurse in the prior example wasn't sure that she could prove false the publicist's manufactured allegations because they were about matters so old that records no longer existed of their truth.

6. ***The scenario implicates the private-figure, private-issue defamation case where the First Amendment offers no protection.*** A resident defamed a neighbor over a petty boundary dispute that the two neighbors had over trees and bushes bordering their adjacent properties. The defamation was innocent in that the resident didn't know what he said was false but was nonetheless damaging.

TORTS WORKBOOK

Framework Exercise for Week 7

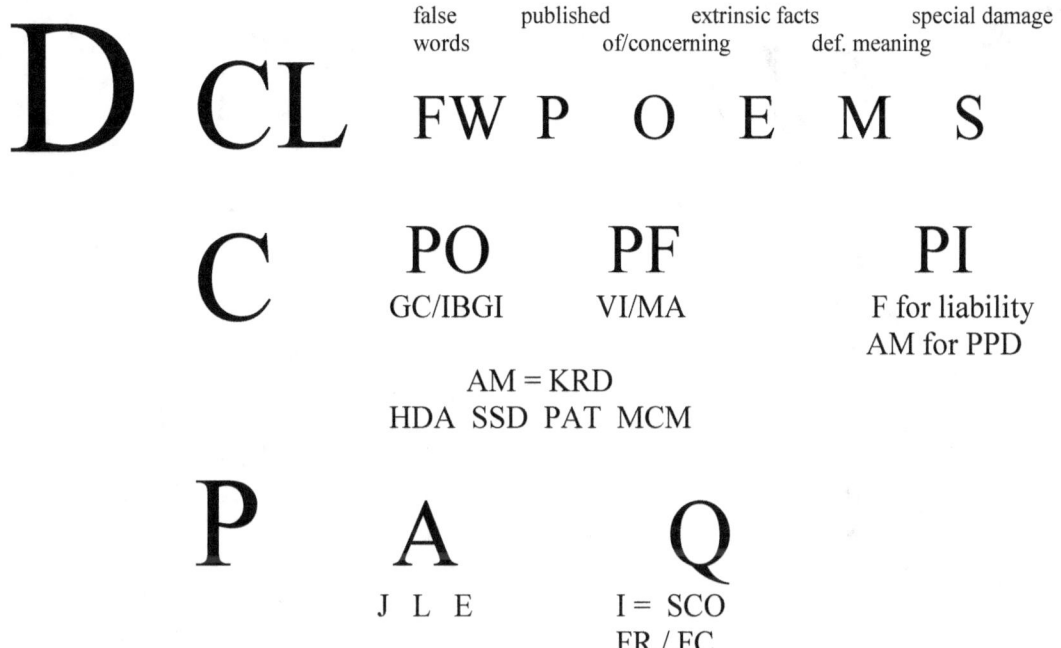

D CL FW P O E M S
(false words) (published) (of/concerning) (extrinsic facts) (def. meaning) (special damage)

C PO PF PI
   GC/IBGI VI/MA F for liability
                   AM for PPD

   AM = KRD
   HDA SSD PAT MCM

P A Q
   J L E I = SCO
          FR / FC

Cover the above and reproduce from memory the framework's abbreviations.

D CL __ __ __ __ __ __

   C   __ __ __

   P   __ __

After checking your answer to be sure it is accurate and complete, try again on the reverse side.

Reproduce the framework again, this time with fewer tips.

D CL

C

P

After checking your answer as accurate and complete, cover it and try a third time below.

D

Check your answer to be sure it is accurate and complete.

Week 8

Invasion of Privacy

BULLET OUTLINE FOR WEEK 8:
INVASION OF PRIVACY
[88]**Four forms:** appropriation, intrusion, public disclosure, and false light
- [89]appropriation is use of another's persona for commercial or other advantage without permission
  - misuse can be of name, likeness, image, or anything associated with person
  - often involves the famous but not always
  - often involves commercial (called commercial exploitation) use but not always
    - can involve political or public-interest uses
  - damages and injunction for forms of relief
- [90]intrusion form arises on highly offensive intrusion into reasonably expected privacy
  - is often into a physical place but can also be into confidential records or information
- [91]public disclosure of private facts arises on highly offensive publication to more than a few persons
  - again, privacy expectation must be reasonable
  - [92]must overcome constitutional protection to publish matters of public interest
- [93]false light arises highly offensive false public depiction

[94]**First Amendment** protects right to intentionally inflict emotional distress if by parody or for public expression

PARAGRAPH OUTLINE FOR WEEK 8:
INVASION OF PRIVACY
[88]The invasion-of-privacy tort takes one of four forms, either appropriation, intrusion, disclosure, or false light. [89]Invasion of privacy's appropriation form involves use of persona for commercial or other advantage without the person's permission, with injunctions and damages for relief. [90]Invasion of privacy's intrusion form arises when there is an unauthorized intrusion into a private place that would be highly offensive to the reasonable person. [91]Invasion of privacy's disclosure form arises when there is publication without legitimate interest to more than a few persons of private facts that would be offensive to the reasonable person. [92]The disclosure form of invasion of privacy must overcome constitutional protection to publish matters of public interest. [93]Invasion of privacy's false light form arises when a person publicly depicts another in a false manner that would be highly offensive to the reasonable person. [94]The First Amendment protects the right of media to intentionally inflict emotional distress if also done for purposes of destroying a person's reputation by parody.

Fluency Cards for Week 8

Cover and uncover the response to each prompt until you fluently recall the exact response.

Intrusion on Seclusion

Invasion where reasonable expectation of privacy, highly offensive to the reasonable person.

Appropriation

Using another's image or persona without permission for pecuniary or other gain.

Public Disclosure

Publication to more than a few of private facts, highly offensive to the reasonable person.

False Light

Public false depiction highly offensive to the reasonable person.

Definitions Worksheet for Week 8

1. What are the four forms of invasion of privacy? (Just name them, don't define.) Which forms do more states recognize?

___

2. Define invasion of privacy's appropriation form. What is the common form of relief?

___

3. Define invasion of privacy's intrusion form. Must the tort involve observation of the person?

___

4. Define invasion of privacy's public-disclosure form. How broad must the disclosure be? Does the law offer any protection for disclosure?

___

5. Define invasion of privacy's false-light form. How does false light differ from defamation?

___

Answer Key for Definitions Worksheet

1. *What are the four forms of invasion of privacy? (Just name them, don't define.) Which forms do more states recognize?* The invasion-of-privacy tort takes one of four forms: (1) appropriation or commercial exploitation; (2) intrusion on seclusion of persona; (3) public disclosure or publicity; and (4) false light. States routinely recognize appropriation and intrusion but may not necessarily recognize public disclosure or false light.

2. *Define invasion of privacy's appropriation form. What is the common form of relief?* Invasion of privacy's appropriation form involves use of name, likeness, or image (persona) for commercial or other advantage without the person's permission. Injunction against continued use is the common relief, plus any provable damages (recovery of amounts wrongfully gained, for instance).

3. *Define invasion of privacy's intrusion form. Must the tort involve observation of the person?* Invasion of privacy's intrusion form arises when there is an unauthorized intrusion into a place where the person has a reasonable expectation of privacy and that would be highly offensive to the reasonable person. The intrusion may involve observation of the person or of private matters such as medical or financial records.

4. *Define invasion of privacy's public-disclosure form. How broad must the disclosure be? Does the law offer any protection for disclosure?* Invasion of privacy's disclosure form arises when there is publication without legitimate interest *to more than a few persons* of private facts that would be offensive to the reasonable person. Where recognized, the disclosure form of invasion of privacy must overcome constitutional protection to publish matters of public interest.

5. *Define invasion of privacy's false-light form. How does false light differ from defamation?* Invasion of privacy's false light form arises when a person publicly depicts another in a false manner that would be highly offensive to the reasonable person. False light involves depictions (images or representations) rather than false words (statements of verifiable fact) like defamation.

Issue-Spotting Worksheet for Week 8

State the law each scenario raises. No analysis. Just spot the issue and state the law.

1. Your client, a multi-media (film, television, song) entertainer, describes an upsetting series of incidents involving paparazzi in general including one so-called investigative journalist whom your client regards as a muckraker. Your client hates that the investigative journalist sells video and photographic images of your client to all kinds of media outlets and just seems to make money off your client's fame. Your client wants to know what you can do. Name the potential tort claims.

2. So you've told the client about several forms of privacy-tort action that might apply. Your client wants to know which one is the most likely to be available and how the law defines it.

3. Your client is concerned not only at losing your client's privacy but also at how the investigative journalist always seem to portray your client in the worst way. Your client wants to know whether the law might do anything to protect your client's wholesome identity and image.

4. Your client learned recently that the investigative journalist may have gone through your client's trash or somehow gotten medical and financial records from some source because your client has seen publications of your client's medical and financial information. Your client wants to know if the law protects medical and financial records.

5. You have convinced the client that you are just the lawyer to help out. The client retains you. Then the client has one last question, which is whether in addition to money damages you can just make the investigative journalist stop.

Answer Key for Issue-Spotting Worksheet

1. ***This question implicates the four forms of the invasion-of-privacy tort.*** The four forms of invasion of privacy are appropriation or commercial exploitation, intrusion on seclusion of persona, public disclosure or right of publicity, and false light.

2. ***The question implicates the varying privacy torts in different jurisdictions.*** Appropriation and intrusion are the common forms of the invasion-of-privacy tort. All or nearly all jurisdictions are likely to recognize both forms of invasion of privacy. The other two forms, public disclosure and false light, are not only less commonly recognized but also face the hurdle of overcoming constitutional protections.

3. ***The question implicates the false-light form of invasion of privacy.*** The false-light form of invasion of privacy protects against false public depictions that negatively impact the claimant's image, identity, persona, or reputation. The depiction must be highly offensive to the reasonable person to be actionable, where recognized.

4. ***The question implicates the scope of the intrusion form of invasion of privacy.*** The intrusion form of the invasion-of-privacy tort protects not only against observations of the person but also against review of confidential medical, financial, and other records, again where the person has a reasonable expectation of privacy and where the review would highly offend the reasonable person.

5. ***The question implicates forms of relief beyond damages.*** While journalists and others have rights of free speech and to make observations of others in public places, when someone invades another's privacy rights, whether by appropriation, intrusion, publicity, or false light, the offended person may be able to obtain an injunction against further invasions.

Comprehensiveness Exercise for Week 8

Insert words at the ^ mark that would make for a more-accurate or more-detailed law statement. Follow the italicized hints for help. Suggested answers are on the next page.

1. The invasion-of-privacy tort takes one of these forms: appropriation ^ and ^ ^ public disclosure. *[Another name for appropriation? And two more forms for a total of four forms.]*

2. States routinely recognize appropriation ^ but may not necessarily recognize public disclosure ^. *[Routinely recognize another form, too. And many states don't recognize one other form, too.]*

3. Invasion of privacy's appropriation form involves use of name ^ for commercial ^ gain. Relief involves any provable damages ^. *[Just name? Just commercial? Just damages?]*

4. Invasion of privacy's intrusion form arises with an ^ intrusion into a place ^ that would be highly offensive ^. *[What kind of instrusion? What kind of place? Offensive to whom?]*

5. Invasion of privacy's disclosure form arises with publication ^ of private facts that would be ^ offensive ^. *[Any publication? How offensive? And offensive to whom?]*

6. Invasion of privacy's false-light form arises when a person ^ depicts another in a ^ manner that would be highly offensive ^. *[Depicts to whom? Any manner? Offensive to whom?]*

Answer to Comprehensiveness Exercise

1. The invasion-of-privacy tort takes one of these forms: appropriation *or commercial exploitation; intrusion on seclusion of persona;* public disclosure; *and false light*.

2. States routinely recognize appropriation *and intrusion* but may not necessarily recognize public disclosure *or false light*.

3. Invasion of privacy's appropriation form involves use of name, *likeness, or image (persona)* for commercial *or other* gain *without the person's permission*. Relief involves any provable damages *and injunction against continued use*.

4. Invasion of privacy's intrusion form arises with an *unauthorized* intrusion into a place *where the person has a reasonable expectation of privacy* and that would be highly offensive *to the reasonable person*.

5. Invasion of privacy's disclosure form arises with publication *without legitimate interest and to more than a few persons* of private facts that would be *highly* offensive *to the reasonable person*.

6. Invasion of privacy's false-light form arises when a person *publicly* depicts another in a *false or misleading* manner that would be highly offensive *to the reasonable person*.

Sameness Exercise for Week 8

Invasion of privacy has four forms, the first two *appropriation (A)* (also known as commercial exploitation or right of publicity) and *intrusion (I)* (also known as intrusion on seclusion of persona) recognized in all states, while the last two *false light (FL)* and *public disclosure of private facts (PD)* recognized only in some states. Working with a seatmate, sort the following fact patterns the applicable invasion-of-privacy form.

____: The car dealership displayed an inflatable Elvis Presley figure for its marathon motor-vehicle sale.

____: The apartment owner concealed a video camera behind the apartment's two-way bathroom mirror.

____: The entertainment website ran a photo of the sports star with a caption suggesting a bizarre drug habit.

____: The private detective displayed old mug shots on its website, of persons the detective traced and caught.

____: The paparazzi pretended to be a shredding service to obtain the papers and records of the film star.

____: The lawyer wrote a blog about the family-law matter in which the opposing party had been a total jerk.

____: The inventor named the invention after a famous entrepreneur to catch the attention of potential licensees.

____: The news service hinted that the resident injured by a home explosion was preparing a terrorist act.

____: The campaign faked ad signatures of several famous figures who had no association with the candidate.

____: Her ex-boyfriend posted scandalous video of her on an anonymous website ostensibly about bad girls.

____: As threatened, the retired caseworker wrote a memoir exaggerating her former boss as a supposed tyrant.

____: The nosey homemaker would sneak out at night to look through the neighbor's garbage before pick-up.

____: The nonprofit decided to use the dead celebrity's silhouette and slogan to attract patrons to the fundraiser.

____: The detective's telephoto lens couldn't capture any images until the detective climbed over the fence.

____: The shopper was shocked to see her insufficient-funds check posted under the retailer's counter glass.

____: The news runner sidled up to the accident scene, unnoticed, to listen to the EMTs and snap a few photos.

____: She couldn't believe that the nursery had used her photo on its billboard by the freeway.

____: The physician blanched at seeing the email string sharing her alleged shenanigans, so greatly exaggerated.

____: The startup's website looked great with the national-brand's colors and logo, and the similar name.

____: The entertainment magazine ran the TV star's juvenile delinquency as part of an "ancient history" section.

____: The custodian had read and scanned the medical records of several of the clinic's better-known patients.

____: The jail guard programmed the hidden camera to take a photo of the shower facilities every minute.

____: The local medical clinic slyly suggested its association with the famous national medical clinic.

____: The news story of the teen's suicide made the parents look heartless, when instead they cared deeply.

____: He claimed he had the right to use his own name for his business even if the same as a leading competitor.

____: The security guard used her master key to enter the executive's office at night to rummage through files.

____: The national retailer took the best product and reproduced it almost exactly as a similar house brand.

Answers are on the back, but please do not turn this sheet over until you have answered all questions fully and conferred with a seatmate to complete and correct your answers.

Answer Key for Sameness Exercise

Invasion of privacy has four forms. The first form *appropriation (A)* (also known as commercial exploitation or right of publicity) involves the unauthorized use of another's name, likeness, or image, for financial or other gain. The second form *intrusion (I)* (also known as intrusion on seclusion of persona) involves the intentional entry into a place where a person has a reasonable expectation of privacy and that is highly offensive to the reasonable person. The third form *false light (FL)* involves a false portrayal or depiction in a manner that is highly offensive to the reasonable person. The fourth form *public disclosure of private facts (PD)* involves the disclosure to more than a few of true but private information, the disclosure of which is highly offensive to the reasonable person. Below are the identified examples.

A: The car dealership displayed an inflatable Elvis Presley figure for its marathon motor-vehicle sale.

I: The apartment owner concealed a video camera behind the apartment's two-way bathroom mirror.

FL: The entertainment website ran a photo of the sports star with a caption suggesting a bizarre drug habit.

PD: The private detective displayed old mug shots on its website, of persons the detective traced and caught.

I: The paparazzi pretended to be a shredding service to obtain the papers and records of the film star.

PD: The lawyer wrote a blog about the family-law matter in which the opposing party had been a total jerk.

A: The inventor named the invention after a famous entrepreneur to catch the attention of potential licensees.

FL: The news service hinted that the resident injured by a home explosion was preparing a terrorist act.

A: The campaign faked ad signatures of several famous figures who had no association with the candidate.

PD: Her ex-boyfriend posted scandalous video of her on an anonymous website ostensibly about bad girls.

FL: As threatened, the retired caseworker wrote a memoir exaggerating her former boss as a supposed tyrant.

I: The nosey homemaker would sneak out at night to look through the neighbor's garbage before pick-up.

A: The nonprofit decided to use the dead celebrity's silhouette and slogan to attract patrons to the fundraiser.

I: The detective's telephoto lens couldn't capture any images until the detective climbed over the fence.

PD: The shopper was shocked to see her insufficient-funds check posted under the retailer's counter glass.

I: The news runner sidled up to the accident scene, unnoticed, to listen to the EMTs and snap a few photos.

A: She couldn't believe that the nursery had used her photo on its billboard by the freeway.

FL: The physician blanched at seeing the email string sharing her alleged shenanigans, so greatly exaggerated.

A: The startup's website looked great with the national-brand's colors and logo, and the similar name.

PD: The entertainment magazine ran the TV star's juvenile delinquency as part of an "ancient history" section.

I: The custodian had read and scanned the medical records of several of the clinic's better-known patients.

I: The jail guard programmed the hidden camera to take a photo of the shower facilities every minute.

A: The local medical clinic slyly suggested its association with the famous national medical clinic.

FL: The news story of the teen's suicide made the parents look heartless, when instead they cared deeply.

A: He claimed he had the right to use his own name for his business even if the same as a leading competitor.

I: The security guard used her master key to enter the executive's office at night to rummage through files.

A: The national retailer took the best product and reproduced it almost exactly as a similar house brand.

Discrimination Exercise for Week 8

Indicate whether each statement *overgeneralizes*, *undergeneralizes*, or *misconceives* the rule, explaining why. *Overgeneralizing* states the rule too broadly, capturing circumstances to which it does not apply. *Undergeneralizing* states the rule too narrowly, omitting circumstances to which it applies. *Misconceiving* states the rule incorrectly.

1. Invasion of privacy involves either appropriation, intrusion, or false light.

   ____OVER/ ____UNDER/ ____MISS/ Why? _____
   _____

2. Invasion of privacy's appropriation or commercial-exploitation form involves use of name, likeness, or image (persona) without the person's permission.

   ____OVER/ ____UNDER/ ____MISS/ Why? _____
   _____

3. Invasion of privacy's intrusion form is physical entry into a place where the person has a reasonable expectation of privacy and that would be highly offensive to the reasonable person.

   ____OVER/ ____UNDER/ ____MISS/ Why? _____
   _____

4. Invasion of privacy's public-disclosure form arises with any publication of private facts that would be offensive to the reasonable person.

   ____OVER/ ____UNDER/ ____MISS/ Why? _____
   _____

5. Invasion of privacy's false light form arises when a person publicly depicts another in a false manner that would be outrageous to the reasonable person, resulting in severe distress.

   ____OVER/ ____UNDER/ ____MISS/ Why? _____
   _____

Answer Key for Discrimination Exercise

1. The statement **UNDERgeneralizes** the rule. The invasion-of-privacy tort takes one of *four* forms, not *three* forms: (1) appropriation or commercial exploitation; (2) intrusion on seclusion of persona; (3) public disclosure or publicity; and (4) false light. States routinely recognize appropriation and intrusion but may not necessarily recognize public disclosure or false light.

2. The statement **OVERgeneralizes** the rule. Invasion of privacy's appropriation form involves use of name, likeness, or image (persona) *for commercial or other advantage* without the person's permission. Injunction against continued use is the common relief, plus any provable damages (recovery of amounts wrongfully gained, for instance).

3. The statement **MISconceives** the rule. Invasion of privacy's intrusion form does not require *physical entry* but instead may be by viewing, listening, or using devices to observe. The intrusion must be unauthorized and into a place where the person has a reasonable expectation of privacy and that would be highly offensive to the reasonable person. The intrusion may involve observation of the person or of private matters such as medical or financial records.

4. The statement **OVERgeneralizes** the rule. Invasion of privacy's disclosure form arises when the publication of private facts offensive to the reasonable person is *without legitimate interest* and *to more than a few persons*, not any publication. Where recognized, the disclosure form of invasion of privacy must overcome constitutional protection to publish matters of public interest.

5. The statement **UNDERgeneralizes** the rule. Invasion of privacy's false light form arises when a person publicly depicts another in a false manner that would be *highly offensive,* not outrageous, to the reasonable person. The tort also may not require severe distress. Outrage and severe distress involve the IIED tort, not false light. False light involves depictions (images or representations) rather than false words (statements of verifiable fact) like defamation.

TORTS WORKBOOK

Sameness Exercise for Week 8

Invasion of privacy has four forms, the first two *appropriation (A)* (also known as commercial exploitation or right of publicity) and *intrusion (I)* (also known as intrusion on seclusion of persona) recognized in all states, while the last two *false light (FL)* and *public disclosure of private facts (PD)* recognized only in some states. Working with a seatmate, sort the following fact patterns the applicable invasion-of-privacy form.

____: The car dealership displayed an inflatable Elvis Presley figure for its marathon motor-vehicle sale.
____: The apartment owner concealed a video camera behind the apartment's two-way bathroom mirror.
____: The entertainment website ran a photo of the sports star with a caption suggesting a bizarre drug habit.
____: The private detective displayed old mug shots on its website, of persons the detective traced and caught.
____: The paparazzi pretended to be a shredding service to obtain the papers and records of the film star.
____: The lawyer wrote a blog about the family-law matter in which the opposing party had been a total jerk.
____: The inventor named the invention after a famous entrepreneur to catch the attention of potential licensees.
____: The news service hinted that the resident injured by a home explosion was preparing a terrorist act.
____: The campaign faked ad signatures of several famous figures who had no association with the candidate.
____: Her ex-boyfriend posted scandalous video of her on an anonymous website ostensibly about bad girls.
____: As threatened, the retired caseworker wrote a memoir exaggerating her former boss as a supposed tyrant.
____: The nosey homemaker would sneak out at night to look through the neighbor's garbage before pick-up.
____: The nonprofit decided to use the dead celebrity's silhouette and slogan to attract patrons to the fundraiser.
____: The detective's telephoto lens couldn't capture any images until the detective climbed over the fence.
____: The shopper was shocked to see her insufficient-funds check posted under the retailer's counter glass.
____: The news runner sidled up to the accident scene, unnoticed, to listen to the EMTs and snap a few photos.
____: She couldn't believe that the nursery had used her photo on its billboard by the freeway.
____: The physician blanched at seeing the email string sharing her alleged shenanigans, so greatly exaggerated.
____: The startup's website looked great with the national-brand's colors and logo, and the similar name.
____: The entertainment magazine ran the TV star's juvenile delinquency as part of an "ancient history" section.
____: The custodian had read and scanned the medical records of several of the clinic's better-known patients.
____: The jail guard programmed the hidden camera to take a photo of the shower facilities every minute.
____: The local medical clinic slyly suggested its association with the famous national medical clinic.
____: The news story of the teen's suicide made the parents look heartless, when instead they cared deeply.
____: He claimed he had the right to use his own name for his business even if the same as a leading competitor.
____: The security guard used her master key to enter the executive's office at night to rummage through files.
____: The national retailer took the best product and reproduced it almost exactly as a similar house brand.

Answers are on the back, but please do not turn this sheet over until you have answered all questions fully and conferred with a seatmate to complete and correct your answers.

Answer Key

Invasion of privacy has four forms. The first form **appropriation (A)** (also known as commercial exploitation or right of publicity) involves the unauthorized use of another's name, likeness, or image, for financial or other gain. The second form **intrusion (I)** (also known as intrusion on seclusion of persona) involves the intentional entry into a place where a person has a reasonable expectation of privacy and that is highly offensive to the reasonable person. The third form **false light (FL)** involves a false portrayal or depiction in a manner that is highly offensive to the reasonable person. The fourth form **public disclosure of private facts (PD)** involves the disclosure to more than a few of true but private information, the disclosure of which is highly offensive to the reasonable person. Below are the identified examples.

A: The car dealership displayed an inflatable Elvis Presley figure for its marathon motor-vehicle sale.

I: The apartment owner concealed a video camera behind the apartment's two-way bathroom mirror.

FL: The entertainment website ran a photo of the sports star with a caption suggesting a bizarre drug habit.

PD: The private detective displayed old mug shots on its website, of persons the detective traced and caught.

I: The paparazzi pretended to be a shredding service to obtain the papers and records of the film star.

PD: The lawyer wrote a blog about the family-law matter in which the opposing party had been a total jerk.

A: The inventor named the invention after a famous entrepreneur to catch the attention of potential licensees.

FL: The news service hinted that the resident injured by a home explosion was preparing a terrorist act.

A: The campaign faked ad signatures of several famous figures who had no association with the candidate.

PD: Her ex-boyfriend posted scandalous video of her on an anonymous website ostensibly about bad girls.

FL: As threatened, the retired caseworker wrote a memoir exaggerating her former boss as a supposed tyrant.

I: The nosey homemaker would sneak out at night to look through the neighbor's garbage before pick-up.

A: The nonprofit decided to use the dead celebrity's silhouette and slogan to attract patrons to the fundraiser.

I: The detective's telephoto lens couldn't capture any images until the detective climbed over the fence.

PD: The shopper was shocked to see her insufficient-funds check posted under the retailer's counter glass.

I: The news runner sidled up to the accident scene, unnoticed, to listen to the EMTs and snap a few photos.

A: She couldn't believe that the nursery had used her photo on its billboard by the freeway.

FL: The physician blanched at seeing the email string sharing her alleged shenanigans, so greatly exaggerated.

A: The startup's website looked great with the national-brand's colors and logo, and the similar name.

PD: The entertainment magazine ran the TV star's juvenile delinquency as part of an "ancient history" section.

I: The custodian had read and scanned the medical records of several of the clinic's better-known patients.

I: The jail guard programmed the hidden camera to take a photo of the shower facilities every minute.

A: The local medical clinic slyly suggested its association with the famous national medical clinic.

FL: The news story of the teen's suicide made the parents look heartless, when instead they cared deeply.

A: He claimed he had the right to use his own name for his business even if the same as a leading competitor.

I: The security guard used her master key to enter the executive's office at night to rummage through files.

A: The national retailer took the best product and reproduced it almost exactly as a similar house brand.

Review Exercise for Week 8
Match these facts with the law on the next page that the facts trigger.

No one was going to believe how badly things had been going for her lately. ____ 1. First, she'd parked her car downtown late one Saturday night and then taken a cab home because she'd had a little too much to drink, only to find out that demolition of a building downtown early Sunday morning had destroyed her car. ____ 2. Then, she couldn't find a lawyer to help her sue the maker of the drug that had made her so sick right after approval of its clinical trials. ____ 3. Next, the home she'd just purchased turned out to have an old termite infestation about the seller had said nothing. ____ 4. Then, the still-new camper that she'd bought from a bank that had repossessed it turned out to have asbestos in its ceiling and floors, with its maker already bankrupt. ____ 5. She'd also been watching public-access television one night when she saw her neighbor falsely accusing her of running a brothel out of her home, in the public-agenda part of the city-council meeting. ____ 6. Then she learned, apparently too late to do anything about it, that her surgeon had implanted a defective hip socket in her hip replacement six years ago, when her hip had felt fine until recently. ____ 7. She then got hurt riding on a ski-doo backwards, which she knew was foolish, but the thing shouldn't have stalled, either. ____ 8. And her employer fired her accusing her of theft that she didn't commit, sure making it hard for her to explain to prospective employers. Some days, she wished she'd gone to law school!

Review Exercise for Week 8
Match this law with the facts on the prior page that the facts trigger.

___A. A discovery rule may toll the limitations period until the plaintiff should have known of the injury and its connection to the defendant's conduct. [Week 1]

___B. Strict products liability provides that merchants who sell products in a defective condition unreasonably dangerous to users are liable for resultant injury. [Week 2]

___C. Comparative negligence is an available defense to products-liability claims in a majority of jurisdictions. [Week 3]

___D. Federal preemption is yet another possible defense, where state tort law would contradict federal statute or regulation. [Week 3]

___E. Strict liability exists for abnormally dangerous activities, defined in the Second Restatement by the inability to eliminate a high risk of harm from uncommon activities of uncertain value. [Week 4]

___F. Silent fraud or fraudulent concealment involves the knowing refusal to disclose under circumstances where disclosure is reasonably expected. Notice that misrepresentation requires intent, desire, or purpose, or what might in the criminal law be thought of as scienter or a guilty mind. [Week 5]

___G. Some courts recognize defamation claims in which circumstances compelled the claimant to self-publish the false statements. [Week 6]

___H. An absolute legislative privilege protects speakers in legislative proceedings against defamation claims made based on any (not just relevant) matters. [Week 7]

Answer key: 1E, 2D, 3F, 4B, 5H, 6A, 7C, 8G

Torts Workbook

Drafting Exercise for Week 8

INTEROFFICE MEMORANDUM

TO: ASSOCIATE
FROM: PARTNER
CLIENT: RABURN / INKLING
SUBJECT: DRAFTING COMPLAINT
DATE: 11/15/2018

Please complete the complaint that I began drafting below. I am in my office if you have any questions. In brief, our client Marsha Raburn was horrified to learn from an acquaintance that a national comedy magazine *You Bet Your Life* published in print and online by Inkling Publications, Inc., had used one of her wedding photographs to depict her as winning an "ugliest bride" contest on page 24 of its May 2016 issue. She had never participated in any such contest and had not given anyone consent to use her photograph. She was aware that the photography service that had taken her wedding pictures had for a brief time displayed some of them on its website and guessed that the magazine had taken the photograph from there. Mrs. Raburn's husband Michael confirms that Marsha has been angry, moody, tearful, withdrawn, depressed, and generally severely distressed over the publication. Mrs. Raburn is now on anti-depressant medication that her treating physician prescribed after noting her sleeplessness, anxiety, shaking, and weight loss. Mrs. Raburn has used up her sick-leave days and has missed some additional work.

STATE OF MICHIGAN
IN THE KENT COUNTY CIRCUIT COURT

MARSHA RABURN,
GC
      Plaintiff,
v

INKLING PUBLICATIONS, INC.,
      Defendant.

No. 16-_____ -

Hon.

COMPLAINT

Nelson P. Miller (P40513)
Fajen & Miller, P.L.L.C.
41 Washington Street, Suite 280
Grand Haven, MI 49417
(616) 846-9875
Attorneys for Plaintiff

Plaintiff Marsha Raburn complains against defendant Inkling Publications, Inc., as follows:

PARTIES, JURISDICTION, AND VENUE

1. Mrs. Raburn is a married individual residing in Kent County.

2. Inkling Publications, Inc., is a New York corporation doing business in Kent County.

3. This case involves damages in excess of $25,000 exclusive of interest and costs.

4. This Court has jurisdiction and venue over this case.

ALLEGATIONS OF FACT

5.

6.

7.

8.

9.

COUNT I: _____

10.

11.

12.

13.

14.

ON THESE ALLEGATIONS, plaintiff Marsha Raburn prays that the Court enter judgment in her favor and against defendant Inkling Publications, Inc., for all damages, costs, interests, and attorney's fees most wrongfully sustained.

FAJEN and MILLER, P.L.L.C.

By:_____

Nelson P. Miller (P40513)
Fajen & Miller, P.L.L.C.
41 Washington Street, Suite 280
Grand Haven, MI 49417
(616) 846-9875
Attorneys for Plaintiff

September 1, 2018

Model Answer for Drafting Exercise: Complaint

* * *

ALLEGATIONS OF FACT

5. Inkling publishes the national comedy magazine You Bet You Life.
6. Inkling published Mrs. Raburn's photograph as "ugliest bride."
7. Inkling's publication was on page 24 of its May 2016 issue.
8. Mrs. Raburn had never participated in an "ugliest bride" competition.
9. Mrs. Raburn did not consent to Inkling using her photograph.
10. Inkling's publication made Mrs. Raburn angry, moody, tearful, withdrawn, depressed, and severely distressed.
11. Mrs. Raburn is now on anti-depressant medication that her treating physician prescribed after noting her sleeplessness, anxiety, shaking, and weight loss because of Inkling's publication.
12. Mrs. Raburn has also used up her sick-leave days and has missed some additional work because of Inkling's publication.

COUNT I: INVASION OF PRIVACY (APPROPRIATION)

13. This reference incorporates the above allegations into this count.
14. As a publisher of a national magazine, Inkling owed Mrs. Raburn a duty not to invade her privacy by appropriating and commercially or otherwise exploiting her name, likeness, image, or persona.
15. Inkling breached its duty and invaded Mrs. Raburn's privacy, committing the appropriation form of invasion of privacy, and did so for commercial, pecuniary, and other gain, when it appropriated and commercially and otherwise exploited her likeness, image, and persona in the manner alleged above.
16. Inkling's invasion of privacy and exploitation of Mrs. Raburn's likeness, image, and persona would have been highly offensive to the reasonable person and was in fact highly offensive to Mrs. Raburn as a reasonable person.
17. As a natural and probable result of Inkling's invasion of Mrs. Raburn's privacy, Mrs. Raburn suffered mental and emotional distress, severe depression, weight loss, hair loss, and other personal and dignitary offense, and incurred medical expense and wage and benefits loss, all of which may continue into the future.

COUNT II: INVASION OF PRIVACY (FALSE LIGHT)

18. This reference incorporates the above allegations into this count.
19. As a publisher of a national magazine, Inkling owed Mrs. Raburn a duty not to invade her privacy by placing and depicting her, using her likeness, image, or persona, in a false light in a way that would be highly offensive to the reasonable person.
20. Inkling breached its duty and invaded Mrs. Raburn's privacy, and committed the false-light form of the invasion of privacy tort, when it falsely depicted her in the manner alleged above, using her likeness, image, and persona.
21. Inkling's invasion of privacy and false depiction of Mrs. Raburn using her likeness, image, and persona would have been highly offensive to the reasonable person and was in fact highly offensive to Mrs. Raburn as a reasonable person.
22. As a natural and probable result of Inkling's invasion of Mrs. Raburn's privacy and depicting her in a false light, Mrs. Raburn suffered mental and emotional distress, severe depression, weight loss, hair loss, and other personal and dignitary offense, and incurred medical expense and wage and benefits loss, all of which may continue in the future.

* * *

Week 9
Damages

BULLET OUTLINE FOR WEEK 9:
DAMAGES
Categories: [95]economic (special) and non-economic (general)
- [96]economic loss begins with medical expense and wage loss
  - [103]claimants may recover for aggravation of pre-existing conditions
    - defendants pay all if parties are unable to distinguish old from new injury
  - [98]spouse of an injured tort victim also has claim for loss of consortium
    - includes lost services, support, love, society, companionship
- [97]non-economic loss is pain and suffering
  - may also include humiliation, shock, fright, mortification, scarring, disfigurement, disability, lost enjoyment of life, etc.
  - avoid duplicating damages

Procedures
- [108]motion in limine asks court to bar inflammatory damages evidence
- [99]motion for remittitur asks court to reduce excessive damages resulting from passion and prejudice
- [100]collateral-source rule bars evidence of health or other insurance, gratuitous payments
  - [101]insurers who pay for loss may have right of subrogation
- [102]defendants may plead plaintiff's failure to mitigate damages
  - plaintiffs must take reasonable action to reduce their loss
- [104]damages caps limit personal-injury plaintiffs' recoveries in many states
  - some states have held caps unconstitutional
- [105]Recoveries on account of physical injury are not taxed
  - recoveries where there is no physical injury are taxed
  - [106]claimants may also structure settlements without tax on the investments' earnings
- [107]contingency fees must be reasonable

Wrongful death action (a procedural device only, not another underlying tort theory)
- [109]allows tort recovery even after death
  - claimants must still have an underlying tort theory such as negligence
- [110]usually brought in the name of the decedent's estate
  - controlled by the estate's personal representative
- [111]spouses and dependent children are typical beneficiaries
  - some states also recognize parents, siblings, and lineal descendants
- [112]acts differ as to the measure of loss
  - some limit to pecuniary loss
  - others allow non-economic loss to beneficiaries
  - some allow loss to the estate

[113]**Survival actions** permit estate to recover for losses the decedent suffered before death

Property damage
- [114]usual measure is market value of property at time of loss
  - [115]personal value to owner only for special items like family heirlooms
- [116]temporary deprivation measured by rental value
- partial destruction measured by reduction in market value

Punitive damages
- [117]where allowed, to punish defendant rather than compensate plaintiff
  - allowed only for more-reprehensible wrongs like willful and wanton misconduct

- [118]Constitution prohibits excessive punitive damages
  - consider ratio to actual damages, reprehensibility, and other available remedies (RRR)

PARAGRAPH OUTLINE FOR WEEK 9:
DAMAGES
[95]There are two main categories of personal injury damages, economic and non-economic, sometimes called special and general. [96]Economic loss typically begins with medical expense and wage loss. [97]Non-economic loss is usually thought of as pain and suffering but may include humiliation, shock, fright, mortification, scarring, disfigurement, disability, and loss of enjoyment of life.

Beyond those two basic categories and their various components or divisions, tort-damages law involves many other special substantive and procedural considerations. For example, [98]the spouse of an injured tort victim may have a claim for loss of consortium, meaning loss of services, love, society, and companionship. [99]On motion for remittitur, the court will reduce or set aside excessive damages verdicts which are the result of passion and prejudice or not supported by the evidence. [100]Where still recognized, the collateral-source rule bars evidence of health or other insurance, gratuitous payments, and other reimbursement for the tort claimant's losses. [101]Insurers who pay for the plaintiff's loss may have the contract right to reimbursement out of the plaintiff's tort recovery or to seek that recovery if the plaintiff has not pursued it.

[102]Tort claimants have the duty to mitigate their damages, meaning to take reasonable action to reduce their loss. [103]Tort claimants may recover for aggravation of pre-existing conditions and hold defendant liable for all disability if the parties are unable to distinguish the old condition from new injury. [104]Damages caps limit personal-injury plaintiffs' recoveries in many states, although some states have held caps unconstitutional. [105]Recoveries on account of physical injury are not taxed, but recoveries where there is no physical injury are taxed. [106]The tax code permits tort claimants to have a third party structure their settlements without tax on the investments' earnings. [107]Contingency fees must be reasonable. [108]Parties may challenge the admissibility of inflammatory damages evidence with a motion in limine heard before trial.

The death of an individual due to a tort creates other special issues. [109]Wrongful-death acts in all 50 states allow tort recoveries for death, but the claimants must still have an underlying tort theory such as negligence. In other words, do not mistake wrongful death as a substantive cause of action. It is really a procedural device for addressing the special considerations the law must address when the tort victim died as a result of the tort. [110]Wrongful-death actions are usually brought in the name of the decedent's estate and controlled by the estate's personal representative. [111]Spouses and children are typical beneficiaries under wrongful-death acts, as may be parents and possibly siblings and other lineal descendants. [112]Wrongful-death acts differ as to the measure of loss, some limited to pecuniary loss while others allow non-economic loss to beneficiaries and some even loss to the estate. [113]Survival actions permit the estate to recover for losses the decedent suffered before death.

Property damage has its own rules different from the rules for personal injury and wrongful death damages. [114]The usual measure of damages for property loss is the market value of the property at the time of loss. [115]Personal value to the owner is not usually considered unless the loss involved an item having the history of a family heirloom. [116]Damages for temporary deprivation may be measured by rental value, whereas damages for partial destruction may be measured by reduction in market value.

Punitive damages are another category of damages, in addition to the broad category of compensatory damages, that some states allow, but with constitutional (due process) limitations. [117]Some jurisdictions allow punitive damages in some cases where there is a more culpable wrong, to punish the defendant rather than compensate the plaintiff. [118]The Constitution prohibits states from awarding excessive punitive damages, measured against the actual damages, the reprehensibility of the tortious conduct, and the nature of other available civil and criminal penalties.

Fluency Cards for Week 9

Cover and uncover the response to each prompt until you fluently recall the exact response.

Damages

Economic loss (medical expense, wage loss) and noneconomic loss (pain and suffering).

Reduction

Remittitur reduces excessive verdicts to the highest amount evidence supports.

Collateral Source

Bars evidence of other payments because health insurers have reimbursement rights.

Limits to Damages

Caps may limit, and plaintiffs must mitigate, damages.

Punitive Damages

Punish reprehensible wrongs, in reasonable ratio to compensatory and other remedies.

Definitions Worksheet for Week 9

1. What are the main categories of personal-injury damages and examples of each?

2. What claim does the spouse of a tort victim have, and for what damages?

3. How do trial courts deal with excessive damage verdicts? What standards do they apply?

4. What is the *collateral-source rule*? Why is it necessary?

5. What is a *wrongful-death* claim? Who brings it? Who gets the money and how much?

6. What are *punitive damages*? How does one measure them, and with what limits?

7. What does the law say on liability for injury to one already ailing before the injury?

Answer Key for Definitions Worksheet

1. *What are the main categories of personal-injury damages and examples of each?* Personal-injury damages have two main categories, economic and non-economic loss, sometimes called special and general damages. Economic loss usually involves medical expense and wage loss. Non-economic loss can include pain, suffering, humiliation, shock, fear, fright, mortification, scarring, disfigurement, disability, and lost enjoyment of life.

2. *What claim does the spouse of a tort victim have, and for what damages?* The spouse of an injured tort victim may have a claim for *loss of consortium*, meaning loss of love, society or companionship, and household services.

3. *How do trial courts deal with excessive damage verdicts? What standards do they apply?* On motion for remittitur, the court will reduce or set aside excessive damages verdicts that are the result of passion and prejudice or not supported by the evidence.

4. *What is the* **collateral-source rule**? *Why is it necessary?* Where still recognized, the collateral-source rule bars evidence of health, disability, or other insurance or gratuitous payments for the tort claimant's loss. Insurers who pay for the plaintiff's loss may have the contract right to reimbursement out of the plaintiff's tort recovery.

5. *What is a* **wrongful-death** *claim? Who brings it? Who gets the money and how much?* Wrongful-death acts allow recovery for death where the claimants have an underlying tort theory such as negligence. Wrongful-death actions are usually in the name of the decedent's estate by the personal representative. Spouses and children are typical beneficiaries, as may be parents and possibly siblings and other lineal descendants. Wrongful-death acts differ as to damages, some limited to pecuniary loss while others loss to beneficiaries and some loss to the estate.

6. *What are* **punitive damages**? *How does one measure them, and with what limits?* Punitive damages are to punish more-culpable, reckless or intentional wrongs. Due process prohibits excessive punitive damages, measured against the actual damages, reprehensibility of the misconduct, and other available civil and criminal penalties.

7. *What does the law say on liability for injury to one already ailing before the injury?* The wrongdoer takes the claimant as the wrongdoer finds the claimant even if the claimant is susceptible to injury. Claimants may recover for aggravation of pre-existing conditions and hold wrongdoers liable for all disability if unable to distinguish the old condition from new injury.

Issue-Spotting Worksheet for Week 9

State the law each scenario raises. No analysis. Just spot the issue and state the law.

1. Your client suffered serious injury as a passenger in a motor-vehicle accident that was obviously the fault of a well-insured driver. Your client's injuries are so severe that your client is very concerned about the client's financial future. Your client wants a sense of how the law will measure your client's monetary recovery.

_____

_____

2. Your client mentions that the client's spouse has grown quite upset about the whole thing and just wonders why the client can't get better so that the household can get back to normal. The marriage is strained.

_____

_____

3. So you've told the client about several damages categories that the law recognizes. Your client, though, admits that the client had off and on for years suffered from a chronic and periodically debilitating circulatory condition. Your client wants to know how that circumstance may affect your client's recovery.

_____

_____

4. Your client discloses having good health insurance except for the substantial deductible and small co-pays. Your client is also fortunate to have purchased disability insurance through the client's employer.

_____

_____

5. More than anything, though, your client is extremely upset that the negligent driver appears to have been using a smartphone at the moment of the accident. Your client wants to know if that fact will change anything in the overall equation.

_____

_____

Answer Key for Issue-Spotting Worksheet

1. ***This question implicates the personal-injury damages categories.*** Personal-injury damages have two main categories, economic and non-economic loss, sometimes called special and general damages. Economic loss usually involves medical expense and wage loss. Non-economic loss can include pain, suffering, humiliation, shock, fear, fright, mortification, scarring, disfigurement, disability, and lost enjoyment of life.

2. ***The statement implicates a spouse's right to recover for loss of consortium.*** The spouse of an injured tort victim may have a claim for *loss of consortium*, meaning loss of love, society or companionship, and household services. A lawyer should promptly tell an injured and married client of that right in the event that the spouse wishes to maintain a claim in the same proceeding.

3. ***The question implicates the law on recovery for pre-existing conditions.*** While the defendant will make much of separating out pre-existing conditions from accident injuries, the wrongdoer takes the claimant as the wrongdoer finds the claimant even when susceptible to injury. Claimants may recover for aggravation of pre-existing conditions and hold wrongdoers liable for all disability if unable to distinguish the old condition from new injury.

4. ***The statement implicates the collateral-source rule.*** Where still recognized, the collateral-source rule bars evidence of health, disability, or other insurance or gratuitous payments for the tort claimant's loss. Insurers who pay for the plaintiff's loss may have the contract right to reimbursement out of the plaintiff's tort recovery.

5. ***The question implicates punitive damages.*** Punitive damages are to punish more-culpable, reckless or intentional wrongs, not generally for simple negligence claims, and not available in every state. Due process also prohibits excessive punitive damages, measured against the actual damages, reprehensibility of the misconduct, and other available civil and criminal penalties.

TORTS WORKBOOK

Comprehensiveness Exercise for Week 9

Insert words at the ^ mark that would make for a more-accurate or more-detailed law statement. Follow the italicized hints for help. Suggested answers are on the next page.

1. Personal-injury damages include economic and non-economic loss. Economic loss can include ^ wage loss. Non-economic loss can include ^ ^ humiliation, shock, fear, fright, mortification, ^ ^ ^ and lost enjoyment of life. *[Not just wage loss but also something even more common. And what other non-economic losses.]*

2. The spouse of an injured tort victim may have a claim for ^ consortium, meaning loss of ^ society or companionship ^ . *[Just consortium or some kind of consortium? What other losses?]*

3. On motion for remittitur, the court may reduce or set aside ^ damages verdicts that are the result of ^ prejudice ^ . *[Any damages? What else besides prejudice? What other grounds?]*

4. The collateral-source rule bars evidence of ^ gratuitous payments for the tort claimant's loss. *[What other kinds of payments?]*

5. Wrongful-death acts allow recovery for death ^ . *[Any death?]*

6. Wrongful-death actions are usually in the name of the decedent's estate ^ . Children ^ are typical beneficiaries ^ . *[Conducted by whom? Who else is a common beneficiary? Any other possibilities?]*

7. Punitive damages punish ^ wrongs. *[Any wrongs?]*

8. Due process prohibits excessive punitive damages, measured against the actual damages ^ ^ . *[Two other measures.]*

Answers for Comprehensiveness Exercise

1. Personal-injury damages include both economic and non-economic loss. Economic loss can include medical expense *and wage loss*. Non-economic loss can include *pain, suffering*, humiliation, shock, fear, fright, mortification, *scarring, disfigurement, disability,* and lost enjoyment of life.

2. The spouse of an injured tort victim may have a claim for *loss of* consortium, meaning loss of *love,* society or companionship, *and household services*.

3. On motion for remittitur, the court may reduce or set aside *excessive* damages verdicts that are the result of *passion or* prejudice *or not supported by the evidence*.

4. The collateral-source rule bars evidence of *health, disability, or other insurance or* gratuitous payments for the tort claimant's loss.

5. Wrongful-death acts allow recovery for death *where the claimants have an underlying tort theory such as negligence*.

6. Wrongful-death actions are usually in the name of the decedent's estate *by the personal representative*. Children *and spouses* are typical beneficiaries, *as may be parents and possibly siblings and other lineal descendants*.

7. Punitive damages punish *more-culpable, reckless or intentional* wrongs.

8. Due process prohibits excessive punitive damages, measured against the actual damages, *reprehensibility of the misconduct, and other available civil and criminal penalties*.

TORTS WORKBOOK

Examples/Non-Examples Exercise for Week 9

Identify whether each fact pattern is an example (E) or non-example (NE) of the **highlighted concept**. Answers follow. In the blanks, generate an additional example and non-example.

1. Personal-injury damages have two main categories, economic and non-economic loss, sometimes called special and general damages. ***Economic loss*** usually involves medical expense and wage loss.
    - ___ The stricken pedestrian missed weeks of work and incurred thousands of dollars in medical expense.
    - ___ The elderly shopper slipped and fell on the puddle of cooking oil, suffering bruising and severe pain.
    - ___ The unwanted sexual touching disgusted the female patron of the ride service, who sued for her upset.

    E: _____

    N: _____

2. ***Non-economic loss*** can include pain, suffering, humiliation, shock, fear, fright, mortification, scarring, disfigurement, disability, and lost enjoyment of life.
    - ___ The injured boater had to be life-flighted to the hospital and spent weeks in intensive care.
    - ___ After the collision, the passenger was screaming in pain until emergency personnel sedated him.
    - ___ The driver's whiplash hadn't seemed severe at the time, but her neck ached for months afterward.

    E: _____

    N: _____

3. The spouse of an injured tort victim may have a claim for ***loss of consortium***, meaning loss of love, society or companionship, and household services.
    - ___ His fall injured him so severely that not only could he not work, but he also couldn't care for his kids.
    - ___ The malpractice kept her from cooking, cleaning, and shopping, chores that her husband had to perform.
    - ___ The friends had been extremely close companions until her chronic illness from the toxic exposure.

    E: _____

    N: _____

4. On motion for remittitur, the court will reduce or set aside ***excessive damages*** verdicts that are the result of passion and prejudice or not supported by the evidence.
    - ___ The jurors were aghast at the perpetrator's actions, and the hundred-times-medicals verdict showed it.
    - ___ The defendant had no idea how he could possibly pay the verdict that doubled the plaintiff's wage loss.
    - ___ The insurer asked defense counsel's opinion on the million-dollar soft-tissue whiplash verdict.

    E: _____

    N: _____

5. Where still recognized, the ***collateral-source rule*** bars evidence of health, disability, or other insurance or gratuitous payments for the tort claimant's loss.
    - ___ The liability insurer disputed that the insured had paid for the coverage for the accident period.
    - ___ The insurer initially disputed the employee's work disability from the accident but finally began to pay.

The hospital admission and discharge records showed that the injured baker had Blue Cross coverage.

E: _____

N: _____

6. ***Wrongful-death acts*** allow an estate's recovery for decedent's death where the decedent would have had a tort claim against the defendant, such as for negligence.

___ The defective scaffold's collapse sent the construction worker on a steep fall to his death.
___ The botched triple-bypass caused the patient's heart fibrillation, resulting first in coma and then death.
___ The drunk driver was going way over the speed limit when careening off road into a tree to her death.

E: _____

N: _____

7. ***Survival statutes*** preserve in the estate's name a claim for someone who lived for a time after the tort but then died of related or unrelated causes. The recovery is an estate asset subject to creditors.

___ The motorist was calling out for help after the roll-over accident but was dead when EMTs arrived.
___ The patient never awoke from the medical procedure that mistakenly overdosed her on anesthesia.
___ The builder lived painfully and disabled for two years after the accident before dying of a heart attack.

E: _____

N: _____

8. ***Punitive damages*** are to punish reckless or intentional wrongs. Due process prohibits excessive punitives, measured against actual damages, reprehensibility of misconduct, and other civil or criminal penalty.

___ The passenger suffered broken hip and neck when the other driver ran the red light, striking the vehicle.
___ The jury awarded a half-million in wage loss, half-million in medicals, and half-million for pain.
___ The ex-boyfriend knew that the heater would explode but didn't care that his ex got severely injured.

E: _____

N: _____

9. A wrongdoer ***takes a claimant as the wrongdoer finds the claimant*** if the claimant is susceptible to injury. Claimants may recover for aggravation of pre-existing conditions, even if not able to separate them out.

___ The twenty-year-old diver suffered severe back injury when the weakened high-dive board broke.
___ The thirty-year-old homemaker tore up her bad knee in the collision so that she couldn't walk.
___ The trauma when the exercise equipment broke made the forty-year-old laborer's bad back much worse.

E: _____

N: _____

Answers: 1 ENN; 2 NEE; 3 NEN; 4 ENE; 5 NEE; 6 EEN; 7 ENE; 8 NNE; 9 NEE

TORTS WORKBOOK

Skills Exercise for Week 9

You are about to give that part of a closing argument in a personal injury case that has to do with this week's subject of *damages*. Your first step, working with a seatmate, is to outline in the space provided below the damages *categories* that you plan to address. Then, still working with your seatmate, list for each category the *facts* that you will address. Your damages argument must combine law (the law of damages) with facts. Then take a few moments to collect your thoughts about the *voice* that you will use, whether firm, polite, friendly, impassioned, or otherwise. Finally, plan your *first* few words and *last* few words so that you feel confident beginning and ending. Although closing arguments may run from about twenty minutes to an hour, practice an outline here by taking about three minutes. Make your closing argument to another student, who at the end of your closing argument will tell you how much they would have awarded if a juror in the case. Then, switch roles to repeat the exercise.

40-year-old, self-employed, married, homemaker Minnie Brown. Mother of two teenage children. Disabling back injury in a motor vehicle accident caused by a truck driver. The trucking company has a primary insurance policy with $100,000 limits. Also has an umbrella policy with $1,000,000 limits. Your client suffered lumbar-spine fractures in the accident. Required hospitalization for three weeks. Two surgeries in which plates and cement were used to stabilize her spine. Restricted to bed at home for an additional 12 weeks. Total medical expense has been $86,000. Will require future medical examination and physical and occupational therapy. It has been nine months since the accident--still ambulates stooped and painfully. Almost totally unable to perform household chores. Has not worked at her home bookkeeping business since her injury. Has engaged in no substantial recreational activities since her injury. Used to walk, jog, and do yard work. Use to play tennis with daughter, hike with son and daughter, and play catch with son. No intimacy with husband since the accident.

EXAMPLE CLOSING ARGUMENT ON DAMAGES:

Jurors, we turn now to the issue of the harm that my client Mrs. Brown suffered. First, please consider what the Court will instruct you to be *economic loss*. You will have for your deliberations Plaintiff's Exhibit 1, photographs of Mrs. Brown's accident injuries, Plaintiff's Exhibit 2, Mrs. Brown's medical records, and Plaintiff's Exhibit 3, a summary and itemization of the $28,645 cost of Mrs. Brown's medical care to date. You also have the testimony of her primary-care physician Dr. Rogers that her future medical care will continue resulting in costs of a like amount, meaning that you should double her medical expense to a subtotal of $57,290 in economic loss.

The Court though will further instruct you in *non-economic loss*, that instruction including Mrs. Brown's pain, suffering, fear, fright, shock, mental and emotional distress, disability, and loss of enjoyment of life. As the Court will instruct you, valuing these non-economic losses is up to you, not defense counsel or even me. Your noneconomic-loss figure could easily be a multiple of the $57,290 economic loss figure to pay Mrs. Brown's medical expense. Very few people whom you met on the street would be willing to undergo what Mrs. Brown has suffered, even for a reasonable multiple of that figure, such as $250,000. We have no way of giving Mrs. Brown her usual life back. The law instead requires that you award full and fair compensation, not what you think that anyone in particular could afford. I simply ask that you follow the law in awarding her full, fair, and just damages. The power and responsibility is yours.

Review Exercise for Week 9
Match these facts with the law on the next page that the facts trigger.

He'd been having one bad day after another, lately. ____ 1. He had learned on Saturday that the Hawaii time-share that he and his wife had purchased didn't exist. ____ 2. Then, he'd run downtown to his office very early Sunday morning to retrieve some papers, when a demolition blast toppled an old building over on his car while he was up in his office. ____ 3. On Monday, a so-called *friend* of his had spread a Facebook rumor that he'd been out all Saturday night drinking and drugging rather than going to his office early Sunday morning. ____ 4. Then, Tuesday, the brand-new laptop computer that he'd just bought completely stopped working, when, he realized, he hadn't bought the express warranty. ____ 5. He was sick on Wednesday and so slept in, only to see someone, looking like that private detective that his ex-wife had once hired, pulling documents from his garbage that he had put out at the curb Tuesday night. ____ 6. Then, on Thursday, he'd found out at his annual physical exam that the heart medication he'd taken about a dozen years ago had caused heart defects in over half of the medication's users. ____ 7. Turns out, the medication's original manufacturer was already bankrupt, although he thought his pharmacist might have gotten him a generic form through a distributor. ____ 8. Finally, his employer had fired him when it learned that his ex-wife had filed *and shared* a motion to reopen their divorce case, falsely alleging that he had fraudulently concealed income and assets from a supposed side business… that didn't even exist. *What would another week bring?!*

Review Exercise for Week 9
Match this law with the facts on the prior page that the facts trigger.

___A. Statutes of repose, typically applying to construction-defect and defective-drug cases, bar future claims a certain number of years after the service or activity that created the risk. Once the period ends, a statute of repose bars claims whether or not they have accrued.^{Week 1}

___B. The Uniform Commercial Code recognizes an implied warranty of merchantability, requiring that the product be fit for ordinary purpose, in all product sales by merchants and an implied warranty of fitness for particular purpose when the customer specifies the use and the seller supplies the product to meet the specification.^{Week 2}

___C. All merchants within the chain of distribution bear the same liability to the injured user as the manufacturer, as do suppliers of defective component parts. Entities in the chain of distribution typically indemnify one another, shifting products liability to the responsible party.^{Week 3}

___D. Under the popular Second Restatement definition, strict liability exists for *abnormally dangerous activities*, defined under a five-factor test including the inability to eliminate a high risk of harm from uncommon activities of uncertain value.^{Week 4}

___E. The public would know misrepresentation or fraud as a scheme, scam, or swindle, like someone fooling or cheating another in a transaction. Law defines misrepresentation as a knowing false material statement made with the purpose and effect of inducing justifiable reliance to the hearer's loss.^{Week 5}

___F. The public would think of defamation as gossip, rumor, innuendo, or *slander*, which is one of the two forms of defamation. Defamation involves false communication published of and concerning another that, together with extrinsic facts, harms the reputation of that other, with special damages except where law presumes damages.^{Week 6}

___G. An absolute judicial privilege protects against defamation claims based on publications in court proceedings, while an absolute legislative privilege protects speakers in legislative proceedings, and an absolute executive privilege protects statements made within the scope of official duties. Absolute privileges protect whether the defendant made the statement in good faith or not.^{Week 7}

___H. Invasion of privacy's intrusion form arises when there is an unauthorized intrusion into a place where the person has a reasonable expectation of privacy and that would be highly offensive to the reasonable person. The intrusion may involve observation of the person or of private matters such as medical or financial records.^{Week 8}

Answer key: 1E, 2D, 3F, 4B, 5H, 6A, 7C, 8G

Torts Workbook

Week 10
Multiple Parties

BULLET OUTLINE FOR WEEK 10:
MULTIPLE PARTIES
Satisfaction and release
- [119]release—plaintiff signs agreement releasing defendant from further liability
  - [124]be sure to release only those persons whom the parties intend to release
    - preserve rights against non-settling defendants
      - old rule was release one, release all
      - avoided in some states by convenant not to sue
      - modern rule is look to intent of parties signing release agreement
  - [121]courts set aside release only for fraud, duress, undue influence, or mutual mistake
- [120]satisfaction—defendant pays money judgment after trial
  - [122]single-satisfaction rule—plaintiffs are entitled to only a single satisfaction of damages
    - even when multiple parties are jointly and severally liable for those damages.
  - [123]partial-satisfaction rule—non-settling defendants get credit for settlements paid by others

Joint-and-several liability
- [125]traditional rule: plaintiff collects all or a portion of the damages from any defendant
  - joint liability means that all defendants share in paying the loss
  - several liability means that any one defendant must pay for all of the loss
- forms
  - [126]concerted action of two or more tortfeasors working together, causing loss
  - [127]independent actors causing indivisible injury (e.g., MV accident with two at-fault drivers)
  - [128]failures in a common duty (e.g., landlord and property manager both owing duty to repair)
- [129]most jurisdictions abolish joint-and-several liability
  - factfinder must apportion fault and judge apportion damages among liable defendants

Vicarious liability
- [130]Vicarious liability holds one party liable for the torts of another.
- forms
  - [131]respondeat superior (employer vicarious liability)
    - for negligence of employees within course of employment
    - [132]Commuting to and from work is not within course of employment
    - personal errands are not within the course of employment
      - employer errands are within course of employment
    - [133]no vicarious liability for intentional torts
      - unless the act furthered employer's mission or
      - employer authorized or ratified the act
    - [134]employers may have direct liability for negligent hiring or entrustment
  - [135]no vicarious liability for independent contractors except where
    - the one hiring the contractor retains control
    - the one hiring the contractor has nondelegable duties
    - the work involves inherently dangerous activities or
    - the contractor has apparent authority to act for the one hiring the contractor
  - [136]joint enterprises meaning common purpose, agreement, interest ($), and direction (PAID)
  - [137]no vicarious liability for bailments except where
    - owner-consent statutes exist for loaned motor vehicles
    - family-purpose doctrine for loaned motor vehicles
    - also watch for direct liability for negligent entrustment

Contribution and indemnity
- [138]contribution requires a defendant to pay a fair share of the damage for which the defendant is liable
  - [140]defendants who settle in good faith are not subject to contribution
    - courts give wide latitude to parties to agree on what is a good-faith settlement
  - [141]contribution actions are not necessary where law apportions liability among defendants
    - no contribution where the law abolishes joint-and-several liability
- [139]indemnity reimburses a defendant who pays the liability of another
  - [142]common-law indemnity where defendant seeking indemnity has only vicarious liability
  - [143]contractual indemnity allocates liability by advance agreement (e.g., insurance)

Successive injuries
- [144]plaintiff suffering successive injuries from separately liable defendants apportions damages
  - [145]if parties cannot separate injuries, then defendant causing successive injury pays all

PARAGRAPH OUTLINE FOR WEEK 10:
MULTIPLE PARTIES

Many tort claims involve more than one party on each side, creating related procedural issues. [119]When parties settle a tort claim, the plaintiff signs an agreement releasing the defendant from further liability, while attempting to preserve rights against non-settling defendants. [120]When parties are unable to voluntarily settle a claim and a money judgment is instead entered after trial, the liability is extinguished when the defendant satisfies the judgment. [121]The courts will set aside a release only for fraud, duress, undue influence, or mutual mistake. [122]Plaintiffs are entitled to only a single satisfaction of their damages even when multiple parties are jointly and severally liable for those damages. [123]Non-settling defendants who are jointly and severally liable get credit for amounts paid by settling defendants. [124]Releases must be carefully considered and crafted to release only those parties and their agents whom the parties intend to release. [125]The traditional rule of joint-and-several liability means that the plaintiff may collect all or a portion of the damages from any defendant. [126]Joint-and-several liability may arise from the concerted action of two or more tortfeasors. [127]Joint-and-several liability may also arise from two independent actors causing an indivisible injury. [128]Joint-and-several liability may also arise from failures in a common duty. [129]Most jurisdictions alter joint-and-several liability to require the factfinder to apportion fault and the judge to apportion damages among liable defendants.

[130]Vicarious liability holds one party liable for the torts of another. [131]A first form of vicarious liability is the respondeat-superior liability of an employer for the negligent acts of employees within the course of employment. [132]Commuting to and from work, and running personal errands, are not within the course of employment, but running employer errands is. [133]There is generally no vicarious liability for intentional torts unless the act was in furtherance of the employer's mission or the employer authorized or ratified the act. [134]Employers may also have direct liability for negligent hiring or entrustment. [135]There may also be vicarious liability for the acts of independent contractors, where the one hiring the contractor retains control or has nondelegable duties or inherently dangerous activities, or the contractor has apparent authority. [136]Another form of vicarious liability arises around joint enterprises, defined by a common purpose, agreement, and pecuniary interest, and shared direction or control. [137]Bailors are not generally liable to third parties who suffer damage from the bailees use of the personal property, but owner-consent statutes commonly change that rule as to vehicles.

[138]Contribution is the claim of a defendant that another party pay a fair share of the damage for which the defendant is liable. [139]Indemnity is the right of a defendant to reimbursement from the party whose fault created the defendant's liability. [140]A defendant who settles liability in good faith is no longer subject to contribution from other parties. [141]Contribution actions are not

necessary or allowed where tort law apportions liability among the liable defendants. [142]Common-law indemnity applies where the defendant seeking indemnity has only vicarious liability. [143]Contractual indemnity allocates the liability for fault by advance agreement among the responsible defendants. [144]When the plaintiff has suffered successive injuries from separately liable defendants, then damages are apportioned to each defendant. [145]When plaintiff is unable to prove which defendant caused which successive injury, the defendants may have the burden of proof to separate the injuries.

Fluency Cards for Week 10

Cover and uncover the response to each prompt until you fluently recall the exact response.

Settlement

Release settling defendants while preserving other claims.

Release Relief

Fraud, duress, mutual mistake, or rush-release statute.

Satisfaction

Non-settling defendants get credit for settlements.

Joint-and-Several Liability

All pay some or one pays all, at plaintiff's option, if concerted action, indivisible injury, or common duties.

Abolition

Many states abolish joint and several, requiring allocation of fault and apportionment of damages.

Vicarious Liability

One party liable for another such as employers for employees acting within the course of employment.

Intentional Torts

No vicarious liability for intentional torts unless authorized or ratified.

Employer/Employee

Employer controls by time, tools, and methods, and hiring, firing, and discipline.

Independent Contractors

Vicarious liability only with retained control, non-delegable duty, inherently dangerous activity, or apparent authority.

Joint Ventures

Vicarious liability only with common purpose, agreement, pecuniary interest, and direction or control.

Bailments

Not liable in common law but liable for motor vehicle under owner-consent statute.

Contribution and Indemnity

Contribute a fair share of the liability or reimburse for paying another's obligation.

Definitions Worksheet for Week 10

1. How do two opposing parties settle a case? Does law offer any relief from settlement?

2. How do parties satisfy money judgment after trial? Are more defendants more money?

3. What is *joint-and-several liability,* when does it arise, and how has law changed it?

4. What is *vicarious liability*, and what forms does it take (when does it arise)?

5. What are *contribution* and *indemnity*? How does law limit contribution actions?

6. How does law treat liability of different defendants for successive injuries to a single plaintiff?

Answer Key for Definitions Worksheet

1. *How do two opposing parties settle a case? Does law offer any relief from settlement?* When parties settle a tort claim, the plaintiff signs an agreement releasing the defendant from further liability, while attempting to preserve rights against non-settling defendants. Lawyers must carefully draft a release to release only those parties and their agents whom the parties intend to release. The courts will set aside a release only for fraud, duress, undue influence, or mutual mistake.

2. *How do parties satisfy money judgment after trial? Are more defendants more money?* When parties are unable to voluntarily settle a claim and the court enters a money judgment after trial, the plaintiff enters a satisfaction of judgment after the defendant pays the judgment. Law entitles plaintiffs to only a single satisfaction of their damages even when multiple defendants are jointly and severally liable for those damages. Non-settling defendants who are jointly and severally liable get credit for amounts paid by settling defendants.

3. *What is **joint-and-several liability**, when does it arise, and how has law changed it?* Joint-and-several liability means that the plaintiff may collect all or a portion of the damages from any defendant. Joint-and-several liability arises from (1) the concerted action of two or more wrongdoers, (2) two independent actors causing an indivisible injury, or (3) failures in a common duty. Most jurisdictions alter joint-and-several liability to require the jury to allocate fault and the judge to apportion damages among liable defendants.

4. *What is **vicarious liability**, and what forms does it take (when does it arise)?* Vicarious liability holds one party liable for the torts of another. Forms of vicarious liability include (1) employer liability for the negligent acts of employees within the course of employment, (2) contractor liability when retaining control or with non-delegable duties or inherently dangerous activities, (3) joint-enterprise liability, and (4) bailor liability but only in special situations such as under motor-vehicle owner-consent statutes.

5. *What are **contribution** and **indemnity**? How does law limit contribution actions?* Contribution is the claim of a defendant that another party pay a fair share of the damage for which the defendant is liable. Indemnity is the common law right of a defendant to reimbursement from the party whose fault created the defendant's vicarious liability or contractual right of reimbursement through insurance or other agreement. A defendant who settles in good faith or as to whom law allocates liability has no contribution liability.

6. *How does law treat liability of different defendants for successive injuries to a single plaintiff?* When the plaintiff suffers successive injuries from separately liable defendants, then law apportions damages to each defendant. When plaintiff is unable to prove which defendant caused which successive injury, the defendants may have the burden to separate the injuries.

Issue-Spotting Worksheet for Week 10

State the law each scenario raises. No analysis. Just spot the issue and state the law.

1. You conveyed the defendant vehicle owner's insurer's $100,000 settlement offer to your client in a motor-vehicle-accident case, which your client has just authorized that you accept. The defendant vehicle driver's insurer has so far offered only $50,000, which your client rejected when authorizing you to make a $200,000 demand. You value the case at a total of about $200,000, meaning that your client has so far recovered about one half of the case's value. How will you take the owner's $100,000 offer while proceeding against the driver for the rest of the case's $200,000 total value?

2. After your client settled with the owner for $100,000, you tried your client's remaining claim against the driver, winning a verdict right at your $200,000 total-case-value estimate. With a $500,000 single-limits insurance policy, the driver has plenty of insurance to pay the driver's liability. Your client wants to know what's next.

3. Complicating the above scenario, your case against the driver also included a claim against a mechanic whom the driver blamed for bad brakes. When the jury returned its $200,000 general verdict, its special verdict was that the driver was 75% at fault and the mechanic 25% at fault. Your client wants to know how those percentages change the client's outcome.

4. Your client had asked before you pled, pursued, and tried the above case what to do with the fact that the defendant driver had been en route from her workplace to a bank to make a deposit for her employer. Your client decided not to sue the employer. The mechanic, having suffered judgment after trial, is now threatening to do so. Your client wants to know how the mechanic could possibly proceed.

Answer Key for Issue-Spotting Worksheet

1. ***This question implicates how to settle a claim while preserving other claims.*** When parties settle a tort claim, the plaintiff signs an agreement releasing the defendant from further liability, while attempting to preserve rights against non-settling defendants. Lawyers must carefully draft a release to release only those parties and their agents whom the parties intend to release. The courts will set aside a release only for fraud, duress, undue influence, or mutual mistake.

2. ***This question implicates how to adjust and satisfy a judgment after trial when other defendants have already settled.*** When parties are unable to voluntarily settle a claim and the court enters a money judgment after trial, the plaintiff enters a satisfaction of judgment after the defendant pays the judgment. Law entitles plaintiffs to only a single satisfaction of their damages even when multiple defendants are jointly and severally liable for those damages. Non-settling defendants who are jointly and severally liable get credit for amounts paid by settling defendants.

3. ***This question implicates the relative liability of two parties whose negligence combined to cause the damage.*** Joint-and-several liability means that the plaintiff may collect all or a portion of the damages from any defendant. Joint-and-several liability arises from (1) the concerted action of two or more wrongdoers, (2) two independent actors causing an indivisible injury, or (3) failures in a common duty. Most jurisdictions alter joint-and-several liability to require the jury to allocate fault and the judge to apportion damages among liable defendants.

4. ***This question implicates employer vicarious liability and contribution claims.*** Vicarious liability holds one party liable for the torts of another. Forms of vicarious liability include (1) employer liability for the negligent acts of employees within the course of employment, (2) contractor liability when retaining control or with non-delegable duties or inherently dangerous activities, (3) joint-enterprise liability, and (4) bailor liability but only in special situations such as under motor-vehicle owner-consent statutes. Contribution is the claim of a defendant that another party pay a fair share of the damage for which the defendant is liable. A defendant who settles in good faith or as to whom law allocates liability has no contribution liability.

Comprehensiveness Exercise for Week 10

Insert words at the ^ mark that would make for a more-accurate or more-detailed law statement. Follow the italicized hints for help. Suggested answers are on the next page.

1. When parties settle a tort claim, the plaintiff signs an agreement releasing the settling defendant from liability. The courts set aside releases for ^^^ mutual mistake. *[And for what else?]*

2. When the court enters money judgment after trial, the defendant must pay the judgment. *[*

3. A ^ satisfaction rule lets the plaintiff collect the judgment ^ from multiple defendants who are jointly and severally liable. The ^ satisfaction rule gives defendants ^ credit for amounts other defendants pay. *[What kind of satisfaction? What kind? Which defendants?]*

4. Joint-and-several liability means that the plaintiff may collect all ^ damages from any defendant. *[All or what?]*

5. Joint-and-several liability arises from concerted action of two or more wrongdoers ^^. *[Two other ways, too,]*

6. Forms of vicarious liability include employer liability for the negligent acts of employees ^, contractor liability when retaining control ^, and bailor liability ^. *[Whenever? Other times? Anytime?]*

7. Contribution is the claim that another defendant should pay a fair share of the damages. A defendant who settles ^ ^ has no contribution liability. *[Any settlement? Only settlement?]*

8. Indemnity is the right of a defendant to reimbursement from the party whose fault created the defendant's vicarious liability ^. *[Only for fault with vicarious liability?]*

Answer Key for Comprehensiveness Exercise

1. When parties settle a tort claim, the plaintiff signs an agreement releasing the settling defendant from liability. The courts set aside releases for *fraud, duress, undue influence, or* mutual mistake.

2. When the court enters money judgment after trial, the defendant must pay the judgment *in exchange for the plaintiff's satisfaction of judgment*.

3. A *single* satisfaction rule lets the plaintiff collect the judgment *only once* from multiple defendants who are jointly and severally liable. The *partial* satisfaction rule gives defendants *who are jointly and severally liable* credit for amounts other defendants pay.

4. Joint-and-several liability means that the plaintiff may collect all *or a portion of* damages from any defendant.

5. Joint-and-several liability arises from concerted action of two or more wrongdoers, *two independent actors causing an indivisible injury, or failures in a common duty.*

6. Forms of vicarious liability include employer liability for the negligent acts of employees *within the course of employment*, contractor liability when retaining control *or with non-delegable duties or inherently dangerous activities*, *joint-enterprise liability,* and bailor liability *but only in special situations such as under motor-vehicle owner-consent statutes*.

7. Contribution is the claim that another defendant should pay a fair share of the damages. A defendant who settles *in good faith or as to whom law allocates liability* has no contribution liability.

8. Indemnity is the right of a defendant to reimbursement from the party whose fault created the defendant's vicarious liability *or contractual right of reimbursement through insurance or other agreement*.

TORTS WORKBOOK

Discrimination Exercise for Week 10

Indicate whether each statement *overgeneralizes*, *undergeneralizes*, or *misconceives* the rule, explaining why. *Overgeneralizing* states the rule too broadly, capturing circumstances to which it does not apply. *Undergeneralizing* states the rule too narrowly, omitting circumstances to which it applies. *Misconceiving* states the rule incorrectly.

1. When a plaintiff and defendant settle a tort claim, the plaintiff signs an agreement releasing all liability for the injury.
____OVER/____UNDER/____MISS/ Why? _____
_____

2. Law entitles plaintiffs to satisfaction of their damages, with non-settling defendants who are jointly and severally liable getting no credit for amounts paid by settling defendants.
____OVER/____UNDER/____MISS/ Why? _____
_____

3. Joint-and-several liability means that the plaintiff may collect a portion of the damages from any defendant.
____OVER/____UNDER/____MISS/ Why? _____
_____

4. Joint-and-several liability arises from the concerted action of two or more wrongdoers or two independent actors causing an indivisible injury.
____OVER/____UNDER/____MISS/ Why? _____
_____

5. Vicarious liability includes employer liability for negligent acts of employees, contractor liability, joint-enterprise liability, and bailor liability.
____OVER/____UNDER/____MISS/ Why? _____
_____

6. Indemnity is the claim of a defendant that another party pay a fair share of the damage for which the defendant is liable.
____OVER/____UNDER/____MISS/ Why? _____
_____

7. When plaintiff suffers successive injuries, defendants have the burden to separate the injuries.
____OVER/____UNDER/____MISS/ Why? _____
_____

Answer Key for Discrimination Exercise

1. The statement **OVERgeneralizes** the rule. When parties settle a tort claim, the plaintiff signs an agreement releasing *the defendant* from further liability, *while attempting to preserve rights against non-settling defendants. Lawyers must carefully draft a release to release only those parties and their agents whom the parties intend to release.*

2. The statement **MISconceives** the rule. When parties are unable to voluntarily settle a claim and the court enters a money judgment after trial, the plaintiff enters a satisfaction of judgment after the defendant pays the judgment. Law entitles plaintiffs to only a single satisfaction of their damages even when multiple defendants are jointly and severally liable for those damages. Non-settling defendants who are jointly and severally liable *get credit for amounts paid by settling defendants*.

3. The statement **UNDERgeneralizes** the rule. Joint-and-several liability means that the plaintiff may collect *all or* a portion of the damages from any defendant. Most jurisdictions alter joint-and-several liability to require the jury to allocate fault and the judge to apportion damages among liable defendants.

4. The statement **UNDERgeneralizes** the rule. Joint-and-several liability arises from (1) the concerted action of two or more wrongdoers, (2) two independent actors causing an indivisible injury, *or (3) failures in a common duty*.

5. The statement **OVERgeneralizes** the rule. Vicarious liability holds one party liable for the torts of another. Forms of vicarious liability include (1) employer liability for the negligent acts of employees *within the course of employment*, (2) contractor liability *when retaining control or with non-delegable duties or inherently dangerous activities*, (3) joint-enterprise liability, and (4) bailor liability *in special situations such as under motor-vehicle owner-consent statutes*.

6. The statement **MISconceives** the rule. *Contribution* is the claim of a defendant that another party pay a fair share of the damage for which the defendant is liable. Indemnity is *defendant's common-law right to reimbursement from the party whose fault created the defendant's vicarious liability or contractual right of reimbursement through insurance or other agreement*.

7. The statement **OVERgeneralizes** the rule. When the plaintiff suffers successive injuries from separately liable defendants, then law apportions damages to each defendant. *When plaintiff is unable to prove which defendant caused which successive injury*, defendants may have the burden to separate the injuries.

TORTS WORKBOOK

Role-Play Exercise for Week 10: Office Consult

CLIENT SCRIPT

Do this office-consult exercise in pairs. Choose roles, one student playing the client and one student playing the lawyer. You are the client. Read this side and only this side. Clients often meet lawyers at the lawyer's office. These office consults typically involve the client sharing information with the lawyer while listening to advice. Share with the lawyer what you know and what you think may be the facts. ***Don't just let the lawyer do all the talking. You don't like lawyers who talk all the time, especially when they talk down to clients. Insist that the lawyer listen to you, hear you, answer your questions, and respect you.***

EXAMPLE CONSULT (YOUR SCRIPT):

[When the lawyer mentions *vicarious liability*:] I have no idea what you are talking about. I'm not a lawyer and don't want to be. I am leaving the legalese to you.

[When the lawyer mentions the driver whose negligence hurt you as a passenger:] Of course I know the driver. What do you think, that I'd be riding around in a vehicle with a teen driver whom I didn't even know? [Let the lawyer drag it out of you that the teen was a neighbor's kid. Make up whatever you want about the details.]

[When the lawyer mentions *collectability*:] You lawyers are always thinking about money. How would I know if the teen had any money, although I can't imagine why the teen would have. Do YOU know of any teens who have a pile of money stashed away?

[When the lawyer again mentions *vicarious liability*:] There you go again with the legalese. Could you just handle that part of it, PLEASE???!!!

[When the lawyer mentions the vehicle that the teen was driving, who owned the vehicle, and whether it was insured:] Of course I know. The vehicle was the dad's vehicle, but how would I know if he had insured the vehicle? Can't YOU find out?

[When the lawyer asks your permission to sue the vehicle owner:] Well, how do you think THAT'S going to go over in the neighborhood when everyone finds out that I *sued my neighbor*?! What do you think I am, a lout?!! If we're going to do this, then we're going to have to find another way. Any ideas?

Role-Play Exercise for Week 10: Office Consult

LAWYER SCRIPT

Do this office-consult exercise in pairs. Choose roles, one student playing the client and one student playing the lawyer. You are the lawyer. Read this side and only this side. Much of law practice involves meeting with clients in your office at other locations convenient to your client. These office consults typically involve a good deal of gathering information from the client. They also involve a good deal of the lawyer educating the client. Gather helpful information from the client while giving the client your advice, educating and informing the client. **Don't just lecture the client. Clients don't like lawyers who talk down to them. Make your communication interactive. Get the client to tell you things as you tell the client your advice.**

EXAMPLE CONSULT (YOUR SCRIPT):

Thank you for the trust and confidence in allowing me to proceed for you against the at-fault driver who caused your injury while a passenger in the vehicle. We have one other important option to consider having to do with *vicarious liability*. Have you ever heard of that?

I understand from the police report that the driver was just seventeen, didn't own the motor vehicle, and may not even have insurance. What can you confirm for me about that?

Only owners of vehicles operated on the public highways have to have liability insurance. You will very likely prove the driver's fault and your injuries but without insurance may not be able to collect the judgment. What can you tell me about the driver's collectability?

Fortunately, the law holds vicariously liable **owners who consent to the use of their vehicle**. The common law might do so, but our state even has a **statute** saying so. Do you understand what I mean by *vicarious liability*?

Now, I don't know yet how much liability insurance this owner had or even if the owner complied with the law and maintained the insurance. But this owner had a nice, new vehicle, probably financed still, and thus probably insured. What can you tell me about that?

The police report shows the name of a small private insurer that sells a high-percentage of high-limits policies. Your recovery in this case would probably come only from the owner's vicarious liability. May I have your permission to include the vehicle owner in your complaint?

Review Exercise for Week 10
Match these facts with the law on the next page that the facts trigger.

She wouldn't want to repeat the last few weeks, that much is sure. ____ 1. First, she'd bought a motorcycle that had a crack in the frame that the seller had hidden with caulk, of all things. ____ 2. Then, the neighbor's sweet little dog had suddenly grabbed her hand and shook it savagely, as she reached down to pet it like she always did. ____ 3. She'd then seen that her old college roommate, the one who left in a huff saying all kinds of nasty things about her, had just posted the same vicious rumors about her on the internet. ____ 4. Then, she'd bought a laptop computer that from the first boot was so glitchy that it didn't accomplish even basic functions, and the screen flickered badly, although she hadn't bought the warranty the online seller offered. ____ 5. On her way to work, she'd seen her own photograph on a billboard advertising cosmetic surgery, from a clinic about which she'd never even heard! ____ 6. On her way home the same day, she'd driven her car through the biggest pothole, breaking the car's steering arm—those darn horrible roads! ____ 7. She'd been practicing juggling, but she cut her hand on the very, very sharp, way-too-sharp blade of one of the three knives that she bought to practice—that darn manufacturer! ____ 8. Then her neighbor falsely accused her to the police of stealing his lawn mower, when she'd only borrowed it and forgot to return it. 9. And her hand where the little dog bit her looked like it was going to have a big, ugly scar on it, right where the scar would be most visible. Gheesh! Things have gotta get better soon.

Torts Workbook

Review Exercise for Week 10
Match this law with the facts on the prior page.

___A. Special notice-of-claim statutes may bar certain claims if the injured person does not notify the responsible agency within a period shorter than the statute of limitations.^{Week 1}

___B. Merchants may disclaim some warranties but not the warranty of merchantability or warranties protecting against personal injury.^{Week 2}

___C. No warning is necessary for obvious risks. Courts will also recognize an open-and-obvious defense.^{Week 3}

___D. Statutes may offer strict liability for dog bites, while under the common law one must show knowledge of the pet's abnormally vicious propensities.^{Week 4}

___E. Active concealment of a condition about which a buyer would want to know can constitute a misrepresentation.^{Week 5}

___F. Defamation in written form is libel, whereas defamation in oral form is slander, with some differences in elements as to each.^{Week 6}

___G. Qualified privileges allow one to protect one's own interests, common interests, or the interests of others, without being subject to defamation claim.^{Week 7}

___H. Invasion of privacy's appropriation form involves use of persona for commercial or other advantage without the person's permission, with injunctions and damages for relief.^{Week 8}

___I. Non-economic loss is usually thought of as pain and suffering but may include humiliation, shock, fright, mortification, scarring, disfigurement, disability, and loss of enjoyment of life.^{Week 9}

Answer key: 1E, 2D, 3F, 4B, 5H, 6A, 7C, 8G, 9I

Week 11
No-Fault Systems

BULLET OUTLINE FOR WEEK 11:
NO-FAULT SYSTEMS
Motor-vehicle no-fault
- [146]motor-vehicle insurance has statutory-minimum liability limits ($20k/$40k in Michigan)
  - [152]insurance often includes uninsured- and underinsured-motorists coverage
- [147]12 states have motor-vehicle no-fault acts (Michigan, New York, and Florida included)
  - [148]those suffering loss first look to their own motor-vehicle insurers for first-party benefits
    - [150]issues of coverage, exclusions, priority, benefits, setoffs, and valuation
    - [151]benefits typically include medical expense, work loss, and replacement service
  - all no-fault states retain some negligence liability
    - [149]bar negligence claims for vehicle damage and minor injuries
  - vehicle owners pay for their own collision coverage
    - allows negligence claims only for a threshold injury
  - serious impairment, permanent serious disfigurement, or death

Worker's compensation
- [153]provides injured employees with limited benefits without respect to fault
  - [154]injury must be incident to employment
  - [155]injury must be accidental
    - progressive conditions not compensated except for occupational disease
- [156]benefits include medical expense and work loss
- [157]benefits are employee's exclusive remedy for employer negligence
  - intentional-tort claims not barred
- [158]resolved through an administrative system
  - contingency-fee lawyers represent injured employees

PARAGRAPH OUTLINE FOR WEEK 11:
NO-FAULT SYSTEMS
There are two areas in which states may alter the tort system in no-fault schemes: motor vehicle accidents and worker's compensation. [146]States require motor-vehicle insurance with varying liability limits. [147]About 12 states have motor-vehicle no-fault acts of varying kind, but all retain some negligence liability in certain situations. [148]In no-fault states, those suffering damage from motor-vehicle accidents first look to their own motor-vehicle insurers for first-party benefits. [149]No-fault acts typically bar liability claims for vehicle damage and minor injuries, allowing negligence claims only for a threshold injury such as serious impairment, permanent serious disfigurement, or death. [150]First-party claims against one's own motor-vehicle insurer involve issues of coverage, exclusions, priority, benefits, setoffs, and valuation. [151]First-party no-fault benefits typically include coordinated medical-expense coverage and limited work-loss and replacement-service-expense benefits. [152]Motor-vehicle insurance often includes uninsured- and underinsured-motorists coverage for liability claims where there is insufficient insurance.

[153]Worker's compensation acts in all 50 states provide injured employees with limited benefits without respect to fault. [154]Worker's compensation benefits depend on showing an employee's

injury incident to employment. [155]Only accidental injuries are compensated, meaning that progressive conditions generally are not, except for occupational disease. [156]Worker's compensation benefits typically include coordinated medical expense and limited work-loss benefits. [157]Worker's compensation acts are an employee's exclusive remedy for injuries caused by employer negligence, although intentional-tort claims are not barred. [158]Worker's compensation claims are resolved through an administrative system in which lawyers working on contingency-fee basis represent the injured employees.

Fluency Cards for Week 11

Cover and uncover the response to each prompt until you fluently recall the exact response.

Motor-Vehicle No-Fault

All states require motor-vehicle insurance. A few have no-fault acts granting some immunity from negligence suits.

No-Fault Benefits

Insurance pays medical expense and work loss, allowing negligence claims only for serious injury.

Worker's Compensation

Employees injured at work get medical and wage benefits without respect to fault.

Exclusive Remedy

Exclusive remedy for workplace injuries but does not bar intentional-tort claims.

Definitions Worksheet for Week 11

1. Should persons injured in vehicle accidents expect liability insurance? If so, then how much?

2. What is a motor-vehicle no-fault act and where would one expect to find it?

3. What are the available first-party benefits?

4. How serious must the injury be for a claimant to recover in negligence liability?

5. What is *worker's compensation*? How does a claimant qualify for it?

6. What benefits does worker's compensation provide?

7. What does the employee lose?

Answer Key for Definitions Worksheet

1. *Should persons injured in vehicle accidents expect liability insurance? If so, then how much?* States require motor-vehicle insurance with varying personal-injury liability limits, often stated as dual limits per person and per accident. Michigan, for instance, requires minimum liability insurance of $20,000 per person and $40,000 per accident. Many vehicle owners nevertheless fail to maintain the required insurance. One's own motor-vehicle insurance thus often includes uninsured-motorist and underinsured-motorist coverage for liability claims.

2. *What is a motor-vehicle no-fault act and where would one expect to find it?* About 12 states, New York, Florida, Pennsylvania, and Michigan included, have motor-vehicle no-fault acts of varying kind. In no-fault states, those suffering damage from motor-vehicle accidents look to their own motor-vehicle insurer for first-party benefits. No-fault acts bar liability claims for vehicle damage and minor injuries but retain some negligence liability for deaths and more-serious injuries.

3. *What are the available first-party benefits?* No-fault acts vary but may provide medical-expense, work loss, survivor's loss, and similar benefits. Michigan's act, for instance, currently provides broad unlimited lifetime medical benefits (including reasonably necessary products, services, and accommodations) plus three years of work loss capped at $5,289 per month and replacement service expense up to $20 per day.

4. *How serious must the injury be for a claimant to recover in negligence liability?* Negligence claims are only for a threshold injury. Threshold standards vary. Michigan's threshold requires serious impairment of body function, permanent serious disfigurement, or death.

5. *What is **worker's compensation**? How does a claimant qualify for it?* Worker's compensation acts in all 50 states provide injured employees with limited benefits without respect to fault. Worker's compensation benefits depend on showing an employee's injury incident to employment. Injuries and disability that are not work-related do not qualify for worker's compensation benefits. Also, only accidental injuries qualify. Progressive conditions such as from aging and ordinary disease do not qualify, except for occupational disease.

6. *What benefits does worker's compensation provide?* Worker's compensation benefits typically include coordinated medical expense and limited work-loss benefits. Michigan, for instance, provides for reimbursement of medical expenses under cost controls and only 80% of take-home wages.

7. *What does the employee lose?* Worker's compensation benefits are an employee's exclusive remedy for injuries caused by employer negligence, although intentional-tort claims are not barred.

Torts Workbook

Issue-Spotting Worksheet for Week 11
State the law each scenario raises. No analysis. Just spot the issue and state the law.

1. Your new client, seeing you for the first time, tells you that she suffered serious injury in a motor-vehicle accident one month ago and needs some advice. Although an adult, she owns no vehicle and has no driver's license, and was a passenger in her friend's vehicle when the accident occurred. Her first concern is that she won't find any insurance for her medical expense, wage loss, and injuries.

_____

_____

2. You, your client, and her vehicle-owner/driver friend all reside in a no-fault state, where the accident occurred. Your client has heard of no-fault but has no clue what it means. You sense a good moment to build your client's confidence in your law knowledge.

_____

_____

3. Your client tells you that she expects some pretty substantial medical bills. While she has health insurance through her local Michigan employer, the insurance recently changed to a $5,000 deductible. She also has just learned that it won't cover the special products and services that her physician recommends for her recovery. Your client is most concerned, though, with not getting a paycheck since the accident and tells you it looks like she might not work for several more weeks.

_____

_____

4. Your client appreciates deeply the information that you have shared with her about her available first-party benefits. She wonders, though, about suing the careless driver who ran the red light and struck her friend's vehicle square in the passenger side where she was sitting. Your client tells you that she has seen online reports of huge cash awards to accident victims.

_____

_____

5. Your client surprises you by mentioning that the accident happened when she and her friend were on a work errand.

_____

_____

Answer Key for Issue-Spotting Worksheet

1. ***This scenario implicates the required motor-vehicle insurance.*** States require motor-vehicle insurance with minimum liability limits such as $20,000 per person and $40,000 per accident, although many vehicle owners fail to insure their vehicles as law requires. One's own motor-vehicle insurance may thus include uninsured-motorist coverage and underinsured-motorist coverage.

2. ***This scenario implicates the basic structure of no-fault acts.*** No-fault acts, matters of state law, require motor-vehicle insurance to pay for medical expense, work loss, and similar benefits but bar liability claims for vehicle damage and minor injuries though not for deaths and serious injuries.

3. ***This scenario implicates the available first-party benefits.*** Michigan's no-fault act provides 100% reimbursement for unlimited lifetime medical benefits including reasonably necessary products, services, and accommodations plus up to three years of work loss capped at $5,289 per month and replacement service expense capped at $20 per day. No-fault medical benefits coordinate with health insurance, but the claimant pays no medical expense.

4. ***This scenario implicates the tort threshold.*** Michigan's threshold for motor-vehicle liability claims requires proof of death, permanent serious disfigurement, or serious impairment of body function. Serious impairment of body function means an objectively manifested impairment of an important body function affecting one's general ability to lead a normal life.

5. ***This scenario implicates worker's compensation benefits.*** Worker's compensation acts provide limited benefits without respect to fault when an employee suffers injury arising out and in the course of employment. Worker's compensation benefits typically include cost-controlled reimbursement of medical expense and work-loss benefits limited to a percentage of take-home pay.

Comprehensiveness Exercise for Week 11

Insert words at the ^ mark that would make for a more-accurate or more-detailed law statement. Follow the italicized hints for help. Suggested answers are on the next page.

1. States require motor-vehicle insurance with minimum liability limits such as $20,000 per person ^. One's own motor-vehicle insurance may include uninsured-motorist ^ coverage. *[Only a per-person limit? Only uninsured coverage?]*

2. Pennsylvania and Michigan ^ have motor-vehicle no-fault acts. *[Other populous states?]*

3. No-fault acts bar liability claims ^ but pay for medical expense ^. *[Bar all liability claims? Pay only medical expense?]*

4. Michigan's no-fault act provides ^ medical benefits plus work loss ^ and replacement service expense ^. *[How much medical? What else related to medical? All work loss? All service expense?]*

5. Michigan's threshold for motor-vehicle liability claims requires proof of death or ^ disfigurement ^. *[What kind? What else?]*

6. Worker's compensation acts provide limited benefits without respect to fault when an employee suffers injury ^. Progressive conditions such as from aging and ordinary disease do not qualify ^. *[Injury when? Any exception?]*

7. Worker's compensation benefits typically include ^ medical expense and work-loss benefits ^. *[Full? All loss or only less?]*

8. Worker's compensation benefits are an employee's exclusive remedy for injuries caused by employer negligence ^. *[Except when?]*

Answer Key for Comprehensiveness Exercise

1. States require motor-vehicle insurance with minimum liability limits such as $20,000 per person **and $40,000 per accident**. One's own motor-vehicle insurance may include uninsured-motorist **and underinsured-motorist** coverage.

2. Pennsylvania and Michigan **and New York and Florida and other states** have motor-vehicle no-fault acts.

3. No-fault acts bar liability claims *for vehicle damage and minor injuries though not for deaths and serious injuries* but pay for medical expense, *work loss, and similar benefits*.

4. Michigan's no-fault act provides **unlimited lifetime** medical benefits *including reasonably necessary products, services, and accommodations* plus *up to three years of* work loss *capped at $5,398 per month* and replacement service expense *capped at $20 per day*.

5. Michigan's threshold for motor-vehicle liability claims requires proof of death or **permanent serious** disfigurement *or serious impairment of body function*.

6. Worker's compensation acts provide limited benefits without respect to fault when an employee suffers injury **arising out and in the course of employment**. Progressive conditions such as from aging and ordinary disease do not qualify, **except for occupational disease peculiar to the employment**.

7. Worker's compensation benefits typically include **cost-controlled reimbursement of** medical expense and work-loss benefits **limited to a percentage of take-home pay**.

8. Worker's compensation benefits are an employee's exclusive remedy for injuries caused by employer negligence **unless the employer commits an intentional tort**.

Torts Workbook

Examples/Non-Examples Exercise for Week 11

Identify whether each fact pattern is an example (E) or non-example (NE) of the *highlighted concept*. Answers follow. In the blanks, generate an additional example and non-example.

1. States require motor-vehicle insurance with varying *personal-injury liability limits*, often stated as dual limits per person and per accident.
   ___ The motor-vehicle-accident claim file indicated that the vehicle owner had 20/40 liability limits.
   ___ The defendant driver owned a mortgaged residence that the driver insured through Farm Bureau.
   ___ The police report showed that the pedestrian that the vehicle struck was uninsured for healthcare.
   E: _____
   N: _____

2. In no-fault states, those suffering loss from motor-vehicle accidents initially *look to their own motor-vehicle insurer* for first-party benefits.
   ___ The motorist demanded that the other driver's vehicle insurance pay for the motorist's collision loss.
   ___ The homemaker submitted her medical bills to her auto insurer after her motor-vehicle accident.
   ___ After the vehicle accident disabled the mason from work, he sent his vehicle insurer a work-loss claim.
   E: _____
   N: _____

3. No-fault acts vary but may provide medical-expense, work loss, survivor's loss, and similar *first-party benefits*.
   ___ The passenger required surgery, occupational therapy, and in-home care due to the roll-over accident.
   ___ The injured vehicle occupant suffered severe pain and had to take a term off from college to recuperate.
   ___ The vehicle collision killed the driver, who earned the sole income for his wife and three minor children.
   E: _____
   N: _____

4. No-fault acts *bar liability claims for vehicle damage and minor injuries* but *retain some negligence liability for deaths and more-serious injuries*.
   ___ The careless driver's vehicle insurer rejected the passenger's request for pain and suffering for whiplash.
   ___ After the accident crushed her spine, her lawyer sent a huge demand to the at-fault driver's auto insurer.
   ___ The delivery truck's collision with the light pole spilled the truck's toxic cargo all over the roadside.
   E: _____
   N: _____

5. *No-fault negligence claims require a threshold injury.* Threshold standards vary. Michigan's threshold requires *serious impairment of body function, permanent serious disfigurement, or death.*
   ___ The police report confirmed that she suffered no accident injury, but she later claimed a sore knee.
   ___ The medical records confirmed three fractured ribs, a displaced hip fracture, and a shattered femur.
   ___ The severe deceleration from the freeway collision caused a heart laceration that led to her demise.

E: _____

N: _____

6. Worker's compensation acts in all states provide injured employees with limited benefits without respect to fault. Benefits depend on showing an employee's injury *arising out of and in the course of employment*.
___ The custodian slipped on the stairway he had just mopped, tumbling down the stairs, breaking his leg.
___ The teacher wrenched her back badly trying to move the classroom desks, requiring a laminectomy.
___ The salesman woke up unable to get out of bed with a neck so stiff that he missed six weeks of work.

E: _____

N: _____

7. Only accidental injuries qualify for comp benefits. *Progressive conditions* such as from aging and ordinary disease *do not qualify, except for occupational disease*.
___ The comp insurer denied benefits when severe coronary artery disease disabled the worker.
___ The hydraulic lift crushed the welder's finger when the operator accidentally raised it too high.
___ The miner's physician diagnosed silicosis from long-term exposure to sand and other mining dust.

E: _____

N: _____

8. Worker's compensation benefits typically include *medical expense and limited work-loss benefits*.
___ The roofer suffered extreme pain and mental and emotional distress after the fall from the roof.
___ The tax preparer could no longer hunt, fish, or run marathons after injuring his hand in the doorway.
___ The clerk had to have the bone set, therapy, and six weeks off work when the machine broke his hand.

E: _____

N: _____

9. Worker's compensation benefits are an employee's *exclusive remedy* for injuries caused by employer negligence, although *intentional-tort claims are not barred*.
___ The press manufacturer forgot to connect the safety guard, so that the operator got severely hurt at work.
___ After the worker slipped and fell, his employer paid comp benefits but not for pain and suffering.
___ The plant owner got so fed up with the manager that he slugged him, breaking his nose and cheek.

E: _____

N: _____

Answers: 1 ENN; 2 NEE; 3 ENE; 4 EEN; 5 NEE; 6 EEN; 7 ENE; 8 NNE; 9 NEE

Skills Exercise for Week 11: Summary-Disposition Motion

You are the injured plaintiff Pam Bertrand's lawyers. Your client suffered serious injury in a motor-vehicle accident. The defendant does not dispute fault. Instead, the defendant maintains that your client's injury does not meet Michigan's tort threshold for *serious impairment of body function*, as Michigan's No-Fault Act requires for a liability claim. The Act defines a serious impairment as an *objectively manifested impairment* of an *important body function* in a way that affects the person's *general ability to lead a normal life*. Look through the medical records, read the following summary, and prepare an argument that Mrs. Bertrand did suffer a serious impairment.

At 8:26 a.m. on April 14, 2016, forty-five-year-old married black female driver Pamela S. Bertrand, 8134 Iroquois Way, Rockville, MI 49412, alone in her own 2011 Subaru Forester motor vehicle, drives east on Wagner Road at its through intersection with Fruitdale Road in suburban Riverview Township, Glen County, Michigan, on her way to a 9 a.m. dental appointment at Family Dental in nearby Morton. She has just dropped off her daughter Sherry Bertrand at high school and after her dental appointment will go to her work as an office manager at Internal Medicine, P.C., also in Morton. She is wearing seatbelt.

At the same time and on the same date, twenty-five-year-old unmarried white male driver Jonathan Q. Carter, 313 Alpine Avenue, Apt. A, Wayfair, MI 48788, alone in his own 2008 Jeep Wrangler motor vehicle, drives north on Fruitdale Road at its stop intersection with Wagner Road on his way to work at Industrial Plastics, Inc., in Riverview Township. A new machine-operator trainee at Industrial Plastics, Mr. Carter is already nearly one-half-hour late for work and is rushing because he already has a couple of other tardy dates for oversleeping. He is wearing seatbelt.

Mr. Carter pulls out of the stop intersection into the path of Mrs. Bertrand's vehicle. The vehicles collide, damaging the front and front quarter panels of both vehicles (passenger front of the Bertrand vehicle, driver front of the Carter vehicle). The collision spins the Carter vehicle while redirecting the Bertrand vehicle forward and to the left, it coming to rest some considerable way east on Wagner. The Bertrand vehicle's stopping distance gives some indication of higher speed in this 45 mph zone.

The collision disables both vehicles. Mr. Carter, shaken but uninjured (he anticipated the collision just instantly enough to pull his head away from the window and stanchion), emerges without difficulty from his vehicle, walking down Wagner to Mrs. Bertrand's vehicle. Mrs. Bertrand, still in the vehicle, complains of right knee and ankle pain, right wrist pain, and neck pain, thinking she may have broken things. Mr. Carter calls 911 at Mrs. Bertrand's urging.

Investigating Officer Bill Barker of the Riverview Township force is at the scene in five minutes, calling for backup to direct traffic (Glen County Officer Brian Voight arrives promptly to do so). Officer Barker asks Mrs. Bertrand questions about what happened as he speaks to her about her condition and calls for an ambulance. Mrs. Bertrand remains seated in her vehicle until the ambulance arrives. Attendants remove and backboard Mrs. Bertrand, transporting her to Riverview Hospital.

Officer Barker then interviews Mr. Carter who says that he didn't see the Bertrand vehicle and that the way to cross Wagner on his way north on Fruitdale Road appeared safe and clear. Mr. Carter has no explanation for why he did not see the Bertrand vehicle, but Officer Barker notices an Android smartphone in the console bucket within Mr. Carter's reach. Mr. Carter admits having had the radio on but denies having used the smartphone.

Officer Barker's reconstruction of the scene with the help of Officer Voight indicates no evasive action by Mrs. Bertrand. While from the vehicle damage and stopping distance the officers are suspicious that her speed exceeded 45 mph, the officers do not arrive at a speed estimate. Because Mrs. Bertrand had the through way, Officer Barker tickets Mr. Carter with two of the several citations that Officer Barker could have issued. Mr. Carter leaves the scene with a friend who picked him up.

Officer Barker indicates C-level injuries for Mrs. Bertrand on the UD-10 official accident report. Officer Barker indicates no injuries for Mr. Carter on the UD-10 official accident report. Officer Barker indicates AAA motor-vehicle insurance for Mrs. Bertrand and Geico motor-vehicle insurance at (431) 988-6321 for Mr. Carter. Weather is cloudy, breezy, cool (43 degrees), and dry.

Mrs. Bertrand has been married to Johnnie P. Bertrand for 19 years. They have one daughter Sherry Bertrand age 15 years. Mrs. Bertrand was working approximately 40 hours per week managing the office of Internal Medicine, P.C., 4598 Medical Drive, Morton, MI 49878, at an annual salary of $82,500.

Mrs. Bertrand has not returned to work and may not do so for months or years, if ever. While Mrs. Bertrand was employed full time, she also was the principal care provider at home for Mr. Bertrand and their daughter Sherry. Since the accident, Mrs. Bertrand has not been able to do any of the shopping, cooking, cleaning, laundry, and other household chores that she did primarily or exclusively before the accident.

Mrs. Bertrand had some pre-existing back pain, likely degenerative rather than traumatic in origin. She had received periodic chiropractic care for it but had not missed any extended period of work. She had from time to time reduced her household chores during episodes of back pain.

Review Worksheet for Week 11

1. What is a statute of limitations? What are typical statutory periods?^{Week 1}

2. What three different products-liability theories do many jurisdictions recognize?^{Week 2}

3. Describe the difference between a design-defect claim and manufacturing-defect claim in products liability. What are the tests for each? Which claim would you rather pursue?^{Week 3}

4. What is the standard for dog-bite liability under the common law? How do dog-bite statutes typically change that standard?^{Week 4}

5. State the definition (elements) of misrepresentation.^{Week 5}

6. How do the elements change for each of the two forms of defamation?^{Week 6}

7. Define the constitutional protection that the First Amendment gives to defamation.^{Week 7}

Answer Key for Review Worksheet

1. *What is a statute of limitations? What are typical statutory periods?* Different statutes of limitation bar different tort actions within different defined periods after the claims accrue. Statutes in different states bar defamation claims after one year, intentional torts after a one or two-year period, negligence after two, three, or four years, and other tort claims after four, five, or six years.

2. *What three different products-liability theories do many jurisdictions recognize?* States recognize negligence, breach of warranty, and strict products liability theories.

3. *Describe the difference between a design-defect claim and manufacturing-defect claim in products liability. What are the tests for each? Which claim would you rather pursue?* While the Second Restatement requires proof of a defective condition unreasonably dangerous under risk-utility or consumer-expectation tests, Third Restatement theories are manufacturing defect, design defect, and failure to warn. Manufacturing defects depart from design, but one still applies the risk-utility or consumer-expectation tests for the other theories.

4. *What is the standard for dog-bite liability under the common law? How do dog-bite statutes change that standard?* Strict liability exists for property damage or injury from wild animals. Strict liability may exist for property damage by roaming livestock, depending on the fence-in, fence-out, or other rules of the jurisdiction. Strict liability exists under the common law for injury from domesticated animals, particularly dogs, when the owner knows that the animal has vicious propensities abnormal to its class. Dog-bite statutes eliminate the knowledge requirement, eliminating the one-free-bite rule.

5. *State the definition (elements) of misrepresentation.* Misrepresentation is a false affirmative representation made knowingly to induce justifiable reliance causing loss. To be actionable, the misrepresentation must be verifiably false, not merely conjecture, salesperson puffing, or opinion. The seller must also know of the statement's falsity for it to be actionable. Honest statements of prediction or intent are not actionable when the predicted event does not occur.

6. *How do the elements change for each of the two forms of defamation?* Slander claims ordinarily require proof of special damages except where the slander is as to loathsome disease, incompetence in one's trade or profession, sex, or crimes of moral turpitude. Libel claims, based on writings or their equivalent, do not require proof of special damages. Special damages mean pecuniary loss from third persons believing and acting on the defamatory statement.

7. *Define the constitutional protection that the First Amendment gives to defamation.* The First Amendment requires that public officials and public figures prove *actual malice*, meaning knowledge of or reckless disregard for the falsity of the defamatory statement. Actual malice may also include a high degree of awareness of falsity, subjective serious doubt as to truth, purposeful avoidance of truth, and deliberate misquotes materially changing meaning.

Problem-Solving Exercise Week 11

Working with a seatmate, read the following example (EX) and non-example (NE) of an unknown new rule (RU), one that the judge writing the opinions and orders has not expressly stated but that you must instead discern and record as your problem solution. To solve the problem, one student vocalize each mental operation taken toward a partial solution, while the other student actively listens, confirming, shaping, correcting, and guiding the other student's vocalizations, until both of you reach and record the final novel rule. Check your answer against the model answer at the bottom when the professor says to do so.

EX OPINION AND ORDER: This case is for motor-vehicle no-fault first-party benefits. The plaintiff alleges that he was loading his pick-up truck, that he insured with the defendant no-fault insurer, with a piece of heavy equipment when he suffered severe back injury as he lifted the equipment into the truck's bed. Plaintiff further claims reimbursement from defendant for no-fault medical-expense and work-loss benefits. Defendant through counsel has moved to dismiss, arguing that plaintiff cannot show, as the No-Fault Act requires, that the loss arose out of the use of a motor vehicle as a motor vehicle. The Court denies defendant's motion, bringing this matter on for jury trial as to the reimbursement amount owed.

NE OPINION AND ORDER: This case is for motor-vehicle no-fault first-party benefits. The plaintiff alleges that she was sitting behind the wheel of her idling sedan, that she insured with the defendant no-fault insurer, when an unknown assailant shot a handgun into the vehicle, striking plaintiff in the shoulder. Plaintiff further claims reimbursement from defendant for no-fault medical-expense and work-loss benefits. Defendant through counsel has moved to dismiss, arguing that plaintiff cannot show, as the No-Fault Act requires, that the loss arose out of the use of a motor vehicle as a motor vehicle. The Court grants defendant's motion, dismissing plaintiff's case with prejudice.

RU _____

_____

_____

_____

_____

Answer: For an injury to arise out of the use of a motor vehicle as a motor vehicle, the use must relate to the vehicle's transportation function, such loading or unloading, and entering into or alighting from the vehicle, and not from an assault and battery that only incidentally occurred in or around a vehicle.

TORTS WORKBOOK

Week 12
Misuse of Legal Procedure

BULLET OUTLINE FOR WEEK 12:
MISUSE OF LEGAL PROCEDURE
Malicious prosecution
- [159]plaintiff must show defendant maliciously caused criminal charges to issue without probable cause
  - charges must resolve in plaintiff's favor before trial
- [160]malice element requires that defendant caused charges to issue for ulterior purpose
- [161]damages are presumed
  - plaintiff may prove compensatory damages for mental distress, lost reputation and income
  - punitive damages may also be available
- [162]some jurisdictions recognize malicious civil prosecution
  - may have to prove special damages in those cases

Abuse of process
- [163]plaintiff must show defendant used legal process for ulterior purposes

PARAGRAPH OUTLINE FOR WEEK 12:
MISUSE OF LEGAL PROCEDURE
Two torts address liability when an individual misuses legal procedures. [159]The tort of malicious prosecution requires plaintiff to show that defendant maliciously caused criminal charges to issue without probable cause, with the charges resolved in the plaintiff's favor. [160]The malice element of malicious prosecution requires plaintiff to show that defendant caused the charges to be issued for a purpose other than to bring plaintiff to justice. [161]Tort law presumes malicious-prosecution damages, although plaintiff may also prove compensatory damages for mental distress and loss of reputation and income, and punitive damages may also be available. [162]Some jurisdictions recognize a malicious prosecution claim for initiating a groundless civil action, but those jurisdictions tend to require proof of special damages in those cases. [163]The tort of abuse of process requires plaintiff to show that defendant used legal process for ulterior purposes. [164]Tort liability extends to protect against harm to commercial interests, either for injurious falsehood, interference with business relations, or unfair competition.

Fluency Cards for Week 12

Malicious Prosecution	**Abuse of Process**
Maliciously causing criminal charges without probable cause, with charges resolved in plaintiff's favor.	Misuse of court procedures for ulterior purpose.

Definitions Worksheet for Week 12

1. What is malicious prosecution? What are the elements of the malicious-prosecution tort?

2. How does law define the *malice* element of the malicious-prosecution tort?

3. Must the malicious-prosecution plaintiff prove damages? Would you if you could?

4. Does law recognize a tort claim for initiating a groundless civil action?

5. What is abuse of process? How does abuse of process differ from malicious prosecution?

6. How does law define abuse of process?

Answer Key for Definitions Worksheet

1. *What is malicious prosecution? What are the elements of the malicious-prosecution tort?* Malicious prosecution is a tort involving the misuse of legal procedures, in effect causing groundless criminal charges to issue. The tort of malicious prosecution requires plaintiff to show that defendant maliciously caused criminal charges to issue without probable cause, with the charges resolved in the plaintiff's favor at an early stage of the proceeding.

2. *How does law define the* **malice** *element of the malicious-prosecution tort?* The malice element of malicious prosecution requires plaintiff to show that defendant caused the charges to be issued for a purpose other than to bring plaintiff to justice on the charge. The law sometimes refers to that other purpose as an *ulterior* purpose.

3. *Must the malicious-prosecution plaintiff prove damages? Would you if you could?* No, tort law presumes malicious-prosecution damages, but yes, a plaintiff should if the plaintiff could. Plaintiff may prove compensatory damages for non-economic loss like mental and emotional distress and economic loss associated with loss of reputation and income. Some states also permit punitive damages.

4. *Does law recognize a tort claim for initiating a groundless civil action?* Not generally. A few jurisdictions may recognize a malicious-prosecution claim for initiating a groundless civil action, but those jurisdictions tend to require proof of special damages in those cases.

5. *What is abuse of process? How does abuse of process differ from malicious prosecution?* Abuse of process is a second tort action, after malicious prosecution, involving misuse of legal proceedings. Abuse of process involves misuse of ongoing legal proceedings rather than causing charges to issue, as is the case with malicious prosecution.

6. *How does law define abuse of process?* The tort of abuse of process requires plaintiff to show that defendant used legal process for ulterior purposes. The legal process itself may be lawful, but the use is a misuse because of the ulterior purpose.

Issue-Spotting Worksheet for Week 12

State the law each scenario raises. No analysis. Just spot the issue and state the law.

1. Your new client is furious. The father of her child went to authorities falsely reporting that she had abused and neglected their child. State workers took the child away for three days before returning the child to her home, while authorities investigated charges. Your client wants you to do something to punish and discourage the father, and set things right again.

_____

_____

2. You have a few questions for your client including what if any evidence the father had of abuse or neglect. Your questions just make your client angrier, causing her to shout at you, *Why do you want to know? Don't you believe in me?*

_____

_____

3. After settling down some, your client begins to describe just how hurtful and expensive the father's false reports were for her, particularly when the authorities briefly arrested her and barred her from her home while searching her home.

_____

_____

4. Your client is also concerned that the father is manipulating their ongoing custody battle. When you ask what your client means by *manipulating*, she says something about getting dragged into court for everything and nothing. She wants the harassment to stop and wants to know what you can do about it.

_____

_____

5. Your client is none too encouraged with your response about another possible tort and so wants to know more specifics about what that tort would require that you prove.

_____

_____

Answer Key for Issue-Spotting Worksheet

1. ***This scenario implicates the malicious-prosecution tort.*** Malicious prosecution is a tort involving the misuse of legal procedures, in effect causing groundless criminal charges to issue. The tort of malicious prosecution requires plaintiff to show that defendant maliciously caused criminal charges to issue without probable cause, with the charges resolved in the plaintiff's favor at an early stage of the proceeding.

2. ***This scenario implicates the definition of*** *malicious*. The malice element of malicious prosecution requires plaintiff to show that defendant caused the charges to be issued for a purpose other than to bring plaintiff to justice on the charge. The law sometimes refers to that other purpose as an *ulterior* purpose.

3. ***This scenario implicates the available damages for malicious prosecution.*** Tort law presumes malicious-prosecution damages, but a plaintiff may also prove compensatory damages for non-economic loss like mental and emotional distress and economic loss associated with loss of reputation and income. Some states also permit punitive damages.

4. ***This scenario implicates the tort of abuse of process.*** Abuse of process is a second tort action, after malicious prosecution, involving misuse of legal proceedings. Abuse of process involves misuse of ongoing legal proceedings rather than causing charges to issue, as is the case with malicious prosecution.

5. ***This scenario implicates the definition of abuse of process.*** The tort of abuse of process requires plaintiff to show that defendant used legal process for ulterior purposes. The legal process itself may be lawful, but the use is a misuse because of the ulterior purpose.

Comprehensiveness Exercise for Week 12

Insert words at the ^ mark that would make for a more-accurate or more-detailed law statement. Follow the italicized hints for help. Suggested answers are on the next page.

1. The tort of malicious prosecution requires plaintiff to show that defendant ^ caused criminal charges to issue ^ , with the charges resolved in the plaintiff's favor ^ . *[Caused how? When? Resolved when?]*

2. The malice element of malicious prosecution requires plaintiff to show that defendant caused the charges to be issued ^ . *[For any purpose?]*

3. Tort law presumes malicious-prosecution damages. Plaintiff may nonetheless prove ^ damages for ^ non-economic loss like mental and emotional distress. ^ *[What type of damages? Just non-economic? Any other damages type available anywhere?]*

4. ^ Jurisdictions recognize a malicious-prosecution claim for initiating a groundless civil action ^ . *[All jurisdictions? Any limitation?]*

5. The tort of abuse of process requires plaintiff to show that defendant misused legal process ^ . *[Any misuse?]*

Answer for Comprehensiveness Exercise

1. The tort of malicious prosecution requires plaintiff to show that defendant *maliciously* caused criminal charges to issue *without probable cause*, with the charges resolved in the plaintiff's favor *at an early stage of the proceeding*.

2. The malice element of malicious prosecution requires plaintiff to show that defendant caused the charges to be issued *for a purpose other than to bring plaintiff to justice on the charge*, sometimes referred to as an ulterior purpose.

3. Tort law presumes malicious-prosecution damages. Plaintiff may nonetheless prove *compensatory* damages for non-economic loss like mental and emotional distress *and economic loss associated with loss of reputation and income. Some states also permit punitive damages*.

4. *A few* jurisdictions *may* recognize a malicious-prosecution claim for initiating a groundless civil action, *but those jurisdictions tend to require proof of special damages in those cases*.

5. The tort of abuse of process requires plaintiff to show that defendant misused legal process *for ulterior purpose*.

Discrimination Exercise for Week 12

Indicate whether each statement *overgeneralizes*, *undergeneralizes*, or *misconceives* the rule, explaining why. *Overgeneralizing* states the rule too broadly, capturing circumstances to which it does not apply. *Undergeneralizing* states the rule too narrowly, omitting circumstances to which it applies. *Misconceiving* states the rule incorrectly.

1. The tort of malicious prosecution requires plaintiff to show that defendant caused criminal charges to issue, with the charges resolved in the plaintiff's favor.
____OVER/ ____UNDER/ ____MISS/ Why? _____
_____

2. The malice element of malicious prosecution requires plaintiff to show that defendant caused the charges to be issued to harm plaintiff.
____OVER/ ____UNDER/ ____MISS/ Why? _____
_____

3. Presumed damages are the plaintiff's recoverable damages under the malicious-prosecution tort.
____OVER/ ____UNDER/ ____MISS/ Why? _____
_____

4. Tort law also recognizes a malicious-prosecution claim for initiating a groundless civil action, not just groundless criminal charges.
____OVER/ ____UNDER/ ____MISS/ Why? _____
_____

5. The difference between malicious prosecution and abuse of process is that a prosecutor brings a malicious-prosecution action while a private party brings an abuse-of-process action.
____OVER/ ____UNDER/ ____MISS/ Why? _____
_____

6. The tort of abuse of process requires plaintiff to show that defendant used legal process unlawfully, in a manner not authorized by the rules.
____OVER/ ____UNDER/ ____MISS/ Why? _____
_____

Answer Key for Discrimination Exercise

1. The statement **OVERgeneralizes** the rule. Malicious prosecution is a tort involving the misuse of legal procedures, in effect causing groundless criminal charges to issue. The tort of malicious prosecution requires plaintiff to show that defendant *maliciously* caused criminal charges to issue *without probable cause*, with the charges resolved in the plaintiff's favor *at an early stage of the proceeding*.

2. The statement **UNDERgeneralizes** the rule. The malice element of malicious prosecution requires plaintiff to show that defendant caused the charges to be issued *for a purpose other than to bring plaintiff to justice on the charge. The law sometimes refers to that other purpose as an ulterior purpose*. Wanting to destroy plaintiff would be an ulterior purpose, but so would wanting to take plaintiff's property, collect a debt from plaintiff, or accomplish other things.

3. The statement **UNDERgeneralizes** the rule. Tort law presumes malicious-prosecution damages, but a *plaintiff may also prove other damages if the plaintiff has evidence of them. Plaintiff may prove compensatory damages for non-economic loss like mental and emotional distress and economic loss associated with loss of reputation and income. Some states also permit punitive damages*.

4. The statement **OVERgeneralizes** the rule. *A few jurisdictions* may recognize a malicious-prosecution claim for initiating a groundless civil action, but those jurisdictions tend to require a limiting element like *proof of special damages in those cases*.

5. The statement **MISconceives** the rule. Private parties bring both a malicious-prosecution action and abuse-of-process action, both of which are private civil claims. Their difference is that abuse of process involves misuse of *ongoing legal proceedings* rather than causing charges to issue, as is the case with malicious prosecution.

6. The statement **UNDERgeneralizes** the rule. The tort of abuse of process requires plaintiff to show that defendant used legal process *for ulterior purposes*. The legal process itself may be *lawful or* unlawful, but the use is a misuse *because of the ulterior purpose.*

Role-Play Exercise for Week 12: Office Consult

CLIENT SCRIPT

Do not read the lawyer script on the next page!

Do this office-consult exercise in pairs. You are the client, and the other student is the lawyer whom you are consulting. Much of law practice involves meeting with clients in the lawyer's office or at other locations convenient to the client. These office consults typically involve a good deal of gathering information from the client. They also involve a good deal of the lawyer educating the client. Share the following information, and listen for the lawyer's advice.

Tell the lawyer only the following, then wait for the lawyer's questions (say it indignantly, like you were understandably horrified by the event): I was shopping when they arrested me.

In answer to the lawyer's questions, hesitatingly, waiting for prompts, explain: A clerk came up to me and said that I had taken something, like I was some kind of shoplifter! *[When the lawyer questions, interject emotionally and combatively: "You don't seem to care! Are you...heartless?!" Continue only when the lawyer settles you down.]* They said they'd seen it on security camera. They called the police! I was so embarrassed and angry that I could hardly breathe! *[Force the lawyer to drag these facts out of you as you respond emotionally rather than rationally:]* I had nothing on me. I had picked up some items but put them all back. *[You choose the items and the store and add other details.]* They let me go only after telling me that they were going to prosecute me! *[Say that you want to sue, but don't immediately disclose that the criminal charges are still pending:]* I want to sue them for every penny they've got! *[Add whatever details you wish about being alone or with friends or family, having witnesses or not having witnesses, etc.]*

Decide whether to hire the lawyer, and tell the lawyer your decision.

Role-Play Exercise for Week 12: Office Consult

LAWYER SCRIPT

Do not read the client script on the prior page!

Do this office-consult exercise in pairs. You are the lawyer, and the other student is the client who is consulting you. Much of law practice involves meeting with clients in your office or at other locations convenient to the client. These office consults typically involve a good deal of gathering information from the client. They also involve a good deal of you educating the client. Listen for the client's information. Elicit more information with questions, prompts, and other active-listening skills.

OBJECTIVES:

1. Inform the client whether the client has a claim.
2. Determine whether to offer to represent the client.

HINTS:

Consider a *malicious-prosecution* claim.
Be sure to articulate the elements of malicious prosecution.

Review Worksheet for Week 12

1. How does the law define *defamation*?^{Week 6}

    _____
    _____
    _____

2. How does the law define actual malice, for the constitutional protection of defamation?^{Week 7}

    _____
    _____
    _____

3. Define invasion of privacy's intrusion form. Must the tortfeasor observe the victim?^{Week 8}

    _____
    _____
    _____

4. What must the estate of a person who died in an accident show to maintain a tort claim against those responsible for the death?^{Week 9}

    _____
    _____
    _____

5. What is vicarious liability, and when does it arise?^{Week 10}

    _____
    _____
    _____

6. When may a person injured in a motor-vehicle accident in a no-fault state like Michigan sue the at-fault driver for the person's injuries?^{Week 11}

    _____
    _____
    _____

Answer Key for Review Worksheet

1. *How does the law define **defamation**?* Defamation involves false communication published of and concerning another that, together with extrinsic facts, harms the reputation of that other, with special damages except where law presumes damages, such as for libel or slander per se.

2. *How does the law define actual malice, for the constitutional protection of defamation?* Actual malice means knowledge of or recklessness with regard to the falsity of the defamatory statement. Actual malice may also include a high degree of awareness of falsity, subjective serious doubt as to truth, purposeful avoidance of truth, and deliberate misquotes materially changing meaning.

3. *Define invasion of privacy's intrusion form. Must the tortfeasor observe the victim?* Invasion of privacy's intrusion form arises when there is an unauthorized intrusion into a place where the person has a reasonable expectation of privacy and that would be highly offensive to the reasonable person. The intrusion may involve observation of the person or of private matters such as medical or financial records.

4. *What must the estate of a person who died in an accident show to maintain a tort claim against those responsible for the death?* Wrongful-death acts in all states require the estate to prove the underlying tort claim, for negligence for instance. Without an underlying tort theory, the estate has no recovery. Wrongful-death acts do not in themselves create claims. They instead preserve claims after death. The estate must also often have to show beneficiary loss. Many acts identify the beneficiaries, typically dependent immediate family members, and limit damages to beneficiary losses.

5. *What is vicarious liability, and when does it arise?* Vicarious liability holds one party liable for the torts of another. Forms of vicarious liability include (1) employer liability for the negligent acts of employees within the course of employment, (2) contractor liability when retaining control or with non-delegable duties or inherently dangerous activities, (3) joint-enterprise liability, and (4) bailor liability but only in special situations such as under motor-vehicle owner-consent statutes.

6. *When may a person injured in a motor-vehicle accident in a no-fault state like Michigan sue the at-fault driver for the person's injuries?* Motor-vehicle-accident victims in no-fault states generally have to prove a more-serious injury to hold the negligent driver and vehicle owner liable for their injuries. In Michigan, the tort threshold is *serious impairment of body function, permanent serious disfigurement,* or *death*, although other states use other standards including monetary-loss standards. No-fault states may also limit tort recovery to non-economic loss, no-fault benefits having already paid some or all of the economic loss like medical expense and wage loss.

Week 13
Business Torts

BULLET OUTLINE FOR WEEK 13:
BUSINESS TORTS
- [164]protects against harm to commercial interests in three forms
  - **injurious falsehood** (2 kinds)
    - [165]slander of title, meaning a false statement calculated to harm plaintiff's pecuniary interest by publication with malice causing special damage
    - [166]trade disparagement, meaning a false statement calculated to harm plaintiff's trade or business, with knowledge or reckless disregard of falsity, causing special damage
  - **interference with business relations**
    - [167]intentional harmful interference with contract or business expectancy by improper means
    - [168]interfering need not be illegal but must violate accepted business standards
  - **unfair competition**

PARAGRAPH OUTLINE FOR WEEK 13:
BUSINESS TORTS

Tort law also recognizes forms of business tort. [165]Injurious falsehood includes slander of title, meaning a false statement calculated to harm plaintiff's pecuniary interest by publication with malice causing special damage. [166]Injurious falsehood also includes trade disparagement, meaning a false statement calculated to harm plaintiff's trade or business, with knowledge or reckless disregard of falsity, causing special damage. [167]Interference with business relations is established by proof of intentional harmful interference with a contract or business expectancy by improper or wrongful means. [168]The interfering conduct need not be illegal so long as it violates generally accepted business standards.

Fluency Cards for Week 13

Cover and uncover the response to each prompt until you fluently recall the exact response.

Injurious Falsehood

False statement harming interest by publication with malice causing special damage.

Falsehood Forms

Slander of title and slander of trade.

Interference with Business Relations

Intentional harmful interference with a contract or business expectancy by improper means.

Definitions Worksheet for Week 13

1. Name two main categories of common-law business tort. How do they differ?

___

2. Identify and define the injurious-falsehood common-law business torts.

___

3. Identify and define the interference-with-business-relations common-law business torts.

___

4. What proof does the improper or wrongful conduct of the interference torts require?

___

Answer Key for Definitions Worksheet

1. *Name two main categories of common-law business tort. How do they differ?* The common law recognizes several forms of (1) injurious-falsehood and (2) interference-with-business-relations torts. The falsehood torts have to do with false statements harming business interests. The interference torts have to do with deliberate wrongful actions harming business interests.

2. *Identify and define the injurious-falsehood common-law business torts.* Injurious falsehood first includes slander of title, meaning a false statement calculated to harm plaintiff's pecuniary interest by publication with malice causing special damage. Injurious falsehood also includes trade disparagement, meaning a false statement calculated to harm plaintiff's trade or business, with knowledge or reckless disregard of falsity, causing special damage.

3. *Identify and define the interference-with-business-relations common-law business torts.* Interference with contract is the first form, defined as intentionally disrupting a contract between others using improper or wrongful means. Interference with prospective economic advantage is a similar tort except that it involves an expectation of a transaction rather than an existing contract. It also requires intentional harmful interference by improper or wrongful means but with business expectancy rather than contract.

4. *What proof does the improper or wrongful conduct of the interference torts require?* The improper-conduct element of the interference torts requires a deliberate wrongful departure from customary business practice, outside the accepted forms of competition. The interfering conduct need not be illegal or even per se tortious as long as it violates generally accepted business standards.

Issue-Spotting Worksheet for Week 13

State the law each scenario raises. No analysis. Just spot the issue and state the law.

1. Your managing partner asks you into her office and then asks you what you know about business torts. You vaguely recall the introduction to Week 13 of Torts II years ago.

2. Impressed with your recall, the managing partner then describes how a competitor to one of the firm's business clients *slandered* the client and the client's services. The partner asks whether you think that the client has a claim.

3. Once again impressed with your law recall, the managing partner adds that the competitor has also done several *nefarious* things to *make a mess* of the client's business. The partner again asks what you think.

4. The managing partner has one more test for you before handing you the file and saying *get to work on it*. She describes one of the several *nefarious things* that the competitor did and asks you *whether that's enough to make it actionable*.

Answer Key for Issue-Spotting Worksheet

1. ***This scenario implicates the common-law business torts.*** The common law recognizes several forms of (1) injurious-falsehood and (2) interference-with-business-relations torts. The falsehood torts have to do with false statements harming business interests. The interference torts have to do with deliberate wrongful actions harming business interests.

2. ***This scenario implicates the definitions of the injurious-falsehood business torts.*** Injurious falsehood first includes slander of title, meaning a false statement calculated to harm plaintiff's pecuniary interest by publication with malice causing special damage. Injurious falsehood also includes trade disparagement, meaning a false statement calculated to harm plaintiff's trade or business, with knowledge or reckless disregard of falsity, causing special damage.

3. ***This scenario implicates the definitions of the interference-with-business-relations business torts.*** Interference with contract is the first form, defined as intentionally disrupting a contract between others using improper or wrongful means. Interference with prospective economic advantage is a similar tort except that it involves an expectation of a transaction rather than an existing contract. It also requires intentional harmful interference by improper or wrongful means but with business expectancy rather than contract.

4. ***This scenario implicates how the law defines the improper-conduct element of the interference torts.*** The improper-conduct element of the interference torts requires a deliberate wrongful departure from customary business practice, outside the accepted forms of competition. The interfering conduct need not be illegal or even per se tortious as long as it violates generally accepted business standards.

TORTS WORKBOOK

Sameness Exercise Week 13 (Problem-Set 1)

Sort the fact patterns into the best business-tort form:
injurious falsehood (IF) or *business interference (BI)*.
Answers are at the bottom of the page.

1. _____ The neighbor recorded the invalid easement to get the owner to grant it when selling the home.

2. _____ For revenge, the jilted supplier secretly paid the winning bidder to abandon the new contract.

3. _____ The media ran the sensational false story that the milk had genetically modified organisms.

4. _____ The entertainer got her friend to stop working with the producer whose politics she didn't like.

5. _____ The owner refused to let the black trainer solicit clients at his fitness club like other trainers.

6. _____ The bank refused to discharge the lien from the car title despite that the owner paid the loan.

7. _____ The patient whose advances the surgeon spurned spread a rumor the surgeon was incompetent.

8. _____ The farmer induced the mill to return the augur it bought so that the seller would bankrupt.

9. _____ The buyer who failed to close recorded a notice of lis pendens anyway to induce the sale.

10. _____ The sales rep got the store buyer to refuse further purchases from a competitor the rep disliked.

11. _____ The graduate removed her despised roommate's resumes from the school's application boxes.

12. _____ The announcer joked that the concession stand had spread salmonella, resulting in its closure.

13. _____ The mechanic filed a lien against the yacht's title even though the owner paid the repair bill.

14. _____ The truck's owner falsely told anyone who would listen that the repair shop cheated on hours.

15. _____ The team secretly paid the star to quit before her contract with a competitor expired.

16. _____ The utility recorded easements across all six properties when it bought easements on only two.

17. _____ The environmentalist falsely told the college that its chemical supplier had poisoned the creek.

18. _____ The developer paid the auctioneer to refuse the rancher's consignments to shutter his business.

19. _____ The shopper wrote viciously false reviews of the online mall's ordering and delivery services.

Answers: 1IF 2BI 3IF 4BI 5BI 6IF 7IF 8BI 9IF 10BI 11BI 12IF 13IF 14IF 15BI 16IF 17BI 18BI 19IF

219

TORTS WORKBOOK

Sameness Exercise Week 13 (Problem-Set 2)

Sort the fact patterns into the best injurious-falsehood tort form **slander of title (ST)** or **trade disparagement (TD)**, or best business-interference tort form **interference with contract (IC), interference with business relations (IBR),** or **interference with prospective economic advantage (IEA)**. Answers are at the bottom of the page.

1. _____ The neighbor recorded the invalid easement to get the owner to grant it when selling the home.

2. _____ For revenge, the jilted supplier secretly paid the winning bidder to abandon the new contract.

3. _____ The media ran with the sensational false story that the milk had genetically modified organisms.

4. _____ The entertainer got her friend to stop working with the producer whose politics she didn't like.

5. _____ The owner refused to let the black trainer solicit clients at his fitness club like other trainers.

6. _____ The bank refused to discharge the lien from the car title despite that the owner had paid the loan.

7. _____ The patient whose advances the surgeon had spurned spread a rumor the surgeon was incompetent.

8. _____ The farmer induced the mill to return the augur it bought so that the augur's seller would bankrupt.

9. _____ The buyer who failed to close timely recorded a notice of lis pendens anyway to induce the sale.

10. _____ The sales rep got the store buyer to refuse further purchases from a competitor the rep disliked.

11. _____ The graduate removed her despised roommate's resumes from the school's application boxes.

12. _____ The announcer joked that the concession stand had spread salmonella, resulting in its closure.

13. _____ The mechanic reported a lien against the yacht's title even though the owner paid the repair bill.

14. _____ The truck's owner falsely alleged to anyone who would listen that the repair shop cheated on hours.

15. _____ The team secretly paid the agent to get the star to quit before her contract with a competitor expired.

16. _____ The utility recorded easements across all six properties when it had bought easements on only two.

17. _____ The environmentalist falsely told the university that its chemical supplier had poisoned the creek.

18. _____ The developer paid the auctioneer to refuse the rancher's consignments to put him out of business.

19. _____ The shopper wrote viciously false reviews of the online mall's ordering and delivery services

---

Answers: 1ST 2IC 3TD 4IBR 5IEA 6ST 7TD 8IC 9ST 10IBR 11IEA 12TD 13ST 14TD 15IC 16ST 17IBR 18IEA 19TD

Examples/Non-Examples Exercise for Week 13

Identify whether each fact pattern is an example (E) or non-example (NE) of the ***highlighted concept***. Answers follow. In the blanks, generate an additional example and non-example.

1. The common law recognizes several forms of ***business torts*** including injurious-falsehood torts and interference-with-business-relations torts.
   ___ The hotdog-stand owner called the health department with false reports on the competitor ice-cream stand.
   ___ The shopper tripped and fell, suffering injury, from an entryway mat that had worn and frayed into strings.
   ___ The artist got his sculptor friend to pull work from the exhibit by lying that the gallery had cheated him.
   E: _____
   N: _____

2. Injurious falsehood includes ***slander of title***, meaning a false publication calculated to harm plaintiff's title to a property interest, with malice and causing special damage.
   ___ The ex-business partner canceled the business's supplier accounts just to give his former partner trouble.
   ___ The lender refused to discharge the mortgage on the premises, trying to secure unrelated credit-card debt.
   ___ The divorcing wife recorded a notice of lis pendens against the marital home she had already relinquished.
   E: _____
   N: _____

3. Injurious falsehood also includes ***trade disparagement***, meaning a false statement calculated to harm plaintiff's trade or business, with knowledge or reckless disregard of falsity, causing special damage.
   ___ When the store canceled the supply contract, the supplier lied to other suppliers that the store didn't pay.
   ___ Desperate at losing patients to the new orthopedist, the old orthopedist spread a rumor the new had HIV.
   ___ The passenger's serious injury in the motor-vehicle accident kept her from operating her home business.
   E: _____
   N: _____

4. ***Interference with contract*** is a first form of interference-with-business-relations tort, defined as intentionally disrupting a contract between others using improper or wrongful means.
   ___ The theater was having a hard time finding help to staff the counter and so advertised a higher wage.
   ___ The orchard offered workers a bonus if they refused to continue harvesting for the competitor orchard.
   ___ The contractor told a competitor's foreman that he'd loan him his boat if he'd help steal carpenter's away.
   E: _____
   N: _____

5. ***Interference with prospective economic advantage*** involves intentional harmful interference by improper or wrongful means, although interference with *business expectancy* rather than interference with contract.

    ___ The nightclub tore down all signs for the bar's special event so that the nightclub didn't lose business.
    ___ The two dry cleaners kept reducing prices and offering special services, knowing only one could survive.
    ___ The tax preparer went around throwing out his new competitor's business cards wherever he found them.

E: _____

N: _____

6. The improper-conduct element of the interference torts requires a ***deliberate wrongful departure from customary business practice***, outside accepted forms of competition.

    ___ The ice-cream-stand owner paid a contractor to cut the power for the new ice-cream store's opening.
    ___ The passed-over fireworks producer snuck out and doused her competitor's fireworks setups with water.
    ___ The gas-station owner decided to offer milk at a discount to try to capture back some of his lost business.

E: _____

N: _____

7. The interfering conduct in the interference torts need not be illegal or even per se tortious as long as it ***violates generally accepted business standards***.

    ___ The coder hacked the agency's server system, posted a defamatory statement, and locked the system.
    ___ The decorator bought all the red fabric to keep her competitor from having any to complete the project.
    ___ The passed-over producer took local stage hands on a fishing trip right during the competitor's big show.

E: _____

N: _____

Answers: 1 ENE; 2 NEE; 3 EEN; 4 NEE; 5 ENE; 6 EEN; 7 NEE

Problem-Solving Exercise Week 13 (Problem 1)

Think-aloud problem solving (TAPS) is a proven method of using vocalization to become a more creative and better problem solver. Professionals are effective problem solvers when they speak aloud to another, speaking aloud to themselves, or let their mental operations taking the silent form of words, concepts, principles, and strategies to reach partial solutions and then chain partial solutions toward final novel solution. Read the following example (EX) and non-example (NE) of an unknown new rule (RU), one that the judges writing their opinions and orders have not expressly stated but that you must instead discern and record as your problem solution. Vocalize each mental operation taken toward a partial solution, until you reach and record the final novel rule. Check your answer against the model answer at the bottom of the next page.

EX   OPINION AND ORDER: In this case, the plaintiff barber claims the defendant bank ran the barber out of business by setting up a competing barber shop, renting out chairs at the shop to new barbers who came to town, and operating the shop at a loss until the plaintiff barber could no longer keep his shop open for lack of customers and income. The Court finds for the plaintiff and awards plaintiff $20,000 in a money judgment against defendant.

NE   OPINION AND ORDER: In this case, the plaintiff local art auction house claims the defendant international art auctioneer ran the local house out of business by setting up a competing auction house in the same local market, soliciting similar art items for auction, and operating at a loss until the plaintiff local house could no longer remain open for lack of consignments and auction revenue. The Court finds for the defendant and dismisses plaintiff's case with prejudice.

RU   _____

_____

_____

_____

The First Amendment requires proof of *actual malice* in a trade-disparagement claim involving a publication addressing a public issue.

Problem-Solving Exercise Week 13 (Problem 2)

Think-aloud problem solving (TAPS) is a proven method of using vocalization to become a more creative and better problem solver. Professionals are effective problem solvers when they speak aloud to another, speaking aloud to themselves, or let their mental operations taking the silent form of words, concepts, principles, and strategies to reach partial solutions and then chain partial solutions toward final novel solution. Read the following example (EX) and non-example (NE) of an unknown new rule (RU), one that the judges writing their opinions and orders have not expressly stated but that you must instead discern and record as your problem solution. Vocalize each mental operation taken toward a partial solution, until you reach and record the final novel rule. Check your answer against the model answer at the bottom of the prior page.

EX   OPINION AND ORDER: In this trade-disparagement case, the defendant newspaper published a story that federal authorities were investigating the plaintiff occupational-therapy clinic for potential criminal-fraud charges, under allegations that the clinic had billed federal social-welfare programs for unnecessary therapy services and for therapy services not actually performed. The publication led to the resignation of clinic care providers, loss of clinic patients, and closure of the clinic. Federal authorities did not file criminal charges against the clinic, which had not billed for unnecessary services or services not performed. The newspaper based the publication on a preliminary investigation report that federal authorities mistakenly released in response to the newspaper's Freedom of Information Act request. The Court finds for the defendant and dismisses plaintiff's case with prejudice.

NE   OPINION AND ORDER: In this trade-disparagement case, the defendant automotive mechanical-service advisor published a newsletter distributed to former and potential customers stating that mechanical-service fraud was rampant in the vehicle-repair and maintenance service industry. The defendant's newsletter gave as an example a purported customer statement complaining about alleged mechanical-service fraud by the plaintiff motor-vehicle-repair shop. The publication led to the plaintiff shop's loss of customers, its landlord's non-renewal of its lease, and its closure. While mechanical-service fraud is rampant, the plaintiff shop had not committed mechanical-service fraud. The defendant advisor fabricated the purported customer and statement. The Court finds for the plaintiff and awards plaintiff $100,000 in money damages against the defendant.

RU   _____

_____

_____

_____

> The *improper means* element of an interference-with-business-relations claim includes the defendant establishing a competing business *outside of the defendant's field* so as to drive the plaintiff out of business, when plaintiff and defendant were not natural competitors in that field.

Torts Workbook

Role-Play Exercise for Week 13: Office Consult

CLIENT SCRIPT

Do not read the client script on the other side!

Do this office-consult exercise in pairs. You are the client, and the other student is the lawyer whom you are consulting. Much of law practice involves meeting with clients in the lawyer's office or at other locations convenient to the client. These office consults typically involve a good deal of gathering information from the client. They also involve a good deal of the lawyer educating the client. Share the following information, and listen for the lawyer's advice.

*Tell the lawyer only the following, then wait for the lawyer's questions (say it **firmly**, like you have a strong financial interest in prevailing and don't want to give up that interest easily):* I bought a commercial property, a SIGNIFICANT investment that was going to make me a LOT of money, but the seller won't close!

In answer to the lawyer's questions, hesitatingly, waiting for prompts, explain: The property is a storage facility, you know, one of those store-and-lock things, 200 units, HUGE, a GOLD MINE! *[Whenever the lawyer questions, interject with things like, "Come on, I was going to make a KILLING!" "Don't you get it? This thing was DIAMONDS!" Continue only when the lawyer settles you down.]* It's the place down by the river. You know it, right? *[Force the lawyer to admit whether the lawyer actually knows the location you are describing.]* We signed the land sale contract, I made the earnest-money deposit, and the guy won't go through with the sale! The closing date came and went, and the guy just wouldn't show up at the title company to close the deal! *[If the lawyer presses you on why not, then admit a little bit of dispute like:]* I was all ready to close, had the financing and everything, and just asked a *little* break on the price because when I inspected it, it was a DUMP! *[End with:]* I want that storage facility because it's going to SET ME UP FOR LIFE! *[Add whatever details you wish about your financial interest, skill, experience, commitment to this deal, etc.]*

Decide whether to hire the lawyer, and tell the lawyer your decision. Also suggest to the lawyer which of the lawyer's recommendations you approve.

Role-Play Exercise for Week 13: Office Consult

LAWYER SCRIPT

Do not read the client script on the other side!

Do this office-consult exercise in pairs. You are the lawyer, and the other student is the client who is consulting you. Much of law practice involves meeting with clients in your office or at other locations convenient to the client. These office consults typically involve a good deal of gathering information from the client. They also involve a good deal of you educating the client. Listen for the client's information. Elicit more information with questions, prompts, and other active-listening skills.

OBJECTIVES:

1. Recommend actions that you can take for the client.
2. Predict for the client the actions that the *other side* may take in response to your recommended actions and the probable outcome.
3. Determine whether to offer to represent the client.

HINTS:

1. Consider and discuss a *specific-performance* claim enforcing the land sale contract.
2. Address with the client that you can and probably should record a *notice of lis pendens* to keep the seller from selling to someone else until the litigation resolves.
3. Discuss that the opposing side, the seller, will very likely file a counterclaim for *slander of title*. Explain what that means.
4. Consider whether you can maintain the action *in good faith* because you, too, along with your client, could well be a counterclaim defendant to a *slander-of-title* claim. Can you represent the client and also defend yourself in the same action? How *would* you handle your own defense to a counterclaim?

TORTS WORKBOOK

Practice Assessments

WEEK 1

1. A client visited a lawyer in the lawyer's office regarding a motor-vehicle accident. The client told the lawyer that the accident had happened a little less than three years earlier. The client still had some pain and disability relating to the accident. The lawyer inquired of the client about how the accident had happened. The client related that the client had been a passenger in a vehicle when the driver had run a red light and collided with another vehicle that had been speeding, and that both drivers were ticketed for moving violations. Which of the following statements best describes the first action that the lawyer should take?
A. Determine the identity of all potential parties to any of the client's potential claims.
B. Determine the applicable limitations period for each of the client's potential claims.
C. Determine the extent of the client's injury to see whether the claim has value to proceed.
D. Determine how the tickets were resolved, whether by plea, conviction, or dismissal.

Answer: B. Different statutes of limitation bar different tort actions within different defined periods after each claim accrues. The client may have had claims barred by one- or two-year limitations periods, and may have a claim about to be barred by a three-year limitations period. A is incorrect because although conflicts checks regarding other parties are important, the lawyer would still need to know and advise the client as to the three-year limitations period before it expires, even if declining the claim. C is incorrect because although injuries document and affect the value of the claim, they do not determine whether the client can maintain the claim at all within a defined period that may momentarily expire. D is incorrect because although the nature and disposition of the tickets may affect liability, they do not determine the period within which the client must act to preserve claims.

2. A physician performed a spinal surgery on a patient. The surgery relieved immediately the patient's numbness in the feet and lower legs, and pain in the lower back. However, over the ensuing months, the patient developed new pain and weakness at the surgery site. Two years of on-and-off physical therapy did not help relieve the pain and weakness. More than two years after the surgery, another surgeon performed an exploratory surgery finding that the first surgeon had left a sponge at the surgical site during the first surgery. The patient visited a lawyer regarding a malpractice claim. The lawyer knew that the applicable limitations period is two years. What action should the lawyer undertake to determine whether the patient has a remedy?
A. Confirm the patient's health insurance because the claim is barred by the period of limitations.
B. Research whether the jurisdiction recognizes pain as a mental disability tolling the limitations period.
C. Research whether the jurisdiction recognizes a discovery rule that would toll the limitations period.
D. Research whether the jurisdiction recognizes leaving a sponge in a patient as obvious malpractice.

Answer: C. A discovery rule may toll the limitations period until the plaintiff should have known of the injury and its connection to the defendant's conduct. A is incorrect because there may be a legal remedy for malpractice, the limitations period for which is tolled for discovery. B is incorrect because although jurisdictions may toll the limitations period for insanity (as the statutes tend to state), pain is not considered a mental disability equivalent to insanity. D is incorrect because the question is whether the claim is barred, and the obviousness of the malpractice does not address that question. It addresses whether expert testimony is necessary to prove the breach.

3. A 17-year-old motorist was injured in a single-vehicle accident. A few weeks later, the motorist visited a lawyer whom the local bar's referral service indicated handled personal-injury cases. The injured motorist explained to the lawyer that a deep pothole had blown out the vehicle's tire, causing it to veer off the road. The injured motorist left a police report and medical records with the lawyer for review, asking that the lawyer get back to the client at the lawyer's convenience with advice on whether the client had a claim against the agency responsible for maintaining the road. Assuming that the limitations period is three years, which of the following is the best initial course for the lawyer to follow in reviewing the claim?
A. Determine whether the jurisdiction has a notice-of-claim statute shorter than the limitations period.
B. Determine whether the jurisdiction has a statute tolling the limitations period for minors under age 18.
C. Determine whether the jurisdiction has a statute of repose for the construction of public highways.
D. Determine whether the jurisdiction has a statute defining when a claim accrues for limitations purposes.

Answer: A. Special notice-of-claim statutes may bar certain claims if the injured person does not notify the responsible agency within a period shorter than the statute of limitations. It has already been a "few weeks" since the accident. Notice-of-claim statutes are common for highway defects and commonly require notice within a few weeks or months. The statute may bar the claim unless the lawyer promptly gives the agency notice for the client. B is incorrect because there is no need for a tolling statute given that the accident occurred a few weeks ago and the limitations period is three years. C is incorrect because statutes of repose typically do not apply to the construction of public highways and, moreover, the immediate concern would be a much shorter notice-of-claim statute, not the typically much-longer statutes of repose. D is incorrect because accrual is not the concern. There is plenty of time to file a lawsuit within the limitations period so long as the lawyer helps the client satisfy any notice-of-claim statute.

4. A child was injured when a defective product exploded. For several years, the parents worked closely with medical-care providers for the child's healing and recovery. When after five years the child had still not fully recovered, the parents consulted a lawyer about products-liability claims on the child's behalf. The lawyer was aware that the jurisdiction has a three-year limitations period for products-liability claims. Which of the following is the best advice that the lawyer can give the parents?
A. Turn attention back to the child's healing and recovery because the limitations period bars the child's claims.
B. Notify the state's consumer-fraud division because with tort claims barred, the state may impose administrative relief.
C. Confirm the jurisdiction's tolling provisions because limitations periods are commonly tolled during minority.
D. Negotiate a settlement after threatening a public recall campaign because the statute bars tort claims.

Answer: C. Filing suit tolls the limitations period. Statutes may also toll limitations periods for minority, insanity, military service, and fraudulent concealment. A is incorrect because the child's claims are probably still valid because of the child's minority. B is incorrect because there is no indication of consumer fraud. Defective products indicate carelessness, not knowing misrepresentations. Administrative relief in these circumstances is highly unlikely. D is incorrect because the child likely has a claim with the limitations period tolled. Also, threatening a manufacturer with a public campaign to induce a private settlement subjugates the public interest for private gain.

5. A building collapsed injuring several people. Within weeks, some of the injured persons retained a lawyer to pursue negligence claims against the building's architect. The lawyer promptly located and made monetary demands on the architect, who had long ago retired. The architect's insurer retained defense counsel to represent the architect. Defense counsel met with the architect who showed defense counsel the building's plans, dated a little less than 20 years before the building's collapse. Which of the following would you most want to know to advise the architect and insurer regarding the claims?
A. The form of liability insurance to ensure coverage.
B. The jurisdiction's laws of immunity.
C. The jurisdiction's statute of limitations.
D. The jurisdiction's statute of repose.

Answer: D. Statutes of repose bar potential future claims a certain number of years after the service or activity that created the risk. With the 20th anniversary of the building's design approaching, and given the substantial lapse of years, knowing the statute of repose could be critical to preserving or pursuing the claim. A is incorrect because the insurer has already retained counsel presumably because of its obligation to defend and indemnify. Retained counsel would have a conflict of interest in advising the insured and insurer as to coverage issues. B is incorrect because there is no indication that immunity would apply (no government or charitable action suggested). C is not as good of an answer because although the limitations period could eventually be important, it has only been weeks since the incident, and limitations periods usually are for one or more years.

6. A six-year-old child was burned when the child accidentally hit a pan handle sticking out from the kitchen range, tipping the pan's hot contents onto the child. The child's mother had left the pan handle sticking out from the range. The child's father had playfully chased the child into the kitchen. Both mother and father felt responsible for their child's injury, the mother for having carelessly left the pan handle sticking out and the father for having carelessly chased the child into the kitchen. The parents consulted a lawyer over whether their injured child had a tort claim against them for their carelessness. Which of the following is the best advice?
A. The child's claim depends on whether the jurisdiction recognizes parent-child immunity.
B. The child's claim depends on whether the jurisdiction recognizes negligent supervision.
C. The child has no claim because tort law does not permit minor children to sue parents.
D. The child has a claim because mother and father were each directly negligent in care of the child.

Answer: A. Many states grant intra-family tort immunity between spouses or between parents and children. A child making a claim against parents would depend on the law of the jurisdiction as to parent-child immunity. B is incorrect because negligent supervision is a theory a third party would maintain against the parents if the child had injured someone due to lack of supervision. The child's claim against the parents, if the parents were not immune, would be direct negligence for having left the pan handle sticking out or having chased the child, not negligent supervision of the child. Supervision is not at issue. C is incorrect because some states do permit minor children to sue parents under some circumstances. D is incorrect because many states offer immunity for parent-child claims. The advice would depend on whether there was immunity, not whether there was negligence, which is apparent from the facts.

7. A husband and wife were driving together to a vacation destination when the husband fell asleep at the wheel. The vehicle left the highway and rolled over in the median, seriously injuring the wife who was a passenger in the vehicle. The accident took place in a jurisdiction that recognizes claims for serious injury caused by a vehicle driver's negligence, subject to applicable statutory and common-law defenses. The husband had in place the statutorily required motor-vehicle insurance. When after several months of extensive medical care the wife had not yet recovered, the husband and wife consulted a lawyer about the wife's claim against the husband for her motor-vehicle-accident injuries. The lawyer then made a claim and demand on the wife's behalf to the husband's motor-vehicle insurer. The insurer's representative consulted defense counsel regarding the claim. Which of the following is the best advice for defense counsel to give the insurer's representative?
A. Inter-spousal immunity exists in all jurisdictions barring these claims based on policy concerns over insurance fraud from collusion between spouses and to preserve domestic tranquility within marriages.
B. Inter-spousal immunity has been abolished in all jurisdictions as a relic of the religious and sacramental treatment of marriages and antiquated family laws treating wives as property of their husband.
C. Although inter-spousal immunity exists in many jurisdictions, it is also commonly waived for motor-vehicle accidents and where there is insurance, making liability depend on the law of the jurisdiction.
D. Inter-spousal immunity exists in many jurisdictions, and where it exists, it uniformly bars claims of this kind involving relatively common motor-vehicle accidents with uncertain liability and disputed injuries.

Answer: C. States recognizing intra-family tort immunity may have exceptions for insurance, motor-vehicle accidents, and changes in the family relationship on which the immunity is based. In this instance, the wife's claim involves a motor-vehicle accident and insurance, both relatively common exceptions to inter-spousal immunity. A is incorrect because some jurisdictions have abolished inter-spousal immunity in all or some cases despite the indicated policy concerns. B is incorrect because some jurisdictions preserve inter-spousal immunity based on the policy concerns expressed in A and for other moral, religious, cultural, and instrumental reasons. D is incorrect because motor-vehicle accidents and insurance are common exceptions to inter-spousal immunity where it exists, and motor-vehicle accidents commonly involve relatively clear liability and injuries.

8. A church member attended a training session in the church library. When the member leaned back in a library chair, the chair broke suddenly, causing the member to fall backward. The member sustained a gash requiring emergency suturing at the hospital and a concussion. The church pastor investigated and found that maintenance personnel knew before the incident that the chair was weakened but had carelessly done nothing about it. The pastor was deeply concerned about the member's unpaid hospital bill and injury and so reported the event to the church's liability insurer. The pastor also consulted a lawyer on the church board. Which of the following is the lawyer's best advice?
A. The church has no negligence liability to the member because the member was injured as a patron of a charitable organization immune to liability.
B. The church may have negligence liability to the member payable by the insurer, depending on whether the jurisdiction has abolished charitable immunity.

C. The church's charitable immunity is of no consequence because the church's insurer will pay for the member's injury without respect to legal liability.

D. The church's charitable immunity and obligation of the liability insurer is of no consequence because the church should pay on moral grounds.

Answer: B. A few states continue to recognize tort immunity for charitable organizations, although most states have abolished charitable immunity. The church is probably liable to the member in negligence depending on whether the jurisdiction is one of the few that still recognizes charitable immunity. A is incorrect because many jurisdictions have abolished charitable immunity and there is no indication whether this jurisdiction has or has not done so. The lawyer would need to know or research immunity before so concluding. C is incorrect because liability insurers pay for loss only where liability is present. If the church is immune, then the insurer would not pay. D is incorrect because although the church may well choose to pay on moral grounds, it would still have an interest in the contractual responsibility of the liability insurer to indemnify the church for the loss. If there is no immunity, then the liability insurer should pay so that the church does not have to expend its own resources when it already paid the insurer's premium for liability coverage.

9. A state employee had state business in another part of the state away from the employee's state office. The employee drove a state vehicle to the location of the business. On the way back to the state office, the employee drove the state vehicle through a red traffic light, negligently crashing into another vehicle that had the right of way. The collision destroyed the other vehicle and seriously injured its driver. The injured driver later consulted an attorney regarding whether the driver had negligence claims against the state employee for the driver's injury and vehicle loss. Which of the following statements would most likely be correct as to the liability of the state and its employee?

A. The state and its employee do not have governmental immunity because the employee's conduct may have amounted to gross negligence, recklessness, or willful and wanton misconduct outside immunity.

B. The state and its employee have governmental immunity because the employee's conduct at most amounted to simple negligence rather than gross negligence, recklessness, or willful and wanton misconduct.

C. The state and its employee do not have governmental immunity because states operating motor vehicles do so subject to the same tort liability of private entities and individuals for negligently caused loss and injury.

D. The state and its employee may have governmental immunity, although many states have either abolished governmental immunity or waived it for specific circumstances commonly including motor-vehicle accidents.

Answer: D. State and federal law may also recognize governmental immunity to tort claims, either broadly or in defined circumstances. Motor-vehicle accidents are one common area where states waive governmental immunity. A is incorrect because the facts indicate negligence, not greater misconduct, and because even if the conduct was more reprehensible than ordinary negligence, some states preserve governmental immunity for all such liability. B is incorrect because some states have abolished governmental immunity or waived it for motor-vehicle accidents caused by simple negligence. In those states, it would not take gross negligence, recklessness, or wanton misconduct to establish liability. C is incorrect because the state may have preserved governmental immunity or may have waived it, depending on common law or statute of the state.

10. A business owner bought several vehicles from a state agency. The vehicles had unreasonably dangerous defects about which agency officials knew but the business owner did not know. The agency had sold the defective vehicles under a program for sale of surplus government goods. The defects caused several instances of personal injury and property damage before they were discovered. Those who suffered losses sued the business owner. The business owner consulted an attorney regarding third-party claims against the agency. Which of the following theories would be most likely to avoid the jurisdiction's limited governmental immunity?
A. The agency's vehicle sales were governmental rather than proprietary functions and discretionary rather than ministerial actions.
B. The agency's vehicle sales were governmental rather than proprietary functions and ministerial rather than discretionary actions.
C. The agency's vehicle sales were proprietary rather than governmental functions and ministerial rather than discretionary actions.
D. The agency's vehicle sales were proprietary rather than governmental functions and discretionary rather than ministerial actions.

Answer: C. Governmental immunity may be waived for proprietary rather than governmental functions and for ministerial rather than discretionary actions, as two common exceptions. Proprietary functions are those typically conducted by private, commercial entities. Ministerial functions are those performed routinely pursuant to established policies and protocols, without discretion. A and B are incorrect because each governmental functions would more likely have immunity than proprietary functions. D is incorrect because discretionary actions would more likely have immunity than ministerial actions.

Essay Question: A business owner prepared financial statements for his own business in January 2002 in which he purposefully wildly exaggerated the business's profits. In December 2004, the owner showed the statements to a prospective buyer for his business, with the fraudulent intent of inducing the buyer to rely on them and purchase the business for substantially more than it was worth. The buyer decided in February 2005 based on the fraudulent financial statement to make the purchase. By July 2005, she had discovered that the statements were fraudulent. She spent the next six months trying to work things out with the owner/seller. In January 2006, she sued the owner/seller for fraud, for which the jurisdiction has a three-year statute of limitations. **Discuss and evaluate whether the buyer timely filed her claim.**

Answer: We are to discuss and evaluate whether a three-year limitations period bars a buyer's fraud claim against the seller of a business.

Statutes of limitation bar claims within a certain period after the claim accrues. The law typically defines accrual as the moment that all elements of the claim are present, although here it would be wise to confirm the specific law of the jurisdiction, given some variety in defining accrual. The facts state the jurisdiction has a three-year limitations period for fraud claims. Law tolls limitations periods for certain things like minority, insanity, and active-duty military service. Many states toll the limitations period until the claimant discovers or should have discovered the concealed circumstances.

When in 2002 the owner/seller first prepared the false financial statements, the buyer did not yet have a fraud claim, not yet having seen the statements and suffered loss as a result. No claim had yet accrued without all elements present. The buyer still had no fraud claim in December 2004 when she saw the statements because she had not yet suffered loss as a result, not yet having bought the business for more than its worth. It was only in February 2005 when the buyer decided based on the false statements to purchase the business that her fraud claim accrued because only then were all elements of the fraud claim, including the last element of loss, present. So, the buyer would have three years from that February 2005 date, or until February 2008, within which to file her fraud claim under the three-year limitation period. She filed in January 2006, well within (more than two years within) the limitations period. The law provides that filing the claim tolls the limitations period. We have no need even to evaluate whether statutory or common law tolling might have been available (reason for the late discovery depending) having to do with her discovering the fraud several months later. The buyer's effort at resolution before filing is certainly an ethical action, one that I appreciate and respect. Fortunately, from procedural, fairness, and efficiency standpoints, her delay did not result in the barring of her action.

In sum, the buyer filed her fraud claim well within the three-year limitations period, which would not bar the claim. The filing of her claim tolls the limitations period, which would not be a defense to the action.

Essay Question: A driver worked for a transportation service operated by a charitable non-profit organization, taking patrons back and forth from an occupational rehabilitation agency to various work sites. On one of those trips, the driver negligently ran a red light, resulting in a collision in which a patron passenger was seriously injured. The driver's wife and minor child, who were not patrons but were along for the ride, were also seriously injured. **Identify the possible immunities relating to the potential claims of the three injured passengers.**

Answer: We are to identify possible immunities relating to potential claims by a charity's patron and the charity's driver's wife and minor child, when the charity's driver negligently ran a red light, injuring the three who were passengers in the charity's vehicle.

A few states recognize charitable immunity, especially for claims brought by patrons of the charity. States also tend to offer immunity to charity volunteers. Some states cap charitable liability at a specific amount, especially when the charity insures itself up to that amount. The few states that do offer charitable immunity tend less to do so for motor-vehicle accidents because of available insurance for motor-vehicle accidents. States may also recognize intra-family immunity. More states preserve parent-child immunity than inter-spousal immunity, but a few states recognize both. Many states waive intra-family immunities for motor-vehicle accidents, available insurance, intentional torts, and if the family relationship ends (in divorce for spouses or emancipation for children).

Here, the driver and charity might have charitable immunity from negligence claims brought by their charitable patron, depending on whether the state recognizes charitable immunity. The driver worked for the charity, presumably meaning that he was not a volunteer but a paid employee. Driving patrons to a rehab service sounds like a daily job, not an occasional volunteer activity, although query why the driver's wife and child had come along for the ride. The organization's activity here, a transportation service, is a high-risk activity as to which the law would require insurance on the vehicles. So charitable immunity could go either way depending on several factors subject to research in the state's law. The driver may also have immunity as to his wife's claim and his child's claim, depending on the state's law, more likely immunity from the child's claim than from the wife's claim.

In sum, charitable and intra-family immunities may well apply to bar all or some claims. These immunity issues are intriguing from economic and social policy perspectives, and I would enjoy doing the research to find out if they are available in the state.

WEEK 2

11. A hedge trimmer injured a woman when part of its blade suddenly sheared and shot back into the woman. The woman had been using the trimmer for the work that she had described to the salesperson who sold her the trimmer. She had been using it in the manner depicted in its advertising on its box and in its instructions. Inspection suggested a defect in the manufacture of the blade and design of its assembly. The woman retained a lawyer to pursue claims for her injury. The lawyer determined to plead all potential theories of products liability. Which of the following should the lawyer's pleading include?

A. Breach of express and implied warranty, negligence, and strict products liability for design, manufacturing, and warning defects.
B. Lack of merchantability, product unfitness for its particular purpose, and unreasonably dangerous marketing of a design.
C. Breach of industry standards, unfitness as to stated warranties, and abnormally dangerous product characteristics.
D. Consumer-protection act violations, consumer-product-safety act violations, and failure to give timely product notice and recall.

Answer: A. Products liability includes not only negligence claims but also claims based on breach of express and implied warranty and strict products liability for design, manufacture, and warning defects. The facts here appear to support possible claims under each theory. B is incorrect because although each of those phrases helps define a possible theory, other theories (negligence, warning failures, etc.) are left out. C is incorrect because breach of contract and misrepresentation are not products-liability theories, and the given facts do not appear to support those claims. D is incorrect because those theories are not products-liability theories, and the given facts do not appear to support those claims.

12. A woman wished to straighten her hair. She went online to read about various straightener products. She chose one the directions for which she could easily follow. The woman purchased the product and used it according to directions. Unfortunately, the product burned her scalp, caused her to lose her hair, and left some scarring. The woman was shocked that the product had failed so catastrophically when she had used it for its advertised purpose and in the manner that the directions indicated. The woman retained a lawyer who filed a breach of express warranty claim against the product's manufacturer. The manufacturer moved for summary judgment arguing that it had given no express product warranty. How should the woman's lawyer best respond to the manufacturer's motion?

A. The Uniform Commercial Code implies a warranty of merchantability when a product's manufacturer gives no express warranty.
B. The Uniform Commercial Code imposes express warranties that consumer products will not injure their users.
C. The product was one of several products advertised to straighten hair, and so it must carry the qualities of hair straighteners generally.
D. The product description, advertising, and directions constituted an express warranty that the product was fit for the advertised purpose.

Answer: D. Manufacturers and retailers may expressly warrant a product's fitness for particular purposes. Product descriptions, advertising, and instructions can constitute an express warranty that the product is fit for the advertised, described, and directed purpose. A is incorrect because the woman's claim is for breach of express warranty, not implied warranty. Also, an implied warranty of merchantability exists whether or not the manufacturer makes an express warranty. B is incorrect because express warranties are made by product manufacturers, not imposed by law. Warranties imposed by law are implied, not express, warranties. Also, the UCC does not impose a warranty that products will not injure, which would constitute a guarantee of personal safety regardless of the product's use and fitness. C is incorrect because it makes no reference to express warranty and is thus not responsive to the manufacturer's summary-judgment motion.

13. A contractor purchased a pair of stilts to use to reach interior ceilings for drywalling. The stilts' manufacturer designed the stilts for that purpose and similar purposes. The stilts carried no advertising, descriptions, instructions, or express warranties. The contractor used the stilts in the ordinary manner for which drywallers use stilts in the drywalling industry. One of the stilts failed suddenly after moderate use, when rivets worked loose from the foot and leg straps. Other manufacturers' stilts used bolts and nuts rather than rivets. The contractor was seriously injured when the stilts failed. The contractor consulted a lawyer regarding potential products-liability claims. Which of the following theories is the best on which to proceed on these facts?

A. The law implies a warranty of fitness for a particular purpose when the user notifies the supplier of the user's particular purpose, which the manufacturer breached in this instance.
B. The law implies a warranty of merchantability, meaning fitness for the product's ordinary purpose, which the manufacturer breached in this instance.
C. The product had a manufacturing defect rendering the product unreasonably dangerous for ordinary use, for which the manufacturer is strictly liable.
D. The manufacturer failed to warn the contractor of reasonable risks involved in the ordinary use of the stilt product, for which the manufacturer is strictly liable.

Answer: B. Manufacturers, distributors, and retailers impliedly warrant a product's merchantability, meaning its fitness for its intended purpose. A is incorrect because the contractor did not notify the manufacturer in such a way that the manufacturer specified the stilts, meaning that there was no warranty of fitness for the particular purpose (only the intended purpose, which is the merchantability warranty). C is incorrect because there is no indication that the manufacturer made the stilts other than as it designed the stilts, meaning that there was no departure from design and hence no manufacturing defect. D is incorrect because warning would not have addressed the unreasonable danger in the sudden failure of the stilts after moderate use.

14. A homeowner purchased several cans of an exterior paint from a local hardware store. The homeowner followed the directions on the paint can for applying the paint to the exterior of the homeowner's home. Within a few weeks, it became clear to the homeowner that the paint was running off with the rain. When the homeowner complained to the hardware store, the storeowner pointed to a sign by the cash register that said all sales were "as is" and without warranties. The homeowner was suspicious that a hardware store could sell such a defective product and so consulted a lawyer. Which of the following is the best advice to the homeowner?

A. The storeowner may disclaim all warranties with signs or other reasonable communications to customers that products are sold "as is" and without warranties.
B. The storeowner may disclaim some warranties, except for those involving personal injury, so that the disclaimer "as is" and without warranties was effective here.

C. The storeowner may not disclaim the implied warranty of merchantability, meaning that the exterior paint would have to have been fit for its intended purpose.
D. The storeowner may not disclaim the implied warranty of fitness for particular purpose, meaning that the storeowner must specify the right product.

Answer: C. Merchants may disclaim some warranties but not the warranty of merchantability or warranties protecting against personal injury. Products must be fit for their intended purpose, when here, the exterior paint was not fit for exterior application. A is incorrect because the implied warranty of merchantability and warranties protecting against personal injury may not be disclaimed. B is incorrect for the same reason. D is incorrect because warranties of fitness for particular purposes may be disclaimed, and the implied warranty of fitness for a particular purpose does not require storeowners to specify products.

15. A contractor hired an electrical subcontractor to supply temporary power to a remote worksite. The electrical subcontractor brought in a large generator on a trailer. After one day's use, the generator failed catastrophically due to its own internal defect. The subcontractor had no other way of supplying temporary power. The contractor was left without power to operate the worksite for many days, causing the contractor to incur substantial expense and lose substantial profits. The subcontractor had no income or assets with which to compensate the contractor. The contractor made a demand on the generator's manufacturer. The manufacturer asked its corporate counsel to respond. Which of the following is the best response?

A. The manufacturer has no liability to the contractor if the jurisdiction follows the economic-loss doctrine barring claims where there is no direct physical impact.
B. The manufacturer has no liability to the contractor because only those in privity have liability claims relating to losses from defective products.
C. The manufacturer has no liability to the contractor because there was nothing wrong with the generator product, which worked perfectly.
D. The manufacturer is probably liable to the contractor but most likely has products-liability insurance to cover fully the contractor's losses.

Answer: A. The economic-loss doctrine, available in most jurisdictions, bars recovery of economic losses where there is no physical impact or injury. Here, the contractor had no such direct physical impact. B is incorrect because privity is not necessary for products-liability theories. All those foreseeably affected may have claims. C is incorrect as a factual matter. The facts state that the generator had an internal defect. Lawyers must not misrepresent facts. D is incorrect because the manufacturer is not liable to the contractor, and an admission of liability would therefore be unwise and may violate a cooperation clause in any insurance policy. Also, corporate counsel would first determine whether there was insurance before responding to a claimant that there most likely is insurance.

16. A woodworker purchased a new table saw from its manufacturer. The table saw came with a rip fence to guide wood into the saw parallel to the saw blade. The particular table saw that the woodworker purchased had the rip fence slightly twisted relative to the saw blade because of a manufacturing defect in the rip fence's alignment. With the table saw's rip fence twisted in manufacture, the saw had a propensity to violently kick back boards toward the saw's operator just as the boards were about to clear the saw blade. The woodworker was seriously injured by one such kickback before discovering the manufacturing defect. The woodworker consulted a lawyer who prepared a demand to the manufacturer in strict products liability. Which of the following best states the strict-products-liability standard?

A. The manufacturer is liable because the table saw as impliedly warranted was not reasonably fit for its ordinary and intended uses.
B. The manufacturer is liable because the table saw was in a defective condition unreasonably dangerous to the woodworker.
C. The manufacturer is liable because its assemblers and inspectors must have been negligent to twist the rip fence in manufacture.
D. The manufacturer is liable because a covenant of good faith and fair dealing is implied in every product-sale contract.

Answer: B. Strict products liability provides that merchants who sell products in a defective condition unreasonably dangerous to users are liable for resultant injury. A is incorrect because it suggests a breach-of-warranty theory like that of merchantability, not a strict-liability theory as the call of the question requests. A is otherwise a reasonable answer. C is incorrect because it suggests a negligence theory, not a strict-liability theory. C is otherwise a reasonable answer. D is incorrect because it suggests a breach-of-contract theory, not a strict-liability theory. Also, the facts do not suggest a violation of good faith and fair dealing.

17. A mechanical-engineering firm designed the control system for a forklift. Consistent with the firm's design, the forklift's control levers poked slightly out from the driver's cage, making the controls easier to operate while standing aside the forklift. Unfortunately, the controls were placed just where workers could accidentally bump them. In one such case, a worker bumped accidentally the forklift controls, sending the forklift forward and crushing and severely injuring another worker. A law firm filed a products-liability action against the mechanical-engineering firm on behalf of the injured worker. During discovery, lead counsel discussed with retained experts the legal standard under which the jury would determine the firm's strict liability for its alleged unreasonably dangerous design. Which of the following best states that standard?

A. The burden of precautions outweighs loss value times probability of loss.
B. The standard of what a reasonable engineer would have done here.
C. A balancing test of social and economic advantages against disadvantages.
D. A risk-utility test weighing design risk, utility, alternatives, cost, and other factors.

Answer: D. A risk-utility test often determines what is *unreasonably dangerous* for purposes of strict products liability. Factors typically include those listed in this answer. A is incorrect because the Learned Hand formula is a negligence formula, not a strict-liability standard, and not one commonly given as a jury instruction. B is incorrect because a reasonable-engineer standard suggests a negligence theory, not a strict-liability theory. Reasonableness is also probably not an appropriate standard for professionals like engineers, where professional custom would instead determine the standard. C is incorrect because a balancing test is not used, and social advantages and disadvantages are not typically a factor, although economics often is a factor.

18. Parents purchased a flotation device labeled a "life preserver" for use by their seven-year-old son in a fishing competition. The son fell overboard during the competition. Although a good swimmer, the son lost his breath in the excitement and cold water and was overcome. The flotation device did not keep the son's head above water. Instead, the son floated for several minutes just below the surface of the murky water, unconscious and unable to breathe. Although rescuers found and revived the son, he suffered moderate brain damage due to oxygen deprivation. The parents retained a lawyer who put the flotation device's manufacturer on notice of a products-liability claim against it. The manufacturer forwarded the notice to its products-liability insurer. The insurer asked its in-house counsel to evaluate the manufacturer's liability. Which of the following is the most applicable legal standard?

A. A risk-utility test.
B. A consumer-expectation test.
C. A reasonable-manufacturer test.
D. A reasonable-engineer test.

Answer: B. Strict products liability includes a *consumer-expectation* test, especially helpful with respect to consumer products as to which the description or common use creates common consumer expectations. Here, marketing the flotation device as a "life preserver" may have created a reasonable expectation that the device would preserve life, making the consumer-expectation test most applicable. A is incorrect because a risk-utility test would be difficult to apply when the issue is really what purchasers like the parents expected the product to do. C and D are incorrect because they suggest negligence standards that would be equally difficult to apply.

19. A marksman borrowed a friend's handgun for target practice. The marksman accidentally discharged the handgun, seriously injuring a bystander. The marksman thought mistakenly that he had the handgun's safety mechanism engaged. Expert inspection established that there was an anomaly in the handgun's safety mechanism that could mislead an unfamiliar user into believing that the safety mechanism was engaged when it was not engaged. The anomaly was not part of the handgun's design and was not mentioned in any of the handgun's literature. The injured bystander retained a lawyer to plead a strict-liability claim in a jurisdiction following the Third Restatement. Which strict-liability theory or theories should the lawyer plead?

A. Design, manufacture, and warning defects.
B. Design and manufacture defects but not warning defect.
C. Manufacture and warning defects but not a design defect.
D. Warning defect but not manufacture or design defects.

Answer: C. The Third Restatement's approach is to classify defects as failures of design, manufacturing, or warning. Here, there is no indication of a faulty design. Rather, the safety mechanism departed from the design in an unsafe manner, suggesting a manufacturing defect, and nothing in the handgun's literature warned of that defective condition. A and B are incorrect because there was no apparent design defect. B is also incorrect because the manufacturer had an opportunity to make reasonable warning of the safety mechanism's proper engagement. D is incorrect because there is an excellent manufacture-defect theory that the handgun departed from its design in a way that rendered it unreasonably dangerous.

20. A worker operated a walk-along lift truck up an incline to deliver raw materials to a production line. A local equipment company had specified and supplied the lift truck for this particular operation. This worker and other workers had operated the lift truck with the same load in the same manner many times without incident. Just as the lift truck neared the top of the incline, it rolled suddenly backward about three feet, catching the worker between the back of the lift truck and a stockpile of raw materials alongside the incline. The incident seriously injured the worker. The worker retained a lawyer who after investigation filed a strict-liability claim against the lift truck's manufacturer, pleading design, manufacturing, and warning defects. The manufacturer moved for summary judgment on the manufacturing defect theory. Which of the following items of evidence discovered by the worker's lawyer would defeat the manufacturer's motion?

A. Engineering drawings showed that the lift truck's drive system was undersized for the rated loads and was likely to fail at any time when used under conditions like those of this incident.

B. Product literature showed operators walking alongside and behind the lift truck up inclines without any instruction, caution, or warning regarding the possibility of sudden backward rolling.

C. Inspection showed that the worker had up until this time always walked ahead of the lift truck rather than beside or behind it in the manner that resulted in the worker's injury in this accident.

D. Inspection showed that this particular lift truck's drive-system gear had been made with an odd chip in it, enabling the drive system to skip and truck to roll just in the manner that caused the accident.

Answer: D. A manufacturing defect exists when at the time of manufacture the product departs from its design. An odd chip in a gear is a good example of a likely manufacturing defect that becomes unreasonably dangerous when it allows a drive system to fail, endangering an operator. A is incorrect because it suggests an unreasonably dangerous design, not a manufacturing defect. B is incorrect because it suggests an unreasonable failure to warn, not a manufacturing defect. C is incorrect because it suggests nothing of a manufacturing defect and instead addresses the operator's potential contributory or comparative negligence.

21. A gardener purchased a hand-crank mulcher to grind up twigs and leaves from his backyard. The manufacturer made the mulcher with a hole in the side of the mulcher's housing near the mulcher's base. One day when the gardener was using the mulcher, the gardener's curious six-year-old daughter stuck her finger in the hole just as the gardener turned its hand crank. The mulcher amputated the daughter's finger. The child's mother retained a lawyer who filed and served a products-liability complaint against the mulcher's manufacturer, alleging a design defect. The manufacturer forwarded the complaint to its insurer who assigned counsel, requesting an evaluation. Which of the following is the best evaluation of the complaint?

A. The mulcher's design was likely unreasonably dangerous and the manufacturer is liable for design defect if as it appears the hole's risk outweighed its utility.

B. The mulcher's design was likely unreasonably dangerous and the manufacturer is liable for design defect because it did not meet the gardener's expectations.

C. The mulcher's design was likely unreasonably safe and the manufacturer is liable for design defect because it involved an abnormally dangerous activity.

D. The mulcher's design was likely reasonably safe and the manufacturer is not liable for design defect because it was the gardener's fault for injuring his daughter.

Answer: A. Design-defect claims depend on showing that the product is not reasonably safe as designed and are commonly determined by risk-utility and consumer-expectation tests. Here, the risk-utility test suggests an unreasonable danger. B is incorrect because the mulcher operated as expected but carried an unanticipated risk. The consumer-expectation test works better than risk-utility when the product does not operate as expected. C is incorrect because abnormally dangerous activity is the definition for strict liability, not strict products liability which instead involves unreasonably dangerous and defective conditions. D is incorrect because although there was almost surely some negligence and probably much negligence on the gardener's part, that negligence would not relieve the manufacturer from liability unless it constituted an unforeseeable misuse. The answer does not refer to unforeseeable misuses, only to fault by the gardener.

22. A technician worked around a production line that cooled glowing-hot metal parts. The contractor who designed and installed the production line had placed guarding at certain points out of concern for injuries if workers should happen to come into contact with the hot parts. The technician slipped and fell on an oily metal platform next to the production line, causing the technician's hand to strike the guarding. Unfortunately, screws holding the guarding had worked loose over time from the production line's vibration. As a result, the guarding collapsed and the technician's hand came into contact with a glowing-hot part, causing severe injury. The technician sued the contractor for design defects in the guarding. After discovery, the contractor's defense counsel moved for summary judgment for lack of design-defect evidence. Which of the following evidence should the technician's lawyer cite to oppose the motion?

A. Design drawings showed that the contractor was to secure the guarding with screws in the same way as installed.
B. Production records showed that plant technicians had twice tightened the screws holding the guarding.
C. An expert testified on deposition that the guard should have been secured by welding rather than screws.
D. An expert testified on deposition that the oily metal platform should have been covered with non-slip grating.

Answer: C. Design-defect claims may require showing an alternative feasible design at the time of manufacture. Welding rather than screws appears to be an alternative feasible design addressing the apparent design defect from the screws working loose due to vibration. A is incorrect because it does not address any defect. It simply shows that the production line was made as designed, a necessary but not sufficient step in proving a design defect. B is incorrect because although it shows the screws' propensity to work loose, at the same time it shows a reasonable means of ensuring continued safe operation. It does not show a feasible alternative safer design. D is incorrect because it addresses a different potential unreasonable danger not necessarily attributable to the contractor who designed and installed the production line.

Essay Question: A rock climber purchased equipment over the Internet from an outfitter. The outfitter advertised one of its manufactured items that the climber purchased, a belaying device, as appropriate for all-season use. The climber did not see the outfitter's advertisement and was not aware that the design of climbing devices might differ depending on whether they would be used in freezing temperatures. The climber used the device climbing in the winter season during freezing temperatures. The device failed as a result, requiring that the climber undergo an embarrassing, hazardous, and expensive rescue in which she suffered exposure and scrapes. **Evaluate and discuss the warranty liability of the outfitter for the climber's injuries.**

Answer: We must evaluate and discuss the warranty liability of a rock-climbing outfitter for an injury that a climber suffered after buying a device advertised for all-season use but that failed in freezing temperatures.

Warranty claims are either express or implied. An express warranty claim depends on an affirmative communication as to the product's characteristics that the product does not in fact have. Advertisement, instructions, and other writings can constitute express warranties even when not in the form of a guarantee. Some jurisdictions require reliance on the communication, while others do not. The law implies a warranty of merchantability in every sale by a merchant. Merchantability means fitness for the product's ordinary purpose. Circumstances may also imply a warranty of fitness for particular purpose, if the buyer specifies the purpose and the seller supplies the product for that purpose. A claimant must prove that the warranty breach caused injury or damage.

Here, the climber may have express and implied warranty claims against the outfitter. The outfitter advertised the device for all-season use, constituting an express warranty of fitness for that use. When the device failed in freezing temperatures, the outfitter may have breached that express warranty because advertising a use for which the product does not work warrants an unsafe use. I would need more detail here about how the device works and also how the device failed, but it seems inferable from the stated facts that the freezing weather had to do with the device's failure. A problem with the climber's express warranty claim is that she did not see the advertisement and thus could not have relied on it for a warranty. I would need to research the law of the jurisdiction on this reliance issue. The climber may have a stronger implied warranty of merchantability claim. The belaying device should have worked for belaying under the advertised conditions (the intended uses). It did not work (it failed in that use), suggesting its unfitness for its ordinary use and constituting a breach of the merchantability warranty. There is probably no warranty of fitness for particular purpose (the other implied warranty) because the climber did not communicate her purpose to the outfitter, meaning that the outfitter had no way of warranting a specific use fit for the climber's specific purpose. Notice that the climber purchased over the Internet without even seeing the advertisement regarding the device's all-season use, confirming no opportunity for the seller to warrant a specific purpose fit for the buyer's particular use. Some states still would hold the seller liable on a fraud-on-the-market theory, from a policy standpoint not to let the seller off simply because this one user did not see the advertisement. The facts that the climber required rescue and suffered exposure and scrapes satisfy the causation and damages elements because rescue costs and stress and personal injury in the form of scrapes are damages.

In sum, the climber likely has breach of express or implied warranty claims. On the other hand, the facts do not seem to state such significant damage as to warrant my taking the case when contrasted with recreational disasters involving death or serious injury. A jury might conclude that the climber was fortunate not to suffer worse. I am also not crazy to represent a recreational climber whom others rescued. I could see a jury believing that climbing has inherent risks and that the climber was fortunate to be rescued, even though neither of these considerations would necessarily be relevant. The facts give no indication that the climber was contributorily or comparatively negligent or assumed the risk of a failing belaying device, a significant issue to investigate.

Essay Question: A craftsman owned a table saw from which he repeatedly removed and replaced the saw-blade guard in order to perform various cutting operations, as shown in the table-saw manual. The craftsman gradually grew weary of removing and replacing the saw-blade guard in the time-consuming manner it required according to design and instructions, and so he decided to simply leave the guard off for all cutting operations. Unfortunately, a piece of material kicked back during a cutting operation, causing Inoue's finger to come into contact with the saw blade, with resulting serious amputation injury. **Choose the most appropriate of the two primary product-defect tests under the Restatement (Second) of Torts §402A, applying the test to evaluate the craftsman's claim.**

Answer: We must choose and apply the most appropriate of the risk-utility and consumer-expectation tests for products liability under the Second Restatement, where a craftsman suffered kickback injury after removing the blade guard from a table saw.

The two primary product-defect tests are the consumer-expectation test and the risk-utility test. The consumer-expectation test simply focuses on what the consumer would expect the product to do, applying best in cases of simple consumer products. The risk-utility test, arising from the Restatement (Second) of Torts §402A, includes seven factors: the product's risk; its utility; whether there is a substitute product; whether design could have eliminated the risk; whether the user was aware of the risk; whether the user could have avoided the risk; and pricing issues surrounding the cost of substitute designs. The risk-utility test applies best in cases involving complex products that consumers do not often use.

Here, the facts make it appear that the saw performed basically as expected. Investigation will confirm, but the facts mention nothing unusual other than the kickback. How often kickback occurs and why it occurs are important questions, but the facts appear to suggest some foreseeable incidence. The risk-utility test may best apply here to this complex product used more often by experts than ordinary consumers and involving a hidden hazard. One could argue a defect in the way that the manufacturer designed the guard for removal and reinstallation. If, as one may presume from the manual (but would need to confirm with investigation), the manufacturer should have anticipated frequent removal of the guard for ordinary uses, then perhaps the guard should have been designed for ready removal and reinstallation so as not to discourage a reasonably prudent user from replacing the guard. The theory could be one that reasonable jurors would reject because the modification of the saw by removing its guard may have relieved the manufacturer from liability. Unforeseeable modifications relieve the manufacturer of liability. But the theory seems plausible insofar as the manual showed how to remove the guard for cutting operations. Obviously, the manufacturer foresaw (not just should have foreseen but actually instructed and thus foresaw) guard removal. Then, applying the seven-factor test, the risk factor may weigh in the user's favor because kickback and blade injury are likely to cause serious physical harm with some frequency. The utility factor may also weigh in the user's favor because there might be little or no utility to a clumsy design for removing and replacing the guard, depending on what the engineers say. The guard would have utility, certainly from its serious-injury-saving capacity, but the design issue is the removal and replacing of the guard. As to the substitute-design factor, there may have been a simpler system for removing and replacing the guard, which is the critical unanswered question needing investigation. In other words, the manufacturer might have had a way to eliminate some of the time it took to remove and replace the guard (the big question for expert testimony). Probably, though, the user was aware of the risk of blade contact or kickback (more investigation like a statement or deposition needed here), and also might well have been able to avoid it by more cautious use. Kickback usually occurs when there is some twisting or other misdirection of the wood into the blade. The price of alternative safer designs (designs that would reduce the trouble in removing and replacing the guard) is simply unknown but likely to be higher, thus weighing in the manufacturer's favor.

On the whole, it seems like a weak case at best that jurors might think the kind to inhibit manufacturers. The saw's modification, the fact that it was a guard that the user removed, and the fairly apparent risk of kickback (perhaps depending on what the manual said about that risk), all make it a problematic case. Although I sympathize for the user over the injury, the manufacturer has much the best of it, and I would prefer to help that manufacturer in its defense. The engineering issues would be fascinating. The call of the question does not ask for defenses, but they would include modification (really, the user's burden to prove non-modification), contributory or comparative negligence (possibly great), product misuse (again, the user's burden to prove foreseeable use or misuse), open and obvious, and possibly even assumption of the risk (voluntarily encountering a known risk).

Essay Question: Husband and wife were riding a snowmobile along state trails when they came to a tree that had fallen across the path. It was clear that other snowmobilers had encountered the tree and managed to cross it in some fashion with their snowmobiles. So husband dismounted from the snowmobile with its front skis part way up over the tree trunk, and asked wife to operate the snowmobile while husband pushed and lifted the rear of the snowmobile to get it over the tree trunk. As wife gunned the engine, the snowmobile track gears rotated sharply, catching and amputating the tips of husband's fingers as he attempted to lift the rear of the snowmobile. **Discuss and evaluate husband's potential manufacturing, design, and warning-defect claims against the snowmobile manufacturer with respect to his injury.**

Answer: We are asked to discuss and evaluate a husband's manufacturing, design, or warning-defect claims against a snowmobile manufacturer for his injury trying to free a snowmobile from an obstacle, coming into contact with track gears.

Under the Third Restatement, a manufacturing-defect claim depends on showing that the product departed from its design, in a way that caused the injury. A design-defect claim requires showing that the manufacturer's failure to adopt a reasonable alternative design left the product in an unreasonably unsafe condition that caused the injury. One may apply consumer-expectation or risk-utility tests to determine the product's reasonable safety. A warning-defect or failure-to-warn claim requires showing that the manufacturer's failure to provide a reasonable alternative warning left the product in an unreasonable unsafe condition, causing the injury.

Here, as to the manufacturing-defect claim, the facts do not indicate that the snowmobile was anything other than as designed. There is no missing or poorly made part mentioned. I see no manufacturing-defect claim. The injured user may claim a design defect. The theory would be that the manufacturer should have made or guarded the snowmobile's track gears so that someone lifting the rear of the snowmobile would not have fingers in contact with the gears. This theory seems plausible. I do not know the incidence of lifting the rear of a snowmobile in ordinary use or foreseeable misuse and would need to investigate, but it seems from the reported events that it might be relatively common. Notice that other snowmobilers had someone managed to get over the fallen tree trunk, presumably meaning that some might have done the same thing as this injured user. The task then becomes applying a consumer-expectation or risk-utility test. I might argue both tests if I were to represent the injured user, which I feel that I would willingly do. Losing fingertips is an awful injury. For brevity's sake, consider only the consumer-expectation test. Consumers would not ordinarily expect risk of serious injury when using a snowmobile in a manner that was probably reasonably foreseeable. I would think that you could lift the back of a snowmobile with losing your fingertips. But again, we would need to learn how the injured user did so and whether his actions were reasonably foreseeable (a liability question) and reasonable (a contributory- or comparative-negligence issue). To argue the risk-utility test, I would need to know a lot more about the particular track and gear design, and alternative guarding and design. Preliminarily, the design-defect claim sounds decent. There may also be a failure-to-warn claim depending on what the proofs show about manual warnings and the injured user's knowledge. A failure-to-warn claim depends on showing that the absence of a warning made the snowmobile unreasonably dangerous. If as it sounds there was a serious injury risk associated with lifting the rear of the snowmobile, then it also sounds like there should have been a warning on the snowmobile or in the manual or both. Perhaps then (a matter for investigation and proof) the injured user would not have lifted the snowmobile's rear.

Although the call of the question does not ask for defenses, I would consider contributory or comparative negligence, product misuse, and possibly open and obvious.

In sum, the husband does not appear to have a manufacturing-defect claim but may well have design-defect and warning-defect or failure-to-warn claims. Those claims are worth investigating with expert engineering consult.

WEEK 3

23. A homeowner purchased a riding mower for the home's hilly lawn. The homeowner mowed the lawn several times using the riding mower without incident. Then the homeowner decided to change the mowing pattern to improve the appearance of the lawn. The homeowner rode the mower across rather than up and down the hilly lawn. At the steepest part of the hill, the mower tipped over, rolling over and seriously injuring the homeowner. The homeowner consulted a lawyer regarding the injury, reporting that he would have mown the hillside by hand if he had known of the mower's propensity to tip over. Which of the following is the best advice regarding the homeowner's potential products-liability claim?

A. The homeowner may have a failure-to-warn claim as to the mower's propensity to tip over on hillsides.
B. The homeowner may have a design-defect claim as to the mower's failure to stay upright on the steep lawn.
C. The homeowner may have a manufacturing-defect claim as to the mower's propensity to tip over on hillsides.
D. The homeowner has no products-liability claims because there was nothing wrong with the mower's performance.

Answer: A. Failure-to-warn claims depend on showing that the omission of a warning made the product unreasonably dangerous. Here, it is at least plausible based on the homeowner's report that the homeowner needed a warning as to the mower's propensity to tip over. Roll-over propensity can be greater or lesser depending on design, arguably requiring warning and instruction. B is incorrect because although a high center of gravity and high incidence of roll-over could involve a design defect, there is no such evidence suggested, while the facts do suggest a direct theory of failure to warn that the homeowner said that he would not have mown across if aware of the danger. C is incorrect because there is no indication that the mower was made other than as designed. D is incorrect because there is at least a plausible failure-to-warn claim, depending on the product literature and roll-over propensity.

24. A mother kept knives stored in a slotted wood block on the kitchen counter. Her child climbed on a chair to reach the kitchen counter. The child pulled one of the knives from the wood block, accidentally cutting herself with it. The mother later contacted a lawyer to see if the lawyer could get the knife manufacturer to pay for the medical expenses relating to the child's injury. The child's mother pointed out to the lawyer that the knife's blade had no warning printed on it saying that it was sharp or that it should be kept out of the reach of children. Which of the following is the best evaluation to give the mother?

A. The manufacturer is liable for failure to warn because printing a blade warning may have made a difference.
B. The manufacturer has no liability for failure to warn because the mother was a sophisticated user.

C. The manufacturer has no liability for failure to warn because child use would be product misuse.
D. The manufacturer has no liability for failure to warn because the risk of knives cutting is open and obvious.

Answer: D. There generally need be no warning as to obvious risks. Courts will recognize an open-and-obvious defense. The risk of a knife cutting is open and obvious. A is incorrect because reasonable persons know that knives are sharp and should be kept from children. There would first be a need for the warning to keep the item from being unreasonably dangerous. B is incorrect because one need not be sophisticated to know that knives have sharp blades capable of cutting. C is incorrect because children do use knives and whether children use knives or not does not address whether knives should carry a warning.

25. An apprentice cabinetmaker purchased a cross-cut saw for use in his home shop. The cabinetmaker read the instructions in the saw's manual. The manual only stated a caution regarding "kickback" without further explanation. The apprentice cabinetmaker had not experienced kickbacks when cutting wood on a cross-cut saw. The first time that the cabinetmaker used the new saw, he cut a piece of wood in a manner that produced violent kickback, throwing a chunk of the wood into his face and blinding him in one eye. The cabinetmaker consulted a lawyer, reporting that he had no idea from the manual's caution that the saw could throw a chunk of wood into his face, seriously and permanently injuring him. Which of the following best states the standard for evaluating the cabinetmaker's failure-to-warn claim against the saw's manufacturer?

A. Warnings must be reasonable, generally meaning that they must make sense when read by an experienced user of like products who is already familiar with their ordinary use but may not appreciate unique hazards.
B. Warnings must be adequate, generally meaning that they must alert users to the product's hazard or injury risk, the nature and severity of the injury that could result, and the means of avoiding the risk.
C. Warnings should reasonably alert users to the need to further investigate the product's properties, proper operation, and unusual hazards, through industry literature on safety.
D. Warnings need alert a user to watch out for the user's own safety by receiving training from those experienced in the field who are familiar with the natural hazards of an operation and its products.

Answer: B. Warnings must be adequate, generally meaning that they should describe the hazard, injury risk, and means of avoiding the risk. The caution here did not adequately address these three elements. A is incorrect because warnings should be for inexperienced users, too, who are unfamiliar with the product. C is incorrect because a warning that merely alerted a user to look elsewhere for safety information would not be sufficient to help a user appreciate the risk, its seriousness, or how to avoid it. D is incorrect because a warning that said to get help from an experienced person would not alert the user to the risk, its seriousness, or how to avoid it.

26. A tradesperson was working in an enclosed area on a jobsite. The area had no natural ventilation. The tradesperson worked alone for long hours using, frequently starting and using a gas-engine-powered cutting tool on the harder parts of the job. The tradesperson grew drowsy and then fell unconscious, overcome by a build-up of carbon monoxide from fumes from the cutting tool's gas engine. The tradesperson was found dead the next day by another worker at the jobsite. A lawyer retained by the tradesperson's estate confirmed that the cutting tool bore no warnings regarding lethal fumes and the need for ventilation. Which of the following is the best evaluation of the estate's failure-to-warn claim against the cutting tool's manufacturer?

A. There is no claim because there is no way of knowing whether the trades-person killed by the engine's fumes would have read and followed a warning, and causation cannot be proven.
B. There may well be a claim because the law does not require proof of negligence elements in the event of a wrongful death, all elements being presumed.
C. There may well be a claim because many jurisdictions would presume that a decedent killed by a product without warning would have read and heeded a warning.
D. There may well be a claim because anytime someone dies relating to a product's use, there is a strict-products-liability claim for the estate to maintain in recovery.

Answer: C. As to causation in failure-to-warn cases, most jurisdictions will presume that the injured user would have read and heeded a warning. A is incorrect because the read-and-heed presumption would satisfy the estate's need to produce evidence on the causation issue. B is incorrect because the law requires proof of an underlying substantive legal theory such as negligence even in the event of wrongful death. The law may presume causation in failure to warn cases, but the estate must still prove the other elements. D is incorrect because no claim will be recognized unless each of its elements are met including duty, breach, causation (cause in fact and proximate cause), and damages. The statement is far too broad.

27. A diabetic used an insulin drug for several years to treat her diabetes. Several physicians had prescribed or renewed prescriptions for the drug over the years, working closely with the diabetic to ensure safe medication at controlled levels. The diabetic died as a result of an overdose of the drug when away on a month-long summer European vacation. The diabetic's estate sued the drug manufacturer for failure to warn of the death risk associated with overdosing. Investigation by a lawyer retained by the manufacturer confirmed that the fourth and last physician who had prescribed the drug to the diabetic had given the diabetic no information as to the drug's risks. The manufacturer's lawyer moved for summary judgment on the estate's failure-to-warn claim. Which of the following is the best argument for the lawyer to make in the motion?

A. The manufacturer of a prescription drug product has no duty to warn consumers who should look to other sources for product risks when drugs cannot be marked with warnings.
B. The manufacturer of a drug product satisfies its duty to warn consumers when it conducts and publishes rigorous studies on the drug's medical risks and performance.
C. The diabetic was a sophisticated user of the insulin drug product who was or should have been warned and informed by several physicians as learned intermediaries.
D. The diabetic had successfully used the insulin drug product for several years without overdosing, so whatever warning the manufacturer gave must have been sufficient.

Answer: C. In failure-to-warn cases, courts will consider the user's sophistication and whether there were any learned intermediaries who should have given warnings. After several years of using the insulin drug under the close management of several physicians, the diabetic knew or should have known of the drug's risks and needed no warning from the manufacturer. A is incorrect because drug manufacturers can and do provide product circulars and warnings on advertising and packaging to ensure that consumers know product risks. The question here is who (physician or manufacturer) should have given that warning as to a prescription drug. B is incorrect because conducting and publishing studies would alone not be sufficient when reasonable care would likely require summarizing the information and giving warnings in product circulars reasonably calculated to reach prescribing physicians. D is incorrect because safe use for several years does not necessarily mean that a better warning would not have prevented death later. A warning as to the death risk associated with overdose may have made a difference. The question is who should have given that warning, the physicians or the manufacturer.

28. A family bought a plastic hockey stick for a young boy. The family bought the stick from a national-chain dollar store. When the boy used the stick to hit a tennis ball, the stick's plastic blade separated from the stick's plastic handle, flying into and seriously injuring the eye of a young girl. Inspection showed that only a defective plastic rivet had connected the blade to the stick. The girl's father could not identify the hockey stick's manufacturer but learned that the family had bought it at the dollar store. The father contacted the dollar store's national headquarters, which indicated that an unknown overseas manufacturer had manufactured the stick, which the dollar store bought from a certain distributor. The father consulted counsel, requesting that counsel sue a responsible party for strict products liability for the defective stick injuring his young daughter. What action should counsel take pursuing the father's lawful objective?

A. Counsel should not sue anyone until identifying the manufacturer.
B. Counsel should name the dollar store and distributor as defendants.
C. Counsel should name only the young boy as a defendant.
D. Counsel should name the young boy's family members as defendants.

Answer: B. All merchants within the chain of distribution bear the same strict products liability to the injured user as the manufacturer, as do suppliers of defective component parts. Counsel should name the dollar store and distributor, both of whom are merchants within the chain of distribution. A is incorrect because the father's objective is to sue a responsible party, and waiting to identify an unidentified manufacturer does not achieve that objective. Counsel may never identify the manufacturer. C is incorrect because the young boy would not be liable in products liability. The young boy is not a merchant. D is incorrect for the same reason, that the family members are not merchants to whom strict products liability would attach.

29. An elderly woman decided to hold a garage sale of her now-adult children's old toys and sporting equipment. Among the items she sold was a lawn-dart set that had been taken off the market many years earlier because of its injury hazard. The manufacturer was long defunct because of liability for deaths and serious injuries connected with the lawn-dart product's unreasonable dangers. A homeowner who purchased the lawn dart at the elderly woman's garage sale later accidentally but seriously injured a boy using the lawn-dart set. The boy's parents made a recovery for the boy in a negligence claim against the homeowner, which was paid by the homeowner's insurer. The insurer then retained a lawyer to evaluate a products-liability claim against the elderly woman. Which of the following is the best evaluation of that claim?

A. There is no claim against the elderly woman who was not in the business of selling such products.
B. There is no valid claim against the elderly woman who was not in privity with the boy whom the product injured.
C. Although there is a valid claim against the elderly woman, pursuing it is pointless unless she has insurance.

D. Only the injured boy would have had a valid claim against the elderly woman, not the homeowner's insurer.

Answer: A. Strict products liability generally does not extend to one-time resellers of used products. The elderly woman was obviously not in the business of selling lawn darts. B is incorrect because although there is no claim against the woman, it is because she was not in the business of selling the product, not because of the absence of privity. Privity is not required. C is incorrect because the woman has no liability, and even if she did, she might have assets to reach even if she had no insurance. D is incorrect because the boy would not have had a valid claim against the woman when she was not in the business of selling and because if there was a claim, then the homeowner's insurer may have had a claim for contribution from the woman (subrogating to the homeowner's rights).

30. A hardware retailer sold an electrical switch to a homeowner who installed it in the home. The home subsequently burned down, with fire marshals tracing the cause to a defect in the switch. The homeowner's lawyer made a demand in products liability on the retailer who forwarded the demand to the retailer's insurer. The insurer retained counsel to investigate other responsible parties. Which of the following evidence that counsel discovered would be most helpful to the retailer and insurer in shifting liability to other parties?

A. The retailer obtained the defective product by buying it in a bulk lot at auction with markings that it was from an overseas supplier.
B. The retailer developed the defective product as an in-house brand working with a small firm that specialized in knock-off products.
C. The retailer had no records of who supplied or manufactured the defective product and no other way of tracing its origins.
D. The retailer had ordered the defective product from a reputable distributor and sold it in its original packaging without inspection.

Answer: D. Entities in the chain of distribution typically indemnify one another, shifting products liability to the responsible upstream party. When the retailer used a reputable distributor and sold the product in its original package without inspection, the retailer increased its likelihood of obtaining common-law and contractual indemnity, or at least contribution, from the upstream distributor and manufacturer. A is incorrect because it indicates great difficulty in tracing the sale to financially responsible entities in jurisdictions where judgments can be readily obtained and enforced. B is incorrect because it indicates the retailer's active involvement and greater responsibility, without indicating parties and theories for indemnity. C is incorrect because it indicates no possibility of passing liability to a financially responsible upstream party.

31. A die-cast machine seriously injured an operator when it accidentally cycled with the operator's hands against a rail supporting the die. State investigators traced the accidental cycling to the failure of a control-box mount. The die-cast machine's manufacturer had assembled the control box to the die-cast machine with a bolt and nut that had worked loose over time with the machine's natural vibration. The worker retained a lawyer to investigate a products-liability claim against the manufacturer. The lawyer learned that the manufacturer no longer mounted control boxes with bolt and nut, instead welding control boxes to the machines to eliminate this hazard. Which of the following best describes how the lawyer should use that evidence in pursuing the products-liability claim?

A. The lawyer should use the manufacturer's subsequent remedial measure to prove that the manufacturer was negligent in using the original nut-and-bolt design.
B. The lawyer should use the manufacturer's subsequent remedial measure to prove the feasibility of the alternative safer design if denied by the manufacturer.
C. The lawyer should use the manufacturer's subsequent remedial measure to establish that the manufacturer controlled the conditions of the machine's design.
D. The lawyer should use the manufacturer's subsequent remedial measure to prove that other similar accidents had occurred for which the manufacturer is liable.

Answer: B. Subsequent remedial changes in design defects are generally inadmissible except to prove disputed feasibility. If the manufacturer denies the feasibility of welding, then its subsequent remedial measure would be admissible. A is incorrect because the evidence would be inadmissible for that purpose, as a policy judgment to encourage remedial measures. C is incorrect because there is no indication that the manufacturer would dispute its control, and the evidence would likely be inadmissible for that purpose because of the policy to encourage remedial measures. D is incorrect because the evidence would be barred for that purpose by the same policy, and proving that the manufacturer is liable for other accidents is not a relevant issue.

32. A baseball player developed the habit of taking home any old wooden bats that other players had discarded as cracked and unsafe for competitive use. The player would carry the old bats around his farm, hitting stones and anything else he happened across, to keep his coordination sharp. On one such occasion, the player's bat shattered, sending the sharp head of the broken bat into the player's knee. When it looked after several months like the incident would result in the player's permanent injury, the player consulted a lawyer about a products-liability claim against the bat's manufacturer. Which of the following best describes how the lawyer should advise the player regarding the effect of the player's own actions?

A. The lawyer should tell the player that the player's products-liability claim would be unaffected by the player's own conduct whether or not unsafe because products liability is strict.
B. The lawyer should tell the player that the player's products-liability claim would likely be barred by contributory negligence or reduced for comparative negligence, depending on the jurisdiction.
C. The lawyer should tell the player that the player's products-liability claim would likely be improved by the stewardship of resources and talent the player showed by his practice.
D. The lawyer should tell the player that the player's products-liability claim would likely be more difficult because the player was not using the bat in competition when it shattered.

Answer: B. Contributory or comparative negligence is an available defense to products-liability claims in a majority of jurisdictions. The player's actions appear to be unsafe, meaning that the player's claim would be barred or reduced depending on the law of the jurisdiction as to contributory or comparative negligence. A is incorrect because contributory or comparative negligence typically is available as a defense to products liability. C is incorrect because although improving a talent and using available resources are good actions, using an unsafe practice rejected by others for competition is likely careless and thus not helpful to the claim. D is incorrect because using the bat in competition or practice should not change the design and manufacturing standards. Bats should be reasonably safe for both competition and practice.

33. A carpenter sued the manufacturer of a saws-all tool when seriously injured after the tool's blade snapped off and hit the carpenter in the face. The manufacturer's lawyer deposed the carpenter, establishing that the carpenter had used the saws-all tool overhead with one hand to cut through a metal strap holding a joist. The deposition further established that the carpenter knew from practice and the tool's instructions that it should only be used with two hands and never used overhead. The deposition further established that the carpenter had broken several blades off the saw in just the same fashion, experiencing a couple of near misses. Which of the following best describes the jury instruction the manufacturer's lawyer should request at trial based on this anticipated evidence?

A. That the jury may find that the carpenter assumed the risk of his injury.
B. That the jury may find that the carpenter's actions were open and obvious.
C. That the jury may find that the tool performed as the carpenter expected.
D. That the jury may find that the manufacturer owed the carpenter no duty.

Answer: A. Assumption of risk is another products-liability defense available in some jurisdictions. Here, the carpenter knew in advance of injury that the carpenter's actions were creating a substantial risk of injury, from prior near misses. B is incorrect because the open-and-obvious defense involves conditions, not actions by the plaintiff. C is incorrect because it is not a law instruction but a proposed finding of fact, when instructions should be as to the law. D is incorrect because the manufacturer would owe the carpenter the duty to design and manufacture a product that was not unreasonably dangerous. The carpenter's conduct does not raise a duty issue.

34. A child was seriously injured when cut by a very sharp metal bracket on the underside of a folding table. The child's parents eventually retained a lawyer who inspected and photographed the table. The lawyer promptly confirmed that the table's metal framework had a date stamped on it indicating the manufacturer and a manufacturing date 11 years earlier. The lawyer also learned from the parents that the accident had happened on the now-14-year-old child's 11th birthday. Which of the following best describes steps the lawyer should take to determine whether the child has a products-liability claim against the table's manufacturer and, if so, to preserve that claim?

A. Determine the jurisdiction's statutes of limitations, tolling, and repose, and preserve the table.
B. Determine the jurisdiction's statutes of products liability and warranty, and dispose of the table.
C. Determine the manufacturer's insurance carrier, and make a demand including the photos.
D. Open a probate case for the child so that the probate court can authorize the parents' action.

Answer: A. The statute of limitations and statute of repose are common products-liability defenses. The limitations period may be affected by a tolling statute. Preserving the product is essential to avoid a spoliation defense. B is incorrect because the first critical step is to determine time periods, and the table should be preserved, not discarded. C is incorrect because there would be no point to making a demand until the periods of limitations and repose are confirmed, and the claim preserved. Making a demand does not toll the limitations period, which in the absence of a tolling statute may be running. D is incorrect because there would be no point to opening a probate case until it was confirmed that there was a viable action not barred by a limitations period or statute of repose.

35. An employer purchased quantities of cleaning fluid for its machinery. The employer required employees to use the cleaning fluid frequently in enclosed places without ventilation or breathing-apparatus protection. The employer had always used this same chemical even though a few workers had complained of difficulty breathing after using it. An employee who suffered from frequent allergies, asthma, and related breathing difficulties was overcome from the cleaning fluid's fumes when using the fluid one day. The incident caused the employee permanent partial disability from breathing problems and related dizziness. The employee sued the employer and the maker of the cleaning fluid claiming failure to warn. Both defendants moved for summary judgment based on the exclusive-remedy provision of the applicable worker's compensation act. Which of the following describes the most likely ruling on the motion?

A. Motion denied as to the employer and denied as to the cleaning-fluid maker.
B. Motion denied as to the employer but granted as to the cleaning-fluid maker.
C. Motion granted as to the employer and granted as to the cleaning-fluid maker.
D. Motion granted as to the employer but denied as to the cleaning-fluid maker.

nswer: D. Exclusive-remedy provisions of worker's compensation acts may bar claims against involved employers but not manufacturers of the injury-causing product. The employer is liable only for worker's compensation benefits (likely through its comp insurer), while the cleaning-fluid maker may be liable in products liability. Each of the other answers is incorrect for these reasons.

36. A team of arborists used chainsaws to trim and cull an urban park's trees. One of the arborists accidentally buried into the opposite side of a large log the tip of one of the smaller chainsaws. Burying the tip of a chainsaw in the timber can result in the chainsaw's kickback into the face, neck, torso, and arms of the chainsaw user. The chainsaw's kickback cut the arborist's carotid artery resulting in the arborist's death. Investigation by a lawyer retained by the arborist's estate revealed that most chainsaw manufacturers make the chainsaws with a tip guard that prevents the user from burying the chainsaw's tip in a log. Investigation further revealed that the team had removed tip guards from all of the team's chainsaws including the chainsaw that killed the arborist, as chainsaw users commonly remove tip guards. How would the court most likely instruct the jury on the legal issue raised by the tip guard's removal?

A. The jury must not consider product alteration or misuse when determining whether the product was unreasonably dangerous.
B. The jury may consider alteration and misuse, but must not consider foreseeability of alteration or misuse, when determining unreasonable danger.
C. The jury may consider alteration, misuse, and foreseeability of alteration and misuse, when determining whether the product was unreasonably dangerous.
D. The jury must find the chainsaw manufacturer not liable because of the product's alteration and misuse.

Answer: C. Product alteration and misuse are products-liability defenses, although manufacturers should anticipate foreseeable alterations and misuses. The chainsaw manufacturer may still be liable for unreasonable failures to guard or warn, if the manufacturer knew or should have known of the product's alteration and misuse, rendering the product unreasonably dangerous. A is incorrect because alteration and misuse may relieve the defendant of liability. B is incorrect because foreseeable alterations and misuses may be relevant to the reasonableness of the design and warning and to the manufacturer's liability. D is incorrect because the jury could conclude otherwise that the manufacturer should have warned or protected against the chainsaw's foreseeable and possibly preventable alteration and misuse.

37. A manufacturer obtained FDA approval to market an anti-hypertensive drug after submitting it to rigorous and extensive testing. The FDA approved the drug under valid federal regulations that specified precise tolerances as to side effects and risks associated with the drug's use in combating hypertensive disease. The FDA had adopted the regulations under federal legislation that included statements that Congress intended federal law to occupy the field to promote development and marketing of drugs to combat the costs and perils of hypertensive disease. The legislation stated expressly that it superseded any contrary state or local enactment. Several patients whose physicians prescribed the drug nonetheless developed heart damage from it. The patients sued the manufacturer under state products-liability law. Which of the following affirmative defenses should the manufacturer's counsel plead in answer?

A. Contributory or comparative negligence.
B. Express and implied consent.
C. Product misuse or alteration.
D. Federal preemption.

Answer: D. Federal preemption is yet another possible defense, where state tort law would contradict federal statute or regulation. A is incorrect because there is no indication from the facts that the patients exhibited any less care for themselves than they should have. B is incorrect because consent is a defense to intentional torts, not products-liability actions. C is incorrect because there is no indication that the patients altered or misused the drug product.

38. A physician's assistant examined, diagnosed, and treated a young child for a childhood disease in the physician's office. When the services were complete, the physician's assistant gave the child a balloon and sucker as reassurance. The child sucked on the sucker and played with the balloon while the child's parents scheduled another appointment and paid the medical co-pay at the reception counter. Unfortunately, in a moment of confusion the child began to suck on the balloon while playing with the sucker, with the result that the child choked on the balloon and required intubation and other invasive medical treatment as life-saving measures. The parents later retained a lawyer who sued the physician's office in products liability for the balloon's unreasonable danger to the child. Which of the following statements best evaluates the merits of the claim?

A. The claim has substantial merit because balloons combined with suckers are unreasonably dangerous for young children.
B. The claim has some merit because physician's assistants generally know that balloons present choke hazards to young children.
C. The claim is without merit because products liability does not attach to transactions that involve primarily services.
D. The claim is without merit because young children must wait until the age of majority before deciding whether to sue.

Answer: C. There is generally no products liability for services that do not involve products as their essential activity. The proper action may be in malpractice or in negligence but not products liability. A and B are incorrect because although the incident may have merit as a negligence or malpractice claim, especially if physician's assistants generally know better than to give young children balloons and suckers, it would not be cognizable as a products-liability action where the medical services were the essential activity. Physicians' offices are not in the business of making and distributing balloons and suckers. D is incorrect because young children need not wait to sue but can sue through their parents or guardians.

39. A patient received a blood transfusion during an emergency procedure following a motor-vehicle accident. The patient was unable to give or deny consent for the transfusion, which medical-care providers instead administered under lawful authority and by customary means. Unfortunately, HIV had contaminated the blood product. The patient retained a lawyer who filed a lawsuit against the medical-care providers. Products liability was one of the claims that the lawyer pled. The medical-care providers' liability insurer asked its corporate counsel to evaluate the claims. Which of the following statements best evaluates the products-liability claim?

A. The court is likely to dismiss the claim on motion based on settled law issues.
B. The court is likely to allow the claim to go to the jury on disputed fact issues.
C. The court is likely to bar evidence of the HIV type of blood contamination.
D. The court is likely to hold the medical-care providers liable as a matter of law.

Answer: A. Products-liability law generally does not consider human blood and tissue as products. Claims involving human blood and tissue may instead be cognizable in negligence or malpractice. There are also classification issues with writings (not usually considered products and left for defamation and misrepresentation law) and animals (sometimes products and sometimes not). B is incorrect because the law likely does not support a products-liability claim involving human blood or tissue. A judge would likely not allow that claim to reach the jury. There are also no apparent disputed fact issues. C is incorrect because there would be no reason to bar the HIV contamination if the claim was cognizable in products liability. The disease type would be important to the damages. D is incorrect because the claim is likely not cognizable in products liability.

Essay Question: A small manufacturer made a gear-shift assembly according to its own design and specifications, and then sold it to a distributor. The distributor supplied it to a racing team. The racing team incorporated it into a race-car it ran for three races at the end of the racing season and then sold to a race family for the following race season. The gear-shift assembly was manufactured out of tolerance in such a manner that it caused the vehicle to lurch forward in a pit area during the family's first race with it, pinning a pit-crew worker against another vehicle and seriously injuring him. Assuming that the accident was due to a manufacturing defect in the gear-shift assembly, **evaluate and discuss the relative products liability of the manufacturer, distributor, racing team, and family to the injured worker.**

Answer: We must evaluate and discuss the relative products liability of a gear-shift manufacturer and distributor, race team that resold the assembly, and family that used it, when the family's crew member suffered injury due to the assembly's defect.

In general, products liability seeks to pass the liability back upstream from the injured user to the party responsible for the product defect. All entities in the product stream who are in the business of selling the product are liable for the defect, but each such entity may seek to pass that liability upstream through indemnity theories. The parties may have indemnity clauses in their contracts, or they may rely on common-law indemnity theories to shift the liability to the responsible party.

Here, the manufacturer of the defective gear-shift assembly would be liable for introducing the defect into the distribution chain and so should bear the ultimate liability to any of the downstream parties who could claim indemnity. The distributor could pass its liability back up to the manufacturer. So, too, would the assembler, which put the defective gear assembly into the vehicle, although one could argue that the assembler, the race team, was not in the business of selling and so would not have downstream liability. The race team holds the odd position of being both an assembler (in that business, apparently, open to investigation) and also a user (a race team). Its downstream liability may depend on whether race teams are not only in the business of racing but also of selling race equipment, a point for investigation. If the race team was simply a one-time seller of a used piece of equipment, then it would not have products liability. The final user, the family, would very probably not have any products liability. It simply bought a used piece of equipment, the defective features of which it would presumably not have known. One would have to find evidence of negligence on the family's part to hold it liable.

In sum, liability should pass back upstream to the manufacturer of the gear-shift assembly that first introduced the defect. I would love to represent the injured pit-crew worker, given the multiple financially and legally responsible parties. I would also learn a lot about the inside of racing—interesting.

Essay Question: A motorcycle owner had the leg protectors—chrome bars that extend around the foot pedals and beyond the operator's legs—removed from her motorcycle because she did not like the looks of them. The dealership where she bought the motorcycle new removed them for her. The motorcycle looked much better without them and was easier to store in the owner's small garage next to her motor vehicle. One day the motorcycle tipped over on the owner when she brought it to a sudden stop at an intersection. The owner's leg was badly injured when crushed under the motorcycle. **Identify, discuss, and evaluate the dealer's defenses to the owner's products-liability claim.**

Answer: We must identify, discuss, and evaluate a motorcycle dealership's defenses to a claim brought by an owner who had the dealership remove the motorcycle's leg protectors but then had the motorcycle tip over and crush her leg without the protectors.

Strict products liability recognizes several defenses based on the plaintiff's own conduct, including contributory or comparative negligence, assumption of the risk, product modification or misuse, sophisticated user, and open and obvious. The time defenses of the statute of limitations and a statute of repose are other potential defenses. The misconduct of a learned intermediary, the injury's unforeseeability, and policy defenses of worker's compensation exclusive remedy, federal preemption, and government specification are other defenses sometimes available.

The first applicable defense, product modification, may also be thought of as part of the plaintiff's case to show non-modification. But treating it as a defense, it raises problematic issues. Removing the leg protectors modifies the original design, but the dealership removed the protectors, not some other party. Presumably (a point for investigation), dealerships may commonly remove leg protectors. I cannot imagine an authorized dealership modifying the authorized product in a way that the manufacturer prohibits. So probably, removing the protectors was no modification of the product but instead a foreseeable adaptation by the manufacturer's own dealer to an intended design and foreseeable use. The better defense is sophisticated user or open and obvious. In the removal of the leg protectors, the injured rider would almost certainly have seen their purpose and understood what she was risking. Notice that the facts say that "the owner had" the protectors removed. She must have given some instruction to do so after having seen them on the motorcycle. She may not have fully appreciated the risks of their removal, but that argument is probably a hard sell. It seems obvious that the motorcycle tipping over without leg protectors might catch the rider's leg. Ask the dealer's employees who dealt with her over the protectors' removal, and you might find some interesting testimony. Assumption of risk is a related applicable defense, that the injured rider voluntarily assumed the risk of a leg crush when she specifically directed that the dealer remove the leg protectors. Product misuse does not really apply because she used the motorcycle without leg protectors when the dealership and probably also the manufacturer foresaw it as an acceptable use. Contributory or comparative negligence may apply as to the specific circumstance of the rider tipping over the motorcycle. Was she going too fast or stopping too suddenly? Did she misapply the brake or negligently fail to keep the motorcycle straight? Investigation would help here. I see no facts to support a statute of limitations, statute of repose, or preemption defense.

In sum, the dealership may well have a good sophisticated-user, open-and-obvious, or assumption-of-risk defense for the injured owner having directed that the dealership remove the leg protectors that would have protected her injured leg. On the whole, I would rather represent the dealership in defense of the case and likely would not take the case as a plaintiff's lawyer.

Essay Question: Homeowner hired a boiler company to install a new gas furnace in his house. The company chose, supplied, and installed a model that, although advertised to handle a house the size of homeowner's house, was in fact inadequate to keep the house heated. As a result, the furnace ran constantly during a very cold spell when the homeowner was away, further resulting in the furnace's complete failure and the freezing and bursting of pipes throughout the house. **Evaluate whether the homeowner has a products-liability claim against the company for the property damage to the house.**

Answer: We must address whether a homeowner has a products-liability claim against a boiler company when the company installed a too-small furnace that failed, causing pipes to burst throughout the house. These facts implicate the question of products liability for a mixed sales-service transaction.

The law resolves mixed products sale-or-service cases by asking which predominated, the product sale or the service? While a company in the business of selling products would have strict products liability, a company only providing a service in some way involving another's product would not have products liability. The predominance test tells whether products liability applies in close cases.

Ordinarily, one might conclude that a homeowner's purchase of a new furnace involves a transaction in which the product sale, not the installation service, predominates. One might compare the cost of the furnace with the installation cost (a point for investigation) as one way to measure. If the furnace was the bulk of the total cost, then again one might conclude that product sale predominated over installation service. But notice here that the facts state that the installer company "chose, supplied, and installed a model" that was inadequate to heat the homeowner's house. It sounds more like the company, a *boiler* company, after all, providing a *gas* furnace, was a contractor ensuring adequate heat (the service predominating) than a sales company ensuring an adequate product (the sale predominating). There is no mention whether the homeowner considered several furnaces, the facts stating to the contrary that the company chose the furnace. The service may have predominated, in which case the company would have no products liability. It would be interesting to know whether the company had several possible furnace-makers and models to choose from, in which case again the installation service may have predominated, or whether the company had an exclusive arrangement with just one furnace maker, in which case product-sale may have been the greater part of the transaction. The facts do state that the furnace was advertised to heat a home this size when it did not, which suggests a warranty theory against the manufacturer, although the call of the question asked only about products liability as the boiler company.

In sum, on a close call, it sounds like the service in this sale may have predominated and that the homeowner would thus *not* have products-liability theories against the boiler company, although the homeowner would have other liability theories such as simple negligence in the specification of a too-small furnace. I would gladly represent any party in this matter, helping them to sort out relative responsibilities and liabilities in this interesting case.

WEEK 4

40. A developer retained an excavator to dig foundations for an urban highrise. The excavator encountered rock that the excavator could only economically remove with blasting. The excavator, who had substantial experience in blasting, followed all reasonable precautions regarding the work. Nevertheless, an unpredictable blast scattered debris over a neighboring auto dealership, ruining the paint job on every vehicle. The dealership's insurer paid for the vehicle damage. The insurer then retained counsel to evaluate a tort claim against the excavator by subrogation into the dealership's rights. Which of the following is the best evaluation of the insurer's claim against the excavator?

A. The insurer has no strict-liability claim because the excavator followed reasonable precautions.
B. The insurer has no strict-liability claim because digging foundations is a reasonable necessity.
C. The insurer has a negligence claim because the excavator must have done something wrong.
D. The insurer has a strict-liability claim based on the conduct of an abnormally dangerous activity.

Answer: D. Strict liability exists for abnormally dangerous activities, defined in the Second Restatement by the inability to eliminate a high risk of harm from uncommon activities of uncertain value. Most likely, blasting in an urban area is sufficiently uncommon of an activity that there would strict liability for resulting injury, even when done with reasonable care. A is incorrect because strict liability does not require proof of unreasonable actions. The liability is strict, not contingent on proof of fault. B is incorrect because although digging foundations may be necessary, blasting is probably a sufficiently unusual means that it would give rise to strict liability for resulting injury or damage. C is incorrect because the facts state that the excavator followed all reasonable precautions.

41. A rancher maintained a small herd of cattle on a feedlot in an area that had grown progressively less open and more settled. The county enacted a provision requiring that ranchers fence in their livestock, contrary to a longstanding custom of allowing livestock to have free range in the area. Not long after, neighbors found the rancher's cattle loose outside his feedlot, wandering through neighboring properties. The rancher's cattle destroyed a neighboring couple's elaborate truck garden out of which the couple had been selling produce. The couple consulted a lawyer asking whether they had any rights against the rancher. Which of the following is the best evaluation?

A. The lawyer first needs to know whether the rancher was careless in letting the cattle loose.
B. The lawyer first needs to determine from research why the county enacted the fence-in rule.
C. The couple has a strict-liability claim for the produce loss given the county's fence-in rule.
D. The couple has no claim because the established custom in the area was to allow free range.

Answer: C. There may be strict liability for property damage by livestock, depending on the fence-in, fence-out, or other rules of the jurisdiction. Here, the county's recent enactment of a fence-in rule likely makes the rancher strictly liable for the couple's produce loss. A is incorrect because there would be strict liability whether or not the rancher was careless. B is incorrect because the purpose of a fence-in rule is reasonably obvious and would not necessarily be disclosed by research but instead determined by circumstance, inference, and reasoning, each of which suggests that it was to protect neighbors and neighboring properties. D is incorrect because the fence-in provision would have contradicted and probably changed the custom.

42. A reptile collector determined to obtain a python. Local ordinance prohibited the keeping of wild animals, specifically including the python species of snake. The collector nevertheless located a pet distributor from whom the collector purchased a python. The distributor indicated to the collector to feed the python nothing larger than rats. Some months later, the neighbor's little dog went missing. The neighbor took the occasion to report the collector's ordinance violation to police authorities, suspecting the python's involvement in the little dog's disappearance, even though there was no indication that the python had left the collector's home. Veterinarians examined the python, confirming for the authorities that the python had eaten the neighbor's little dog. The neighbor filed a small claim against the collector for loss of the little dog. A magistrate heard the small claim. How should the magistrate rule?

A. For the neighbor based on the collector's negligent failure to confine the python.
B. For the neighbor based on strict liability for property damage from a wild animal.
C. For the collector if he reasonably believed the python ate nothing larger than rats.
D. For the collector so long as he kept the python reasonably confined within the home.

Answer: B. There may also be strict liability for property damage or injury from wild animals, generally defined as those not common to the region. Here, the python was surely a wild animal not common to the region, insofar as ordinance prohibited its keeping. There would thus have been strict liability for the property damage constituting loss of the little dog. A is incorrect because there is no evidence of negligent failure to confine the python. The facts state that there was no indication the python left the home. C is incorrect because fault and reasonableness are of no consequence when, as here, there is a claim for strict liability. D is incorrect because whether or not the collector confined the python, strict liability would apply for the loss.

43. A family determined that the children would benefit by having the responsibility of a dog. The family chose a breed often used for this purpose and a breeder who had the reputation of raising sound dogs. The breeder recommended a year-old neutered male dog that the breeder knew to be quiet and without viciousness. The family took the dog for obedience lessons and followed the advice in several books regarding proper dog management. A boy unfamiliar to the dog ran past the dog one day pursuing a kite. Without any warning, and even though it was on a leash and had never bothered anyone, the dog lunged at the boy and bit him severely. The boy's parents were in need of financial assistance to pay for the boy's medical care from the dog bite. Would it be worthwhile for the boy's parents to consult a lawyer regarding a financial recovery?

A. Yes because there may be statutory or common-law strict liability for dog bite.
B. Yes because of strict liability for the dog's abnormally dangerous propensities.
C. No because the family did it right in choosing, training, and caring for the dog.
D. No because the boy's running past the dog after a kite was clearly provocation.

Answer: A. There may be strict liability under statute or common law for dog bites. There are a variety of strict-liability regimes for dog bites, and there is at least some prospect that the jurisdiction has a strict-liability regime that does not add other conditions. B is incorrect because although there may be strict liability under the common law for injury from a pet's abnormally dangerous propensities, there is no indication that this dog had any such propensities. C is incorrect because although the family did everything right so far as the facts indicate, many states provide for strict liability where the reasonable care of the dog's owners and keepers would not matter. D is incorrect because although provocation is a defense in many statutory or common-law regimes, running past a dog is very likely not provocation. Provocation would more likely be an act directed at the dog under circumstances where the actor knew or should have known that the act would provoke the dog to bite.

44. A dairy farmer impounded substantial animal and minimal human sewage in containment ponds, planning to turn the waste into fertilizer. The location and soil used for containment had unusual properties that allowed the impounded sewage to leach gradually into surface waters on neighboring properties. The dairy farmer, who had followed the advice of responsible extension officials in establishing and maintaining the ponds, neither knew nor should have known of the unusual properties that permitted the leaching. The neighboring property owners lost substantial productive uses of their properties because of the leaching. A group of them retained a lawyer to investigate their rights to recover from the dairy farmer. The lawyer's initial research disclosed no statutory basis but some common-law authority for recovery. Which of the following best describes the likely common-law theory?

A. Negligence for establishing an unreasonable practice.
B. Trespass for an entry onto the neighboring properties.
C. Strict liability for an abnormally dangerous activity.
D. Products liability for an unreasonably dangerous condition.

Answer: C. Strict liability for environmental harm is typically a subject for statute but may also exist as an abnormally dangerous activity under the common law. There is some possibility that containing waste in ponds is sufficiently risky of an activity that liability for harm from it would attach even given the best of care in the practice. A is incorrect because there is no indication of any negligence or unreasonableness in the practice. B is incorrect because the dairy farmer neither intended that the waste enter the neighboring properties nor knew to a substantial certainty that it would do so. D is incorrect because the waste would not be considered a product and the condition was probably not unreasonably dangerous given the responsible advice under which the farmer established it.

45. An ammunition manufacturer made armor-piercing bullets and marketed them to the general public without restriction. The armor-piercing bullets had no apparent purpose other than to kill individuals wearing bullet-proof vests. A terrorist purchased the bullets and used them in an attack on a military base that resulted in the deaths of several service members, each of whom was wearing a bullet-proof vest that would have stopped ordinary bullets. The decedents' estates retained a plaintiffs' lawyer who sued the ammunition manufacturer for making and marketing the armor-piercing bullets. The plaintiffs' lawyer pled several counts. The manufacturer's insurer retained defense counsel who moved to dismiss each count. Which of the following counts would the court most likely dismiss?

A. Negligence.
B. Breach of the implied warranty of merchantability.
C. Strict products liability.
D. Strict liability for abnormally dangerous activities.

Answer: D. Strict liability for abnormally dangerous activities generally applies to conditions on land, not the manufacture of products. There would probably not be strict liability for manufacturing and marketing the armor-piercing bullets. A is incorrect because the manufacturer owed those foreseeably affected by its actions a duty to protect against unreasonable dangers of its products. It may have been careless for the manufacturer to market the product to the general public without restriction. B is incorrect because the bullets may not have been merchantable, meaning fit for the ordinary use of bullets. That they pierced bullet-proof vests may have been a characteristic that made them unfit for marketing to the general public without restriction. C is incorrect because the bullets may have been unreasonably dangerous and defective under the seven-factor risk-utility test or other test for strict products liability.

46. A rancher bred, trained, and sold bucking bulls for use in rodeos often conducted to benefit charities. A rodeo producer purchased one of the rancher's bulls and kept it in a field. A neighboring farmer had his jacket blow off of his tractor and into the producer's field in sight of the bull. The farmer entered the field to retrieve his jacket, knowing that the bull might charge, having seen it do so on several prior occasions and knowing that the rancher had bred, trained, and sold the bull for its high spirit. The bull seriously injured the farmer in its charge. The farmer retained counsel who sued the rodeo producer for strict liability for a wild animal and abnormally dangerous activity. Counsel served the complaint on the producer who forwarded it to the producer's defense lawyer for answer. Which of the following defenses should the lawyer plead?

A. Assumption of risk and disclaimer of warranties of fitness.
B. Assumption of risk and contributory or comparative negligence.
C. Contributory or comparative negligence and consent.
D. Contributory or comparative negligence and charitable immunity.

Answer: B. Assumption of risk and comparative negligence may be defenses to strict liability. The farmer knew of and voluntarily encountered the bull's charging risk. The farmer was also careless for the farmer's own safety. A is incorrect because there is no indication of disclaimers or limitations, which would not be defenses to strict liability but only warranty claims. C is incorrect because consent is a defense to an intentional tort, and here the rodeo producer had no intent to injure the farmer. Assumption of risk would be the defense for voluntarily encountering a known risk, not consent. Consent goes not to known risks but permitting intentional actions. D is incorrect because a rodeo producer is not a charity, even if rodeos are often conducted to benefit charities. Rodeo production is a commercial activity. Charitable immunity has also been abolished in most jurisdictions, and the farmer would not have been a patron of the charity if charitable immunity exists and applies only to patrons.

47. A farmer maintained a herd of cows to produce milk for the farmer's sale to a cooperative. A rancher sold a nearby property for mining. The mine operator periodically set off dynamite charges that the farmer could hear and sometimes feel when working with his cow herd. The dynamiting disturbed the cows, and the farmer noticed a significant drop-off in the herd's milk production associated with the dynamiting. The famer met with the mine operator. Both agreed that they did not initially expect the dynamiting to upset the cow herd and reduce the quantity of produced milk. The mine operator later consulted a lawyer regarding the operator's potential liability to the farmer. Which of the following best describes the mine operator's potential liability for the drop-off in milk production?

A. No strict liability because the harm must be that which makes the activity dangerous.
B. No strict liability because there is no indication that the operator did something wrong.
C. Strict liability because it applies whether or not the particular harm was foreseeable.
D. Strict liability because dynamiting is unusual and abnormally dangerous in any region.

Answer: A. For there to be strict liability, the harm must ordinarily be that which makes the activity abnormally dangerous. Here, the dynamiting risk is rock debris, not cows put off their milk production. (Recall the mink case.) B is incorrect because strict liability does not depend on showing wrong conduct (carelessness or intent to harm). Strict liability attaches without respect to the actor's state of mind and reprehensibility of the conduct. It depends on the danger of the conduct. C is incorrect because the harm was not that which makes the activity of dynamiting abnormally dangerous. In that sense, foreseeability of the harm is a factor in determining whether the activity was abnormally dangerous as to that claimant for the particular harm. D is incorrect because dynamiting might actually be usual and not abnormally dangerous in certain regions where, for instance, mining is common. And whether or not dynamiting is unusual and abnormally dangerous in any region, the particular harm here was not that which makes dynamiting dangerous.

Essay Question: A mother's daughter stables a horse at a private stable, where the mother often visits while her daughter rides. One evening, the mother heard whining coming from a stall at the end of the stable hallway. Approaching the closed stall door, the mother noticed a hand-written sign tacked to the door stating, "Watch out—dog may bite." The mother peered cautiously over the stall boards and into the stall, where she saw a cute Dalmatian wagging its tail vigorously and acting playfully. "Aw," she said, "You don't look mean," as she reached her hand into the stall to pet the Dalmatian. The dog suddenly snapped at her hand with its mouth, tearing the mother's skin and severing tendons. The mother's daughter later told the mother that although the dog is generally kind, the stable's owners had told her that it gets defensive when in closed areas and had snapped at others. **Analyze the mother's strict-liability claim in a jurisdiction having no dog-bite statute but recognizing a traditional form of strict liability for animals.**

Answer: The question requires analyzing a strict liability claim by the mother of a horseback rider, when the mother reached into a stall marked with a warning about a biting dog to pet the whining dog inside, and the dog tore the mother's hand tendons. The jurisdiction has no dog-bite statute but follows traditional law.

Dog-bite statutes tend to assign strict liability without regard to the owner's or keeper's knowledge of the dog's abnormally dangerous propensities. By contrast, the common law tends to require the owner's or keeper's knowledge of the dog's vicious propensities abnormal to its class, without which the owner or keeper would have no liability. Provocation may be a defense under dog-bite statutes, as may the presence of a warning sign or trespassing by the victim. The common law is less clear about such defenses. Comparative negligence and assumption of risk may also be defenses to strict liability in some jurisdictions.

Here, the owners clearly knew of the dog's vicious propensities abnormal to its class. Dalmatian dogs are likely not normally vicious biters. The sign on the stall, "dog may bite," is perfect evidence that the owner knew of the dog's biting propensity. So also would be the daughter's testimony that the owners had told her that it gets defensive and snaps in closed areas. Given the common law's strict liability, the dog's vicious propensities abnormal to its class (few dogs or Dalmatian dogs get defensive and bite), and the owners' knowledge, the injured mother's claim meets the basic conditions for strict liability. Problems arise, though, from the mother's action reaching in to pet the dog after reading the sign, which may give rise to defenses, depending on whether the jurisdiction recognizes defenses to strict liability (a point for research investigation). Because the mother clearly knew from the sign and her statement, "You don't look mean," that the owners or keepers were warning that the dog would bite, she certainly voluntarily encountered a known risk, constituting assumption of risk, and very probably breached a standard of reasonable care with respect to her own safety, constituting contributory or comparative negligence. The question is really whether the jurisdiction recognizes those defenses. Some do, while others do not. The mother did not appear to provoke the dog (provocation another possible defense, depending on the law of the jurisdiction) because she was trying to pet it kindly, not aggravate it.

On the whole, this case is not the best plaintiff's case because of the mother's careless action in encountering a known risk after reading the warning sign, and thus one that I would hesitate to counsel the mother to pursue. I would want to do the research on what defenses the jurisdiction recognizes, though, before meeting with the mother (or, for that matter, the owners). Otherwise, it would look like I had no answer for what would likely be the dispositive legal issue in the case—not a good start for an otherwise competent lawyer. Know the law of your jurisdiction, or find it out quickly.

Essay Question: Over neighborhood opposition, a media corporation won a court battle for the right to erect a radio tower adjacent to a subdivision. High winds one night during the tower's construction toppled a portion of the tower, damaging three subdivision residences. State safety and police investigations determined that the tower's fall was due to a combination of the high winds and vandalism. The corporation and its contractors were absolved of any wrongdoing. **Discuss and evaluate the homeowners' strict-liability claims for an abnormally dangerous activity, assuming that the jurisdiction's law of strict liability is unclear.**

Answer: The question requires discussing and evaluating the strict-liability claims of three homeowners on whose residences a media corporation's tower toppled during construction, on the theory that the construction was an abnormally dangerous activity.

Restatement (Second) of Torts §520 offers a six-factor test to determine whether there is strict liability for an abnormally dangerous activity. The six factors include: the extent of the harm if realized; the ability of the actor to eliminate the risk; the frequency of the risk being realized; the social value of the activity; whether the activity was uncommon; and the characteristics of the location where it occurred.

Here, the harm factor weighed in the homeowners' favor when the tower's portion toppled because the toppling of a high tower can certainly cause great personal injury (up to death) and property damage (the destruction of buildings). It carries a lot more force than a balloon landing in your vegetable garden, for instance. The steel of the tower falling from a high height is ultrahazardous. The next factor is more difficulty to analyze. The construction company seems to have had some ability to eliminate the risk insofar as it occurred "one night during the tower's construction." It presumably was not secured as it would have been when completed. Yet the official investigation found no wrongdoing. I would want to make my own investigation with private experts. Perhaps construction experts would conclude that the contractors should have protected against vandalism and anticipated and protected against high winds. Even if the contractors had no ability to eliminate the risk of a toppling tower, which seems unlikely, the factor may still weigh for the homeowners because that is where strict liability makes sense, that the one conducting a hazardous activity should internalize (pay) its unavoidable costs. Notice that the homeowners protested the tower's construction. When the corporation forced the activity upon the homeowners, it just seems equitable that it should bear all costs, perhaps especially those costs against which there was no precaution. The next factor, frequency, is hard to judge. I might need data on construction accidents or the estimates of experts to say. The next factor having to do with social value probably weighs in favor of the corporation. Notice the result of the court battle, which may have explicitly or implicitly depended on social value (public policy judgments). The next factor, the uncommonness of the activity, probably weighs in the homeowners' favor because high towers are probably relatively uncommon, at least in neighborhood locations. The last factor weighs heavily in the homeowners' favor because the area in which the corporation built the tower was plainly residential. Witness the lawsuit. We generally preserve residential areas for non-hazardous activities. Introducing into a residential area where there would be families and children with homes and personal property, what is more like an industrial or commercial activity (the high tower) with its attendant risks, makes the corporation and contractors look like they should bear the activity's cost.

In sum, I would love to represent the homeowners here, who likely have a reasonably strong to very strong strict-liability claim based on application of the Restatement's six factors. The theme of an uncaring commercial entity forcing a high-risk activity into this area over local protest is compelling. The case has a great "I told you so" appeal. The court decision to allow it may have been a bad one, and the corporation and contractors should pay for it.

WEEK 5

48. A young man posted a bulletin-board note that he had a Cartier watch to sell. A young woman contacted the young man because she was interested in buying the watch for her father but only if it was genuine. The young man reassured the young woman that the watch was an original Cartier made of 14k gold, purchased by his mother for his father's 50th birthday. He explained that he had inherited it when his father passed away but needed funds to complete college. The young woman bought the watch from the young man but later learned that it was not a genuine 14k gold Cartier. The young woman consulted a lawyer regarding maintaining a fraud claim against the young man. Which of the following evidence would be most helpful to proving that claim?

A. The young man had no knowledge or expertise regarding watches and their values.
B. The young woman paid the value of a knock-off watch, not an original Cartier.
C. The young man's father had not passed away, and the watch was not inherited.
D. The young man spent the funds that the woman paid for the watch to buy drugs.

Answer: C. Misrepresentation is a knowing false material statement made with the purpose and effect of inducing justifiable reliance to the hearer's detriment. Evidence that the young man's father had not passed away and that the watch was not inherited would certainly support that the young man knew that he was lying (making material false statements). A is incorrect because it would tend to have the opposite effect, to show that the young man might have been innocently mistaken. B is incorrect because if the woman paid only what the watch was worth, then she may not have relied on the young man's false statement to her detriment. She would not have been harmed if all that she paid was fair value. D is incorrect because the fact that the young man spent the funds in a manner other than what he represented, although indicating dishonesty, is not dishonesty suggesting the authenticity of the watch. The other lies about his father passing away and his inheriting the watch go to the watch's authenticity and are much more clearly material to the transaction.

49. A homeowner determined to sell his home. The state in which the sale would take place required that the homeowner complete a statutory disclosure form and make it available to prospective buyers. The homeowner seller skipped the disclosure form's question about basement leaks, knowing that a "yes" answer would cost thousands in the home's sale. A purchaser bought the home, only to find out during the first hard rain that the basement leaked. Basement repairs cost the purchaser thousands. The purchaser consulted a lawyer regarding claims against the seller. Which of the following claims would be the best to advise the purchaser to plead in a claim against the seller?

A. Innocent misrepresentation.
B. Negligent misrepresentation.
C. Fraudulent misrepresentation.
D. Fraudulent omission.

Answer: D. Silent fraud, fraud in the omission, fraudulent omission, or fraudulent concealment involves the knowing refusal to disclose under circumstances where disclosure is reasonably expected. Here, the statutory disclosure form required a response to that specific question. A non-response could have been a fraudulent omission. A is incorrect because there was no affirmative misrepresentation, and the omission was not innocent. B is incorrect because there was no affirmative misrepresentation, and the omission was not negligent. C is incorrect because although there was fraud, there was only fraudulent omission, not a fraudulent misrepresentation. There was no affirmative misrepresentation.

50. A homeowner determined to sell her home in a state where there was a statute requiring the disclosure of home defects. The homeowner obtained and completed a disclosure form, checking "no" on the disclosure form's question about roof leaks. The homeowner was not aware of any roof leaks, even though a reasonable inspection of the attic might have disclosed several roof leaks, and shoddy work the homeowner had done on the roof was the cause of the leaks. The homeowner sold the home to a buyer who later discovered the roof leaks when storing items in the attic. The buyer had a contractor repair the roof leaks at a cost of thousands of dollars. The buyer then sued the home's seller, pleading several counts. The seller moved for summary judgment. Which of the following counts would the court most likely dismiss?

A. Fraudulent misrepresentation.
B. Negligent misrepresentation.
C. Innocent misrepresentation.

D. Negligence.

Answer: A. There is no evidence on these facts that the seller knew of the false statement about the absence of roof leaks. Fraud requires proof of scienter, meaning that the seller must have known that there were leaks in order to hold the seller liable for fraud. B is incorrect because some jurisdictions recognize negligent misrepresentation claims involving not a knowing but a careless false statement of fact. C is incorrect because some jurisdictions recognize innocent misrepresentation claims, and it appears that the seller's misrepresentation might have been merely innocent. D is incorrect because the seller engaged in shoddy work, and there is at least a possibility that a court would recognize a negligence claim based on a duty that the repairing homeowner would have owed to future homeowners.

51. A restaurateur grew tired of hearing chefs complain about restaurant blenders. The restaurateur determined to buy the best blenders that the restaurateur could reasonably afford. The restaurateur made a special trip to a kitchen-equipment specialty store, where the restaurateur explained the need to a sales clerk. The sales clerk showed the restaurateur a blender, bragging that it was the best one on the market in its price range. The restaurateur bought several of the blenders, but chefs complained worse than ever about the new blenders. The restaurateur later saw a consumer survey showing that the blender was an unpopular model and brand. The restaurateur faxed the survey to the specialty store demanding a refund, but the specialty store refused despite that the sales clerk admitted that the clerk had known of the survey. The restaurateur then consulted counsel about a fraud claim. Which of the following is the best evaluation of that claim?

A. There is an actionable claim for fraud because the sales clerk knew the statement was false.
B. There is an actionable claim for fraud because the restaurateur relied on the sales clerk.
C. There is no actionable claim for fraud because the restaurateur had sophisticated chefs.
D. There is no actionable claim for fraud because the sales clerk's opinion was not verifiably false.

Answer: D. To be actionable, a misrepresentation must be verifiably false, not merely conjecture, salesperson puffing, or opinion. A sales clerk's statement that a product is the best on the market in its price range is probably opinion or puffing that one would expect to hear rather than a verifiably true or false statement. A and B are incorrect because the statement would still have to be verifiably false. Just because a consumer survey indicates otherwise does not mean that the sales clerk is incorrect as to the clerk's opinion, which would not be verifiably false in any case insofar as it constitutes an opinion. Knowledge and reliance are necessary but alone not sufficient. C is incorrect because although the statement may be true that the chefs were sophisticated, it is a non-sequitur. The restaurateur did not rely on the chefs to choose the blender. The restaurateur relied on the sales clerk, but the sales clerk's statement was probably merely an opinion and puffing.

52. A junk dealer had agreements with several nursing homes and apartment complexes to clean out vacated units. A collector made a practice of visiting the junk dealer from time to time to see if there were valuable items to purchase for collecting. On one of those visits, the collector spied a plaster parrot. The junk dealer knew that similar plaster parrots were a dime-a-dozen but skillfully used the collector's excitement to negotiate a $100 sale price. The collector soon discovered similar plaster parrots available at virtually no cost. The collector reported the

junk dealer to a consumer-fraud protection agency, whose official consulted a lawyer regarding the matter. Which of the following is the best evaluation of the junk dealer's conduct under the common law of fraud?

A. The junk dealer had no duty to disclose under these arm's-length circumstances.
B. The junk dealer had no duty to disclose unless knowing that the collector was relying.
C. The junk dealer had a duty to disclose to avoid misleading the collector into overpaying.
D. The junk dealer had a duty to disclose to maintain a reputation as an honest broker.

Answer: A. Bare nondisclosure, without a duty to disclose arising out of the relationship or circumstances, is not actionable. This transaction was at arm's length between two individuals of like standing where there would be no duty to disclose knowledge of the market for plaster parrots. B is incorrect because there is no basis to claim reliance. The only question was the market for plaster parrots. C is incorrect because arm's-length transactions do not require sellers to disclose market values. Buyers should investigate and determine the market before buying. Buyer and seller may act to maximize their own interests so long as not engaging in fraud. D is incorrect because it would be up to the dealer to decide what reputation the dealer wanted. Not disclosing the market is not necessarily a question of dishonesty as much as sharp practice. It may be a wise or unwise, moral or immoral business practice, but the law of fraud does not condemn it.

53. A horse owner grew tired of several annoying habits of her horse, despite the horse's beauty, athleticism, and training. Those annoying habits included cribbing, windsucking, and weaving. The only way that the horse owner knew to stop those habits was to keep the horse's head tied on a short rope to a solid wall of a stall. If the horse was loose in a stall or paddock, it would crib, weave, and windsuck, to the owner's annoyance and to some detriment to the horse. The horse owner advertised the horse for sale. When a buyer came to look at the horse, the seller tied the horse up tight in the stall so that the buyer would not see that the horse was a cribber, windsucker, and weaver. The buyer purchased the horse for a few thousand dollars less than the seller had asked. The buyer later grew tired of the horse's cribbing, windsucking, and weaving, and demanded rescission of the sale. Buyer and seller worked with a mediator to try to resolve their differences. Which of the following is the best evaluation of the common law of fraud applicable to this dispute?

A. The seller's active concealment of the horse's habits was actionable misrepresentation as confirmed by the seller's willingness to reduce the sale price.
B. The seller's active concealment of the horse's habits could constitute an actionable misrepresentation so long as the buyer did not know of those habits.
C. The buyer's negotiating a price reduction of a few thousand dollars less than the seller's asking price bars any fraud claim because the buyer must have known.
D. There is no actionable misrepresentation because the sale was an arm's-length transaction where the buyer must beware of and investigate concealed conditions.

Answer: B. Active concealment of a condition about which a buyer would want to know can constitute a misrepresentation. The seller's tying the horse up tight was an active attempt to conceal the horse's annoying and detrimental habits. So long as the buyer did not know, that concealment was actionable. A is incorrect because although there was active concealment, the price reduction could have been for any reason including that the buyer might have known. C is incorrect because the buyer may have negotiated the sale price for a variety of reasons not necessarily including the horse's annoying habits. That factual question must be resolved. D is incorrect because active concealment, making it more difficult or impossible to discover the true condition of the thing sold, can be actionable.

54. A franchisee was looking for a prime location to open another outlet. The franchisee met with the owner of a large piece of real estate at a freeway overpass where there was no freeway exit. The property owner told the franchisee that the state was planning to construct an exit off the freeway right by the property. The franchisee purchased the property expecting to open a franchise location as soon as the state completed the freeway exit. The state never did so. The franchisee demanded rescission and, when the property owner refused, consulted a lawyer. Which of the following would be most important to the lawyer's evaluation of the franchisee's rights to rescind for fraud?

A. The property still had substantial value without the state's construction of a freeway exit.
B. The franchisee had no other property on which the franchisee could construct a franchise.
C. The property owner had lobbied state officials for years to build the freeway exit.
D. At the time of the sale transaction, the state was planning to construct the freeway exit.

Answer: D. The seller must know of the statement's falsity for it to be actionable. Honest statements of prediction or intent are not actionable when the predicted event does not occur. Because the state was planning a freeway exit as the property owner stated, there was no actionable misrepresentation. A is incorrect because there would still be a difference in value, meaning that there would still be some damage if the statement was otherwise actionable. B is incorrect because the unavailability of other properties would have nothing to do with whether this transaction was fraudulent. C is incorrect because the important question would be whether the state had plans when the owner said so, not whether the owner had any role in bringing about those plans by lobbying.

55. A partnership involved in packaging and transporting wood shavings for sale decided to sell its business. A business broker told the partners that although they were reputable and their asking price was fair, they would still need financial statements to sell the business. The partners looked through their check registers for the past few years to prepare the financial statements. The broker gave the statements to some interested parties who were impressed enough to buy the business. The buyers soon realized that they were not making anything like what the partners' financial statements had suggested. Working from the check registers, an accountant confirmed that the partners had carelessly prepared the financial statements. The buyers sued under state law that recognized their claim for negligent misrepresentation. Which of the following describes their most likely damage recovery?

A. Out-of-pocket losses associated with the purchase.
B. Benefit-of-the-bargain damages.
C. The full purchase price.
D. The business' value as represented.

Answer: A. Where recognized, negligent-misrepresentation claims may be limited to recovery of out-of-pocket losses rather than benefit-of-the-bargain damages. The buyers would be limited to that recovery rather than receive the full measure of damages available in fraudulent misrepresentation cases. B is incorrect for the same reason. C is incorrect because the full purchase price is not a damages recovery even for fraud, unless there is rescission, which is not mentioned. The buyers appear to still own the business. D is incorrect because value-as-represented is not a measure of damages even for fraud (no less negligent misrepresentation) where the purchased property has some value. The fraud measure is the benefit of the bargain. The negligent-misrepresentation damages tend to be out-of-pocket losses.

56. A boater determined to buy a used boat. The boater located a classified advertisement for a boat within the boater's established price range and specifications. The boater arranged to meet with the seller and see the boat. At the meeting, the seller told the boater that the boat was seaworthy. The boater nevertheless hired a mechanic from the local marina to inspect the boat, paying the mechanic's usual boat-inspection fee for a report on the boat's condition. The boater then purchased the boat. The boat proved to have several leaks in its hull requiring extensive repair. The buyer demanded that the seller refund enough of the purchase price to pay for the repairs necessary to make the boat seaworthy. The seller asked a lawyer whether the law required the seller to do so. Which of the following would you most like to know before giving the seller an opinion?

A. What the classified advertisement stated regarding the boat's price range and specifications.
B. Whether the buyer knew from the mechanic's inspection that the boat had several leaks in it.
C. What were the purposes that the boater disclosed to the seller that the boater had for the boat.
D. Whether the seller can afford to give a refund or has already spent the boater's money.

Answer: B. The fraud claimant must show that the claimant's reliance on the misrepresentation was justifiable. Here, the boater may or may not have relied on the seller's representation that the boat was seaworthy, and that reliance may or may not have been justifiable, depending on whether the buyer knew from the mechanic that the boat had leaks in it. A is incorrect because although there may have been other misrepresentations in the classified advertisement, the misrepresentation critical to the boater's demand is the boat's seaworthiness, as to which the seller made a direct statement. The boat's price range and specifications are not the disputed issues. C is incorrect because the boater's purposes would have been largely irrelevant to whether or not the boat was seaworthy, which the seller represented and the boater evidently required, from the use to which the boater apparently put the boat. D is incorrect because although it may be a practical issue important to the short-term resolution of the claim, the first question is whether the claim is valid, including whether the boater relied and whether the reliance was reasonable.

57. A builder constructed a structure that the builder planned to complete when a buyer purchased it and specified its particular use. Because the builder did not finish the structure, local building officials had not yet approved the building's construction. The builder ran into financial trouble requiring that the builder sell rather than finish the structure. The builder showed the structure to a buyer and the buyer's contractor, telling the buyer that the structure complied with all local building codes. The builder knew to the contrary that the structure did not comply with all local building codes. The buyer purchased and attempted to finish the structure but could not get local building official approval without incurring substantial costs for extensive modifications to correct the non-compliance. The buyer consulted a lawyer regarding whether the buyer had a fraud claim against the builder. Which of the following best describes the legal issue that these circumstances raise?

A. Whether the builder's statement was a non-actionable misrepresentation of law or an actionable implication of false underlying facts.
B. Whether the builder made the statement that the structure complied with all codes with the intent that the buyer rely on that statement.
C. Whether the builder's financial trouble requiring that the builder sell was related to the structure's non-compliance with codes.
D. Whether the buyer's particular use was one that the builder anticipated when constructing the structure.

Answer: A. Misrepresentations of law are generally not actionable unless falsely implying underlying facts. The builder may have merely misstated the law or may have falsely implied underlying facts regarding the structure's construction. Whether the builder committed fraud is likely to turn on that question. Notice that the buyer had a contractor along. Perhaps the buyer was able to determine all facts. B is incorrect because it would be rather obvious that the builder made the statement with the intent that the buyer rely. Why else would the builder make the statement? It also raises a fact issue rather than a legal issue as the call of the question requested. C is incorrect because although it may be an interesting factual issue, it does not implicate a legal issue. The call of the question asked for the legal issue. D is incorrect because it would not bear on the question of liability for fraud.

58. An accountant had a longstanding professional relationship with a client manufacturer. The manufacturer often requested the accountant to prepare financial statements in various ways that were inconsistent with standard accounting practices but met the manufacturer's particular needs for internal board, management, and staff financial reviews. The statements were inaccurate under accounting standards, even though useful for internal reviews. The manufacturer maintained a line of credit with a local bank. The bank requested financial statements to review and approve the line of credit. At the manufacturer's request, the accountant faxed the statements to the bank, knowing that the bank was reviewing the manufacturer's line of credit. When the manufacturer later defaulted on the line of credit and declared bankruptcy, the bank consulted its corporate counsel regarding a fraud claim against the accountant. Which of the following is the best evaluation of that fraud claim?

A. The accountant is not liable because the bank was not the accountant's client toward whom duties are owed.
B. The accountant is not liable because the manufacturer requested that the accountant prepare those statements.
C. The accountant is liable based on overt action toward the third party with knowledge of that party's reliance.
D. The accountant is liable for having departed from accounting standards and prepared inaccurate statements.

Answer: C. Professionals who misrepresent facts are liable to third-parties only when they know of their reliance and take some overt action in support of it. Here, the accountant knew of the bank's reliance and yet faxed the statements to the bank, which is an overt action. A is incorrect because fraud liability will extend to third parties where the professional knows of the third party's reliance and takes overt action to facilitate it. B is incorrect because the manufacturer's request, though presumably reasonable for one purpose, does not insulate the accountant from liability when the accountant knows that the bank will use the statements for another purpose. D is incorrect because the accountant had a reason to depart from standards, and preparing inaccurate statements alone would not be actionable as fraud without some overt action toward the third party with knowledge of that party's reliance.

59. A seller listed real property for sale, indicating that it was a natural woodland and describing its natural features. A buyer inspected the property in winter when snow covered the ground. The buyer indicated to the seller that the buyer was looking for an unspoiled woodland to enjoy and preserve. The buyer purchased the property that winter. The following spring when the snow melted, the buyer discovered old home foundations, garage pads, driveways, and other substantial evidence of prior human habitation. The buyer sued the seller in fraud for rescission and damages. At trial, the parties contested the buyer's knowledge and reliance, and the seller's intent in misstating the property's condition. The lawyers for the parties then submitted proposed jury instructions for the trial judge's approval. How should the trial judge instruct the jury on the burden of proof?

A. The seller has the burden to disprove fraud by a preponderance of the evidence.
B. The buyer has the burden to prove fraud beyond a reasonable doubt.
C. The buyer has the burden to prove fraud by a preponderance of the evidence.
D. The buyer has the burden to prove fraud by clear and convincing evidence.

Answer: D. Because it is thought to be easy to allege fraud (to allege a false material statement relating to a transaction), it is generally held that claimants must prove fraud by clear and convincing evidence. A is incorrect because the plaintiff buyer has the burden of proof. B is incorrect because the buyer's burden is not as high as the burden for proving a criminal charge, which is beyond a reasonable doubt. C is incorrect because the plaintiff's burden to prove fraud is higher than the usual civil standard, which is a preponderance of the evidence.

60. A coin dealer advertised on the dealer's website that the dealer had just purchased a valuable collection from a well-known and recently deceased coin collector's estate. The coin dealer advertised that the dealer was selling portions of the collection to the first buyers to meet the dealer's asking prices. Another coin dealer bought one of the parts of the collection sight unseen, relying on the advertisement that the coins were mint. The buyer had the coins insured and shipped. The coins proved not to be mint as advertised. If that part of the coin collection had indeed been mint as the seller had advertised, then the buyer would have made a small fortune. Which of the following best describes the greatest measure of damages that the common law of fraud is most likely to support in these circumstances?

A. The seller's undue gain.
B. The coin's market value.
C. The buyer's out-of-pocket loss.
D. The buyer's lost benefit of the bargain.

Answer: D. A majority of jurisdictions measure fraud damages by the lost benefit of the bargain, although some limit damages to out-of-pocket loss. The facts indicate that the buyer lost a small fortune, which would be greater than any other damages measure. A is incorrect because although the seller presumably had some undue gain, the facts suggest that the buyer would have made a small fortune if the coins had been as advertised, which suggests a greater benefit-of-the-bargain loss than the seller's undue gain. B is incorrect because the market value of the misrepresented item is not a measure of damages. That market value may be a factor in determining damages, such as the difference between market value and benefit of the bargain, but it is not alone the damage measure. C is incorrect because although out-of-pocket loss is a permissible measure, and the buyer had costs in insuring and shipping, those losses would likely be substantially less than the small fortune due as lost benefit of the bargain.

Essay Question: An artist designs and crafts expensive jewelry for fine jewelers using 14-kt gold and diamonds. She also designs and crafts much less expensive rings and bracelets for herself and friends using 14-kt gold and fake diamonds—a side-interest that she does not hide from her fine-jeweler customers. Her fine jewelry can cost from $2,000 to $20,000. She often gives away the jewelry she crafts using fake diamonds or, for more elaborate pieces, sells it for amounts generally under $200. Over the course of a year, the artist spent considerable time crafting an incredibly detailed and ornate 14-kt gold ring. It took her so much time and it was so attractive that she did not want to sell it to her fine-jeweler customers, so she set a fake diamond in the ring and wore it herself. One of those fine-jeweler customers saw the artist's ring and insisted that she sell it to him. Without saying anything to the customer about its fake diamond, the artist told him that she would have to have $3,000 for it. The customer bought it instantly, only to find out later to his great surprise and disappointment that the diamond was fake. **Discuss and evaluate the customer's misrepresentation claim against the artist.**

Answer: The question requires discussing and evaluating a jewelry customer's misrepresentation claim against an artist who sold the customer a fake-diamond ring for $3,000.

Misrepresentation, also known as fraud, involves a false representation made knowingly to induce justifiable reliance causing loss. The representation must ordinarily be an affirmative one rather than silence, given the other's duty of due diligence and the rule of buyer beware, unless one has a special relationship or finds a statute that would require disclosure. The misrepresentation must be provably false, not a subjective statement of opinion. It must also be presently false rather than a prediction that does not come true. While fraudulent misrepresentation requires the intent to defraud, some states recognize negligent or even innocent misrepresentation, like a contract-rescission claim and typically limiting damages in those cases to recovery of the amount that the misrepresenter gained.

Here, the customer has an arguable fraud claim against the artist and a better negligent or innocent misrepresentation claim for rescission, assuming the jurisdiction recognizes it (only some do). The representation element is problematic because the artist did not state that the diamond was real. At most, the artist may have misleadingly omitted to disclose that the diamond was fake, in a supplier relationship where the course of dealing or custom of trade may have required disclosure (a question to investigate). Notice that the artist had supplier relationships, so there would have been a course of dealing and probably also a custom of trade. Do artists (suppliers) generally disclose whether a gem is fake or real? One would think so, but investigation is required. If the omission constituted actionable misleading, then certainly there is falsity (the next element) in the sense that the diamond was fake, not real, and knowledge, in that the artist knew that the diamond was fake rather than real. Proof that the artist intended to induce (the next element) the customer into believing it was real would be circumstantial at best and may depend on other detail. It does not seem like the artist was a schemer or scammer based on the ongoing relationships with fine jewelers, but then, there may be other evidence that she did have a motive (dislike for this jeweler, sudden need for money, etc.). We would need to find out. The customer did clearly suffer resulting loss (the next elements, causation and damages), constituting the difference in value between the fake diamond and a real one (a common measure of loss).

In sum, the customer would probably lose a fraud claim because of the weak representation and inducement elements but might win rescission if the jurisdiction recognizes negligent or innocent misrepresentation. If I were to advise the artist of these uncertainties, I would recommend returning the money to preserve reputation and relationship. It is not solely about the legal claim. There are also business (financial), moral, political, and social issues on which I can and should give counsel as a lawyer.

WEEK 6

61. A property owner operated a strip mall in which a restaurant was located. The property owner wanted the restaurant tenant to leave in order to lease the restaurant space to a new tenant at a higher rent. The property owner had flyers printed and put on the windshields of vehicles parking in the strip-mall parking lot. The flyers falsely asserted that diners at the restaurant had suffered food poisoning. The restaurant lost so much business that it closed and relinquished the space to the property owner, only later finding out about the property owner's flyers. Which of the following best evaluates the restaurant's defamation claim against the property owner?

A. The restaurant has a strong defamation claim for which all elements are readily satisfied.
B. The restaurant has a weak defamation claim, lacking substantial evidence on some elements.
C. The restaurant has no defamation claim, lacking any evidence on at least one element.
D. The restaurant would have a defamation claim only if it was a sole proprietorship.

Answer: A. Defamation involves false communication published of and concerning another that, together with extrinsic facts, harms the reputation of that other, with special damages except where damages are presumed. The facts state a clear case of defamation. B and C are incorrect because there is substantial evidence on each element. D is incorrect because corporations and partnerships can also be defamed, not merely individuals.

62. A politician received word that a speaker was saying false and potentially defamatory statements about the politician. The politician arranged to discretely attend the speaker's next speech. The speaker told several outright falsehoods about the politician and the politician's marriage, fidelity, honesty, and compliance with the law. At times, it looked and sounded to the politician like the speaker was reading from a letter as the speaker made the false statements. The politician was unable to obtain a copy of that writing or a recording of the speech, and had only the memory of those attending the speech from which to prove defamation. The politician consulted a lawyer, asking whether the speech was libel or slander, and what difference it would make. Which of the following is the best answer to the politician's questions?

A. The speech was slander rather than libel given that it was a speech read in part from a letter or similar writing. The politician would not need to prove special damages, special damages being presumed for slander.
B. The speech was libel rather than slander given that it was a speech read in part from a letter or similar writing. The politician would need to prove special damages or an exception, special damages not being presumed for libel.
C. The speech was slander rather than libel given its oral presentation and that it was not memorialized in a distributed writing or recording. The politician would need to prove special damages or an exception.
D. The speech was libel rather than slander given its oral presentation and that it was not memorialized in a distributed writing or recording. The politician would need to prove special damages or an exception.

Answer: C. Defamation in written form is libel, whereas defamation in oral form is slander. Where there is some question as to the form, courts tend to ask whether the defamation was memorialized in some manner more permanent and more widely distributed than oral statements. In the case of slander, the plaintiff must prove special damages or one of the four exceptions for crime of moral turpitude, loathsome disease, sexual misconduct, or incompetence in trade or profession. A is incorrect because special damages must be proved for slander. B is incorrect because the speech was not libel, it not having been written or recorded in a distributed form. D is incorrect because the speech was not libel, and if it was, special damages need not be proved.

63. An official completed a complex public-finance matter involving an unpopular private developer. Members of the public made sworn statements to the local prosecutor alleging the official's criminal wrongdoing in that matter. The prosecutor filed criminal charges against the official but voluntarily dismissed those charges after meeting at length the next day with the developer. The local newspaper accurately published that the prosecutor had charged the official with wrongdoing. The official's public support plummeted as a consequence, notwithstanding the charge's voluntary dismissal reported by the newspaper the following day. The official demanded that the newspaper retract its publication of the criminal charges, or the official would sue for defamation. The newspaper consulted a lawyer regarding its obligation to retract. Which of the following is the best advice to the newspaper regarding retraction?

A. The newspaper should immediately retract because it will have otherwise defamed the official.
B. The newspaper should retract as prudent business even though it did not defame the official.
C. The newspaper should not retract because to do so will establish actionable defamation.
D. The newspaper has no obligation to retract because it published nothing other than the truth.

Answer: D. Although it is often said that truth is a defense to defamation claims, more accurately, the defamation claimant has the burden to prove falsity. Here, the newspaper published nothing false, so it has no duty to retract. A is incorrect because the newspaper did not defame the official, having published nothing false. Also, retraction does not eliminate but only mitigates defamation. B is incorrect because there is nothing to say that retraction is prudent business. It may be imprudent to retract when what the newspaper published was truthful. C is incorrect because retraction does not establish defamation, even though it may tend to confirm that what was published was untruthful.

64. A corporation completed a study comparing its regulatory compliance with the compliance of one of its major competitor. The study reflected well on the corporation but drew no conclusions regarding the competitor. The corporation's public-relations office prepared a press release summarizing the study. The press release inaccurately reported the study's results in a way that made the competitor appear to be substantially out of legal compliance. The office printed many copies of the press release for distribution and authorized a clerk to deliver the copies to a media distribution center. The corporation's public-relations officer discovered the inaccuracy and immediately contacted the corporation's counsel, who was just able to intercept the clerk before the clerk delivered the inaccurate statement to the media center. Which of the following best describes the corporation's defamation liability to its competitor?

A. No liability because the press release was merely inaccurate and did not accuse of crime.

B. No liability because the corporation did not publish the inaccurate press release to another.
C. Liability because the corporation printed many copies and gave them to a clerk for delivery.
D. Liability although damages will be limited because of the corporate counsel's prompt action.

Answer: B. To satisfy the publication element of a defamation claim, the false statement must reach and be understood by another. Here, the corporation's counsel kept the press release from reaching the media for distribution, from which one should infer that the press release did not reach another. A is incorrect because the violation of regulations could harm the reputation of a corporation, as the press release itself would indicate. Accusation of crime would not be needed. C is incorrect because the printing and handing to a clerk would not constitute publication so long as that information was not distributed outside the corporation to another. D is also incorrect because there was no publication.

65. A nonprofit agency fired an employee after an acrimonious dispute over the agency's management. The fired employee wrote a lengthy private grievance to the agency's board of directors, detailing allegations of financial improprieties, inaccurate grant reports, and program mismanagement. A stringer for the local newspaper heard about the dispute and asked the fired employee for a copy of the private grievance. The fired employee gave the stringer a copy of the grievance telling the stringer it was confidential but hoping and believing that the stringer would deliver it to the newspaper for publication. The newspaper published details of the grievance, causing a sharp decline in public contributions to the agency. The agency consulted a lawyer about a defamation claim against the fired employee for the newspaper publication. Assuming that the agency can prove that the published details were false, which of the following is the best evaluation of the agency's defamation claim against the fired employee for the newspaper publication?

A. Certain claim because it does not matter how the newspaper obtained the grievance.
B. Strong claim based on the employee's reasonably anticipating the newspaper's republication.
C. Weak claim based on the employee's telling the stringer to keep the grievance confidential.
D. No claim based on the employee's telling the stringer to keep the grievance confidential.

Answer: B. Primary publishers must reasonably anticipate republication and pay for resulting damage from defamatory statements. Here, the employee hoped and believed that the stringer would give the grievance to the newspaper, which would seem a reasonable anticipation given the role of a stringer to collect story leads. A is incorrect because the defendant in a defamation action must have published the allegedly defamatory material, including reasonably anticipated republication. If the newspaper obtained the details by other means, then there would be no defamation action against the fired employee for the newspaper's unrelated publication. C and D are incorrect because a reasonable anticipation of the publication would be enough, notwithstanding the contrary instruction.

66. A blogger wrote regularly about the activities of a labor-union board. An Internet service provider supported the electronic site to which the blogger regularly posted. Several of the blogger's posts included false allegations that officers of the union board had embezzled funds and committed voting fraud in connection with union elections. The board retained counsel who demanded that the Internet service provider remove the blogger's posts. The Internet service provider declined. The board requested counsel to sue the Internet service provider for defamation. Which of the following best describes the action that counsel should take?

A. Decline the board's request, explaining that Internet service providers have statutory immunity from defamation liability when not the content provider.
B. Accept the board's request, drafting and filing a complaint against the Internet service provider for defamation liability for the blogger's false posts.
C. Modify the board's request, drafting a complaint against the Internet service provider and sending it as a threat but not filing it because of immunity.
D. Interpret the board's request, drafting a complaint against the blogger instead of the Internet service provider because the blogger has no immunity.

Answer: A. Internet service providers have statutory immunity from defamation liability when they are not the information content provider. This provider did not supply the content. The blogger did. B is incorrect because the provider has statutory immunity. Counsel would be subject to sanction and grievance if counsel were to file a complaint without legal basis. C is incorrect because counsel should also not make threats without legal basis. D is incorrect because the choice of whom to sue is the client's choice, not counsel's choice. Counsel could legitimately advise the board to sue the blogger rather than the provider, but counsel must not sue a party whom the client board did not authorize to be sued.

67. A securities broker employed a licensed financial advisor to manage client brokerage accounts. The securities broker fired the financial advisor, falsely alleging on federal filings that the advisor had willfully violated federal securities-trading regulations for the advisor's own financial gain. Several other securities brokers refused to hire the fired advisor when the fired advisor disclosed the broker's false allegations. The fired advisor sued the securities broker for defamation. The broker retained counsel to defend the advisor's actions. Counsel prepared a memorandum evaluating the claim and reflecting the applicable law on the disputed aspects of the defamation claim. Which of the following best describes law that the memorandum should include on disputed issues?

A. Federal regulations required the fired advisor to disclose the broker's false allegations to prospective employers.
B. Federal regulations required securities brokers to report fired advisors for the conduct this broker falsely alleged.
C. The state law of defamation requiring that slander claims include proof of special damages like lost employment income.
D. The state law of defamation requiring that the harmful words be provably false rather than mere puffing or opinion.

Answer: A. Some courts recognize defamation claims in which circumstances compelled the claimant to self-publish the false statements. When the securities broker fired the advisor on deliberately false charges, it knew that the advisor would have to tell the regulators and future employers that false reason for the firing. The fired advisor would have a claim for what was, in effect, self-defamation. B is incorrect because the regulations may have required honest brokers to report firing dishonest advisors but would not require brokers to make false allegations of anything. C is incorrect because the matter involves libel (the federal filings) and not slander, where no special damages need be proven, and because the false allegations involve crimes of dishonesty and incompetence in profession, both exceptions to special damages. D is incorrect because the facts do not suggest puffing or opinion and instead clearly indicate false allegations, which thus do not raise a disputed fact issue.

68. An engineering firm engaged in vigorous competition for clients with an established company providing construction services. As the competitor firm gained more clients from the company, the company developed progressively more aggressive marketing strategies. One of those strategies involved negative Internet posts wherever someone mentioned the competitor firm. The company made a series of negative Internet posts one day, falsely alleging incompetent performance by the competitor firm. The competitor firm learned of those posts from a potential client whom the posts had scared away. A little more than one year later, when viewers could still see the posts on the Internet, the competitor firm consulted a lawyer about a defamation claim. The jurisdiction has a one-year statute of limitations for defamation. Which of the following is the best advice the lawyer could give the competitor firm regarding the defamation claim?

A. There are no defamation claims between commercial entities in competition for clients.
B. The false allegation of incompetent performance amounts to non-actionable opinion.
C. Under the single-publication rule, the statute of limitations bars the defamation claim.
D. Under the single-publication rule, a new defamation claim exists for each viewing.

Answer: C. Under a single-publication rule, most jurisdictions treat the original publication date as the date the cause of action arose, rather than treating subsequent printings as additional accrual dates. Although the rule developed as to print media, courts have held the single-publication rule to apply to Internet posts. A is incorrect because defamation law gives no immunity for competitive behaviors. Defamation law applies equally to commercial and non-commercial communications. B is incorrect because incompetence is not a matter of opinion but provably true or false based on comparisons to professional standards. Incompetence can be a matter of fact, not merely opinion. D is incorrect because the single-publication rule treats the defamation claim as arising with the first publication (the first Internet posting), not that new claims arise with subsequent publications or viewings.

69. A small-town resident disagreed vigorously with the mayor's policy of declining to enforce an ordinance regarding adult bookstores. After the resident's public advocacy failed to change the mayor's policy, the resident posted flyers in public places around town falsely alleging sexual improprieties by unnamed town residents. While the flyers mentioned no names, they did refer to the title and office of the mayor. The mayor retained counsel who filed a defamation claim against the resident. When the case came to trial, the trial judge asked counsel for each party to draft a jury instruction on the of-and-concerning element of defamation. Which of the following is the best instruction?

A. The mayor must prove that the resident's publication identified the mayor, meaning that the publication must have used the mayor's name so that there could be no doubt to whom the publication referred.
B. Although the mayor must prove that the resident's publication identified the mayor, identification need not be by name if persons acquainted with the matter would understand to whom the publication referred.

C. The mayor need not prove that the resident's publication identified the mayor, if the publication's allegations were sufficiently defamatory to reduce the reputation of anyone to whom the publication might apply.

D. The mayor need not prove that the resident's publication identified the mayor, if persons might be able to use the publication against the mayor in advocating for enforcement of the ordinance regarding adult bookstores.

Answer: B. Defamation's of-and-concerning element requires that the publication identify the claimant, although not necessarily by name if the circumstances make it sufficiently clear to whom the publication refers. If town residents would know from the circumstances of the resident's dispute with the mayor that the flyers referred to the mayor, then there is actionable defamation. A is incorrect because there is no requirement that the publication use the defamed person's name, if those who saw the publication would understand it to refer to the mayor. C is incorrect because the mayor must satisfy the of-and-concerning element. That the publication would defame anyone to whom it might apply does not help identify the mayor. D is incorrect because the mayor must still meet the of-and-concerning element. It would not be sufficient simply to show that persons could use the publication against the mayor in a political issue. The publication must identify the mayor.

70. A college sports team of 13 members hired dancers to entertain the team at an informal season-ending party not attended by any team coaches or college officials. One of the dancers later made false accusations of sexual misconduct by certain team members at the party. Based on the false accusations, a college newspaper published that the team had facilitated, supported, and committed criminal sexual misconduct. The publication referred only to the team, not naming individual members. Two members of the team, who suffered death threats and whom the college suspended based on the publication, filed a defamation claim against the college newspaper. The newspaper's counsel moved to dismiss the claim, arguing that the publication did not identify the two team members. Which of the following best describes the most likely ruling on the motion?

A. Motion granted because the publication did not identify the individual team members, meaning that the facts do not satisfy defamation's of-and-concerning element.

B. Motion granted because the publication referred only to a team of 13 members, and 13 is too large a number for the reasonable person to identify individuals.

C. Motion denied because there may be evidence discovered later that the publication's authors intended to refer to the individual team members making the claim.

D. Motion denied because a reasonable person would take the publication to have included the individual team members as having participated in the misconduct.

Answer: D. A publication can defame an individual by referring to a group of which the individual was a member, so long as the reasonable person would identify the individual in that manner (for reasonably small groups). A reasonable person would construe a story accusing a team of just 13 members of having committed criminal sexual misconduct to reach individual team members. A is incorrect because the publication need not name individuals if the group is small enough that readers would believe the individuals to be included. B is incorrect because 13 is a small enough number to identify individual members as having participated. C is incorrect because the authors' intent is not an element of a defamation claim. The law resolves the question of identification based on the reasonable reader's impression.

71. A manager had a running dispute with a worker whom the manager supervised, involving a variety of work and non-work topics. One of those topics involved the manager's treatment of a female co-worker whom the worker had defended against the manager's charges of incompetence. The dispute reached the point that the manager shouted a false and profane allegation that the worker, who was married, was having an affair with the female co-worker. The manager had shouted the allegation at the worker in the presence of several co-workers, deeply upsetting the accused worker. The worker consulted a lawyer regarding a defamation claim against the manager. Which of the following is the best evaluation of that claim?

A. Tenable slander claim, because the manager accused the worker of sexual misconduct.
B. Tenable slander claim, because the worker's deep upset constituted special damages.
C. No slander claim, given that there is no proof that the worker suffered special damages.
D. No slander claim, because the worker wrongly interfered with the manager's supervision.

Answer: A. Slander claims ordinarily require proof of special damages except where the slander is as to loathsome disease, incompetence in one's trade or profession, sex, or crimes of moral turpitude. Here, the manager falsely accused the worker of sexual misconduct (an affair while married). B is incorrect because deep upset is not special damages. Special damages require pecuniary loss. C is incorrect because although slander claims ordinarily require proof of special damages, and the facts mention no special damages, the facts do fit the sexual-misconduct exception to special damages. D is incorrect because whether the worker had any business interfering with the manager's supervision of the female co-worker is not relevant to whether the worker has a defamation claim. The defamation claim would stand alone on its merits.

72. A woman maintained a reputable home business doing word processing and other office support for independent business operators in her small town. One of her clients made sexual advances on the woman that the woman promptly and firmly refused. She also terminated the client's business services, not wanting to have anything to do with the client. The client then sought to antagonize and distress the woman for spurning his advance. When those efforts seemed unavailing, the client printed and posted anonymous handbills around the neighborhood, making scurrilous false accusations about the woman. Several people whom the woman knew began avoiding her, so thoroughly distressing her that she consulted a lawyer and sued for defamation. The court referred the matter to mediation. Which of the following best describes how the mediator should evaluate the legal merits of the woman's defamation claim, when developing mediation strategies?

A. There is no claim because slander is not actionable without proof of special damages.
B. There is only a weak claim based on an exception to the requirement of special damages.
C. The claim is strong because libel is actionable for harm to reputation without special damages.
D. The claim would be strong only if the accusations involved the woman's sexual misconduct.

Answer: C. Libel claims, based on writings or their equivalent, do not require proof of special damages. The woman could recover for her loss of reputation and distress, without proving pecuniary loss. A is incorrect because the printed handbills support a claim of libel, not merely slander. Slander involves oral false statements rather than false writings. B is incorrect because there is no requirement of special damages, the postings being libel rather than slander, and there is no evidence yet of an exception (accusation of loathsome disease, incompetence, sexual misconduct, or crime involving moral turpitude). D is incorrect because the claim is strong as its stands. There would be no need to prove that the accusations involved the woman's sexual misconduct. Other libelous accusations would also be actionable.

73. A homeowner purchased home insurance through an independent insurance agent. The homeowner soon made a claim under the insurance policy for home damage. The insurance company denied the claim through its own adjusters, not in any way involving the independent insurance agent who sold the homeowner the insurance. The homeowner falsely told several acquaintances around town that the insurance agent had misrepresented the claim to the insurance company, causing its denial. The agent heard about the homeowner's false statements. The agent inquired of a lawyer whether the agent had a defamation claim against the homeowner. Which of the following additional information would the lawyer most want to know to evaluate the claim properly?

A. The reason that the insurance company denied the claim through its adjusters was that the company was trying to meet targets.
B. The relationship between the homeowner and the several acquaintances the homeowner told the false statements about the agent.
C. The identity and relationship of the persons through whom the agent heard about the homeowner's false statements.
D. The agent noticed a steep decline in customer calls beginning right after the false publication, seriously affecting the agent's income.

Answer: D. Special damages must be shown for slander claims, unless there is an exception. Special damages are shown by proof of pecuniary loss from third persons believing and acting on the defamatory statement. The agent's noticing a steep decline in customer calls is arguably evidence of a pecuniary impact from the publication. A is incorrect because it would not strengthen or weaken the agent's claim against the homeowner to know why the insurer denied the claim. B is incorrect because the homeowner's relationship with the acquaintances would not matter. What would matter is whether the statements affected the agent's reputation causing special damages. C is incorrect because the identity and relationship of the persons through whom the agent heard of the homeowner's statement would not establish harm to reputation or pecuniary loss.

Essay Question: A public-school charter academy has a financial audit every school year as required by state and federal law. The latest audit report showed that the academy complied with generally accepted accounting practices and had adequate cash reserves but that a time clock should be installed to reduce the probability of over- or under-payment of three part-time, hourly employees. The academy board treasurer, a respected local accountant, moved that the audit report be adopted, and it was unanimously. One week later, the local journal ran an editorial titled, "Where's the money?" The journal editorial stated that the academy board was "siphoning off" and "misusing" funding once reserved for traditional public schools. The journal editorial stated that the academy was "cash rich" and had inadequate financial controls, that employees were overpaid, and that there was "missing money." The editorial did not name any academy board members but did refer repeatedly to the academy board. The journal editorial was published during the academy's enrollment period, and enrollment had dropped off. The academy's treasurer has said that she needs to resign to protect her professional practice. **Identify, discuss, and evaluate the common-law elements of the academy's defamation claims and claims of any board members against the Journal.**

Answer: The question requires identifying, discussing, and evaluating the common-law elements of a public charter academy's defamation claim, and the claims of any board members including its treasurer, against a local journal that ran an editorial casting aspersions at the academy's financial practices.

Defamation is the publication of false words of and concerning, or identifying, the claimant that, together with extrinsic facts, carry a meaning that lowers the claimant's reputation among at least a respectable minority of individuals, causing special damages unless an exception to the special-damages requirement exists. The defamatory statement must be objectively, measurably false rather than mere opinion or prediction. Group libel, which is an individual's defamation claim based on a statement about a group of which the individual was a member, is a tenable theory so long as the public would attribute the defamatory statement to individual members of the group (a functional definition). Governmental entities have no right to maintain defamation claims.

Here, the academy is a public charter school academy, a governmental entity, and as such has no defamation claim. The individual academy board members may have claims, notwithstanding that they are public officials. The journal's titling "Where's the money?" together with the phrases "siphoning off" and "misusing" funding probably carry a sufficient sting to lower the board members' reputations. A permissible implication is that they were diverting funds to unauthorized purposes. Reasonable jurors could find the journal's meaning to be defamatory, satisfying that element. Whether those words were also false is likewise a somewhat close issue but one that reasonable jurors could find in the board members' favor. The fact that the audit report recommended a time clock might be some evidence that some hourly employees were overpaid (and some underpaid), which could in its extreme be taken as a misuse of funding. But to modestly overpay an employee is probably not the equivalent of "siphoning off" and "misusing" funding, in the public's mind. The context here is that the journal's editorial board appears to have been a political supporter of traditional public schools and opponent of public charter academy schools (a popular stance among teacher-union members), and may have overly shaped the information to support that political view. As to the publication element, the journal certainly published the story reaching third persons, as the facts indicate but also as the enrollment decline may show. We need more information on why enrollment declined, but if we could find some witnesses confirming that it was the perception of the academy as financially and corruptly mismanaged, based on the story, then that evidence would support the defamatory meaning element while also proving damages. Note, too, the treasurer's statement that she needs to resign to protect her professional practice, which is an indication both of the publication and its potential harm. The of-and-concerning element might be thought somewhat problematic because the story only referred repeatedly to the board without naming individual members. It may depend on the size of the board, but probably, the public would attribute these negative actions to all members of even a reasonably large board of 20 or more members, especially noting that the board was unanimous in adopting the audit report. So any board member may well sue and prevail. The extrinsic facts that tend to support the editorial's defamatory meaning include such things as the role of the board, purpose of audits, and use of time clocks. As to the last element of special damages, no such proof is required because the editorial was libel (a writing) rather than slander, and libel is an exception to the special damages requirement. Even if the editorial was merely slander (oral), it may have been enough to attribute a crime of moral turpitude (misuse of public funds) to board members, which is another exception (along with loathsome disease, incompetence in trade or profession, and sexual misconduct). And the treasurer's concern over her professional reputation may suggest that witnesses could be found who would confirm that they declined her professional services because of the article, which would be special damages.

On the whole, it seems that the board members have pretty strong claims, independent of the constitutional issues that the call of the question do not ask me to address. Whether I would take the case may depend in part on how I feel about these public-education and public-funding issues, or what my personal and professional relationship was with the school community and its board members, but the challenge of the case intrigues me.

WEEK 7

74. A candidate was running for election to the school board. The local television news station reported on the evening news that the candidate had failed to file income-tax returns for several years. The report was untrue. The candidate had filed all required income-tax returns. After losing the election, the candidate sued the news station for defamation for its false report. The news station assigned the defense of the lawsuit to counsel who drafted a motion for summary judgment. Which of the following statements to which the news station's reporter can truthfully attest would defense counsel best use to support that motion?

A. The news reporter had no first-hand knowledge of the report's truth or falsity.
B. The news reporter learned of the report from a usually reputable source.
C. The television news station had exhibited no particular political bias or agenda.
D. The candidate lost to another candidate whose public record was spotless.

Answer: B. The First Amendment requires public officials and public figures to prove actual malice in defamation claims. Evidence that the reporter relied on a usually reputable source would tend to indicate that the reporter and news station acted without actual malice. A is incorrect because lack of knowledge alone could mean that the reporter had no basis for making the report, from which one could infer actual malice. C is incorrect because the absence of bias would not establish a basis for the report. The news station needs to show a basis for the report. D is incorrect because it would only tend to indicate that the false report may have made a difference in the election's outcome, helping the candidate's case, not the defense.

75. A journalist reported for a tabloid magazine on the arrest of a film star for driving while intoxicated by alcohol consumption. Police reports documented the presence of illegal drugs in the vehicle the film star operated at the time of arrest. Police reports also documented that a passenger in the vehicle had multiple sex- and drug-related convictions. From these facts, the journalist fabricated an entertaining story of the film star's pre-arrest exploits that included prostitution and drug use. The tabloid published the journalist's fabricated story. In the film star's defamation lawsuit against the tabloid, the trial judge ruled as a matter of law that the film star was a public figure, leaving the remaining issues for jury trial. Which of the following best describes the instruction that the trial judge should give the jury on the tabloid's First Amendment defense?

A. The film star must prove actual malice, meaning knowledge of or recklessness regarding the publication's falsity.
B. The film star must prove fault, meaning careless action outside of the standard of care for tabloid journalism.
C. The tabloid must prove that it did not act with actual malice, meaning that it must prove a source for the story.
D. The tabloid must prove that it did not know that the journalist was fabricating the story to make it compelling.

Answer: A. The First Amendment requires that public figures prove actual malice in claims of defamation. Actual malice means knowledge of or recklessness with regard to the falsity of the defamatory statement. B is incorrect because public figures must prove more than mere fault (negligence). They must prove actual malice. Also, query whether there is a standard of care for tabloid journalists. That formulation of fault is in itself problematic. C is incorrect because the plaintiff film star would have the burden of proof on each element as a matter of constitutional law. The burden is not on the defendant tabloid. Also, a source for the story would not alone be sufficient if the tabloid knew or acted recklessly as to the source's unreliability. D is incorrect because the film star, not the tabloid, would have the burden of proving actual malice, and also, the tabloid would not relieve itself of liability by distancing itself from its own journalist for whose knowledge and actions it would be liable.

76. In exchange for a few dollars and a free meal, an informant told a news reporter that a police officer was under internal-affairs investigation for receiving and using illegal drugs in return for helping a drug dealer avoid arrest and other law-enforcement action. The reporter knew that the informant was notoriously unreliable, especially when offered inducements like cash and food. The reporter knew that he could readily confirm or contradict the informant's allegations through an internal-affairs source. The reporter despised the officer for personal reasons and so published a story on the informant's information without further investigation. The officer consulted a lawyer about a defamation claim, honestly stating that the story was untrue. Which of the following is the best evaluation of the officer's claim?

A. The officer has no claim because the officer is a public official who must prove actual malice, and the news reporter had an informant as a source for the publication.
B. The officer has only an arguable but very weak claim because reporters have no general duty to comply with standards of care such as to investigate through other sources.
C. The officer has a good claim because actual malice includes a high degree of awareness of falsity, subjective serious doubt as to truth, and purposeful avoidance of truth.
D. The officer may have a good claim, but the reporter has a better defense based on the public interest in learning about serious wrongdoing by law-enforcement officers.

Answer: C. Supreme Court decisions further define actual malice to include (that is, to be satisfied by proof of) a high degree of awareness of falsity, subjective serious doubt as to truth, and purposeful avoidance of truth, each of which appear to be present here from the reporter's actions. A is incorrect because having a source would not alone be sufficient if the reporter knew of or had subjective serious doubt as to the publication's falsity, and yet purposefully avoided the truth, which was here pretty much the case. B is incorrect because although breach of a standard of care would not alone avoid the constitutional defense, here the failure to investigate amounted to purposeful avoidance of the truth, where the reporter knew that the informant was unreliable but refused to confirm the story because of a personal loathing for the officer. The reporter's conduct amounted to recklessness and actual malice. D is incorrect because public interest is not a defense. The actual-malice standard is a constitutional standard based on First Amendment rights. There are policies supporting those rights, and the actual-malice standard supports those policies, but arguing public interest without resort to the actual-malice standard does not address the legal issue.

77. A city commissioner maintained a public campaign for more law-enforcement resources for the ward that had elected the commissioner. To bring more attention to that campaign, the commissioner made several controversial statements that the local newspaper published. One of those published statements falsely alleged that criminal interests had privately influenced the county sheriff into not providing law-enforcement resources to the city. The commissioner directed the false charges at the sheriff, with the sheriff's re-election campaign in full swing. The sheriff sued the commissioner for defamation. The trial judge ruled in pretrial proceedings that the First Amendment standard for public officials applied to the sheriff's claim. Which of the following best describes the definition of public official that the trial judge should apply in reaching that conclusion?

A. A public official is any public employee, meaning any employee who works for the government receiving public compensation no matter at what level or in what capacity or office.
B. A public official is any public employee about whose qualifications the public would want to know, beyond the public's general interest in the qualifications of all public employees.
C. A public official is any elected official, meaning any public employee who seeks or gains public office through a contested election in which citizens vote based on candidate qualifications.
D. A public official is any elected official or official appointed by an elected official but not other public employees who are not elected or appointed directly by an elected official.

Answer: B. A public official includes any public employee about whose qualifications the public would want to know, beyond the general interest in the qualifications of all public employees. In other words, public officials do not include low-level public employees about whom the public would have no concern beyond the employee's general fitness for public employment. A is incorrect because low-level employees whose specific qualifications (beyond their general fitness) are not of interest to the public are not treated as public officials. C is incorrect because one does not have to be elected to be a public official. Elected officials would be public officials, but so would appointed officials like cabinet, department, and agency heads, and other public employees occupying positions where the public would want to know their specific qualifications rather than merely general fitness. D is incorrect because the definition does not follow a categorical, bright-line rule over election or appointment but instead follows a functional inquiry over public interest.

78. A prominent actress participated so frequently and openly in social and political causes against child abuse and hunger in foreign lands, that the media commonly described her, and the public also knew her, as an activist. She also benefited from several product endorsement arrangements. An Internet blog reported falsely that law-enforcement authorities in a foreign country had arrested the actress on child-trafficking charges. Several print media republished those false Internet reports as if the reports were accurate, even though they were completely without any factual basis. The actress consulted a lawyer about suing those print media. Which of the following is the best conclusion as to the status First Amendment law would assign to the actress, if the lawyer were to file her defamation action?

A. A public official, but not a universal or limited public figure.
B. A public official, and a universal and limited public figure.
C. Not a public official, but a universal and limited public figure.
D. Not a public official or limited public figure, but a universal public figure.

Answer: D. A public official is a government employee of some standing in whose qualifications the public has an interest beyond an ordinary interest in general qualifications. A universal public figure has prominence and influence, whereas a limited public figure has media access from engaging in conduct around which one would expect public interest. Here, the actress was not a public employee and so not a public official. She certainly had the notoriety to be a universal public figure, as her endorsements show. She was not a single-issue limited public figure. A, B, and C are incorrect because they identify her as either a public official or limited public figure, which she was not.

79. A lawyer represented a woman in a civil lawsuit alleging her long-term imprisonment in slavery by a man. The lawyer knew that the case might someday produce a media blitz, when the media discovered its bizarre and compelling nature. When news of the lawyer's bizarre case broke into the national news, a tabloid published a false story that the lawyer had replaced the man as the woman's slave master. The lawyer filed a defamation claim against the tabloid. The trial judge asked the judicial clerk to prepare draft jury instructions. Which of the following best states the law on the tabloid's First Amendment defense?

A. The tabloid must prove that the civil lawsuit involved a matter of significant policy about which the public would have a right to know.
B. The lawyer must prove that the civil lawsuit had merit such that the maintenance of it was protected by public policy.
C. The lawyer must prove the tabloid's actual malice to establish liability and fault for presumed and punitive damages.
D. The lawyer must prove the tabloid's fault to establish defamation liability and actual malice for presumed and punitive damages.

Answer: D. If as here the publication concerns a private figure but is on a public issue, then the private figure must show fault for liability and actual malice for presumed and punitive damages. A is incorrect because policy questions are not the only issues protected by the First Amendment (not the way the law defines a public issue). The tabloid also does not have a proof burden. The lawyer does. B is incorrect because the First Amendment standard has nothing to do with whether the lawsuit has merit. C is incorrect because the lawyer is not a public official or figure and so would not need to prove actual malice for liability. Actual malice would be necessary for presumed and punitive damages on a public issue.

80. Several patients sued a physician for medical malpractice in a series of lawsuits over a three-year period. Each patient suffered serious injury following the physician's highly questionable medical procedures. The state medical licensing board investigated the physician. The physician's insurer settled several of the lawsuits for substantial payments. As part of a public debate over health-care reform including restricting the right of patients to sue for medical malpractice, a local columnist published an editorial citing the physician's gross incompetence. The physician sued the columnist for defamation. The attorneys for the parties prepared joint proposed jury instructions. Which of the following best describes the physician's burden of proof?

A. Because the common law presumes that assertions of incompetence are false, the columnist has the burden to prove the statement true.
B. Because the publication concerned a private figure relating to a public issue, the physician has the burden to prove the statement false.
C. Because the publication concerned a private figure relating to a public issue, the physician has the burden to prove the columnist's actual malice.

D. Because the publication concerned a public figure relating to a public issue, the physician has the burden to prove the columnist's actual malice.

Answer: B. If the publication concerns a private figure but is on a public issue, then the private figure must retain the burden of proof to prove the statement false. The physician is a private figure, having taken no steps to be involved in any public issue. The columnist was writing on a public issue of health-care reform. The First Amendment requires that the physician retain the burden to prove the publication false. A is incorrect because although the common law may in some circumstances have presumed falsity, the First Amendment requires that the plaintiff physician prove falsity on publications relating to a public issue. C is incorrect because actual malice is not necessary for a private figure's claim of defamation for a publication relating to a public issue. D is incorrect because the physician was not a public figure, and actual malice is not necessary for a private figure's claim of defamation relating to a public issue.

81. A builder depended on a line of credit with the local bank to finance construction of homes on speculation. The builder had always timely paid bills and never been insolvent or bankrupt. A local credit bureau employed a teenager to review court filings and compile credit-bureau reports on local businesses. The teenager mistakenly compiled a report stating that the builder had filed for bankruptcy to forestall civil enforcement related to several substantial payment delinquencies. The credit bureau published the false report without knowing of the usually reliable teenager's mistake. When the report ruined the builder's ability to obtain financing, the builder made a demand on the credit bureau on a claim for defamation. The credit bureau's counsel prepared a memorandum evaluating the First Amendment issues relating to the builder's defamation claim. Which of the following best describes those issues?

A. There are no First Amendment issues.
B. The issue is whether there is fault.
C. The issue is whether there is actual malice.
D. The issue is who has the burden to prove falsity.

Answer: A. Private-figure/private issue cases are unaffected by the constitutional standards. The builder was a private figure, and the builder's creditworthiness was a private issue. B is incorrect because the First Amendment does not require proof of fault for private figure/private issue cases. C is incorrect because the First Amendment does not require proof of actual malice for private figure/private issue cases. D is incorrect because the First Amendment does not address the burden of proof in private figure/private issue cases.

Essay Question: A monthly newspaper's readers are college students who rent housing in the city. Landlords are not popular in the city. The student union had recently distributed flyers objecting to high rents and poor living conditions, and calling for reforms. One landlord is particularly unpopular for renting subsistence housing at high prices close to campus. The newspaper ran an article stating that the landlord is a "slumlord" who makes "outrageous profits," and that the landlord had been "convicted of rental housing crimes" for bad plumbing, roof leaks, non-working smoke detectors, and other safety and use issues. The article pondered whether he might have "done hard time" had he not "made friends in high places," and asked whether he had "paid the right people off." The city's public records show that the landlord had been cited less often than other rental property owners, doing relatively well in constantly repairing his dilapidated properties. He had a heart for students, was charging just enough rent to cover the costs of his expensive and declining properties, lived frugally, and took enforcement action only because he had to and did not want paying students to subsidize deadbeats. The city treats rental housing violations as a civil infraction rather than a crime. The landlord's default rates skyrocketed after the article, requiring that he exhaust his modest cash savings, and he had several anonymous telephone threats and could not go anywhere in the city without embarrassment. The newspaper's only "source" for its article was the student union flyer and interviews with student union representatives. **Discuss and evaluate the newspaper's constitutional defense to the landlord's defamation claim.**

Answer: The question requires discussing and evaluating a newspaper's constitutional defense to a landlord's defamation claim, after the newspaper ran an article criticizing the landlord as a "slumlord" and asserting his "conviction" for housing "crimes."

Under NY Times v Sullivan, the First Amendment protects defamers of public officials and public figures unless the claimant can prove actual malice. A public official is one who controls government or a public employee in whose qualifications the public has more interest than its general interest in any public employee's qualifications. A public figure is either universally well known or a limited public figure who voluntarily inserts himself or herself into a public issue and has media access. If the claimant is instead a private figure but the publication was on a public issue, then the claimant must prove fault for liability and actual malice for presumed or punitive damages, and must retain the burden of proof. The Supreme Court defined actual malice in the NY Times case as knowing or reckless disregard of the truth and in Garrison as "high degree of awareness," St. Amant as "subjective serious doubt," and Harte-Hanks as "purposeful avoidance of the truth."

Here, the newspaper may raise its First Amendment rights under NY Times v Sullivan and its progeny, in defense of the landlord's claim – that is, to raise the proof burden and alter the elements by which the landlord must prove his claim. The analysis of the newspaper's constitutional defense begins with classifying the landlord as a public or private figure. The landlord is certainly not a public official (not a government employee) or universal public figure. He has no general acclaim. The public does not know him. He appears not to be a voluntary limited public figure either, because he did not inject himself into any single public cause or issue. His ownership of rental housing is very probably not the kind of voluntary activity from which he could have expected publicity to develop. There is some argument in the newspaper's favor on this point, given that housing is occasionally an issue in settings like this college town, and the student union had recently distributed flyers calling for housing reform. But the landlord appears to have owned his housing before the issue became public. There is some argument that the landlord is an involuntary limited public figure given these same considerations. He may even have some access to the media with which to defend himself, now that the newspaper has publicly identified him as a "slumlord," although I very much doubt it. Who wants to hear from a slumlord? If the landlord is a public figure, then he would have to prove NY Times malice, which is not actual malice but rather the newspaper's reckless disregard for the falsity of that which the newspaper published. The newspaper's negligent failure to investigate would not alone be sufficient to satisfy the constitutional standard as to a public figure. The newspaper's sole reliance on an anonymous "official source," if that is all that the newspaper had in the way of information, would probably constitute NY Times malice under either Garrison's "high degree of awareness," St. Amant's "subjective serious doubt," or Harte-Hanks' "purposeful avoidance of the truth" tests. Anonymous sources are notoriously unreliable and avoided by responsible publishers, we might want to confirm from industry experts opining on journalism trade practices. The newspaper could readily have discovered the falsity of the statements by inspecting the public records. The severity of the newspaper's characterizations of the landlord's conduct would pretty obviously warrant some investigation beyond accepting an anonymous source. Responsible people just do not publicly suggest felony crimes ("hard time") without reliable attribution. If the landlord is not a public figure, the newspaper would have some constitutional protection if the issue was of public concern, which it likely was, given the student union's activity and the general student concern over rents and living conditions. However, under Gertz, that constitutional protection would only require the landlord to prove negligence rather than NY Times malice for liability (actual malice for presumed and punitive damages), which for the above reasons the landlord almost surely could. A reasonably prudent editor would not have published accusations of criminal conviction, on the basis of an anonymous source, without checking the public record – though further investigation is necessary to determine the nature and identity of that "official source." Although the landlord would have to prove actual malice for presumed and punitive damages, which he might as indicated above, he can also show actual damages from the loss of rents and exhausting of his savings. So he is likely to meet even that constitutional proof burden on damages and have an argument for presumed and punitive damages.

On the whole, the newspaper's constitutional defenses are probably weak at best, although there remains important investigation especially as to the source. I would actually appreciate the intellectual challenge of defending the newspaper, to be involved in that inside inquiry about sources and practices. But if it were a matter purely of money (earning a fee) and justice (protecting the earnest and powerless), I would much rather represent the landlord. He provides an important service and is deserving of representation.

Essay Question: A temp agency provided temporary personnel to an industrial concern on a contract basis. The industrial concern terminated the temporary contract with respect to a temp employee's services. The agency requested that the industrial concern complete its questionnaire on the employee's performance, which the industrial concern did, indicating that on two occasions tools were found missing in the employee's area during her shift and that surveillance tapes indicated suspicious behavior supporting that the employee may have stolen the tools. As a result, the agency removed the employee from its approved-employee list and refused to offer her further employment. **Evaluate the industrial concern' defense of qualified privilege in the employee's defamation suit against it.**

Answer: The question requires evaluating whether an employer has a qualified-privilege defense to an employee's defamation suit, after the employer reported missing tools and suspicious behavior, resulting in the employee's termination and de-listing from a temp agency.

A qualified privilege of self-interest and interest in common protects otherwise defamatory statements when the defendant makes those statements in good faith. Courts may variously define good faith as the absence of actual malice, that is, no knowledge or reckless disregard of the truth, or as no ulterior purpose, such that the defendant made the statements only for the purpose of pursuing the interest that the statements reflected.

Here, if the industrial concern has published a false statement to the agency of and concerning the employee lowering her reputation for honesty and competence in her trade, then the employee would ordinarily have a defamation claim against the industrial concern. Yet here, the industrial concern published that statement only out its own interest and the common interest of the agency to maintain an honest and competent workforce. The facts give no indication that the industrial concern published the statement in any respect other than on the agency questionnaire, which would have been for evaluation purposes. The industrial concern' information was relevant to its evaluation and the evaluation of the agency. We have no indication of any bad faith by the industrial concern. To the contrary, with the missing tools and suspicious activity on the surveillance tape, the industrial concern appears to have acted in good faith in publishing the statement on the questionnaire.

In sum, whether or not the statement is false and defamatory, the industrial concern would very likely have a qualified privilege here.

Essay Question: A restaurant critic published in the local newspaper that the local truckstop diner was not the sort of place to which one would want to go "if the customer had a clean premises, safe food, and good health in mind." The diner's restaurant receipts sharply declined following the publication, with the wait-staff noticing a big dropoff in local customers. In the diner's defamation suit against the newspaper, the trial-court judge denied the newspaper's motion for summary judgment, holding that the quoted material and other like criticism, juxtaposed against false factual references to the diner's having failed health-department inspections, could constitute a false and defamatory publication, and that there was also supporting evidence of actual malice. **Describe the defamation damages the diner's could pursue under the common law and the evidence it might offer to prove them.**

Answer: The question requires describing the defamation damages that a diner could pursue under the common law, and the evidence appropriate to prove those damages, after a newspaper published an allegedly defamatory restaurant review, and sales fell.

Defamation damages can include nominal, compensatory, and punitive damages depending on the state's law and evidence of actual malice. Economic loss, such as lost customers and sales, and loss of business goodwill, and in individual cases non-economic loss such as embarrassment over harm to reputation, typically are the measure of compensatory damages. Punitive damages are to punish, not to compensate, and may depend on proof of the defendant's resources and ability to pay. Factfinders may measure punitive damages based on the size (the wealth or economic resources) of the defendant, the reprehensibility of the wrong, and other civil or criminal penalties, within constitutional limits.

In this case, the compensatory damages would be the big dropoff in local customers. The diner should contrast its receipts before and after the defamatory publication to prove that the defamation reduced its earnings by that amount. The diner could project those past damages into the future. Because of the newspaper's malice, the diner may also be able to prove punitive damages again depending on the state's law. The diner should discover the revenue of the newspaper to show its ability to pay punitive damages.

WEEK 8

82. A homeowner sued the proprietor of an adjacent vehicle-repair facility when the homeowner and proprietor were unable to resolve a boundary dispute, and the proprietor continued to park vehicles on what the homeowner reasonably believed was the homeowner's land. The proprietor filed an answer that denied the homeowner's allegations while alleging falsely that the homeowner, who was an accountant by profession, was a tax-cheating, child-molesting, wife-abusing, incompetent swindler. The proprietor's answer pled no counter-claim, leaving the boundary dispute as the only matter at issue. When a news reporter and several accounting clients called the homeowner asking questions about the dispute, the homeowner consulted the homeowner's lawyer regarding a defamation claim against the proprietor based on the proprietor's answer. Which of the following is the best evaluation of that claim?

A. Absolute privilege protects all court papers, meaning that the homeowner has no defamation claim based on the proprietor's pleading.
B. Absolute privilege protects relevant court papers, and the homeowner has no claim because the proprietor's allegations were relevant.
C. Although privilege protects relevant court papers, there is a strong defamation claim because the proprietor's allegations were irrelevant.
D. There is no privilege regarding court papers, which defamation law instead judges by the same standard as publications in other public forums.

Answer: C. An absolute judicial privilege protects lawyers, judges, and others from defamation claims based on relevant publications made in court proceedings. Here, the only matter at issue was the boundary dispute. The homeowner's professional honesty and competence, and personal comportment with respect to children and wife, were irrelevant falsehoods not protected by the absolute judicial privilege. A is incorrect because the judicial privilege protects only relevant court papers, not all court papers, and the homeowner has a defamation claim. B is incorrect because the homeowner has a claim based on the irrelevant falsehoods. Tax cheating, child molesting, wife beating, and incompetence as an accountant have no relevance to who owns adjacent lands. D is incorrect because there is an absolute judicial privilege.

83. An activist decried a city administration's treatment of homeless persons. The activist used every possible public forum to embarrass city leaders into acceding to the activist's demands for more equitable treatment of the homeless. On one occasion, the activist attended a public hearing of the city commission where the activist scandalized a private developer with false statements that the developer was defrauding a public housing authority while having a sexual affair with the city manager. Consistent with established practice, the commission's stenographer recorded the activist's scurrilous statements for anyone to read in the commission record and archive. The developer brought a defamation claim against the activist. The activist moved to dismiss the developer's defamation claim. Which of the following is the activist's best argument for dismissal?

A. The activist has absolute 1st Amendment immunity for statements to the commission.
B. The activist has conditional 1st Amendment protection for good-faith arguments.
C. An absolute judicial privilege protects the activist from state-law suit for defamation.
D. An absolute legislative privilege protects the activist's statements to the commission.

Answer: D. An absolute legislative privilege protects speakers in legislative proceedings against defamation claims made based on any (not just relevant) matters. The activist made the statements to the commission in public hearing, where there was an absolute privilege. A is incorrect because the 1st Amendment does not afford absolute immunity or privilege. It only changes the conditions for liability. The activist would not have absolute 1st Amendment immunity for statements made with actual malice, meaning those made in knowing or reckless disregard of the truth. B is incorrect because good-faith is not the constitutional 1st Amendment standard. The standard for public officials and figures is actual malice, while the standard for private figures on public issues is fault (with actual malice for presumed and punitive damages). Scurrilous and scandalous false statements about a sexual affair do not appear to be in good faith, even if good faith was the constitutional standard. C is incorrect because a judicial privilege, though absolute, would not apply to statements made in a legislative hearing. It would apply only within a judicial proceeding.

84. A consumer agency investigated multiple reports of infant deaths and injuries allegedly relating to a toy's choking hazard. The agency's chief issued an agency statement warning consumers of the toy's alleged choking risks. The agency chief's statement identified the toy and its manufacturer. The manufacturer later established to the agency's satisfaction that the toy had no choking hazard and that the agency chief's statement was false in several particulars. The false statement devastated sales of the toy and other products made by the manufacturer. The manufacturer requested that its corporate counsel obtain an outside opinion from a law firm whose lawyers had significant experience in civil litigation, as to whether the manufacturer had a defamation claim against the agency chief. Which of the following would be the best opinion?

A. The manufacturer has no defamation claim against the agency chief who has an absolute executive privilege.
B. The manufacturer has no defamation claim against the agency chief because the chief is a public official.
C. The manufacturer has a defamation claim against the agency chief because the manufacturer is a private figure.
D. The manufacturer has a defamation claim against the agency chief because presumed damages are unnecessary.

Answer: A. An absolute executive privilege, protecting statements made within the scope of official duties, extends to all administrative-branch officials at the federal level but in most states only as to higher officials at the state level. B is incorrect because it is the plaintiff's status (the manufacturer's status), not the defendant agency chief's status, that the 1st Amendment would have us classify for purposes of the *NY Times* actual-malice standard. C is incorrect because the manufacturer has no defamation claim. Also, although the manufacturer was possibly a private figure (a disputed issue), the agency chief's statement was still on a public issue (the safety of infants from choking death or injury), meaning that the manufacturer would have to prove fault under the 1st Amendment standard (*Gertz*), which would require investigation. The 1st

Amendment defense might help the agency chief (the executive privilege is here much stronger) but would surely not help the manufacturer. D is incorrect because although it is true that the manufacturer can show actual losses and would need no presumption (need not show actual malice), there is no defamation claim because of the absolute executive privilege.

85. A stay-at-home resident heard reports from neighbors of daytime thefts from their garages. The resident vowed to keep a quiet lookout for suspects. The resident kept careful notes of neighborhood youths and young adults moving around the neighborhood during the daytime. The resident made particular note of what looked to the resident like probable thefts from neighbors' garages. The resident reported those suspected thefts to the police. When doing so, the neighbor mistakenly included the name of an innocent suspect whom the resident observed, but who had permission for activities in and around neighborhood garages. The innocent suspect suffered some expense and substantial embarrassment and distress over the matter. When the resident declined to apologize and continued to regard the innocent suspect with suspicion, the innocent suspect consulted a lawyer regarding a defamation claim against the resident. Which of the following is the best evaluation of that claim?

A. The innocent suspect has no claim because the resident has 1st Amendment rights to address public figures on public issues.
B. The innocent suspect has no claim because the resident had a qualified privilege to protect the interests of others.
C. The innocent suspect has a claim because the resident kept careful notes but failed to confirm the suspect's permission.
D. The innocent suspect has a claim because the matter involves a private figure and private issue without 1st Amendment protection.

Answer: B. Qualified privileges allow one to protect one's own interests, common interests, or the interests of others, without being subject to defamation claim. Here, it appears that the resident merely reported suspicious activity following thefts. Even if ultimately found to be mistaken, the resident would not be liable in defamation. The resident's refusal to apologize and continued suspicion are irrelevant where there is no claim. A is incorrect because the innocent suspect was not a public figure, and the thefts may not have been a public issue. The matter is more one of a privilege to report on issues of private concern. C is incorrect because the suspect has no claim. Just because the resident kept careful notes does not mean that the resident need have confirmed permission. D is incorrect because there is no claim, notwithstanding that there may be no 1st Amendment protection. There is a qualified privilege to report on a matter involving the interest of others.

86. A local retailer terminated a manager's employment. The manager complained to the retailer and then to an administrative agency that the termination was unlawfully discriminatory. When the retailer refused to address and resolve the manager's complaints, the manager filed a court complaint under state civil-rights statute. The manager's complaint falsely alleged that the retailer had made racial slurs and unlawful demands for sexual favors. In its daily summary of new court filings, the local newspaper reported verbatim the manager's false allegations against the retailer, clearly identifying the manager's complaint as the source of the allegations. The retailer demanded a retraction. The newspaper consulted its retained counsel. Which of the following best describes the newspaper's defamation liability to the retailer?

A. The newspaper has no liability to the retailer because of the fair-reporting privilege.

B. The newspaper has no liability to the retailer because the retailer fired the manager.
C. The newspaper is liable to the retailer because the newspaper is a secondary publisher.
D. The newspaper is liable to the retailer because the false allegations alleged sexual misconduct.

Answer: A. There is a qualified common-law privilege of fair reporting to make accurate summary of an official proceeding containing defamatory publications. The newspaper clearly identified its report as coming from the manager's complaint in an official (court) proceeding. The report was privileged. B is incorrect because the manager's firing would not justify false allegations by the manager or the newspaper's repeating those false allegations in its publication. C is incorrect because there is no liability and because although secondary publishers are ordinarily liable to the same extent as original publishers, newspapers have a common-law privilege of fair reporting on official proceedings. D is incorrect because there is no liability and because although false allegations of sexual misconduct would create an exception to the special damages requirement for slander, the newspaper publication was a writing and would therefore have been libel if not privileged, without respect to special damages.

87. A television station showed a photograph of an innocent man in connection with a news story on a suspect wanted for serious crimes involving the robbery and stabbing death of another individual. The station recklessly disregarded information that the station had the wrong man's photograph. The innocent man retained a lawyer who sent by hand delivery and certified mail a letter demanding that the station immediately air an apology and retraction. The station refused for fear that the innocent man would use the retraction against it in a defamation lawsuit. The innocent man, who operated a T-shirt shop in a resort town, suffered extreme distress and embarrassment, substantial diminution of his reputation, and loss of half of his T-shirt sales for the ensuing summer. Which of the following best describes the innocent man's remedies against the station if he decides to sue for defamation?

A. Only nominal and punitive damages.
B. Only nominal damages and compensatory damages for non-economic loss.
C. Only nominal damages, compensatory damages for economic loss, and punitive damages.
D. Nominal damages, compensatory damages for economic and non-economic loss, and punitive damages.

Answer: D. Defamation remedies may include nominal damages, compensatory damages for economic and non-economic losses, and punitive damages, although some states first require demand for retraction. The above facts support each measure of damages. A is incorrect because it omits compensatory damages for economic and non-economic loss, both of which the man suffered. B is incorrect because it omits compensatory damages for economic loss, which the man suffered, and punitive damages, which the law may permit a jury to award. C is incorrect because it omits compensatory damages for non-economic loss, which the man suffered.

88. Over the course of a marriage, a wife told her husband several secrets in confidence. The secrets included incidents of childhood sexual abuse by an older male relative and the challenges the incidents created with intimate relationship. In time, the husband and wife grew estranged and then separated for other reasons. The estranged husband then told several of the wife's friends about the wife's secrets. The wife was shocked, embarrassed, and humiliated by the estranged husband's disclosures, each of which was true but would have deeply offended the reasonable person. She instructed her attorney to include a tort claim in her divorce complaint, as the jurisdiction's laws permitted. Which of the following best describes the wife's tort claim?

A. Appropriation of likeness.
B. Intrusion on seclusion of persona.
C. Public disclosure of private facts.
D. False light.

Answer: C. The invasion-of-privacy tort takes one of four forms, either appropriation, intrusion, disclosure, or false light. Here, the estranged husband disclosed shameful secrets, which would have been private facts, to several friends, which would have been public disclosure, satisfying the elements of that invasion-of-privacy tort. A is incorrect because the husband did not appropriate the wife's likeness for commercial exploitation. B is incorrect because the husband did not intrude on the wife's seclusion. They were close at one time, and she voluntarily disclosed the secrets to him. D is incorrect because the husband did not place the wife in a false light. The secrets were true. He just should not have disclosed them.

89. A car dealership developed and pursued a new marketing strategy centered on tent and other outdoor summer events. The dealership used various props to attract the curious, including a spotlight at night, large helium-filled balloon on a long rope, and a huge inflated likeness of a popular film star the dealership had a local company construct. The film star's likeness attracted local media coverage, which was then posted to the Internet where it was observed by representatives of the film star's agency. With the film star's authority, the agency retained counsel to challenge and end the dealership's use of the film star's likeness. Which of the following best describes the film star's legal claim on which to base that challenge?

A. Interference with prospective economic advantage and business relations.
B. Invasion of privacy for appropriating likeness for commercial exploitation.
C. Invasion of privacy for intrusion on seclusion of persona.
D. Ex parte temporary restraining order followed by preliminary injunction.

Answer: B. Invasion of privacy's appropriation form involves use of persona for commercial or other advantage without the person's permission, with injunctions and damages for relief. The dealership clearly appropriated the film star's likeness for the dealership's commercial exploitation, without the film star's permission. The film star would succeed in this challenge. A is incorrect because although it describes a recognized business tort, the dealership was not interfering with the film star's contracts or other business interests but was instead trading for its own benefit on the film star's publicity value. C is incorrect because although it identifies a recognized tort, the dealership did not intrude on the film star's privacy or seclusion. It traded on the film star's publicity value, which is commercial exploitation, not intrusion. D is incorrect because it describes a legal procedure rather than the underlying legal claim. There is also no indication that the order and injunction could be pursued ex parte (out of the dealership's hearing) because notice to the dealership of the challenge would not result in greater harm. It would instead probably end the harm (end the dealership's use of the film star's likeness).

90. A famous movie star and politician married the daughter of a famous political figure. The couple then had twin children, whom they made every effort to shield from public scrutiny. Paparazzi clamored to photograph the twins. On one occasion when the couple was vacationing at a secluded seaside resort, a photographer climbed to a balcony, pulled the curtains aside on the

open balcony door, and photographed the couple's sleeping twins. The couple learned of the photographs and sued the photographer for invasion of privacy. The court ordered the photographs destroyed and scheduled the couple's damage claim for trial, requesting that counsel draft an instruction defining the couple's tort claim for the jury. Which of the following is the best jury instruction?

A. Appropriation and commercial exploitation of likeness arises with an unauthorized use of a person's image for commercial gain.
B. Interference with business relations and prospective economic advantage arises when unlawful means are used to diminish business expectancy.
C. Intrusion on seclusion arises when there is an unauthorized intrusion into a private place that would be highly offensive to the reasonable person.
D. Public disclosure of private facts arises when there is an unauthorized and highly embarrassing disclosure to the public of confidential information.

Answer: C. Invasion of privacy's intrusion form arises when there is an unauthorized intrusion into a private place that would be highly offensive to the reasonable person. The photographer's intrusion into this private place to photograph the twins would very probably have been highly offensive to the reasonable person. A is incorrect because although it defines another form of invasion of privacy, the facts did not indicate commercial exploitation. The photographs were recovered and destroyed, leaving only the intrusion claim for trial to the jury. B is incorrect because the claim is for invasion of privacy, not interference with business relations. D is incorrect because public disclosure is not the claim. Disclosure of the twins would not have been highly embarrassing. Intrusion was the offense, not public disclosure.

91. Police identified a local accountant as a suspect in the robbery of a jewelry store. The accountant cooperated fully with police, resulting in the determination that the accountant was not involved in the robbery. The police investigation nonetheless documented that the accountant had fathered a child at age 14 and had two affairs in the five years of his marriage. A local newspaper reporter obtained copies of the police reports and wrote a news story including those details of the accountant's personal life. The newspaper's editor-in-chief showed the story to corporate counsel for an opinion before its publication. Which of the following describes the best opinion as to the legal consequences of the story's publication?

A. The story's publication could result in the accountant having an abuse of process claim for misuse of legal proceedings.
B. The story's publication could result in the accountant having an invasion of privacy claim for public disclosure of private facts.
C. The story's publication could result in increased attention to the robbery leading to tips that would solve it after further investigation.
D. The story's publication could result in the accountant's son discovering the identity of his father bringing together a family.

Answer: B. Invasion of privacy's disclosure form arises when there is publication without legitimate interest to more than a few persons of private facts the disclosure of which would be offensive to the reasonable person. Fathering a child at age 14 and having affairs during marriage are private matters the public disclosure of which could be highly offensive to the reasonable person. A is incorrect because the newspaper would not have initiated or employed any legal proceeding by publication. Abuse of process is the wrong form of action. C is incorrect because the editor-in-chief would be seeking corporate counsel's opinion on the legal consequences to the paper, not the effect of publication on the solving of the crime. D is incorrect because the call of the question asks for legal consequences, not familial consequences. Also, the facts do not indicate that the son is unaware of the father's identity.

92. A prominent local businessman was arrested and charged for first-degree criminal sexual misconduct involving a young woman. A radio station owned and operated by an acquaintance of the businessman sent a reporter to the businessman's preliminary examination, at which defense counsel required the prosecutor to disclose the victim's name. The radio-station reporter then disclosed the victim's name in a news report about the crime. State statute prohibited media disclosure of rape-victim names. The news report resulted in death threats and other harassment of the young woman. She consulted a lawyer about suing the radio station for violating the state statute. Which of the following best describes the woman's invasion-of-privacy claim against the radio station?

A. The radio station is not liable to the woman because there is no invasion-of-privacy claim for reporting truthfully on matters that media judge interesting.
B. The radio station is liable to the woman because it placed her in a false light relative to her individual rights not to be identified as the victim of a rape.
C. The radio station would be liable to the woman for intrusion on seclusion of persona except for the intrusion having been made by the prosecutor and police.
D. The radio station would be liable to the woman for public disclosure of private facts except for the constitutional protection to publish matters of public interest.

Answer: D. The disclosure form of invasion of privacy must overcome constitutional protection to publish matters of public interest. The radio station disclosed a highly private matter the disclosure of which would surely highly offend the reasonable person, but the matter may also have been of public interest over the discovery and conviction of the wrongdoer and resolution of the serious criminal charge. A is incorrect because public disclosure of private facts is a recognized form of invasion of privacy even where the reported information is truthful and interesting. B is incorrect because although false light is a form of invasion of privacy, it does not apply here. The radio station did not inaccurately portray the woman in any respect. C is incorrect because the radio station did not enter a private place to obtain the information. It reported on a court proceeding. There was no intrusion, that being the wrong form of invasion of privacy for this case.

93. A developer planned to raze portions of a popular but decrepit arts district to build new downtown housing. Although city officials supported the developer's plans, public sentiment did not. A local arts magazine hired a photographer to illustrate a negative story on the developer's proposed plans. The arts magazine then published a photograph of the developer standing in front of an adult bookstore, in a manner that suggested that he was a patron of the adult bookstore when he had only been walking by when stopped by an arts-magazine representative for the photographer to take the photograph. Influenced by the arts magazine's story and public response to it, city officials nixed the developer's plans. The developer asked its retained counsel for an opinion regarding the liability of the arts magazine to the developer. Which of the following best describes that liability?

A. The arts magazine is not liable to the developer because the First Amendment protects its actions.

B. The arts magazine is not liable to the developer because there is no tort claim for taking public photographs.
C. The arts magazine may be liable to the developer for misrepresentation for having induced the plan's demise.
D. The arts magazine may be liable to the developer for the false light form of invasion of privacy.

Answer: D. Invasion of privacy's false light form arises when a person publicly depicts another in a false manner that would be highly offensive to the reasonable person. The arts magazine portrayed the developer in a false negative light that would likely have been highly offensive to the reasonable person. A is incorrect because the First Amendment does not protect deliberate manipulations to place a person in a false light. B is incorrect false light can protect a person against deliberate manipulations of circumstances that then place the person in a highly offensive false light. C is incorrect because misrepresentation involves a communication by the defendant to the plaintiff that induces the plaintiff to take action detrimental to the plaintiff, not actions or communications that cause others to decline to deal with the plaintiff.

94. A feminist scholar at a private university made it her career's work to urge legal challenges to the pornographic exploitation of women. To attack the feminist scholar's credibility, an adult magazine crudely portrayed the feminist scholar being violently sexually victimized. The adult magazine's portrayal caused the feminist scholar severe emotional distress resulting in physical manifestation. The scholar retained legal counsel who filed a claim against the magazine for intentional infliction of emotional distress. The magazine's counsel filed a motion to dismiss based on the First Amendment. The trial judge assigned the briefs to a law clerk for a bench memorandum. Which of the following describes the best evaluation?

A. The magazine likely has a First Amendment defense to parody a public figure.
B. The magazine likely has a First Amendment defense to destroy a public official.
C. The magazine likely has no First Amendment defense for intentional infliction.
D. The magazine likely has no First Amendment defense to destroy credibility.

Answer: A. The First Amendment protects the right of media to intentionally inflict emotional distress if also done for purposes of destroying a person's reputation by parody. Although the feminist scholar is likely a voluntary public figure for her public stance against pornography, the Supreme Court has in a similar case protected intentional infliction of distress. B is incorrect because the scholar was not a public official but a public figure, and the right is not to destroy so much as to challenge or criticize by parody. C is incorrect because there likely is a First Amendment defense even for intentional infliction, as the Supreme Court has held in a similar case. D is incorrect because there likely is a defense to attack and, if successful, then to destroy credibility.

Essay Question: A bride was horrified to learn from an acquaintance that a national comedy magazine had used one of her wedding photographs to depict her as participating in and winning an "ugliest bride" contest. She had never participated in any such contest and had not given consent to anyone to use her photograph. She was aware that the photography service that had taken her wedding pictures had for a brief time displayed some of them on its website and guessed that the magazine had taken the photograph from there. What form of tort action does the bride have against the magazine, if any? **Analyze and evaluate the bride's likelihood of prevailing.**

Model Answer: The question requires analyzing and evaluating whether a bride has some form of tort action, particularly invasion of privacy, against a comedy magazine that used her wedding photograph without permission in a mock "ugliest bride" competition.

One finds four different forms of invasion-of-privacy tort in the common law: intrusion on seclusion of persona; appropriation or commercial exploitation; public disclosure of private facts; and false light. Intrusion is a highly offensive invasion into a place or matter in which the claimant has a reasonable expectation of privacy. Appropriation involves the use of another's name, likeness, or image without consent, for economic or other gain. While person's claiming the appropriation tort are often celebrities whose name, likeness, or image has value, the claimant need not be a celebrity. Use of the name, likeness, or image is alone enough. Public disclosure of private facts is the highly offensive disclosure of true facts as to which the claimant has a reasonable expectation of privacy. The false-light form, recognized in fewer states, is similar to the defamation tort except that the false-light tort involves the claimant's false depiction or portrayal more so than false statements of fact, lowering the claimant's reputation or subjecting the claimant to ridicule in a manner highly offensive to the reasonable person. Not all states recognize all four forms, so we would need to investigate whether the state law applicable to the bride's claim does recognize the form or forms that the bride would need to plead here.

Here, the bride may have a cause of action for invasion of privacy. The first form she may pursue is the appropriation form of invasion of privacy. Although the misuse without consent is often commercial, as is likely the case here (query whether the magazine publication is a for-profit publication), the use need not be for commercial gain. By using the bride's likeness, meaning her wedding photograph, the magazine has appropriated that which belonged to the bride. Simply because the magazine may have found her image on the internet does not mean that the magazine may use her image for anything it wishes. The fact that the magazine also held the bride up to ridicule for allegedly winning an ugly bride contest that she did not in fact enter suggests that the magazine may also have committed the false-light tort. The bride would certainly be reasonably and highly offended by the magazine's portrayal of her as entering and winning an ugly bride contest, which was patently false insofar as she had never entered any such contest nor given consent to her photograph's use in any such story. Intentional infliction of emotional distress is another potential theory, although the conduct may or may not be so outrageous as to be beyond all bounds of decency in civil society.

In sum, the bridge surely has an invasion-of-privacy claim in the appropriation form and likely also in the false-light form if available in the jurisdiction. The bride's challenge, though, is a practical one, that pursuing the claim may draw more attention to the embarrassing story than simply ignoring it. Assuming the bride's goal is to preserve or restore her peace of mind and reputation, then pursuing civil litigation that calls attention to the magazine story may have the opposite effect of prolonging her embarrassment and increasing the harm to her reputation. Although the bride would very likely prevail, as a near certainty, she would still need to think carefully about the wisdom of pursuing the claim. I would want to be sure, too, that the magazine was collectible and, indeed, would want to know more about the bride's harm and distress.

WEEK 9

95. An elderly woman entered a Laundromat carrying a plastic hamper of soiled clothing. The elderly woman tripped and fell when her heel caught in several frayed loops of an old mat on the floor just inside the door of the Laundromat. The woman broke her elbow in the fall, requiring medical treatment in the form of casting and causing her much pain and to incur substantial medical expense. She retained counsel to make a negligence demand on the Laundromat's liability insurer. Counsel turned the file over to a law clerk to draft the demand. Which of the following best describes the damages that the demand should include?

A. Nominal damages consisting of humiliation and embarrassment and punitive damages for allowing a dangerous condition to persist.
B. Compensatory damages consisting of pain and suffering, lost enjoyment of life, loss of consortium, and loss of services and support.

C. Economic or special damages consisting of the medical expense and non-economic or general damages consisting of pain and disability.
D. Economic or special damages consisting of loss of earnings and non-economic or general damages consisting of scarring and disfigurement.

Answer: C. There are two main categories of personal injury damages, economic and non-economic, sometimes called special and general. The elderly woman had economic loss in the form of medical expense and non-economic loss in the form of pain and disability. A is incorrect because nominal damages are unnecessary where there are compensatory damages to claim, humiliation and embarrassment would actually involve compensatory not nominal damages, and using a frayed rug is probably not so egregious a form of misconduct (such as gross negligence or recklessness) as to warrant punitive damages. B is incorrect because although compensatory damages often include these categories, there is no evidence of consortium loss (no spouse mentioned) or loss of services and support. D is incorrect because there is no evidence of lost earnings or of scarring and disfigurement.

96. A carpenter drove his pickup truck to lunch from a jobsite during the height of the construction season. On the way back to the jobsite, a negligent driver ran a motor vehicle into the carpenter's pickup truck. The collision fractured the carpenter's hip, putting him in the hospital for several weeks. The carpenter later consulted with a lawyer regarding the potential damages value of a negligence claim, in a jurisdiction where there is no no-fault act to modify the common law. Which of the following best describes the carpenter's economic loss supporting the damages element of his negligence claim?

A. The carpenter's damaged or destroyed truck meant that he would lose the value of the earnings he could have made with it.
B. The carpenter's inability to work from the broken hip meant that he would lose customers and profits from his construction business.
C. The carpenter's broken hip from the motor-vehicle accident meant that he had mounting medical expense and loss of earnings.
D. The carpenter's broken hip from the motor-vehicle accident meant that he had substantial pain, suffering, disability, and lost enjoyment of life.

Answer: C. Economic loss typically begins with medical expense and wage loss. Several weeks in the hospital would mean substantial medical expense and a period of complete disability from carpentry work. A is incorrect because the more substantial economic losses would be the medical expense and work loss, and because although damage to the truck would be one economic loss, it would be measured by diminution in the truck's value, not what the carpenter could have earned using the truck. He must mitigate his damages by renting another truck. B is incorrect because it omits the substantial medical expense as a typical form of economic loss and because lost earnings (the wage value of work that the injured person was unable to perform), not loss of business profits, is the general measure for work loss. D is incorrect because it describes non-economic rather than economic loss.

97. A teenager had mental disabilities that would keep the teenager from gainful employment throughout her life. The teenager subsequently suffered permanent physical disability when a paragliding enthusiast negligently crashed into the teenager. Health insurance maintained by the teenager's parents paid the substantial cost of the teenager's medical care from the paragliding injury. Unable to enjoy physical activity, the teenager grew despondent, as if she had quit on life. The teenager's parents consulted with counsel about the teenager's non-economic damages in a negligence claim against the paragliding enthusiast. Which of the following best describes those non-economic damages?

A. Pain from the paragliding crash into the teenager and from the subsequent medical treatment.
B. Pain, suffering, mental and emotional distress, depression, disability, and loss of enjoyment of life.
C. Loss of earnings and earning capacity, loss of work benefits, and expense of medical care.
D. Loss of love, society, services, companionship, and other support known as loss of consortium.

Answer: B. Non-economic loss is usually thought of as pain and suffering but may include humiliation, shock, fright, mortification, scarring, disfigurement, disability, and loss of enjoyment of life. The teenager's despondency presumably indicates substantial mental and emotional distress and loss of enjoyment of life. A is incorrect because it describes only a small portion of the total pain and total non-economic loss. Non-economic loss includes much more than simply the pain from the initial injury and from medical treatment. C is incorrect because it describes economic, not non-economic, loss. D is incorrect because loss of consortium involves losses from an injured spouse, and here the teenager has no spouse.

98. A wife maintained the home while her husband worked. The wife had a surgery in which substandard medical care resulted in her severe permanent injury and physical disability. The couple did not initially realize and plan for the impact that the wife's injury would have on their household and relationship. The husband gradually realized that he would have to take over some household chores and hire help to handle others. The wife was also unable through her pain to express any intimacy toward the husband. The wife and husband consulted a trial lawyer regarding a medical-malpractice claim. Which of the following best describes the husband's right to recover for the above losses?

A. The husband has no right to recover because it was the wife whom the substandard medical care injured.
B. The husband has no right to recover, but the wife may recover for the husband's loss of love, society, and services.
C. The husband may recover for his loss of love, society, and services, whether or not the wife has a malpractice claim.
D. The husband may recover for his loss of love, society, and services, under a derivative claim for loss of consortium.

Answer: D. The spouse of an injured tort victim may have a claim for loss of consortium, meaning loss of services, support, love, society, and companionship. The spouse's claim is derivative, meaning that the injured spouse must first have the right to recover. A is incorrect because the husband does have a loss of consortium claim on the given facts. B is incorrect because the husband's right to recover is his own right, even though derivative of the injured wife's right. C is incorrect because the husband's claim is derivative, meaning that the wife must first have a right to recover, without which the husband has no right.

99. A drunken driver let his motor vehicle wander from the road and into an adjacent marked bicycle lane, striking and breaking the arm of a child bicyclist. The child's parents filed suit against the driver for the child's injury. A year later, well after the child's arm had healed, the court tried the case to a jury. During the trial, the driver surprised his own counsel by testifying that bicycle lanes were a bad idea and that the child was stupid for using the lane. The driver's testimony visibly angered several jurors. After deliberations, the jury returned a $6 million award for the child's broken arm. The driver's trial counsel then advised the driver and his insurer regarding appropriate post-trial proceedings. Which of the following describes the best advice?

A. The driver and insurer should pay as much of the verdict as they can as quickly as possible to avoid judgment interest and collection action.
B. The driver should appeal because the appellate court might agree that bicycle lanes are a bad idea and that the child was responsible.
C. The driver should file a motion for remittitur to reduce or set aside the verdict inflamed by prejudice aroused by the driver's insensitive testimony.
D. The driver should file a motion for new trial based on a verdict against the great weight of the evidence as to liability and damages.

Answer: C. On motion for remittitur, the court will reduce or set aside excessive damages verdicts which are the result of passion and prejudice or not supported by the evidence. Here, the jury was likely inflamed by the driver's insensitive testimony because $6 million for a child's broken arm that healed well within one year is an excessive verdict. A is incorrect because there are substantial grounds to have the verdict reduced or set aside rather than paying the verdict. The insurance is likely to be less than the damage award, and the driver is unlikely to have the money to pay the uninsured portion of the verdict. B is incorrect because there are grounds to have the verdict remitted, and an appeal over bicycle lanes being a bad idea would be frivolous. D is incorrect because the verdict is not against the great weight of the evidence as to liability, and when a verdict amount exceeds the evidence, the proper course is to challenge it in the trial court first by motion for remittitur rather than motion for new trial.

100. A worker suffered a serious abdominal injury when a jackhammer he was using malfunctioned. Health insurance paid 80% of the injured worker's medical expense, and disability insurance paid 60% of the wage loss. A trial lawyer whom the worker retained traced the malfunction to a defect in the jackhammer. The trial lawyer filed the worker's products-liability claim against the jackhammer manufacturer. Shortly before trial, the trial lawyer filed a motion in limine to bar evidence of the health- and disability-insurance payments. Under the common law, which of the following best describes the correct ruling on the motion?

A. Grant the motion, barring evidence of insurance and payments, and allowing proof of 100% of medical expense and wage loss.
B. Grant the motion, barring evidence of insurance and payments, and allowing proof of 20% of medical expense and 40% of wage loss.
C. Deny the motion, allowing evidence of insurance and payments, and allowing proof of 100% of medical expense and wage loss.
D. Deny the motion, allowing evidence of insurance and payments, and allowing proof of 20% of medical expense and 40% of wage loss.

Answer: A. Where still recognized, the common-law collateral-source rule bars evidence of health or other insurance, gratuitous payments, and other reimbursement for the tort claimant's losses. The worker would be entitled to prove and recover 100% of medical expense and wage loss. B is incorrect because the worker would get to prove 100% of medical expense and wage loss. C and D are incorrect because the court would grant the motion, not deny it. D is also incorrect because the worker would get to prove 100% of medical expense and wage loss.

101. Two friends hit baseballs together in one friend's yard. One friend accidentally hit the other friend in the head with the baseball bat under circumstances where the friend with the bat was obviously negligent. The injured friend sustained a head injury that required hospitalization and substantial medical treatment. The uninjured friend had homeowner's insurance that would have covered the negligence liability to the injured friend. The injured friend nonetheless decided not to pursue the negligence action against his friend because health insurance paid the substantial medical bills. The health insurer consulted its retained counsel regarding its rights to recover for those insurance payments. Which of the following best describes those rights of the health insurer?

A. The health insurer may have a right of subrogation to the injured friend's claim against his uninjured friend, to recover its payments from the homeowner's insurer.
B. The health insurer may have a right of contribution from the injured friend that would force the injured friend to sue his uninjured friend for homeowner's insurance.
C. The health insurer has no rights because the injured friend can choose whether or not to sue, and the health insurer has its own obligation to pay for medical care.
D. The health insurer has no rights because the injured friend lost the right to maintain a negligence claim when the health insurer paid for the injured friend's loss.

Answer: A. Insurers who pay for the plaintiff's loss typically have the contract right to reimbursement out of the plaintiff's tort recovery or to seek that recovery in subrogation if the plaintiff has not pursued it. Here, the health insurer could subrogate to the injured friend's negligence claim against the uninjured friend, in effect to recover medical payments from the homeowner's insurer. B is incorrect because the health insurer's right would not be contribution from the injured friend. It would be a contract right to subrogate to the injured friend's rights in negligence against the uninjured friend. C is incorrect because the health insurer very probably has a right of subrogation in the same health insurance contract that requires it to pay for medical care. D is incorrect because the injured friend would still have a right to sue in negligence not only for other damages like pain and suffering but also for the medical expense, although the injured friend may have to reimburse the medical insurer out of any recovery.

102. A homeowner hired a plumber to install a new kitchen sink. The plumber installed one of the high-pressure water lines incorrectly, leading to a significant and continuous leak in the cabinet below the sink. The homeowner noticed the leak immediately but delayed in calling the plumber back for several days. When the homeowner did call back the plumber, they discovered that the leak had ruined cabinetry, flooring, and insulation, requiring substantial expensive repairs. The homeowner demanded that the plumber's general liability insurer pay for the repairs. The insurer consulted retained counsel, who interviewed the plumber regarding possible defenses. Which of the following true statements by the plumber would be most helpful to the insurer's defense of the homeowner's claim?

A. The homeowner could have paid for the expensive repairs out of petty cash given the homeowner's high income.

B. The homeowner could have prevented 90% of the water damage by calling the plumber when first noticing the leak.
C. The homeowner could have done the repairs without the plumber's help if the homeowner had a little plumbing skill.
D. The plumber's insurance has high enough policy limits and broad enough coverage to pay for all of the repairs.

Answer: B. Tort claimants have the duty to mitigate their damages, meaning to take reasonable action to reduce their loss. The homeowner should have called the plumber immediately, and the failure to do so was surely a failure to mitigate damages. A is incorrect because the homeowner's ability to pay for the damages is not a basis on which to defend the claim. It is irrelevant to the homeowner's right to recover. The rich have the same tort rights as the poor. C is incorrect because the homeowner may not have had any plumbing skill, and the homeowner's skill is not the issue. The homeowner's delay is the issue giving rise to the failure-to-mitigate defense. D is incorrect because the availability of insurance, though helpful to the plumber as a practical matter, does not help the plumber's legal defense to the homeowner's claim.

103. A bricklayer developed a bad back from years of physical labor. A motorist negligently operated a vehicle such that it collided with the bricklayer's truck one day when the bricklayer was on the way home from a construction site. Trauma from the collision triggered additional severe symptoms in the bricklayer's back, for which doctors recommended and performed expensive back surgery, putting the bricklayer out of work for months. The bricklayer's trial lawyer presented a detailed claim to the negligent motorist's insurer. The insurer retained counsel to investigate the claim. The retained counsel confirmed that medical records showed extensive pre-accident treatment for the bricklayer's bad back and that doctors were unable to say whether the surgery would have been necessary even without the trauma from the motor-vehicle accident. Which of the following is retained counsel's best evaluation of the law, assuming no applicable no-fault provision changing the common law?

A. The motorist is liable only for the bricklayer's back injury that the bricklayer can separate from the pre-existing bad back.
B. The motorist is liable for aggravation of the bricklayer's bad back including the cost of and work loss due to the surgery.
C. The motorist is not liable for the bricklayer's back injury because of the previous treatment and inability to sort it out.
D. The motorist is not liable for the bricklayer's back injury because the severe symptoms could have been triggered by the work.

Answer: B. Tort claimants may recover for aggravation of pre-existing conditions and hold defendants liable for all disability if the parties are unable to distinguish the old condition from new injury. The motorist would be liable for aggravation of the bricklayer's bad back and for the surgery and work loss even though the physicians could not separate its traumatic cause from the pre-existing condition. A is incorrect because aggravation of a pre-existing condition is recoverable, and when the condition and the injury are inseparable, the defendant is liable for both. C is incorrect because the motorist would be liable for any additional back injury or aggravation, of which there is evidence of some, and then for all injury when it cannot be separated out. D is incorrect because the facts state that trauma from the collision triggered the severe symptoms.

104. A young man used a kerosene stove on a camping trip to cook for several friends. The kerosene stove exploded, causing third-degree burns over much of the young man's body. The young man would suffer a lifetime of severe pain from the third-degree burns and disfiguring scarring over his entire body. A trial lawyer whom the young man retained developed a case showing that the kerosene stove had a manufacturing defect causing the explosion. The trial lawyer tendered a multi-million demand to the stove's manufacturer. In pre-suit settlement negotiations, which of the following would the manufacturer cite to most influence the negotiations?

A. Tests showing that the stove's design was the safest feasible.
B. Medical evidence that there were no further treatments.
C. A state statute limiting non-economic damages to $250,000.
D. An umbrella insurance policy with $10,000,000 in liability limits.

Answer: C. Damages caps limit personal-injury plaintiffs' recoveries in many states, particularly as to non-economic damages, although some states have held caps unconstitutional. The case presents huge non-economic damages (severe lifetime pain and disfiguring scarring), most of which the damages cap would bar. A is incorrect because the claim was for a manufacturing defect, not a design defect. The design may have been quite safe, but the stove departed from the design. B is incorrect because although no further treatment would mean no further medical expense, the non-economic damages for severe lifetime pain and disfiguring scarring are the greater part of the damages. D is incorrect because the umbrella policy would show coverage for the trial lawyer's multi-million demand, thus supporting rather than contesting the demand.

105. A local newspaper published an investigative story in which it carelessly misidentified a young couple as responsible for sexual abuse of children at a local daycare. The young couple retained local counsel on a contingency-fee basis. Counsel sued the media company that owned the newspaper, for defamation and invasion of privacy. The media company offered the young couple $100,000 to settle their claims. The young couple calculated that if they accepted the $100,000 offer, after the attorney's one-third contingency fee there would be just enough for them to buy a new home in a new town where they would have a clean reputation. Which of the following best describes advice that counsel should give to the young couple about the offer and settlement?

A. That a bird in hand is worth two in the bush, and to take the offer.
B. That reputation is easily won and lost, so not to rely on a new town.
C. That if they discover other claims and losses, they can sue again.
D. That there are federal income taxes on the settlement proceeds.

Answer: D. Recoveries on account of physical injury are not taxed, but recoveries where there is no physical injury are taxed. Here, the young couple had no physical injury, and so there would be federal income taxes. They would need to know that before accepting the settlement offer because the taxes could make a big difference in their net proceeds and plans to use them. A is incorrect because it is an evaluation of the offer that may or may not be reliable, is overly directive rather than advisory, and relies on a platitude rather than evaluation. B is incorrect because the impact of the defamation, the embarrassment of the invasion, and the significance of a fresh start, are personal judgments for the young couple to make, not matters on which counsel should speculate. C is incorrect because the settlement agreement is almost certain to contain a release of all claims for any damage, whether known or unknown.

106. A young woman suffered a serious and permanent injury while a spectator at a sports event. The young woman's attorney made a negligence demand on the event's producer, who forwarded the demand to the producer's liability insurer. At a subsequent mediation, the insurer offered $1,500,000 to settle the young woman's claim. The young woman needed only a fraction of the settlement offer for her present needs because she still lived with her parents. Which of the following best describes what the mediator should address with the parties and their counsel, regarding the potential settlement?

A. The tax advantages to the young woman's attorney of the settlement.
B. The tax advantages to the young woman's parents of the settlement.
C. The tax advantages to the young woman of structuring the settlement.
D. The tax advantages to the liability insurer of reaching the settlement.

Answer: C. The tax code permits tort claimants to have a third party structure their settlements without tax on the investments' earnings. The parties must structure the settlement before the funds are conveyed to the claimant, not later. The mediator should cover that option with the parties and make it a part of the settlement if they agree. The tax advantage of structuring helps parties settle cases. A is incorrect because the attorney would know the tax treatment (not advantages, of which there are none—earned proceeds are taxable income to the attorney). B is incorrect because there are no tax consequences for the parents. D is incorrect because the insurer would already know of the tax consequences of its settlement, that being its business.

107. A collision between a truck and van seriously injured and permanently disabled a schoolteacher riding as a passenger in the van. Police attributed the collision to the negligence of the van's driver and owner, who had insurance with a million-dollar liability limit. The schoolteacher retained a law firm on a one-third contingency fee to pursue her negligence claim against the van's driver. Lawyers from the firm quickly prepared a demand, convincing the insurer to pay the full million-dollar liability limits. The lawyers had spent about 10 hours on the case for which their contingency-fee agreement provided that they would receive one third of the million-dollar recovery. Which of the following best describes the lawyers' duty to their client regarding that fee?

A. The lawyers may charge the agreed-upon fee given that the schoolteacher agreed and consented to it.
B. The lawyers may charge the agreed-upon fee if they can get the schoolteacher to specifically approve it.
C. The lawyers must charge no more than their usual hourly rate because the contingency fee is excessive.
D. The lawyers must charge no more than a reasonable fee, meaning its reduction to that amount if necessary.

Answer: D. Contingency fees must be reasonable. One third of one million dollars would be approximately $333,333 or what would amount to $33,333 per hour, which is very likely excessive. The lawyers must reduce the fee to a reasonable amount. A is incorrect because the parties entered into the fee agreement not knowing what work the case would ultimately require. The fee now appears excessive. The schoolteacher's consent to one third was not consent to $33,333 per hour. B is incorrect because even if the schoolteacher consents, the fee must still be reasonable. The schoolteacher might change her mind later and contest the fee after the lawyers had taken it, subjecting them to discipline if it was excessive whether or not she approved it. Moreover, the phrase "if they can get" the schoolteacher to approve it suggests some extent of persuasion of the teacher when the lawyers would have their own interest adverse to hers, and when the standard is reasonableness, not consent. C is incorrect because the lawyers can charge more than their usual hourly rate so long as the total fee is still reasonable. Contingency-fee cases carry risks of non-recovery, unlike most hourly fee cases, justifying higher per-hour recoveries. They also often require financial investment (advanced costs) and greater skill warranting higher per-hour recoveries.

108. A motorcyclist gunned his motorcycle away from a friend's house, as was his custom, despite neighborhood complaints regarding the safety of young children. In looking back over his shoulder at his friend's reaction in doing so, the motorcyclist accidentally ran over and killed one of those young children. The parents of the child sued the motorcyclist for the child's death under provisions of the jurisdictions wrongful-death act. The motorcyclist's lawyer moved just before trial to prohibit the parents' lawyer from offering into evidence photographs of the dead child, taken by police at the scene. Which of the following describes the most likely ruling on the motion?

A. Grant the motion, barring the photographs as inflammatory damages evidence.
B. Grant the motion, barring the photographs as having no admissible foundation.
C. Deny the motion, allowing the photographs as relevant evidence of damages.
D. Deny the motion, allowing the photographs as relevant evidence of liability.

Answer: A. Parties may challenge the admissibility of inflammatory damages evidence with a motion in limine heard before trial. Photographs of the dead child are likely highly upsetting and inflammatory of the jury. B is incorrect because the police and others at the scene could readily establish the photographs' foundation for admissibility. C is incorrect because the judge should grant the motion and because the photographs may not necessarily even be relevant damages evidence. There is no dispute that the child died, and the parents or other immediate family members may not have seen the child's death (relevant to a bystander's claim for emotional distress). D is incorrect because the judge should grant the motion and because the photographs may not be relevant liability evidence. The motorcycle would probably admit fault, removing other inflaming evidence of the prior complaints.

109. The father of three young children died in a motor-vehicle accident at a construction site. Police determined that a highway contractor's carelessness was responsible for the father's death. The father's death left his children's mother, from whom the father was divorced, without any child support. The personal representative of the father's estate retained counsel to evaluate and prepare the estate's wrongful-death claim against the contractor. Which of the following best describes the most likely treatment of the children's loss of their father's support, as part of the wrongful-death case?

A. Include the children as beneficiaries, counting the children's loss of their father's support as damages in the wrongful-death claim.
B. Include the mother as beneficiary, counting the mother's loss of the child support as damages in the wrongful-death claim.
C. Include the children as beneficiaries, but count only the loss of the father's love and society as damages in the wrongful-death claim.

D. Exclude the children as beneficiaries, not counting the children's loss of their father's support as damages in the wrongful-death claim.

Answer: A. Wrongful-death acts in all 50 states allow tort recoveries for death, so long as the claimants have an underlying tort theory such as negligence. Although the acts vary, they tend to include dependent children as beneficiaries and their loss of financial support as damages. The children would likely recover, although their recovery would be held in trust for them and managed by an adult (possibly the mother but possibly a relative of the father). B is incorrect because the acts do not include divorced spouses as beneficiaries. The mother should end up with child support, but it would be damages paid on behalf of and held for the children, not the mother, whom the father had divorced. C is incorrect because the father's financial support would most likely be included. Damages might also include loss of love and society, but they would more likely and most likely include the loss of financial support. D is incorrect because the child would be included, not excluded, as beneficiaries.

110. A wealthy financier with a large extended family died in a boating accident. Authorities quickly concluded that another boater was negligent in causing the financier's death. An insurance representative for that boater quickly contacted the financier's family offering to meet regarding settling the liability as soon as the family had completed funeral plans. Before the financier's body had even been buried, the family was arguing over whether and how to proceed with litigation. One family member consulted a lawyer regarding the right of individual family members to proceed. Which of the following best describes the family members' individual rights?

A. Family members should each seek and retain their own counsel to maintain wrongful-death actions in their individual names unless everyone agrees.
B. Family members should identify and consult with the estate's personal representative through whom the wrongful-death action would proceed.
C. Family members should choose their own representative by any reasonable means by which to impose order and proceed through that representative.
D. Family members have no individual or collective rights because any negligence action would pass away with the financier's death, there being no right left.

Answer: B. Although there is some variation in the acts, wrongful-death actions must usually be brought in the name of the decedent's estate and are controlled by the estate's personal representative. The financier's will, and if no will, then the law for intestate administration, would designate the priority for choosing the personal representative. A is incorrect because the acts do not generally authorize individual actions, where bedlam might ensue from a multiplicity of cases and results. C is incorrect because wills, wrongful-death acts, and probate laws and rules designate the estate's representative. Family members may voice preferences and raise objections but do not control the designation.

111. A construction accident killed a subcontractor. At the time of his death, the subcontractor had five minor children with his wife, one minor child out of wedlock with another woman, and one adopted minor child. The personal representative of the subcontractor's estate retained counsel to investigate a wrongful-death claim against the general contractor whose negligence caused the subcontractor's death. Counsel prepared a demand to submit to the general contractor's liability insurer. Which of the following beneficiaries should counsel include in the damages portion of the demand?

A. The subcontractor's wife and five children with his wife.
B. The subcontractor's wife, five children with his wife, and one child born out of wedlock with another woman.
C. The subcontractor's wife, five children with his wife, and one adopted child.
D. The subcontractor's wife, five children with his wife, one child born out of wedlock with another woman, and one adopted child.

Answer: D. Spouses and children are typical beneficiaries under wrongful-death acts, as may be parents and possibly siblings and other lineal descendants. Children typically include all biological and adopted children. It likely violates equal protection to exclude out-of-wedlock children. A is incorrect for omitting the out-of-wedlock and adopted children. B is incorrect for omitting the adopted child. C is incorrect for omitting the out-of-wedlock child.

112. A wealthy, reclusive former rock star killed a school principal who spurned the rock star's pursuit. After the local prosecutor obtained the rock star's criminal conviction, the personal representative for the principal's estate evaluated the estate's wrongful-death claim. The decedent principal was making about $100,000 per year at the time of her death. She left no family. Her will left everything to school causes. The rock star had unlimited financial assets. Which of the following best describes the estate's wrongful-death damages in a state whose wrongful-death laws limit recovery to pecuniary loss to dependent beneficiaries?

A. The principal's $100,000 salary for as many years as she would have worked and her loss of enjoyment of life for as many years as she would have lived.
B. The principal's $100,000 salary for as many years as she would have worked.
C. The principal's pain and suffering.
D. None.

Answer: D. Wrongful-death acts differ as to the measure of loss, some limited to pecuniary loss to designated immediate-family dependent beneficiaries while others allow non-economic loss to beneficiaries and some even loss to the estate. If the principal left no dependent beneficiaries, then there would be no one to recover any loss under laws that limit recovery to pecuniary loss to dependent beneficiaries. A is incorrect because no dependent beneficiary suffered the $100,000 loss, while the law limits recovery to pecuniary loss of dependent beneficiaries. Also, the principal's loss of enjoyment of life would only be recoverable in a jurisdiction recognizing loss to the estate. B is incorrect because no dependent beneficiary suffered that loss, while the law limits recovery to pecuniary loss of dependent beneficiaries. C is incorrect because any conscious pain and suffering (of which the facts mention none) would be under a survival statute, not a wrongful-death act limiting recovery to pecuniary loss to dependent beneficiaries.

113. A fan attended a soccer match at which a grandstand collapsed due to the promoter's negligence in overselling tickets and failing to limit access to the grandstand. Although rescue workers pulled the fan from the wreckage and hospitalized him, the grandstand had crushed one of the fan's legs. The fan survived, conscious but in pain and mental distress, for only three days following his injury, when he died in a motor-vehicle accident while in transport to another medical facility. The fan's family members retained counsel to investigate tort claims arising out of the fan's death. Which of the following best describes law necessary to allow tort recovery for the fan's pain and suffering after the grandstand injury and before the motor-vehicle accident?

A. A survival statute.
B. The wrongful-death act.
C. Motor-vehicle civil-liability laws.
D. Probate law.

Answer: A. Survival actions permit the estate to recover for losses the decedent suffered before death. Survival statutes preserve the decedent's actions that arose while the decedent was still living. B is incorrect because wrongful-death acts provide recoveries for death caused by tortious conduct. The wrongful-death act would provide recovery for the motor-vehicle accident, not the grandstand event. C is incorrect because motor-vehicle civil-liability laws would provide liability only for motor-vehicle accidents and not the grandstand event. D is incorrect because probate laws do not create substantive tort rights to maintain survival actions. They govern distribution of assets of an estate.

114. Fire destroyed a home. Fire officials investigated, tracing the fire's cause and origin to an electrical contractor's negligent installation of a recessed ceiling light. After the homeowner insurer reimbursed the homeowners for the fire loss, the insurer retained counsel to make a demand to the electrical contractor's general-liability insurer on its subrogation claim. The general-liability insurer agreed that it should reimburse the fire insurer but disputed damages. The fire destroyed the home at a time when its market value was around $225,000. The fire insurer paid the homeowners $275,000. A year later, when the insurers agreed to settle, the home would have been worth $150,000. The cost to rebuild the home would have been $300,000. Which of the following would be the usual measure of property damages for the fire insurer's subrogation claim?

A. The $225,000 market value at destruction.
B. The $275,000 the fire insurer paid the homeowners.
C. The $150,000 the home would have been worth at settlement.
D. The $300,000 it would take to rebuild the home.

Answer: A. The usual measure of damages for property loss is the market value of the property at the time of loss, in this case $225,000. B is incorrect because amounts others pay to reimburse for the loss are not the measure of property damages. The fire insurer may have overpaid or paid for other expenses not constituting property damages. C is incorrect because the home's fall in value was fortuitous, and damages are measured at the time of loss, not later. D is incorrect because repair or replacement cost is not the usual measure of property damage.

115. A woman shipped her personal property by truck to her new residence. The truck slid from the highway and into a water-filled ditch, due to the driver's negligence, ruining the woman's personal property. The woman retained counsel who made a demand on the driver's insurer for the personal-property damage. The driver's insurer agreed to the value of all items except the woman's wedding dress handed down to her through three generations. The woman and the driver's insurer submitted the dress value to arbitration. Which of the following best describes the damages measure that the arbitrator should apply?

A. The wedding dress' sentimental value to the woman.

B. The wedding dress' market value in a resale shop.
C. The wedding dress' original cost when first purchased.
D. The wedding dress' replacement cost if made again now.

Answer: A. Personal or sentimental value to the owner is not usually considered unless the loss involved an item having the history of a family heirloom. The wedding dress would qualify as an heirloom under these circumstances where it was passed from generation to generation. B is incorrect because although market value is the typical property-damage measure, the rule may change for heirlooms. C is incorrect because original cost does not allow for inflation, depreciation, or in this case sentimental value. D is incorrect because repair or replacement cost is not the usual property-damage measure.

116. A winter outdoor enthusiast owned a snowmobile. The enthusiast's friend took the snowmobile for a week without the enthusiast's permission. At the end of the week, the friend operated the snowmobile to a local bar to drink beer until the bar closed. In a drunken escapade, the friend then operated the snowmobile down the center of paved and gravel roads until arrested by police. The friend's escapade deprived the enthusiast of the snowmobile's use, destroyed the snowmobile's track, made the snowmobile inoperable, and substantially reduced its value. The friend later agreed to pay the enthusiast the full measure of property damages associated with his drunken escapade, to ease or forestall prosecution. The enthusiast consulted a lawyer to learn the full measure of damages the friend would owe. Which of the following best describes that measure of damages?

A. Cost of a new snowmobile to replace the one that the friend damaged, together with transaction expenses.
B. Market value of the enthusiast's snowmobile at the time that the friend destroyed its track on the roads that night.
C. Rental value of a replacement snowmobile during deprivation, and reduction in market value for its partial destruction.
D. Repair costs for a new track, and the enthusiast's mental and emotional distress while missing the snowmobile.

Answer: C. Damages for temporary deprivation may be measured by rental value, whereas damages for partial destruction may be measured by reduction in market value. This instance involved both temporary deprivation and partial destruction, making both measures applicable for full compensation. A is incorrect because the snowmobile still has value. Even if it was totally destroyed, cost of a new snowmobile would not be the measure of damages. Market value at destruction, meaning depreciated value, would be the measure of damages for total destruction. B is incorrect because although a correct measure for total destruction of property, the snowmobile was not totally destroyed. The answer also omits the rental-value damages. D is incorrect because repair cost is not a measure of property damage in the typical case, and neither is mental and emotional distress. Property damages are limited to economic losses.

117. A neighbor approached a homeowner about using the homeowner's side yard for the neighbor to drive his motor home around the back of his house for periodic maintenance and storage. The homeowner declined the neighbor's request. The neighbor then offered to purchase an easement for that purpose from the homeowner. The homeowner again declined the neighbor's request. To spite and intimidate the homeowner for refusing to agree to the easement, the neighbor then cut down the homeowner's ornamental tree. Which of the following describes the largest tort damages measure that the homeowner might claim against the neighbor, recognized in at least some jurisdictions?

A. Nominal damages for the trespass.
B. Compensatory damages for the ornamental tree.
C. Non-economic damages for the homeowner's frustration.
D. Punitive damages to punish and deter the neighbor.

Answer: D. Some jurisdictions allow punitive damages for property damage, in some cases where there is a more culpable wrong, to punish the defendant, in addition to compensatory damages to compensate the plaintiff. This matter involved an intentional and highly invasive and aggravated tort. Where allowed, punitive damages are often greater than or even a multiple of compensatory damages, as the Constitution allows. A is incorrect because nominal damages are usually one dollar or another minimal amount. B is incorrect because although the ornamental tree may have had substantial value, punitive damages are often measured by increasing or even multiplying the compensatory damages, as the Constitution allows. C is incorrect because non-economic damages are not allowed for property damage, and although there is a trespass here where a court might allow some form of non-economic damage for the invasion, punitive damages typically allow for an award greater than compensatory damages.

118. A classic-car buff anticipated a bidding war at an auction of a prized vehicle coveted by a wealthy collector. The buff won the bidding when the collector was delayed. The buff then refused to sell the vehicle to the collector who offered to double the sale price. When the buff refused, the collector angrily tossed a trash can on the vehicle's hood, causing significant vehicle damage. The buff sued the collector, claiming punitive damages as state law allowed. The jury returned a million-dollar punitive-damages award that was 100 times the $10,000 compensatory loss that the vehicle owner had suffered. The collector's lawyer filed a motion challenging the punitive-damages award. Which of the following is the lawyer's best argument to make on behalf of the collector under the Constitution?

A. The punitive-damages award is excessive when measured against the collector's ability to pay.
B. The punitive-damages award is excessive when measured against the actual damages.
C. The punitive-damages award is unnecessary when considering other available criminal penalties.
D. The punitive-damages award is prohibited considering the lack of reprehensibility of the conduct.

Answer: B. The Constitution prohibits states from awarding excessive punitive damages, measured against the actual damages, the reprehensibility of the tortious conduct, and the nature of other available civil and criminal penalties. The Supreme Court has held excessive punitive-damages awards that are 100 times the compensatory-damages verdict. The allowable multiple is probably closer to eight times compensatory damages. A is incorrect because the collector is said to be wealthy, and although wealth is often allowed as a factor under state law, the constitutional factors are those mentioned above, not including wealth. C is incorrect because other available civil or criminal penalties are a factor in judging constitutionality but do not rule out punitive damages. The court is to compare and contrast other available penalties, not use them to bar punitive damages. D is incorrect because the conduct is intentional and violent, and thus sufficiently reprehensible. Even grossly negligent or reckless conduct may warrant punitive damages in some jurisdictions. Property damage can warrant punitive damages, not just death or personal injury.

Essay Question: A 22-year-old college student suffered a closed-head injury and ruptured spleen in a motor vehicle accident caused by the negligence of an automobile's driver. The student was taken from the accident scene to the hospital by ambulance, where exploratory abdominal surgery was performed and the student's spleen removed. No empirical evidence suggests that the removal of the spleen has any adverse impact on life-span, wellness, or capacity. The student's closed-head injury resulted in frequent headaches, sleep disruption, emotional volatility, and an inability to concentrate on his college studies. As a result, the student's roommate and significant other ended their relationship, and the student had to withdraw from college and move back in with his parents. **Identify the categories of recoverable damages and the proofs in support.**

Answer: The question requires identifying categories of recoverable damages and supporting proofs for a 22-year-old college student who suffered a ruptured spleen and closed-head injury in a vehicle accident.

The main compensatory damage categories in any personal-injury case are economic loss usually consisting of medical expense and wage loss and non-economic loss including pain, suffering, mental and emotional distress, fear, fright, shock, embarrassment, mortification, and lost enjoyment of life. A spouse may also recover consortium loss in the nature of lost love, society, services, intimacy, and companionship. Punitive damages are not usually available particularly for ordinary negligence. Evidence proving medical expense can include medical records, care-provider testimony, billing and account statements, and expert testimony on prognosis. Evidence proving wage loss includes personnel file, wage records, and testimony of employers and vocational-rehabilitation experts. Evidence supporting non-economic loss begins with the claimant's testimony but can also include testimony of family members, friends, and experts on rehabilitation and prognosis.

Here, the college student suffering personal injury due to the motorist's negligence required ambulance, hospitalization, exploratory surgery, and likely some follow-up care for the ruptured spleen (a point to investigate), and likely some investigation and therapy relating to the closed-head injury, which may continue into the future (points to investigate). Those services had associated expenses, which the student would prove with medical records, billing and account statements, and care-provider and account-manager testimony. The student appears not yet to have incurred wage loss but might in the future from the closed-head injury, another point to investigate through expert consult. As to non-economic loss, the student would present his own testimony and the testimony of family, friends, and treating care providers about his pain, suffering, limitations, and lost enjoyment of life. The student's girlfriend would not have consortium-loss damages even if losing love, society, support, and services because she was not a spouse, and consortium loss is limited to spouses. No punitive damages would be available because the case involved only ordinary negligence, a motor-vehicle accident.

In conclusion, the student would have the classic economic and non-economic damages claimed in any personal-injury case other than wage loss depending on proof of future work disability.

Essay Question: The estate of a 55-year-old married woman is maintaining a wrongful-death claim against the manufacturer of an allegedly defective product. The woman suffered severe electrical shock from the product's use, suffered cardiac arrest, and, though hospitalized for ten days, never regained consciousness. The woman, who had been separated from her husband for five years up to the time of her injury and death, was survived by a 30-year-old son and 16-year-old daughter. The woman had not seen her son since her separation from her husband but cared for her daughter at home with the daughter attending high school. The husband paid the woman child support, and the woman worked part-time as a book-keeper for a local business. **Itemize the estate's wrongful-death claim damages.**

Answer: The case requires itemizing an estate's wrongful-death damages in a claim involving the death of a part-time book-keeper separated from her husband for five years and caring for one of their two minor children.

Wrongful-death actions depend on state statutes, which vary as to the form of damages. Typically, though, the estate will maintain the action through the personal representative to recover funeral and burial expenses and amounts on behalf of beneficiaries including any spouse and minor children. Some statutes extend the beneficiaries to other close relatives or dependents. Some statutes measure damages by loss to the beneficiaries, particularly economic loss but possibly also for services or even society and companionship, while other statutes measure damages by loss to the estate, meaning the total loss of the decedent's income and lost enjoyment of life, sometimes reduced by personal consumption. Survival statutes permit recovery for loss that the decedent suffered while still living after the injury but before the death, subject to claims against the estate.

Here, the decedent was a part-time book-keeper, and so the estate's loss could include all of the book-keeper's lost income for the duration of her work-life expectancy if in a loss-to-the-estate jurisdiction. If instead in the more-common loss-to-the-beneficiaries jurisdiction, then the estate's loss would begin with the decedent's lost support to the minor at-home daughter and possibly lost services and society and companionship to that child also, at least until the age of majority and possibly beyond depending what the specific statute allows. The adult son would not have a minor child's beneficiary claim and, not being dependent or in contact at all, had no loss of services, support, love, society, or companionship. The husband would also likely have little or no claim given the five-year separation and no mention of spousal support. Indeed, the husband was instead paying the decedent child support, suggesting no lost support going from decedent to husband. The estate would also have a survival claim for the ten-day hospitalization, although because the decedent did not regain consciousness, those damages would only include the medical expense and any wage loss from the part-time book-keeping work during that period. The estate would also recover any expenses associated with the final demise, funeral, and burial.

In sum, damages in this wrongful-death case would center on the 16-year-old daughter's loss of her decedent mother's financial support, household services, and love, society, and companionship, plus the estate's expenses for the decedent's final ten-day hospitalization and funeral and burial expenses.

Essay Question: An investor owned stock she pledged to a bank to secure a short-term loan. The loan agreement permitted the investor to prepay the loan at any time through any means including by her sale of the pledged stock. When the investor saw that her stock had risen to new highs, she directed the bank loan agent to sell her stock to prepay the loan and to release the remaining funds to her. The agent wrongfully refused. In the 60 days that it took the investor to convince the bank that she had the right to sell her stock to prepay the loan, the stock crashed to no value. **Identify the measure of damages in the investor's conversion action against the bank.**

Answer: The question requires identifying the measure of damages in an investor's conversion action against a bank that wrongfully refused to relinquish stock that the bank held as pledged security for a loan.

The measure of property damages is the reduction or diminution in value caused by the wrongful act. A plaintiff ordinarily compares the fair market value of the property before the wrong to the fair market value of the property after the wrong. The difference in values is the amount of the loss for the defendant to compensate.

Here, the damages measure would be the value of the stock at the time that the investor directed its sale at the high mark minus the difference in value of the stock when she was able to convince the bank to let her sell it, which the facts state was zero value. So the investor would have as a damages measure the full value of the stock at its high value when she directed its sale and the bank wrongfully refused.

Essay Question: A homeowner suffered severe depression, post-traumatic stress, and mental and emotional disability causing wage loss, after a repairman attempted a sexual assault on her at her home. Evidence supported that the repairman's employer knew when it hired the repairman and assigned him to the homeowner's work order that the repairman presented a sexual assault risk to its customers. Assuming that punitive damages are available in the jurisdiction in which the homeowner will try her tort claim against the employer, **identify the criteria on which punitive damages may be awarded, so that counsel may investigate punitive damages and plan trial proofs and arguments.**

Answer: The question requires identifying the criteria on which courts measure punitive damages, so that counsel for a homeowner may investigate and plan proofs in a negligent-hiring-and-retention action against the employer of a repairman who sexually assaulted the homeowner.

Punitive damages are to punish the defendant rather than to compensate the plaintiff. Typical measures for punitive damages begin with the reprehensibility of the wrong. A highly reprehensible wrong deserves greater punishment than a bare wrong. Another typical measure for punitive damages is the relationship of the punitive award to the compensatory award. When a plaintiff suffers significant compensatory damages, the punitive award should also be significant, although limited by due process to a multiple up to about ten times the compensatory award. Another typical measure for punitive damages is the ability of the defendant to pay. A punitive-damages award of a certain size would punish a wealthy defendant less than a poor defendant. A last measure for punitive damages is to show the size of other available civil or criminal remedies.

Here, sexual assault is a very serious wrong, and the employer's ignoring a known risk of sexual assault is a very serious wrong, warranting greater punitive damages. The homeowner's proofs would begin with showing the assault and the employer's knowledge of that risk. Here, the homeowner should show her compensatory loss including mental and emotional distress and any medical expense or wage loss. The homeowner should also discover and prove the employer's financial resources to show the relative size of a punitive-damages award. The homeowner might want to research and prove that criminal restitution or civil sanctions for violent crime of this type warrant certain penalties.

WEEK 10

119. A passenger was seriously injured in a collision in which the driver of the vehicle in which the passenger was riding, the driver of the other vehicle, and the repairer of the other vehicle were each negligent contributing to the collision. Near trial, the plaintiff's lawyer conducted settlement negotiations with the insurer for the repairer of the other vehicle, whom the plaintiff and lawyer regarded as least culpable. The plaintiff had been demanding $100,000 in total from all defendants but accepted that defendant's offer of $35,000, expecting that later settlements from or judgments against the other defendants would make up most of the difference. Which of the following best describes the document that the plaintiff's lawyer should prepare or approve for the plaintiff's signature to effectuate the settlement?

A. A release of the liability of all persons and entities, and their insurers, agents, and employees, in consideration of that defendant's settlement.
B. A release of the liability of that defendant and its insurers, agents, and employees, reserving rights against other persons and entities.
C. A release of liability for negligent vehicle repair, reserving rights as to all other negligent actions under which anyone may be liable.
D. A release of liability for $35,000, reserving rights to recover more than that amount from anyone other than the settling defendant.

Answer: B. When parties settle a tort claim, the plaintiff signs an agreement releasing the settling defendant and its insurers and agents from further liability, while attempting to preserve rights against non-settling defendants. The passenger should release the vehicle repairer and its insurer and agents but reserve rights as to other defendants. A is incorrect because the passenger wishes to preserve the remaining claims against other non-settling defendants (the two drivers). C is incorrect because release liability for actions would not forestall suing the same defendants for other actions, and no defendant would settle for actions leaving open the possibility of liability for other actions. Releases are as to persons and entities, not actions. D is incorrect because the release should be of the settling party, not as to the amount. The passenger may wish to recover less than $35,000 from other non-settling parties.

120. A shopper tripped and fell when the heel of her shoe caught in the strings of a worn rug at the entrance to an antique shop. The shopkeeper was aware of the risk from prior incidents. The shopper broke her wrist and clavicle in the fall, requiring casting of the lower arm and hand, and a sling for the shoulder. The shopper made a premises-liability claim against the shopkeeper. The shopkeeper's insurer declined to settle the case, which proceeded to trial. The jury returned a $100,000 verdict that the judge entered as a court judgment against the shopkeeper. The insurer indicated that it would pay the entire judgment amount rather than appeal, instructing defense counsel to proceed accordingly. Which of the following best describes the steps that defense counsel should take?

A. Make an offer of compromise and settlement to plaintiff's counsel for the entire judgment amount and wait for reply.
B. Obtain a release and settlement agreement from plaintiff's counsel in exchange for the insurer's draft for the total judgment.
C. Obtain a signed satisfaction of judgment from plaintiff's counsel in exchange for the insurer's draft for the total judgment.
D. File a motion to set aside the judgment and to dismiss the case based on the insurer's willingness to pay the judgment.

Answer: C. When parties are unable to voluntarily settle a claim and a money judgment is instead entered after trial, the liability is extinguished when the defendant satisfies the judgment. Because the insurer has indicated that it will pay the entire judgment, and the trial judge already entered judgment, defense counsel must obtain a satisfaction of judgment from plaintiff's counsel in exchange for the insurer's draft. A is incorrect because plaintiff can execute on the judgment once the appeal period and its automatic stay expire. Making an offer and waiting does not bring the matter to conclusion or protect against execution, which could be embarrassing and inconveniencing. B is incorrect because a release and settlement agreement does not address the judgment already on file. The court records need to reflect the judgment's satisfaction. A release and settlement agreement, together with a dismissal of the action, would have been appropriate before the entry of judgment, not after. D is incorrect because there is no basis to set aside the motion or to dismiss. The trial judge entered judgment. It must now be timely satisfied to forestall execution.

121. The collapse of a scaffold erected by a construction company injured a worker employed by a painting subcontractor. The construction company prepared an incident report. The construction company's insurer hired an adjusting company to settle the worker's negligence claim against the construction company. The adjusting company obtained a copy of the incident report and provided it to the worker along with a settlement offer. Relying on the incident report, the worker accepted the offer and signed a settlement agreement and release in exchange for the settlement funds. The injured worker later learned that the construction and adjusting companies had altered the incident report to cover-up the construction company's gross negligence. The injured worker consulted a lawyer regarding the worker's rights against the construction company. Which of the following best describes those rights?

A. The worker has the right to have the release set aside for fraud and to pursue the claim to its proper resolution.

B. The worker has the right to have the construction company held in contempt and fined or otherwise sanctioned.
C. The worker has the right to summary judgment in its favor on the worker's claim against the construction company.
D. The worker has the right to keep the settlement proceeds only and nothing further, having signed a release.

Answer: A. The courts will set aside a release only for fraud, duress, undue influence, or mutual mistake. A company's altering an incident report on which the settling claimant relied is a clear example of the kind of fraud that the court will recognize to set aside a settlement. B is incorrect because the facts do not describe the filing of an action, and hence there is no violation of court order or proceeding to hold the company in contempt. The fraud is on the claimant worker, not the court, at this point. C is incorrect because although summary judgment may be an appropriate remedy for the spoliation of evidence, the facts do not say that the report was destroyed, and the court would instead first have to set aside the release. D is incorrect because the worker can have the release set aside for fraud.

122. Two vehicles collided at a four-way stop intersection. Each vehicle skidded into the intersection because of excessive speed on icy road surfaces. The collision badly injured a passenger in one of the vehicles. The passenger obtained a single $50,000 judgment of joint and several liability against the drivers of each vehicle. The passenger collected that $50,000 judgment from the insurer of one of the two drivers. The passenger's lawyer then advised the passenger regarding the passenger's rights against the other driver. Which of the following best describes the passenger's remaining rights as to the other driver?

A. The passenger has the right to pursue the other driver for the $50,000 judgment amount until paid by that driver.
B. The passenger has the right to pursue the other driver for whatever amount greater than $50,000 but less than $100,000 the other driver is able to pay.
C. The passenger has no remaining rights against the other driver unless the other driver has more insurance up to $100,000.
D. The passenger has no remaining rights against the other driver because the passenger is due only a single satisfaction.

Answer: D. Plaintiffs are entitled to only a single satisfaction of their damages even when multiple parties are jointly and severally liable for those damages. The passenger could have pursued either driver for the whole judgment or each for a portion but neither for more than the total $50,000 received from each together. The driver who paid (the driver's insurer who paid) may possibly pursue the other driver for contribution, but the passenger's rights are extinguished by the $50,000 payment. A and B are incorrect because the passenger has already received the $50,000 judgment and is due no more than that amount. C is incorrect because the passenger has no rights to more whether or not the other driver has insurance.

123. A collision occurred between two vehicles as their drivers both attempted to change lanes on the interstate at the same time without looking for and yielding to the other vehicle. The collision caused one of the vehicles to leave the road surface and come to rest in the median ditch, injuring a passenger. The passenger settled her claim against one of the drivers for that driver's $20,000 insurance policy limits. The passenger's lawsuit against the other driver resulted in a $25,000 judgment. The passenger's lawyer made a demand on the second driver's insurer to fully satisfy the $25,000 judgment out of the insurer's $100,000 policy limits. The insurer consulted its retained counsel. Which of the following best describes the proper amount for the second driver's insurer to pay?

A. Pay $100,000 representing the full amount of the policy limits.
B. Pay $25,000 representing the full amount of the judgment.
C. Pay $5,000 after $20,000 credit against the $25,000 judgment.
D. Pay $20,000 like the other driver's insurer paid for equal liability.

Answer: C. Non-settling defendants who are jointly and severally liable get credit for amounts paid by settling defendants. The non-settling defendant who suffered a $25,000 judgment would get credit for the settling defendant's $20,000 payment because the drivers were jointly and severally liable. A is incorrect because the judgment amount was $25,000 and credit $20,000. Insurers do not pay their policy limits unless there is that amount of liability. B is incorrect because the $25,000 judgment would be reduced by the $20,000 settlement. Judgments represent full damages, when some of those damages have already been compensated by the settlement. D is incorrect because the judgment amount is $25,000 and credit $20,000. Just because the other driver's insurer paid $20,000 does not mean that this driver owes the same amount.

124. A teenage owner of a motor vehicle loaned his vehicle to a friend for the friend to deliver newspapers on the teenager's motor route. The friend allowed his foot to slip from the vehicle's clutch, causing the vehicle to lurch forward into a pedestrian in a crosswalk. The vehicle collision injured the pedestrian's knee. The teenager's motor-vehicle insurer offered its $20,000 policy limits to the pedestrian in exchange for a release that included all agents, employees, and employers of the insured teenager. The pedestrian consulted a lawyer regarding the release. Which of the following describes the best advice regarding the effect of the pedestrian's signing the release?

A. The pedestrian may sign the release, relinquishing the claim as to the teenager while pursuing the newspaper and friend.
B. The pedestrian may sign the release, relinquishing the claim as to the teenager and friend while pursuing the newspaper.
C. The pedestrian may sign the release, relinquishing all claims unless the pedestrian changes his mind and returns the $20,000.
D. The pedestrian should sign the release only if the pedestrian intends to relinquish all rights as to the teenager, newspaper, and friend.

Answer: D. Releases must be carefully considered and crafted to release only those parties and their agents whom the parties intend to release. Signing a release of all agents, employees, and employers would release the vehicle-owner teenager and his putative employer newspaper and employee friend. A is incorrect because the release would include the newspaper and friend, who were putative employer and employee, not just the teenager. B is incorrect because the release would release the newspaper, also, as the putative employer. C is incorrect because once a release is signed and consideration paid, there is no changing one's mind and returning the money. A court would set aside the release only for fraud, duress, coercion, or mutual mistake.

125. An engineering firm surveyed a suburban lot for its owner to build a new residence. An architect designed the residence relying on the survey. Part way into the construction it became apparent that the survey was incorrect and the residence out of code compliance as designed for and sited on the lot. The owner had to retain others to properly re-survey, relocate, and redesign the residence, at a $100,000 loss to the owner. The owner's retained counsel sued the engineering firm and architect, resulting in a $100,000 judgment for joint and several liability. The engineering firm had $300,000 in insurance policy limits while the architect was uninsured. Which of the following describes the owner's best legal course to collect on the judgment?

A. Collect half of the $100,000 judgment from the insured engineering firm and pursue the architect's income and assets for the other half.
B. Collect all of the $100,000 judgment from the insured engineering firm and pursue none of the architect's income and assets.
C. Collect $300,000 from the insured engineering firm and then refund $200,000 to the architect to net the $100,000 judgment amount.
D. Pursue the $100,000 judgment amount solely out of the architect's income and assets for not having maintained any insurance.

Answer: B. The traditional rule of joint-and-several liability means that the plaintiff may collect all or a portion of the damages from any defendant. The owner may collect all of the $100,000 joint and several judgment from the insured engineering firm. A is incorrect because joint and several liability allows the owner to collect all, not just half, of the judgment from the insured engineering firm. Why stop at half? C is incorrect because the liability is limited to $100,000, meaning that the owner has no basis to collect $300,000 from the engineering firm. There is also no reason to give $200,000 back to the architect who was also liable. D is incorrect because the owner's objective is to collect on the judgment. Although the owner could pursue the full judgment amount from the architect, that pursuit would not achieve the owner's goal as readily as collecting the insurance from the engineering firm. The architect is likely to resist collection, whereas the insurance company is certain not to resist, its contractual obligation to the engineering firm being to indemnify.

126. The owner of a small machine shop determined to expand. The owner retained a builder who marked the location of an underground water line servicing the shop. An excavator then dug footings for the shop's addition but struck and severed a water line that the builder had failed to locate and mark. The water-line break flooded a portion of the machine shop, damaging expensive equipment and requiring extensive repairs. The owner retained a construction expert who determined that both the builder and excavator had breached standards of reasonable care leading to the damage. The owner then consulted an attorney regarding their tort liability. Which of the following best describes the relative liability of the builder and excavator under the traditional common law?

A. The builder would have primary liability and the excavator secondary liability for damage resulting from their sequential action.
B. The excavator would have direct liability and the builder vicarious liability for damage resulting from their relative actions.
C. The builder and excavator would have joint and several liability for damage resulting from their concerted action.
D. The builder and excavator would have several liability but not joint liability for damage resulting from independent action.

Answer: C. Joint and several liability may arise from the concerted action of two or more tortfeasors. The builder and excavator were acting in concert, meaning coordinating their work toward a common end. Acting in concert is one basis for joint and several liability. A is incorrect because the law does not recognize sequential action as a basis for primary and secondary liability. The terms have no legal meaning in this context. B is incorrect because both parties acted in ways that they participated directly in causing the loss, even if the excavator's actions were the more immediate. Both would have direct rather than merely vicarious liability. Their concert of action would make them jointly and severally liable. D is incorrect because their action was in concert (coordinated toward a common end) rather than independent, and they would therefore have joint and several, not merely several, liability.

127. A driver took her vehicle to a mechanic for brake inspection and repair. The driver later drove the vehicle into the rear of another vehicle, causing injury to a passenger in the other vehicle. A police officer ticketed the driver for speeding and negligent failure to stop, even though the driver complained that the brakes had failed. Investigation revealed that the mechanic had carelessly neglected to properly attach the brake pad, making it harder for the speeding driver to stop the vehicle in time. The injured passenger made a demand on the driver's liability insurer who consulted its retained counsel about the mechanic's relative liability. Assuming a common-law jurisdiction with no no-fault laws, which of the following best describes the relative liability of the driver and mechanic to the passenger?

A. The driver and mechanic have joint and several liability for having caused an indivisible injury.
B. The driver and mechanic have several but not joint liability for having caused an indivisible injury.
C. The driver and mechanic have joint but not several liability for having caused an indivisible injury.
D. Neither the driver nor mechanic has liability because neither alone would have caused the injury.

Answer: A. Joint and several liability may also arise from two independent actors causing an indivisible injury. Here, the driver and mechanic each contributed to the passenger's injury. Although acting independently, they caused an indivisible (a single) injury and so are jointly and severally liable. B is incorrect because they do have joint, not just several, liability. C is incorrect because they do have several, not just joint, liability. The passenger could collect all or part from either. D is incorrect because although it is possible that neither alone would have caused the injury (the facts are not that clear), even independent actors whose negligence together causes an injury have joint and several liability.

128. A hotel employed a security company to lock doors and arm a security system at the hotel each night for guest security. A hotel clerk carelessly dropped several room key cards on the sidewalk outside the hotel entrance. That same evening, the security company mistakenly failed to schedule anyone to lock the doors and arm the security system. An unidentified individual entered an unlocked door and used the dropped room key cards to assault and rob two hotel guests. The hotel consulted its counsel regarding its liability and the liability of the security company. Which of the following best describes the relative liability of the hotel and security company?

A. The hotel and security company are neither jointly nor severally liable but are each separately liable.

Torts Workbook

B. The hotel and security company are jointly but not severally liable for common failures made independently.
C. The hotel and security company are severally but not jointly liable for independent failures.
D. The hotel and security company are jointly and severally liable for failures in a common duty.

Answer: D. Joint and several liability may also arise from failures in a common duty. Here, the hotel and security company each owed hotel guests duties of ordinary and reasonable care for hotel security. They each failed in that duty, causing the hotel guest's loss. They are jointly and severally liable. A, B, and C are incorrect because the hotel and security company have both joint and several liability.

129. A hunter and his friend took the hunter's pickup truck to hunt up north. The hunter drove through the dark of the early morning at slightly above the speed limit. A deer stepped out into the road ahead of the pickup truck, requiring the hunter to slam on the brakes. A mechanic had carelessly failed to replace one of two brake shoes during the pickup truck's most recent servicing. As a result of the pickup's truck speed and poor braking, the pickup truck collided with the deer and ran off the road, injuring the passenger. The passenger filed suit against the driver and mechanic to recover for his personal injuries as the jurisdiction's law permitted. That law also required the jury to allocate fault. Which of the following describes the most likely evaluation of relative fault?

A. The mechanic was solely at fault because his carelessly servicing brakes came before the driver's speeding.
B. The driver was solely at fault because his speeding came after the mechanic's carelessly servicing brakes.
C. The mechanic's fault probably exceeds the driver's because the driver's excessive speed was slight.
D. The driver's fault probably exceeds the mechanics because speed is worse than carelessly servicing brakes.

Answer: C. Most jurisdictions alter joint-and-several liability to require the factfinder to allocate fault and the judge to apportion damages among liable defendants. Both parties were at fault, the driver for slightly excessive speed and the mechanic for carelessly servicing brakes. Because the speed's excessiveness was slight, the mechanic's carelessness seems the greater. A and B are incorrect because the order of the negligence is of no particular consequence so long as both contribute to the injury. D is incorrect as a judgment call with C because the driver's excessive speed was slight.

130. A large tent collapsed on a wedding party, injuring several guests. The wedding producer had retained a contractor to specify the tent. The contractor did so and then had retained a tent company to locate it on the wedding grounds. The tent company did so and then had retained a crew to erect the tent. The crew did so and then had left it to a caterer to secure shut certain tent door flaps. The injured guests retained counsel to investigate tort claims. Of the producer, contractor, tent company, crew, and caterer, only the tent company had liability insurance coverage. Which of the following research topics would most help determine the tent company's liability for negligent acts by the others?

A. The law of joint and several liability.
B. The law of vicarious liability.
C. The law of allocation of fault.
D. The law of satisfaction and release.

Answer: B. Vicarious liability holds one party liable for the torts of another. Research on that topic would help the lawyer determine whether the tent company was liable for the negligence of the others. A is incorrect because joint and several liability has to do with the direct liability of multiple parties, not the liability of one party for the negligence of another. C is incorrect because allocation of fault involves determining relative percentages of fault among negligent parties, not the liability of one party for the negligence of another. D is incorrect because satisfaction and release involves the settlement of one party's liability, not the liability of one party for the negligence of another.

131. A restaurant manager instructed a cook to drive the restaurant's catering van to the grocer for fresh produce for the night's fare. On the way back to the restaurant from the grocer's, the cook ran a red light, collided the van into the side of a sedan, and injured a passenger. The passenger retained counsel to plead the allowable tort claims in a jurisdiction that had no no-fault act. Which of the following best states those tort claims?

A. Negligence as to the cook and vicarious liability as to the restaurant.
B. Negligence as to the cook and vicarious liability as to the manager.
C. Negligence as to the cook, manager, and restaurant.
D. Vicarious liability as to the cook, manager, and restaurant.

Answer: A. A first form of vicarious liability is the respondeat-superior liability of an employer for the negligent acts of employees within the course of employment. The cook was negligent in running the red light. The cook was acting with the course of restaurant employment making the restaurant vicariously liable. B is incorrect because the manager did not employ the cook. The restaurant employed the cook and owned the van. Respondeat-superior liability would not extend to the manager. C is incorrect because the manager and restaurant were not negligent on the given facts. D is incorrect because the cook would have no vicarious (only direct) liability, and the manager would have no vicarious or other liability.

132. A pet store employed a sale clerk. The sales clerk took a lunch break, driving his own vehicle to a nearby fast-food store. On the way back to the pet store, the sales clerk dropped off the pet store's cash deposit at the pet store's bank as instructed. On the way out of the bank's parking lot, the sales clerk turned in front of a van carrying elderly nursing-home residents to an outing, resulting in a collision. The collision injured one of the elderly residents, who sued the sales clerk for negligence and pet store for respondeat-superior liability. The pet store's insurer retained defense counsel. Which of the following describes the pet store's best defense?

A. File a motion for summary judgment challenging respondeat-superior liability.
B. Cross-claim against the sales clerk for negligence to allocate fault.
C. Deny respondeat-superior liability but admit the sales clerk's fault.
D. Coordinate the pet store's defense with defense of the sales clerk.

Answer: D. Commuting to and from work, and running personal errands, are not within the course of employment, but running employer errands is. The sales clerk was clearly on an employer errand when the accident occurred, meaning that the pet store would have respondeat-superior liability for any negligence by the sales clerk. The two defendants had better coordinate their defense. A is incorrect because there is no factual or legal basis on which to challenge respondeat-superior liability. B is incorrect because cross-claiming against the sales clerk would only serve to benefit the elderly resident by confirming the pet store's own respondeat-superior liability. Respondeat-superior liability is all or nothing of the liability of another, not an allocation of fault as to that other. C is incorrect because admitting the sales clerk's fault would establish respondeat-superior liability for that fault. The pet store must dispute the sales clerk's fault if it is to avoid liability, provided that there is a factual basis to do so, as the facts leave open.

133. A night club employed a bouncer to maintain order and eject unruly patrons. The bouncer used more zeal than necessary to shove a drunken and disorderly patron from the night club. The bouncer's shove caused the patron to break his wrist when the patron fell off the night club's front stoop. The patron retained a trial lawyer who sued the night club in vicarious liability for the patron's injury. The night club's defense counsel filed a motion for summary judgment arguing that there is no vicarious liability for intentional torts. Which of the following describes the trial lawyer's best response?

A. There is vicarious liability for all intentional torts committed by an employee while on duty, meaning while at the employer's premises during working hours.
B. Although there is generally no vicarious liability for intentional torts, there remains vicarious liability for intentional acts ratified afterward by the employer.
C. Although there is generally no vicarious liability for intentional torts, there remains vicarious liability for authorized intentional acts furthering the employer's business.
D. Concede that the defense counsel's argument is correct, and request leave to amend to allege the employer's direct liability for negligent hiring and supervision.

Answer: C. There is generally no vicarious liability for intentional torts unless the act was in furtherance of the employer's mission or the employer authorized or ratified the act. The night club employed the bounce to eject unruly patrons, which is an intentional act furthering the night club's business. Excessive zeal in that act may be carelessness for which the night club would be vicariously liable. A is incorrect because it states the vicarious liability much too broadly. There is generally no vicarious liability for intentional torts, except with the noted exceptions (the bouncer rule). B is incorrect because although the option correctly states another exception (ratification), there is no evidence here of ratification. The facts do not state that the night club approved later of the bouncer's action. D is incorrect because although the option correctly states an alternative theory of direct liability (negligent hiring and supervision), there is no evidence of negligent hiring or supervision, and there is no need to concede on vicarious liability.

134. A courier service employed a bevy of bicyclists to carry deliveries including cash deposits on the crowded downtown streets of a metropolis. One courier bicyclist converted many thousands of dollars in cash deposits from several courier-service customers before authorities discovered the conduct and arrested the bicyclist. The customers retained counsel who determined from investigation that the bicyclist had a long record for crimes of dishonesty included fraud and conversion. Which of the following describes the best claim for counsel to plead on behalf of the customers and against the courier service?

A. Vicarious liability for the negligence of the bicyclist.
B. Vicarious liability for the conversion by the bicyclist.
C. Direct liability for negligent hiring and entrustment.
D. Contribution and indemnity against the bicyclist.

Answer: C. Employers may have direct liability for negligent hiring or entrustment, where an employee commits an intentional tort consistent with the employee's history that the employer should have discovered before hiring and entrusting. Here, no responsible employer would hire and entrust a criminal defrauder and converter to handle cash deposits. A and B are incorrect because there is generally no vicarious liability for intentional torts. The bicyclist acted intentionally in converting the cash, not negligently. None of the exceptions (the bouncer rule, authorization, or ratification) apply here. A is also incorrect because the bicyclist acted intentionally, not negligently. D is incorrect because the call of the question asked for claims against the courier service, not the bicyclist. It would also likely do little good to sue the bicyclist who has been arrested and will likely be without assets. If the courier service did sue the bicyclist, it would be for common-law indemnity, not contribution.

135. A property owner leased a facility to a metal-coating shop. The shop went out of business. When the property owner tried to sell the property, soil testing showed toxic waste from the metal-coating shop. The property owner hired a contractor to clean up the toxic waste, but some of the toxic waste contaminated the neighbor's land during the contractor's clean up. The neighbor retained counsel to investigate tort claims. Investigation showed that the contractor was uninsured and without substantial assets but that the property owner had applicable liability insurance. Which of the following describes the best advice to the neighbor regarding claims against the property owner?

A. The property owner owes vicarious liability to the neighbor for an inherently dangerous activity.
B. The property owner owes vicarious liability to the neighbor for retaining control of the clean-up work.
C. The property owner owes direct liability to the neighbor for negligent hiring and entrustment.
D. The property owner owes contribution and indemnity to the neighbor for the contamination of the land.

Answer: A. There may also be vicarious liability for the acts of independent contractors, where the one hiring the contractor retains control or has nondelegable duties or inherently dangerous activities, or the contractor has apparent authority. Here, the clean up of toxic waste was probably an inherently dangerous activity not delegable to another without liability. B is incorrect because there is no evidence that the property owner retained control. C is incorrect because there is no evidence of negligence in hiring or entrustment. D is incorrect because contribution depends on direct liability of which there is none here, and indemnity depends on a relationship not present here. Neither contribution nor indemnity apply.

136. Two sailors purchased a sailboat together, agreeing that they would share the purchase, maintenance, and other costs associated with using the sailboat in their sea tour business. The seller of the sailboat instructed the sailors in how to unhook the battery to the small engine in the sailboat when not in use, to prevent accidental fire. The sailboat later caught fire, destroying the dock at the marina. Investigation revealed that the last sailor to use the sailboat had not removed

the battery as the seller instructed, resulting in the fire. The marina's owner consulted counsel regarding the liability of the two sailors for the dock's destruction. Which of the following best describes that liability?

A. Both sailors are directly liable, each for their own negligence.
B. The last sailor to use the sailboat is liable in negligence and the other sailor vicariously liable.
C. The last sailor to use the sailboat is liable in negligence and the other sailor not liable.
D. Neither sailor is liable, there having been no negligence.

Answer: B. Another form of vicarious liability arises around joint enterprises, defined by a common purpose, agreement, and pecuniary interest, and shared direction or control. The sailors had a common purpose, agreement, and pecuniary interest in using the sailboat in their sea-tour business. One was directly liable and the other vicariously liable. A is incorrect because one sailor was not negligent but was still vicariously liable. C is incorrect because the other sailor who was not negligent was still vicariously liable. D is incorrect because both sailors were liable, one directly and the other vicariously.

137. A young man wanted transportation to a party. The young man asked to borrow a neighbor's car, saying that he needed to visit his grandmother in the hospital. The neighbor loaned her vehicle to the young man, who drove the vehicle to the party. The young man got drunk at the party and, on his way home, crossed the center line and crashed his neighbor's car into an oncoming vehicle. The young man had no liability insurance. The neighbor had motor-vehicle liability insurance. The occupants of the oncoming vehicle consulted a trial lawyer about the neighbor's liability. Which of the following best describes a legal basis for the neighbor's liability in a jurisdiction having no motor-vehicle no-fault act?

A. The family-purpose doctrine for vicarious liability.
B. The vicarious liability of a joint venturer.
C. Respondeat-superior liability.
D. The existence of a motor-vehicle owner-consent statute in the jurisdiction.

Answer: D. Bailors are not generally liable to third parties who suffer damage from bailees' use of the personal property, but owner-consent statutes commonly change that rule as to vehicles, making the owner liable. Consent to use of the vehicle is consent to all use. When the neighbor loaned the young man the neighbor's car, the neighbor would be liable for any injury or damage caused by the young man's negligence using the car. A is incorrect because there was no family relationship between the young man and neighbor. B is incorrect because there was no joint venture. C is incorrect because there is no employer-employee relationship.

138. A homeowner hired a general contractor to add an addition to the home. The general contractor hired a roofer to install the shingles on the addition's roof. The roofer used an unstable old ladder from which the articulated feet had long ago broken off. The homeowner fell from the ladder when the roofer invited the homeowner to inspect the roof, and what remained of the ladder's broken feet skidded out. The homeowner fell onto a pile of jagged debris that the general contractor had left in violation of safety regulations for a clean workplace. The homeowner sued the roofer for negligence to recover for the homeowner's resulting injuries. Which of the following best describes the roofer's common-law rights as to the general contractor?

A. The roofer has the right to contribution from the general contractor.
B. The roofer has the right to indemnity from the general contractor.
C. The roofer has no rights because the roofer was actively negligent.
D. The roofer could sue the general contractor for vicarious liability.

Answer: A. Contribution is the claim of a defendant that another party pay a fair share of the damage for which the defendant is liable. Here, the roofer was negligent in providing the broken ladder, but the contractor was negligent in leaving the pile of debris into which the homeowner fell. The roofer could seek contribution from the contractor. B is incorrect because there is no indication of a contract for indemnity, and both parties were actively negligent so that common-law indemnity does not apply. C is incorrect because the roofer has a right of contribution. Active negligence does not bar a claim for contribution. D is incorrect because the general contractor is not vicariously liable for the roofer's negligence. It does not fit any of the bases for vicarious liability on the given facts. Even if it did, vicarious liability would be a claim that the injured homeowner would make, not the roofer.

139. A camp manager and his younger assistant took the manager's pickup truck into town to buy groceries. The manager allowed the assistant to drive the pickup truck on the way back to the camp. The assistant failed to stop at a stop sign, resulting in a collision that injured another motorist. The jurisdiction had no motor-vehicle no-fault act. The manager had minimum liability insurance but the young man additional liability insurance through a vehicle that the young man owned. When the manager received from the motorist a substantial settlement demand larger than the manager's insurance limits, the manager consulted a lawyer. Which of the following describes the best advice regarding the manager's excess liability over the manager's insurance limits?

A. The manager must pay the excess liability out of his own assets and earnings without recourse against anyone for reimbursement of that personal liability.
B. The manager may seek contribution from the assistant and assistant's insurer for all liability including the excess liability over the manager's insurance limits.
C. The manager may seek indemnity from the assistant and assistant's insurer for all liability including the excess liability over the manager's insurance limits.
D. The manager has no excess liability because the motorist's recovery is limited to the manager's insurance limits. The balance of the damages will go unpaid.

Answer: C. Indemnity is the right of a defendant to reimbursement from the party whose fault created the defendant's liability. Here, the manager's liability would be vicarious, by law from an owner-consent statute. The assistant was negligent, would be directly liable, and would owe the manager common-law indemnity for the whole liability including the excess liability. In effect, the two insurers would ensure that the total limits were paid before either insured had any personal liability. A is incorrect because the manager has recourse against the actively negligent driver-assistant, for common-law indemnity. The assistant's insurer would have to cover the excess liability up to its insurance limits. B is incorrect because indemnity is the correct claim, not contribution. The manager would claim contribution only if the manager was at fault in part, which the manager was not. D is incorrect because insurance limits do not limit excess liability. The insured pays the excess liability.

140. Two motor-vehicle drivers collided due to excessive speed on the part of one and a failure to yield on the part of the other. Police ticketed both drivers, and each driver acknowledged fault. A vehicle passenger injured in the collision settled with one of the drivers whose insurer paid a small portion of the driver's available insurance limits. The passenger then made a demand on the other driver for three times the first driver's settlement amount. The insurer for the non-settling driver consulted its in-house counsel regarding the liability of the settling driver to help settle the remaining claim. Which of the following best describes the settling driver's liability?

A. The settling driver is liable in contribution because that driver underpaid.
B. The settling driver is not liable in contribution if the settlement was in good faith.
C. The settling driver is liable in indemnity because of their common fault.
D. The settling driver is vicariously liable because of their dependent fault.

Answer: B. A defendant who settles liability in good faith is no longer subject to contribution from other parties. The settlement was only a small portion of the insurance limits and a third of the motorist's demand on the other driver, but neither of those facts is clear evidence of bad faith. A is incorrect because the small settlement may not have been underpayment, and underpayment alone is not evidence of bad faith. C is incorrect because there is no basis for common-law or contractual indemnity. They were both actively at fault. D is incorrect because there is no basis for vicarious liability. Dependent fault is not a basis for vicarious liability.

141. A motor-vehicle accident seriously injured a pedestrian, permanently ending the pedestrian's ability to work. The pedestrian sued the driver of the car that hit the pedestrian. The pedestrian also sued the driver of a truck that the car driver had tried to avoid when the car hit the pedestrian. Following the trial judge's correct instructions on the applicable law, the jury awarded $1,000,000, allocating 90% of the fault to the car driver and just 10% to the truck driver. The trial judge entered judgment against the car driver for $900,000 and truck driver for $100,000. The car driver had the state's $20,000 minimum liability insurance limits. The truck driver had $1,000,000 limits. Which of the following best describes the pedestrian's liability-insurance recovery?

A. The pedestrian will recover all $1,000,000 of the judgment in insurance because of rights of contribution.
B. The pedestrian will recover all $1,000,000 of the judgment in insurance because of rights of indemnity.
C. The pedestrian will recover the car driver's $20,000 limits and $100,000 of the truck driver's $1,000,000 limits.
D. The pedestrian will recover no insurance because the judgment was against the drivers, not their insurers.

Answer: C. Contribution actions are not necessary or allowed where tort law apportions liability among the liable defendants. Liability is limited to the allocated fault and apportioned damages. The car driver's insurer would pay its $20,000 limits, and the truck driver's insurer $100,000 of its $1,000,000 limits. The pedestrian would have to seek the car driver's personal assets and earnings for the unpaid balance. A is incorrect because allocation of fault ends rights of contribution. B is incorrect because there is no basis for common-law or contractual indemnity in the given facts. The two drivers appear to have been strangers to one another, each actively negligent. D is incorrect because the insurers have contractual (and possibly statutory) duties to the drivers to pay for liability up to their insurance limits.

142. A plastics plant hired a general contractor to construct an addition to the plant. The general contractor selected and hired a subcontractor to do the steel work. Because they had worked together before, their agreement was only as to the scope and price for the work. The subcontractor's careless handling of a steel girder resulted in serious injury to a building inspector on the site. The inspector sued the subcontractor in negligence and the general contractor for vicarious liability. The general contractor's insurer retained counsel to respond to the inspector's complaint. Which of the following best describes how the general contractor's counsel should plead the general contractor's rights against the subcontractor?

A. Plead nothing. There are no rights.
B. Plead contribution.
C. Plead contractual indemnity.
D. Plead common-law indemnity.

Answer: D. Common-law indemnity applies where the defendant seeking indemnity has only vicarious liability. Here, the inspector pled only the general contractor's vicarious liability. Although there was no contract term for indemnity between the general contractor and subcontractor, there would have been common-law indemnity. A is incorrect because of the right to common-law indemnity. B is incorrect because the general contractor was not actively negligent, and contribution is for allocation of fault between two or more actively negligent parties. C is incorrect because there was no contract term for indemnity.

143. The cap to a pressurized tank exploded, causing serious injury to a worker. Investigation traced the explosion to a manufacturing defect in the cap. The worker retained a trial lawyer who sued the tank's distributor. The distributor provided its counsel with the contract between the distributor and manufacturer. A contract clause stated that the manufacturer would hold the distributor harmless from any liability for injury or loss caused by defective products. Which of the following best describes how the distributor's counsel should plead the distributor's response to the worker's complaint?

A. Plead a counter-claim against the worker for not suing the manufacturer.
B. Plead a third-party claim against the manufacturer for products liability.
C. Plead a third-party claim against the manufacturer for contractual indemnity.
D. Plead a third-party claim against the manufacturer for contribution.

Answer: C. Contractual indemnity allocates the liability for fault by advance agreement among the responsible defendants. The manufacturer promised to hold the distributor harmless for injury from defective products, constituting contractual indemnity. A is incorrect because there is no counter-claim for failure to sue. The distributor's recourse would be to bring the manufacturer in as a third party. B is incorrect because the distributor was not injured and has no products-liability claim, and pleading a claim against the manufacturer for products liability would be to admit the distributor's own products liability. D is incorrect because contribution is a right of action between parties who are actively negligent. Here, the distributor's liability is passive as a pass-through entity for the manufacturer's active negligence in creating the manufacturing defect.

144. A driver carelessly fell asleep at the wheel, allowing the vehicle to drift into the median and crash. The crash injured a vehicle passenger. The passenger received medical treatment for accident injuries, in which the physician's malpractice worsened the original injury. The passenger retained counsel who sued the driver and physician. The trial judge asked counsel to draft a jury instruction stating the apportionment of damages between the driver and physician. Which of the following best describes that apportionment?

A. The jury should not separate damages for the successive injuries whether or not it is able, because each defendant is liable for the full amount of the damages.
B. The jury should separate damages for the successive injuries whether or not it is able, because some apportionment even if arbitrary is more just than not.
C. The jury should separate damages for the successive injuries if it is able, representing the relative degrees of fault of the driver and physician.
D. The jury should separate damages for the successive injuries if it is able, so that the physician will be liable for only the results of the physician's own actions.

Answer: D. When the plaintiff has suffered successive injuries from separately liable defendants, then damages are apportioned to each defendant. If the damages can be separated, then the jury should make the driver pay for the accident injuries and the physician for the malpractice injuries. A is incorrect because the physician should not have to pay for the damages from the prior motor-vehicle accident because the physician was not negligent in bringing about that accident and did not cause it. The physician should pay for only the malpractice damages. B is incorrect because juries separate damages only when able. They do not make arbitrary judgments. C is incorrect because the driver and physician did not cause the same injury. Juries allocate fault only among defendants causing the same injury. If defendants cause different injuries, then juries apportion damages among those different injuries.

145. A homemaker tripped and fell on a large crack in the interior concrete floor of a home-products retailer, injuring her left knee. A truck driver ran a red light, driving his truck into the homemaker's vehicle while the homemaker was on the way to a medical clinic for treatment to her injured left knee. The collision injured the homemaker's left knee. When the homemaker's knee failed to recover, she sued both the retailer and truck driver. The proofs at trial were inconclusive as to which part of her knee injury the homemaker's trip and fall or motor-vehicle accident caused. Which of the following best describes how the trial judge should instruct the jury regarding the inconclusive proofs?

A. Where proofs as to the causes of successive injury are inconclusive, defendants bear no liability for the injury.
B. Where proofs as to the causes of successive injury are inconclusive, the burden shifts to defendants who are liable.
C. Where proofs as to the causes of successive injury are inconclusive, the plaintiff must file separate suits.
D. Where proofs as to the causes of successive injury are inconclusive, the jury must apportion damages equitably.

Answer: B. When plaintiff is unable to prove which defendant caused which successive injury, the defendants will have the burden of proof, meaning that they will share liability. The plaintiff has the burden of proof to show which negligent actor caused which successive injury, by a preponderance of the evidence, unless the plaintiff cannot prove them separate, in which case the defendants will both bear liability. A is incorrect because courts and the Restatement have held that the defendants will then bear the burden. C is incorrect because filing separate suits would not resolve the problem. The court and jury in the separate suits would face the same problem of how to treat successive injuries by separate tortfeasors. D is incorrect because there is no basis for equitable apportionment where proofs are inconclusive. Equity must rest on proofs, not conjecture. The rule is instead to shift the burden of proof, leaving the defendants liable.

Essay Question: An entrepreneur operated a car-detailing business out of the back of a business owner's do-it-yourself carwash. The entrepreneur and one employee would spend all day picking up corporate and rental cars for hand cleaning. Throughout the day, they would also check the do-it-yourself car wash for the carwash owner to be sure that the garbage pails were empty, the stalls clean of debris, and the coin- and bill-changers operating. They would also take complaints and give refunds for the carwash owner. In return, the carwash charged the entrepreneur no rent for the use of the back area on the premises, although the entrepreneur gave the carwash owner some cash now and then to help with the water and electric bills. They had only one sign out front for both the owner's do-it-yourself carwash and the entrepreneur's detailing service. Most people thought that they were partners, and they did not discourage the impression, although they kept their own books and filed their own tax returns. The carwash owner paid the entrepreneur's helper to mow the grass. A customer of the carwash owner lost an eye using one of the owner's carwash wands and sued both the carwash owner and entrepreneur. Discuss and evaluate the entrepreneur's vicarious liability for the carwash owner's alleged negligence.

Model Answer: The question requires discussing and evaluating an entrepreneur's vicarious liability for the alleged negligence of a carwash owner, when one of the owner's customers suffered an eye injury from a wash wand.

One ordinarily has vicarious liability only for the torts of an employee or agent acting in the course or scope of the employment or agency (respondeat-superior liability) and for the torts of a joint venturer. A joint venture depends on common purpose, agreement, monetary interest, and direction or control. One ordinarily does not have vicarious liability for the acts of an independent contractor or bailee. Law distinguishes an employee from an independent contractor variously, but the basic test for an employee is one of control. One may also look to whether the employer dictated the time, provided the tools, and dictated the methods, and had a process to hire, fire, and discipline.

Here, first as to an employer-vicarious-liability or respondeat-superior theory, the carwash owner does not appear to employ the entrepreneur, the facts giving no indication of wages and instead only free rent. We have no indication that the carwash owner hired, fired, or disciplined the entrepreneur or gave the entrepreneur the time, tools, or methods to work. The carwash owner does not appear to control the entrepreneur's work. So the entrepreneur is probably not an employee under the common control and economic-reality tests for employment. And the reverse, that the entrepreneur employed the carwash owner, would certainly not meet these tests, with no facts supporting control or the other factors of time, tools, methods, and hiring, firing, and discipline. On the other hand, the entrepreneur may possibly be a joint venturer with the carwash owner. The facts indicate that people thought that they were partners, which they did not discourage. The carwash owner and the entrepreneur seem to agree on the conduct of the carwash business, and they may share a common purpose in cleaning cars. I would like to see their sign out front, whether it distinguishes their two businesses. They might even to some degree share common direction or control over use and maintenance of the facility. Yet it does not appear that they share in the business income. Indeed, they appear to have separate businesses, the carwash owner for the carwash and the entrepreneur for the detailing. The facts state that they keep separate books and file their own tax returns. I would like to know how long that arrangement has gone on and whether they share any financial interest beyond the free rent. The facts indicate that the entrepreneur has an employee, further distinguishing his detailing business from the carwash owner's carwash. I think that the customer has only the slimmest of chances of proving them joint venturers.

In sum, I highly doubt that the entrepreneur has vicarious liability for any negligence on the carwash owner's part in causing the customer's injury. I wonder whether the entrepreneur has business-liability insurance, too, and what the customer expected to gain by suing the entrepreneur in addition to the carwash owner. The carwash owner probably has the only coverage, although we would need to confirm. I would like to defend the entrepreneur who seems to have a good small business going and probably needs to get out of the suit at low cost and without liability, for himself and his employee. Small service businesses are important contributors to local economies, vocational development of individuals, and well being of families.

Essay Question: A plumber and an electrician worked in coordination on a construction project. Through a combination of negligent errors by each during the course of their work, a carpenter suffered severe electric shock and associated burns. The carpenter sued the plumber, whose insurer negotiated a settlement figure on the plumber's behalf with the carpenter. What terms would you include on the plumber's and his insurer's behalf in the settlement agreement with the carpenter to ensure the greatest rights and greatest protections with respect to the joint liability of the electrician? Explain your answer.

Answer: The question requires determining what terms to include in a plumber's settlement agreement with a carpenter shocked and burned on the plumber's project, when the carpenter may continue to pursue claims against an electrician with whom the plumber coordinated work.

A good-faith settlement bars contributions claims from non-settling defendants. Settling parties will execute a settlement agreement stating the settlement terms. Settling parties may include an agreement that the claimant indemnify the settling respondent for any expense to which the claimant's continued pursuit of the claim causes the respondent. In a common-law state, a settling party may also obtain the release of non-settling parties and then pursue contribution claims against them.

Here, the settlement agreement would need to ensure that the electrician could not, if sued by the carpenter, seek to join the plumber as a third-party defendant for the plumber to contribute. The plumber's good faith in settling with the carpenter would ordinarily bar such a third-party claim by the electrician, but settling defendants typically include an indemnification clause requiring the plaintiff to pay for any expense and damages that the settling defendant incurs as a result of any other action by the plaintiff to pursue remedies against other defendants. So the plumber could include an indemnification clause requiring the carpenter to pay for the plumber's defense and any damages the plumber pays to any other party because of the carpenter's action. The plumber may also want to see that the electrician contributes to the settlement that the plumber paid to the carpenter. The plumber could arrange for the electrician's contribution by obtaining from the carpenter a release of the electrician (as well as the plumber) and an assignment of the carpenter's action against the electrician. These provisions would give the plumber the greatest rights and protections as to the electrician who should bear joint-and-several liability with the plumber for breach of common duties owed to the carpenter.

In sum, the settling plumber and carpenter should take care in executing a settlement agreement that provides for the carpenter's indemnity of the plumber. They may wish to have the carpenter grant the electrician a release so that the plumber could pursue the electrician for contribution.

Essay Question: A skateboarder seriously injured his elbow in a skating-boarding accident on a public sidewalk outside of his home. His mother got him in the family vehicle to drive him to the emergency room. On the way, as the skateboarder's mother was driving through an intersection, a truck driver ran a stop sign in another vehicle and collided with the passenger side of the vehicle in which the skateboarder was riding. The skateboarder's elbow injury from the skating-boarding incident was aggravated, and the skateboarder also suffered a serious leg injury. An ambulance took the skateboarder to the emergency room, where a doctor negligently treated the skateboarder's leg, considerably worsening the leg injury. Describe the truck driver's and doctor's liability for the skateboarder's elbow and leg injuries.

Answer: The question requires that we describe the liability of a truck driver for a skateboarder's leg injury and aggravation of the skateboarder's elbow injury when the truck driver ran a stop sign colliding with the vehicle in which the skateboarder rode as a passenger, and the liability of a doctor who negligently treated and worsened the leg injury.

Under rules for liability involving successive injuries, a tortfeasor does not pay for harm subsequent to the tortfeasor's wrong, which makes sense given that the tortfeasor would have no control over those subsequent events. Jurisdictions recognize an exception, though, when the subsequent harm is foreseeable as in the case of malpractice during treatment for the injury that the tortfeasor caused.

Authority holds the tortfeasor liable not just for the direct harm but also for the malpractice injury. Another rule has to do with liability for a pre-existing condition, of which the tortfeasor naturally has none, given that the tortfeasor did not cause the pre-existing condition. Yet an exception to that rule holds that the tortfeasor will pay for all of the harm, both the pre-existing condition and its aggravation, when the tortfeasor is unable to prove the distinction.

Under these rules, the truck driver will pay for aggravating the skateboarder's elbow injury, not the pre-existing elbow condition, unless the truck driver is unable to prove the difference, in which case the truck driver will pay for all of the skateboarder's elbow injury. The truck driver will also pay for the skateboarder's leg injury, which her negligence directly caused, plus also pay for the doctor's worsening of the skateboarder's leg injury, which would have been foreseeable to the truck driver. The doctor will pay only for the aggravation he caused to the skateboarder's leg injury unless the doctor cannot separate the aggravation from the pre-existing condition, in which case the doctor will pay for all of the leg injury. The skateboarder will not get a double recovery, though. The single-satisfaction rule will prevent it.

In sum, the law requires separating out the damages to only those injuries that the truck driver and doctor each individually caused, except that the truck driver will also pay for the doctor's foreseeable negligence, and if the doctor cannot separate out his aggravation of the injury from the original injury, then the doctor will pay for all of that injury.

WEEK 11

146. A young motor-vehicle driver on a cell phone failed to observe a vehicle stop ahead of him and slammed his vehicle into the rear of the other vehicle. The collision caused serious injuries to the driver and three passengers in the other vehicle. The young driver had the lowest motor-vehicle insurance liability limits allowed by state law, $20,000 per person and $40,000 per occurrence. The four injured occupants in the other vehicle tendered demands ranging from $50,000 to $100,000 on the young driver, who notified his motor-vehicle insurance carrier. The motor-vehicle insurance carrier consulted its in-house counsel indicating its willingness to pay its insurance limits. Which of the following best describes how the four occupants would divide those limits?

A. The four occupants must divide the $40,000 limit based on relative injury value with none receiving more than $20,000.
B. The four occupants must accept $20,000 each no matter the relative value of their injuries, totaling $80,000.
C. The four occupants must accept $40,000 each no matter the relative value of their injuries, totaling $160,000.
D. The four occupants may receive from the insurance carrier as much as their injury values warrant with no limit.

Answer: A. States require motor-vehicle insurance with varying liability limits. The limits are commonly double limits, the first amount a limit on payment to any one person and the second amount a limit for each accident. The four occupants would divide the total $40,000 occurrence limit with none receiving more than $20,000. The division would be based on the relative value of their injuries. B is incorrect because the occurrence limit is $40,000. C is incorrect because the person limit is $20,000 and occurrence limit $40,000. D is incorrect because the limits are $20,000 per person and $40,000 per occurrence.

147. A high-speed motor-vehicle collision occurred on a three-lane wide portion of the interstate when two vehicles passed a third vehicle in the middle lane and then tried to merge into the center lane. The collision killed one vehicle passenger and seriously injured others. The motor vehicle accident occurred in New York, a no-fault state, between two New York-resident motorists. After notifying her insurer, one of the vehicle drivers consulted a lawyer regarding her potential liability. Which of the following best describes that potential liability?

A. An at-fault driver will be liable for the death and for serious injuries meeting the state's tort threshold, and no more than the state's minimum insurance limits.
B. An at-fault driver will be liable for the death and for serious injuries meeting the state's tort threshold, covered up to the motor-vehicle insurance's limits.
C. An at-fault driver will be liable only for the death but not for any serious injuries, covered up to the motor-vehicle insurance's limits.
D. There is no liability, the state's no-fault act barring all liability and requiring all persons and estates to look to first-party motor-vehicle no-fault benefits.

Answer: B. About 12 states have motor-vehicle no-fault acts of varying kind, but all retain some negligence liability in certain situations. Death and very serious injuries meet the tort thresholds. Insurance will pay that liability up to its limits, after which the at-fault driver will be liable for the excess over insurance limits. A is incorrect because the driver will be liable for any excess over insurance limits. C is incorrect because there is liable for serious injuries exceeding the tort threshold. D is incorrect because there is liability for death and for serious injuries exceeding the tort threshold.

148. A motor-vehicle driver drove faster than icy conditions warranted, resulting in his inability to stop the vehicle at a four-way stop sign. His vehicle struck another vehicle that had already entered the intersection after stopping. The collision caused each vehicle some damage and also involved medical expense for an emergency-room visit by the driver of the other vehicle, who was not seriously injured. The collision took place in Michigan, a no-fault state, between vehicles owned and operated by Michigan residents who had in place the required motor-vehicle insurance. The driver whose vehicle was struck and damaged, and who visited the emergency room, consulted a lawyer regarding recovering those expenses. Which of the following best describes the source of recovery?

A. The driver would look to the at-fault driver's insurer for vehicle-damage coverage and medical-expense reimbursement.
B. The driver would look to the at-fault driver's insurer for vehicle-damage coverage and to his own motor-vehicle insurer for medical expense.
C. The driver must look to his own motor-vehicle insurer for vehicle-damage coverage and to the at-fault driver for medical expense.
D. The driver must look to his own motor-vehicle insurer for vehicle-damage coverage and medical-expense reimbursement.

Answer: D. In no-fault states, those suffering vehicle damage, work loss, or medical expense from motor-vehicle accidents look to their own motor-vehicle insurers for first-party benefits. The driver who owned and operated the vehicle would look to the driver's own insurer. A is incorrect because the driver would not look to the at-fault driver's insurer for any vehicle-damage coverage or medical expense. It is a no-fault system. B is incorrect because the driver would not look to the at-fault driver's insurer for vehicle-damage coverage. C is incorrect because the driver would look to his own insurer for medical expense, which is a first-party benefit.

149. A vehicle owner took his friend for a pleasant drive in the country. The friend fell asleep. The vehicle owner and driver then also fell asleep on a curve in the country road. The vehicle drifted off the road and into a tree, causing a violent collision. The force of the collision fractured the passenger's spine at three levels, leaving the friend with permanent partial paralysis and total work disability. The vehicle owner and driver implored the friend to consult an attorney regarding his $300,000 in motor-vehicle insurance limits, which the friend finally did. Which of the following best describes the liability claim's evaluation, assuming that the accident occurred in Michigan, a no-fault state, involving Michigan residents?

A. The friend has no liability claim because the accident occurred in a no-fault state in which there is no motor-vehicle liability.
B. The friend has no liability claim because there was only a single-vehicle accident and no other vehicle driver or owner to sue.
C. The friend has a strong liability claim based on serious impairment of body function or permanent serious disfigurement.
D. The friend has a strong liability claim only for the work loss and medical expense associated with the accident injuries.

Answer: C. No-fault acts typically bar liability claims for vehicle damage and minor injuries, allowing negligence claims only for a threshold injury such as serious impairment, permanent serious disfigurement, or death. The at-fault owner and driver would be liable to the friend for the permanent partial paralysis and total work disability, which surely constitute threshold injuries. A is incorrect because no-fault states still allow recovery from the at-fault driver for threshold injuries. No-fault acts bar liability for minor to moderate injuries. B is incorrect because passengers may recover from at-fault drivers of the vehicle in which the passenger was riding, so long as the tort threshold is met. D is incorrect because a no-fault carrier would pay work-loss and medical-expense benefits as first-party benefits, not as a liability claim. The liability claim would be for pain and suffering, disability, loss of enjoyment of life, and excess economic loss, not for work loss and medical expense.

150. A motor-vehicle owner insured a vehicle, falsely representing to the insured that there were no minor relatives living with the owner who would have permissive use of the vehicle. The owner's minor son lived with the owner and drove the vehicle frequently with the owner's (his father's) permission, despite having a restricted driver's license for a prior motor-vehicle accident. The son, who had his own insured vehicle, was in another motor-vehicle accident driving his father's insured vehicle with his father's permission. The owner and son claimed first-party medical-expense benefits from the insurer. The insurer requested its in-house counsel to review the claim. Which of the following best describes any first-party issues that the claim raises?

A. The claim raises a benefits issue regarding whether the son's medical expense was reasonably necessary and accident related.
B. The claim raises a coverage issue based on the insured's misrepresentation and a priority issue regarding the son's own vehicle insurance.
C. The claim raises an exclusion issue regarding the son's and father's intentional acts in the vehicle's permissive use and operation.
D. The claim raises no first-party issues, meaning that the insurer should promptly pay the claim rather than risk a bad-faith denial.

Answer: B. First-party claims against one's own motor-vehicle insurer involve issues of coverage, exclusions, priority, benefits, setoffs, and valuation. Here, the owner's misrepresentation raises a coverage issue that the policy may be void, and the son's own vehicle insurance raises a priority issue, that coverage is personal and portable and may first come from the son's insurer before reaching the father's insurer. A is incorrect because the facts do not place in dispute the necessity and accident-relationship of the medical expense. There is not yet a benefits dispute. C is incorrect because the accident was not an intentional tort. The son's operation of the vehicle and the father's loan of the vehicle, though both intentional, do not make the accident intentional. The intentional-acts exclusion would not apply. D is incorrect because there are coverage and priority issues. Denying the claim would not necessarily be in bad faith.

151. A woman suffered moderate injuries in a single-vehicle accident on the way to work. She was not ticketed, although her speed and poor vehicle maintenance contributed to the accident. The woman was a New York resident, and the accident was in New York, a no-fault state. The woman had thousands of dollars in reasonably necessary accident-related medical expense. She also missed several weeks of work and had to hire some home help around the house to get through her recovery, which was complete. The woman consulted a trial lawyer when the insurer began to question some of her medical expense. Which of the following best describes her likely first-party no-fault benefits?

A. The woman may have recovery for pain and suffering, loss of enjoyment of life, and disability.
B. The woman may have first-party benefits for repair or replacement of her vehicle and rental expense.
C. The woman may have medical-expense benefits only and is not entitled to other first-party benefits.
D. The woman may have medical-expense, work-loss, and replacement-service-expense benefits.

Answer: D. First-party no-fault benefits typically include coordinated medical-expense coverage and limited work-loss and replacement-service-expense benefits. The woman had medical expense, missed work, and had to hire household help, so that she may be due all three of those first-party benefits. A is incorrect because it describes non-economic losses not recoverable as first-party benefits. B is incorrect because it describes collision coverage not mandated as a first-party benefit. Also, the woman sought the lawyer's advice when the insurer questioned medical expense, not over vehicle damage. C is incorrect because the woman may also have work-loss and replacement-service-expense benefits.

152. A professional had her finances including insurances reviewed annually by an independent financial advisor to ensure prudent management. She was also an avid recreational enthusiast, including golf, skiing, and running. A 16-year-old driver operated his motor vehicle through a red light, colliding with a vehicle operated by the professional. The collision badly injured the professional, who as a result missed a full year of any work and would never golf, ski, or run again. The 16-year-old driver's insurer contacted the professional offering the $20,000 in insurance limits. The professional consulted a lawyer regarding the offer. Which of the following describes the best advice?

A. The professional should accept the $20,000 offer because recovery of anything more is highly unlikely.

B. The professional should reject the $20,000 offer because the 16-year-old driver should pay more out of pocket.
C. The professional should first determine whether the 16-year-old driver was living with a parent who had more insurance.
D. The professional should first determine whether the professional had purchased underinsured-motorist coverage.

Answer: D. Motor-vehicle insurance often includes uninsured- and underinsured-motorist coverage for liability claims where there is insufficient insurance. The insured may need to invoke that coverage before settling an underinsured liability claim, or the UDIM coverage may be lost. A is incorrect because the UDIM coverage, if available, may be lost by accepting the $20,000 before invoking the UDIM coverage. B is incorrect because although the 16-year-old driver would be liable for excess damages beyond liability limits, it is relatively unlikely that the driver has assets or substantial income to contribute to a settlement, and the $20,000 might be available whether or not the insurer obtains the driver's release. Policies often permit tender of the limits without respect to the insured's release. C is incorrect because the facts indicate that the driver was driving his own vehicle. Living with a parent does not make the parent liable.

153. An employee worked at a meat-processing plant around cutting equipment. The employee suffered a serious injury when the employee tripped over a loose shoelace and fell up against one of the pieces of cutting equipment. The state's Occupational Safety and Health Administration (OSHA) investigated but ruled that the employer had not violated any safety regulations relating to the employee's serious injury. OSHA attributed the employee's serious injury entirely to the employee's own fault. The employer consulted its corporate counsel regarding its liability to the injured employee. Which of the following best describes that liability?

A. The employer will have statutory liability for worker's compensation benefits.
B. The employer will have common-law liability for an unreasonably dangerous workplace.
C. The employer will have strict liability for an ultrahazardous activity.
D. The employer will have no liability given that the employer was not at all at fault.

Answer: A. Worker's compensation acts in all 50 states provide injured employees with limited benefits without respect to fault. The employee suffered accidental injury in the course of employment and would be entitled to worker's compensation benefits. B is incorrect because there is no indication of an unreasonable danger. The worker's compensation act's exclusive-remedy provision would also bar common-law negligence claims. C is incorrect because there is no indication of an ultrahazardous activity of the type for which there is generally strict liability. Also, the worker's compensation act's exclusive-remedy provision would also bar common-law strict-liability claims. D is incorrect because worker's compensation benefits are due without respect to fault.

154. A bartender worked for a national chain grill and pub. Fights outside the front of the pub were relatively common on late summer weekend nights, interfering with pub business. The pub's manager encouraged the pub's staff to step outside from time to time to ask patrons to come inside or move along, and to discourage fights. The bartender suffered injury when trying to quell a fight between patrons outside the bar one night. When the pub's manager discouraged the bartender from making any claims for the bartender's medical expenses and wage loss due to the injuries, the bartender consulted a lawyer. Which of the following describes the best advice to the bartender to recover medical expense and wage loss?

A. Sue the patrons who injured the bartender in the fight.
B. Claim worker's compensation benefits from the pub.
C. File a cause of action for negligence on the part of the pub.
D. Nothing other than check for health and disability insurance.

Answer: B. Worker's compensation benefits depend on showing an employee's injury incident to employment. There is a good argument that the bartender was acting incident to employment when accidentally injured breaking up the fight between patrons outside the pub. The facts specifically state that the pub's manager had asked staff to discourage fights outside the pub because they were interfering with business. A is incorrect because the patrons may be difficult to identify and collect. The call of the question asks for medical-expense and wage-loss recovery. Worker's compensation benefits would provide both. C is incorrect because the worker's compensation act's exclusive remedy provision bars employee negligence actions against the employer. D is incorrect because worker's compensation would likely provide medical expense and wage loss. The bartender may have health insurance and probably does not have disability insurance. Although it would be wise to check for both, the answer choice states "Nothing other than" check for insurance, when the lawyer should advise a worker's compensation claim.

155. A construction company employed a roofer for many years. The roofer's work required that he repeatedly bend over at the waist to set and staple shingles. Over a period of years, the roofer developed a chronically bad back from that shingling work. The roofer's surgeon recommended repair of the herniated discs in the roofer's back from the work. The roofer's back finally gave out at home when he took out the garbage, causing the roofer to accept the surgeon's recommendation and have the surgery. The roofer claimed worker's compensation medical-expense benefits for the surgery and wage-loss benefits for the recovery time off from work. The worker's compensation carrier retained counsel to respond to the claim. Which of the following is the best evaluation of the claim?

A. The surgery is likely compensable under the worker's compensation act because directly related to the shingling work and incident to the employment.
B. The surgery is likely compensable under the worker's compensation act because the act requires all medical expense to be paid during employment.
C. The surgery is likely not compensable under the worker's compensation act because of the progressive condition rather than accidental injury.
D. The surgery is likely not compensable under the worker's compensation act because it was probably the employee's fault for not getting help sooner.

Answer: C. Only accidental injuries are compensated, meaning that progressive conditions generally are not, except for occupational disease. A bad back developed over years of work is a progressive condition treatment for which is likely not compensable under the act without a showing of sudden traumatic injury. A is incorrect because incident to employment is only one condition. Accidental injury is another condition likely not satisfied here. B is incorrect because the injury is likely not compensable, and worker's compensation acts do not require employers to pay all medical expense during employment. D is incorrect because fault is not a part of the worker's compensation equation, and it is not clear that the employee was at fault for not getting help sooner.

156. An employee operated a forklift as a routine part of her job. The forklift started to roll backward with the employee standing next to it. The employee lunged and jumped for the forklift's controls, managing to stop the forklift's roll but injuring her back in the process. Severe back pain from the incident kept the employee out of work for several weeks. The employee made several visits to the chiropractor and had acupuncture in attempts to return to work, finally managing her return on limited-duty status after ten weeks. The employee's supervisor asked the employee not to make a workplace-injury claim because the employer had a perfect record of no workplace injuries. The supervisor asked the employee to apply for unemployment compensation for the time she lost and use her health insurance to cover most of the medical expense. The employee consulted a lawyer. Which of the following best describes the employee's workplace-injury rights?

A. The employee has no workplace-injury rights because there is no indication of anyone's carelessness in causing the injury.
B. The employee has no workplace-injury rights because the employee can recoup the loss through health insurance and unemployment.
C. The employee is due medical-expense and wage-loss damages in a negligence claim against the employer or a fellow employee.
D. The employee is due medical-expense reimbursement and work-loss benefits as worker's compensation act rights.

Answer: D. Worker's compensation benefits typically include coordinated medical expense and limited work-loss benefits. The employee suffered accidental injury incident to her employment and is due those benefits. A is incorrect because worker's compensation is paid without respect to fault. Worker's compensation acts bar negligence claims against the employer and fellow employees. B is incorrect because the availability of some health insurance or unemployment benefits does not bar worker's compensation claims. The benefits may be coordinated. Also, unemployment benefits are not due for the employee's inability to work due to workplace injury. Worker's compensation should pay work-loss benefits. C is incorrect because the worker's compensation act's exclusive-remedy provision bars negligence claims against the employer and fellow employees. Also, there is no indication of anyone's negligence.

157. An employer processed radioactive isotopes used in medical equipment as part of its routine business. A transporter accidentally shipped isotopes to the employer in defective containers that failed to contain the radioactivity. The radioactivity set off the employer's alarms. The employer knew that the conditions would expose employees to harm from radiation but had them perform their usual duties to keep production on schedule. The radioactivity did in fact harm employees just as the employer expected. The employer paid the employees worker's compensation benefits for medical treatment, medical monitoring, and time missed from work related to that harm. The employees consulted a lawyer regarding other claims against the employer. Which of the following describes the best evaluation of those other claims?

A. The employees may have intentional-tort claims against the employer.
B. The employees may have negligence claims against the employer.
C. The employees may have vicarious liability claims against the employer.
D. The worker's compensation exclusive-remedy provision bars all claims.

Answer: A. Worker's compensation acts are an employee's exclusive remedy for injuries caused by employer negligence, although intentional-tort claims are not barred. Here, the employer knew that the employees would be harmed, that knowledge likely satisfying the intent element for intentional-tort claims not barred by the exclusive-remedy provision. B is incorrect because the exclusive-remedy provision would bar negligence claims against the employer. C is incorrect because there is no theory for vicarious liability and would be none given the exclusive-remedy provision. Vicarious liability depends on an underlying negligence action. Employees may not use vicarious liability as a way around the exclusive-remedy provision. D is incorrect because the exclusive-remedy provision does not bar intentional-tort claims.

158. A construction accident involving the collapse of a temporary barrier injured an employee at work. The injured employee required several weeks of rest, physical therapy, and strengthening exercises to prepare to return to work. Shortly before the injured employee was ready to return to work, the employee learned that the employer had fired her without notice weeks earlier, shortly after her workplace injury. The employee was shocked that she had not even had a chance to recover and return to work following her injury. The employee spoke with a lawyer friend about how to get legal help. Which of the following best describes a procedure through which the employee may get help?

A. The employee may sue the employer in a state court of general jurisdiction with the help of a court-appointed lawyer.
B. The employee may pursue arbitration with any health or disability insurers relying on her own self-representation.
C. The employee may pursue an administrative complaint against her employer with the state's occupational safety administration.
D. The employee may locate a contingency-fee lawyer to pursue her worker's compensation claim through an administrative filing.

Answer: D. Worker's compensation claims are resolved through an administrative system in which lawyers working on contingency-fee basis represent the injured employees. This employee likely has a worker's compensation claim. The contingency-fee lawyer would pursue that claim through an administrative procedure. A is incorrect because there is no clear cause of action that would not be barred by the worker's compensation act's exclusive remedy provision and there are no court-appointed lawyers for worker's compensation claims like this one. B is incorrect because there is no indication of any health or disability insurers and no indication of any right to or need for arbitration against them. Also, self-representation in arbitration is not a preferred procedure. C is incorrect because an administrative complaint against the employer for an unsafe workplace may get the employer sanctioned but is not likely to be of any substantial help to the employee.

Essay Question: A contractor's vehicle ran a red light colliding violently with a mother's 2002 Ford Pinto. The collision totaled the mother's vehicle. The collision also required emergency and follow-up treatment of the mother's fractures. The contractor's vehicle was uninsured. He had lost his job recently and not paid the premium. The mother maintained motor vehicle insurance but had opted for no collision coverage. The mother's husband from whom the mother was separated also had coverage. The mother was living at the time with her mother-in-law who also had coverage. The mother-in-law had to help the mother with bathing, dressing, and walking for several weeks. The mother-in-law's husband (the mother's step-father) cut the mother's lawn and did other errands for her. The mother had health insurance, but it only covered 80% of her accident care. The mother was self-employed and could not work for 12 weeks. Her income fell drastically. The contractor also had significant medical expense related to his accident injuries. Identify and evaluate the contractor's and mother's first- and third-party motor-vehicle no-fault rights and claims.

Answer: The question requires identifying and evaluating the first- and third-party rights of a contractor and mother each injured in a motor-vehicle accident after the contractor ran a red light colliding with the mother's vehicle.

This answer presumes the application of Michigan No-Fault Act laws. The answer would be different in jurisdictions have different no-fault acts or having only the common law. Law requires that owners of motor vehicles operated on the public highways have vehicle insurance in place, failing which they lose rights of recovery and are liable without respect to no-fault immunity. First-party rights are for 100% of accident-related allowable expense for reasonably necessary products, services, and accommodations for care, recovery, and rehabilitation, plus up to three years of replacement-service expense at up to $20 per day and up to three years of work loss capped at just over $5,000 per month. Third-party claims are for serious impairment of body function, permanent serious disfigurement, or death, also requiring proof of negligence. Vehicle damage is usually recoverable only through collision coverage and from the at-fault driver only up to the $1,000 mini-tort amount.

Because his vehicle was uninsured, the contractor has no first- or third-party rights and claims. If as the facts indicate the contractor owned a motor vehicle operated on the public highway, then law requires that he insure the vehicle, and under the No-Fault Act one consequence of not maintaining the required insurance is that the claimant loses all first- and third-party rights. Otherwise, the contractor could have claimed first-party benefits for medical expense and any potential work loss (although he had already lost his job, making a work-loss claim problematic). The mother has first-party rights and claims for 100% of accident-related medical expense, which would cover the 20% not covered by her health insurance. These expenses would include the mother-in-law's attendant care. The mother also has the right to up to three years of replacement-service expense at up to $20 per day for the things that others like the stepfather were doing for her (the lawn cutting and errands) that she ordinarily did for herself (or dependents). The mother would also have the right to up to three years of work loss capped at just over $5,000 per month. Work loss includes loss of self-employment income. The mother may also have a third-party claim for her serious impairment of body function based on the fractures and related injuries meeting that tort threshold. If the mother proves serious impairment, then she would recover her non-economic loss (pain and suffering) from the at-fault driver and owner of the vehicle driven negligently. In this instance, though, because the contractor was uninsured, the mother need not prove a threshold injury and may sue for the contractor for all injury, damage, and loss including her vehicle damage, usually recoverable only through collision coverage and from the at-fault driver only up to the $1,000 mini-tort amount.

In sum, the mother has substantial first-party rights and may also have a third-party claim, even without proving the tort threshold because the contractor was unlawfully uninsured. The contractor has no first-party rights because he was uninsured.

Essay Question: A worker was injured while cleaning a plastic-injection molding machine at her workplace. The electrical circuitry was exposed in an area where the worker reached to vacuum dust and debris, with the result that the worker received a severe high-voltage shock, burns to the hands, and nerve injuries. A manufacturer made the machine, which the workplace installed. The worker does not expect to return to work for at least several months. Reports by OSHA investigators indicate that the worker's injury was the result of a combination of the worker's carelessness, workplace training and guarding violations, and a machine defect. What are the worker's legal rights for recovery for her injury?

Answer: The question requires stating a worker's recovery rights when she was hurt in the workplace using a machine having a manufacturing defect and violating guarding requirements, where the worker was also careless and lacked workplace training.

State worker's compensation disability acts require employers to provide security (typically insurance) for accidental personal injuries within the course and scope of employment. A personal injury must be a new pathology, typically a traumatic injury caused at and by work, rather than a slow onset of a degenerative condition caused gradually over time from wear and tear. Comp benefits are typically 100% of medical expense and 80% of work loss. The comp act's exclusive remedy provision bars an employee's negligence claims against the employer but not negligence or products-liability claims against others who are not the worker's employer. A comp carrier would have a lien to recover comp benefits out of any third-party recovery.

Here, the worker may recover worker's compensation benefits from her employer workplace or its comp insurance carrier. The facts make clear that the worker suffered an accidental rather than intentional injury in that she was trying to clean the machine, not trying to hurt herself, when she received a severe shock due to a machine defect. The worker's severe shock causing burns and nerve injuries clearly would qualify as a traumatic work injury and thus satisfy the comp act's personal-injury requirement. The worker's accidental personal injury occurred within the course and scope of her employment as she cleaned a machine at her workplace, qualifying her for the comp act's benefits, typically a 100% medical-expense benefit and 80% work-loss benefit. The comp act's exclusive remedy provision bars her other claims against the workplace for careless training and guarding. Her exclusive remedy against her employer is comp benefits. The worker may however pursue a products-liability claim against the machine's manufacturer, which would pay the worker's economic and non-economic loss subject to the comp carrier's lien to recover comp benefits paid to the worker. The facts indicate that the machine had a defect. If that defect made the machine unreasonably dangerous, then the worker would be able to maintain a tort claim (negligence, strict products liability, or warranty) against the manufacturer. The worker's tort recovery will be reduced by her comparative negligence.

WEEK 12

159. A homeowner kept chickens in an enclosure and structure behind her house, consistent with a local ordinance. A neighbor objected to the presence of the chickens because it lowered home values in the neighborhood. The homeowner disagreed and kept the chickens. The neighbor then reported to police that the homeowner had beaten a neighborhood child, causing the prosecutor to issue assault and battery charges. The homeowner retained criminal defense counsel, maintaining her utter innocence to and perplexity what she believed were false charges. Which of the following best describes the elements that the homeowner must prove to establish the neighbor's malicious prosecution?

A. The police and prosecutor had a conspiracy or other common purpose to harm the homeowner by bringing false charges.
B. The neighbor had made other false police reports like this one, so that the police should not have believed the neighbor.
C. The neighbor had no probable cause and acted with ulterior motive, and the court must dismiss the charges for lack of evidence.
D. The homeowner must plead to a lesser conviction than that charged, or the jury must find a lesser conviction after trial.

Answer: C. The tort of malicious prosecution requires plaintiff to show that defendant maliciously caused criminal charges to issue without probable cause, with the charges resolved in the plaintiff's favor. The homeowner must show that the neighbor had no probable cause and instead acted with malice, meaning with ulterior purpose or ill will. The homeowner must also succeed in having the charges dismissed for lack of evidence. A is incorrect because the police and prosecutor need not be involved in the false report. The neighbor alone may know that the report is false, and that alone would establish malicious prosecution. The tort is complete when a private individual causes charges to issue. B is incorrect because the tort does not require prior false reports. They may be helpful to prove lack of probable cause and malice, but they would not be necessary. The homeowner's gaining dismissal of the charges would be necessary. D is incorrect because the homeowner would not have a tort claim if the homeowner pleads to or the jury convicts of a lesser charge. Plea or conviction would tend to establish probable cause, when the homeowner must prove that there was no probable cause and must obtain the charges' dismissal.

160. A farmer enjoyed the solitude of tending his several fields. A neighbor contacted the farmer asking to buy a small parcel of land at the far edge of one of those fields, adjoining the neighbor's tiny home site. The farmer declined, reasonably suspecting that the neighbor had previously planted marijuana in the farmer's fallow field. The neighbor called the police alleging that the farmer was growing a marijuana crop, in order to pressure the farmer into selling the land. The police used the neighbor's report to obtain charges against the farmer from the local prosecutor. The prosecutor dismissed those charges after further investigation including the farmer's lie-detector test and interview. Which of the following describes the best evidence of the neighbor's malice in the farmer's malicious-prosecution claim against the neighbor?

A. The neighbor probably planted the marijuana in the farmer's fallow field.
B. The neighbor intended the allegation to pressure the farmer into selling land.
C. The police accepted the neighbor's report as a basis to obtain the charges.
D. The prosecutor dismissed the charges after further investigation, test, and interview.

Answer: B. The malice element of malicious prosecution requires plaintiff to show that defendant caused the charges to be issued for a purpose other than to bring plaintiff to justice. The neighbor's motive to pressure the farmer into selling the land was ulterior to the alleged crime report and thus readily satisfies the malice element. A is incorrect because the farmer's belief that the neighbor planted the marijuana would only go to the farmer's intent in not selling the land, not to the neighbor's bad faith in making the police report. C is incorrect because the willingness of the police to accept the neighbor's report tends to show good faith on everyone's part (no knowledge of falsity) rather than bad faith or malice on the neighbor's part. D is incorrect because the prosecutor's dismissing the charges only shows that they were likely without basis, not that the neighbor knew that they were without basis. It is not evidence of the neighbor's malicious state of mind.

161. A small-town, part-time mayor employed at a modest salary stood for re-election. During the mayor's re-election campaign, a citizen who supported the opposing candidate made a false report to a police detective that the mayor had illegally converted tenant security deposits in the mayor's private property-management business. The citizen's report resulted in the prosecutor filing criminal charges against the mayor. The mayor lost the election and had to seek counseling during the debacle over the false charges, which the court later dismissed for lack of evidence. The mayor retained a local lawyer to sue the citizen for malicious prosecution. Which of the following best describes the damages that the lawyer should plead for the mayor in the complaint in that action?

A. Presumed damages, compensatory damages for mental distress, counseling, and loss of reputation and income, and punitive damages if the jurisdiction recognizes punitives.
B. Nominal damages, compensatory damages for pain, suffering, mental and emotional distress, and loss of enjoyment of life, and interference with prospective economic advantage.
C. Work loss, medical expense, replacement-service expense, loss of insurance and related job benefits, lost opportunity for advancement, and other out-of-pocket economic loss.
D. Property-loss damages for loss of office, income, reputation, and amenities, at fair market value for those goods and services, both past and future, plus taxable costs and interest.

Answer: A. Tort law presumes malicious-prosecution damages, although plaintiff may also prove compensatory damages for mental distress and loss of reputation and income, and punitive damages may also be available if recognized in the jurisdiction. The mayor had each of these losses. B is incorrect because nominal damages are unnecessary and not helpful, there is no indication of pain and suffering or loss of enjoyment of life (except perhaps based on the counseling), and there is no business-tort claim for interference with prospective economic advantage. C is incorrect because there is no replacement-service expense, no mention in the facts of lost insurance and job benefits (the compensation may have been cash wages without benefits), no indication of lost advancement, and no other out-of-pocket loss apparent. D is incorrect because there is no property loss and no claim for lost amenities. Also, fair market value is not the measure for personal damages (only property damages). Taxable costs and interests are not really a form of damage. They are procedural costs, not tort damages.

162. A developer retained a contractor to excavate for footings on which to build a new commercial structure. The neighboring landowner opposed the development on competitive grounds. To thwart the developer's new project, the neighbor made a false report to the police that the developer's excavation was a trespass onto the neighbor's land. The prosecutor filed criminal trespass charges but later dismissed them when the developer provided a survey. The neighbor also filed a civil lawsuit on the same false allegations. The developer sued the neighbor for malicious prosecution based on both the criminal charges and civil lawsuit. The neighbor retained counsel to defend. Which of the following describes the best basis for defense counsel to move to dismiss that portion of the developer's claim based on the civil lawsuit?

A. Malicious prosecution is for false criminal charges, not frivolous civil matters.
B. The developer must prove that there was no probable cause for the criminal charges.
C. The developer must prove malice as to the neighbor's filing of the civil lawsuit.
D. The developer must prove special damages as to the neighbor's filing of the civil lawsuit.

Answer: D. Some jurisdictions recognize a malicious prosecution claim for initiating a groundless civil action, but those jurisdictions tend to require proof of special damages in those cases. The developer must prove that the developer suffered some pecuniary loss because of the false report, of which the facts give no indication. A is incorrect because some jurisdictions recognize malicious prosecution for instituting groundless civil lawsuits, where the action causes special damages. B is incorrect because although true that a malicious-prosecution plaintiff must prove the criminal charges are without probable cause, the question here has to do with the civil lawsuit, not the criminal charges. Also, the facts state that the neighbor made the false report to thwart the development, which indicates that there was no probable cause and was instead malice. So this challenge would not help. C is incorrect because malice would be evidence from the false report made to thwart the development. Malice is an ulterior motive, and that motive was present here. The challenge would fail.

163. The human-resource manager of a private company fired an employee for repeated work absences. The fired employee filed a civil lawsuit challenging the firing as discriminatory and moved for a preliminary injunction. When the fired employee learned that the company president was to host a press conference announcing the company's initial public offering, the fired employee obtained a hearing date on his motion at the same time and day as the announcement. The fired employee then obtained a court subpoena requiring the president to attend the hearing in the civil lawsuit. The company's corporate counsel requested that the fired employee adjourn the hearing by a day or permit the president to provide deposition testimony at no cost to the fired employee, so that the president could attend the announcement. The fired employee refused. Which of the following is the best evaluation of whether the company has a counterclaim against the fired employee?

A. The company has no counterclaim, the fired employee having a privilege to lawful process.
B. The company has no counterclaim, the fired employee having a need for testimony.
C. The company has a counterclaim for malicious prosecution without probable cause.
D. The company has a counterclaim for abuse of lawful process for harassing ulterior purpose.

Answer: D. The tort of abuse of process requires plaintiff to show that defendant used legal process for ulterior purposes. The fired employee could have adjourned the hearing for a day or used the president's deposition testimony. Given the employee's refusal, there is a strong inference that the employee had the ulterior purpose of interfering with the company's initial public offering. A and B are incorrect because lawful use of civil proceedings becomes tortious and creates an abuse-of-process claim when the lawful use is for an ulterior harassing purpose. C is incorrect because malicious prosecution involves the issuance of criminal charges without probable cause or filing of a civil lawsuit without basis, not the misuse of civil proceedings for ulterior purpose. The civil lawsuit may have been without basis, but probable cause is a term of art attached to criminal charges, not civil proceedings.

Essay Question: The law-enforcement officer who had signaled a driver to pull over for a non-working tail-light regretfully informed her that she was going to jail—as courteous as she had been and as small of an infraction as was the darkened tail-light. Stunned, the driver asked why. The officer replied that there was a bench warrant for the driver's arrest for uttering and publishing. Later the next day—after the driver spent the night in jail and missed work the next morning—the driver learned that a rental-business owner had falsely complained to the police that she had written the owner a bad check. At the preliminary hearing on the owner's false charges, the driver established to the magistrate judge's satisfaction that she had properly stopped payment on her check the moment she found out that the owner had fraudulently double-billed her. The charge was dismissed. Identify, discuss, and evaluate the driver's tort claim against the owner.

Answer: The question requires identifying, discussing, and evaluating a driver's malicious-prosecution claim against a rental-business owner, when the owner made a false report of a bad check on which police arrested and jailed the driver when stopped for a non-working tail-light.

Malicious prosecution requires the plaintiff to show that the defendant maliciously caused criminal charges to issue without probable cause, with the charges resolved in the plaintiff's favor. The malice element requires the plaintiff to show that the defendant caused the charges to issue for a purpose other than to bring plaintiff to justice. The charges must resolve by dismissal or abandonment, or otherwise in a way confirming that authorities had no probable cause on which to proceed but for the false report.

Here, the driver may well have a malicious-prosecution claim against the owner. The owner clearly caused the criminal charge of uttering and publishing to issue against the driver, when the owner complained to the police that the driver had written a bad check. That charge also clearly resolved in the driver's favor when the magistrate judge dismissed the charge, early enough to show no probable cause. The only potential issues here may be the driver's proving that the owner had no probable cause and proving the owner's malice. The malice element requires the plaintiff to show that the defendant caused the charges to issue for a purpose other than to bring plaintiff to justice. If the owner had in fact believed that the driver had written a bad check, then the owner's complaint would have been with probable cause. The driver stopped payment on the check, meaning that the bank did not honor the check, from which the owner might have believed that the driver's account had insufficient funds and that the driver had in fact written a bad check. But the facts state that the owner *falsely* complained to police, leaving at least an implication that the owner knew when complaining to police that the driver was disputing the billing, not writing checks on insufficient funds. Moreover, the facts indicate that the owner had fraudulently double-billed the driver. Fraud is an intentional tort, meaning that the owner would have known and intended his actions to be part of a scheme to defraud the driver. One can readily argue that every subsequent action including reporting the driver's putative obligation to the police was therefore malicious. The owner's purpose was to complete the fraud, not to collect on a legitimate billing. The owner would thus have acted with malice.

In sum, the driver here should be able to prove malicious prosecution when the owner made a false report of a bad check. The owner should not have used the criminal justice system to address what may have been a civil dispute or to perpetrate a fraud.

Essay Question: A corporation filed suit against its competitor to resolve disputed rights to the use and maintenance of the border between their mining properties. During the course of the litigation, the competitor's engineers worked closely with the competitor's retained counsel to draft discovery requests that would disclose to the competitor the design of proprietary equipment and nature of secret methods used by the corporation in its mining operations. The corporation complied with the discovery requests on counsel's assurance that the disclosures would be used solely in defense of the corporation's action. The corporation discovered after the settlement of the litigation, from a former competitor employee whom the corporation hired, that the competitor was now using the corporation's proprietary designs and secret methods in the competitor's mining operations. Discuss and evaluate whether the corporation has claims against the competitor or counsel for abuse of process.

Answer: The question requires discussing and evaluating whether a corporation has abuse-of-process claims against a competitor and the competitor's counsel for using discovery requests to obtain and use proprietary information on mining practices.

The tort of abuse of process requires the plaintiff to show that the defendant misused existing legal procedures for an ulterior, improper purpose, other than that for which the courts designed those procedures. The abuse is typically of complaints, summonses, and subpoenas. Parties and their counsel may both be liable for abuse of process.

Here, the competitor used a legal procedure when its retained counsel who drafted discovery requests to get the corporation to disclose the design of proprietary mining equipment and nature of secret mining methods. While abuse-of-process claims more typically involve complaints, summonses, and subpoenas rather than discovery requests, the corporation can nonetheless probably show the first element of the use of a legal procedure because discovery is such a procedure. The competitor later used those disclosures in mining operations, with that use clearly improper given the assurance (common in such litigation) that discovery disclosures were only for the litigation. If as the facts imply the corporation can indeed show that the competitor used those discovery requests for that ulterior purpose of stealing the designs and methods for use in its own mining operations, and if counsel also knew of the competitor's intent, then the corporation has claims against both for abuse of process. If on the other hand the competitor manipulated its lawyer counsel and counsel did not know of its intent, and counsel instead only conducted the discovery as a responsible lawyer would have, then only the competitor would be liable for abuse of process.

In sum, the corporation likely has an abuse-of-process claim against the competitor for misusing discovery procedures to steal and use secret methods, as was apparently the competitor's plain intent. Whether counsel is also liable depends on counsel's knowledge of the scheme and intent to misuse otherwise typical discovery requests.

WEEK 13

164. Two diners, one at each end of a small town, struggled to survive hard economic times. The proprietors of each diner admitted to anyone who would listen that only one of them could survive. They each used many means to drive the other out of business. They undercut one

another's prices. They hired away one another's help. They bad-mouthed one another's business to customers. They reported one another to local police. They tried to get the local bank to refuse one another further credit and to foreclose on loans. They even sued one another over spurious allegations. The court ordered their civil lawsuit to mediation before a lawyer who began by addressing their liability to one another for the above acts. Which of the following best describes that liability?

A. The proprietors may have liability to one another for fraudulent, negligent, and innocent misrepresentation.
B. The proprietors may have liability to one another for commercial disparagement and interference with business relations.
C. The proprietors may have liability to one another for competing to drive one another out of business without interest.
D. The proprietors have no liability to one another given the common law's policy to protect economic interests and liberty.

Answer: B. Tort liability extends to protect against harm to commercial interests, either for the commercial disparagement form of injurious falsehood or for interference with business relations, including forms of unfair competition. The above facts describe several acts that could constitute one or more forms of injurious falsehood. A is incorrect because the facts do not describe actions in which either was trying to get the other to rely upon a false statement. They were not scamming one another but instead competing by improper means. C is incorrect because competition alone is not an improper motive, and here the proprietors were competing out of their own interest in surviving. The law protects competition of this type. D is incorrect because the common law, while protecting economic interests and liberty, does not protect improper and wrongful conduct of the type described that harm economic interests and liberty.

165. A developer offered to purchase a property owner's vacant land adjacent to the developer's ongoing project. The property owner told the developer that the property owner was interested and would study the developer's offer. When the developer followed up with the property owner one week later, the property owner said that she was going to sign the offer. When the developer followed up again one week later, the property owner said that she had initially signed but then torn up the offer when she received a better offer. The developer recorded a lien against the property owner's title based on the property owner having signed but not delivered the offer. When the other interested person rescinded the other offer because of the developer's lien, the property owner's counsel demanded that the developer remove the lien because the owner had never delivered the offer, but the developer refused. Which of the following best describes the legal rights and liabilities of the developer and property owner?

A. The developer has a claim against the property owner for specific performance.
B. The developer has a claim against the owner for interference with business.
C. The property owner has a claim against the developer for slander of title.
D. The owner has a claim against the developer for commercial disparagement.

Answer: C. Injurious falsehood includes slander of title, meaning a false statement calculated to harm plaintiff's pecuniary interest by publication with malice causing special damage. The developer did not have an interest in the vacant land because the owner never delivered the signed offer. The developer knew that there was no basis for the lien, which caused the owner to lose the higher offer. A is incorrect because there was no contract, the owner not having delivered the signed offer. B is incorrect because the owner used no improper or wrongful means and did not interfere with the developer's business expectancy or relations with a third party. D is incorrect because the developer did not disparage the owner's trade or business and instead slandered the owner's title to the real property.

166. A grocer grew concerned that a new national chain-store competitor was affecting the grocer's business. Whenever the subject of the new store came up, the grocer told customers that the national chain was under state investigation on price-gouging charges. The manager of the new store heard of the grocer's false statements and reported them to the national chain's corporate counsel. Which of the following is the best evaluation of the grocer's liability for the statements?

A. The grocer is liable for commercial disparagement on the given facts that the statements were false and aimed to discourage customers from using the new store.
B. The grocer is liable for trade disparagement if the new store can prove that the grocer knew the statements were false and caused the new store to lose customers.
C. The grocer is liable for interference with business relations if the new store can show that the grocer violated an ethical standard applicable to competing grocers.
D. The grocer has no liability under any circumstances because the grocer is trying to survive in competition with a more sophisticated and resourceful competitor.

Answer: B. Injurious falsehood also includes trade disparagement, meaning a false statement calculated to harm plaintiff's trade or business, with knowledge or reckless disregard of falsity, causing special damage. The new store must show knowledge or reckless disregard and special damage, not yet given in the facts. A is incorrect because knowledge or reckless disregard and special damages are additional elements not yet satisfied by the given facts. C is incorrect because although improper or wrongful conduct is an element of interference with business relations, the tort also requires proof of special damage of which there is as yet no evidence given. Also, the better claim is trade disparagement, given the grocer's aim to generally discredit the new store rather than interfere with specific contracts or anticipated transactions. D is incorrect because competition as a policy does not protect knowing falsehoods. Competition must be fair. Also, the sophistication and resourcefulness of a competitor does not justify unfair competition.

167. A banker grew concerned about the success of a rival bank in attracting away business customers. The banker learned that his bank and the rival bank used the same software licensor. The banker paid an employee of the licensor for a confidential list of the competitor's customers. The banker then used the list to solicit those customers, with some success, for their banking business. The bank's internal auditors discovered the arrangement and reported it to the bank's corporate counsel. Which of the following best evaluates the bank's potential liability for the arrangement?

A. There is no liability because the banker was merely competing for business.
B. The bank may have liability to the software licensor for injurious falsehood.
C. The bank may have liability to its rival for commercial trade disparagement.
D. The bank may have liability to its rival for interference with business relations.

Answer: D. Interference with business relations is established by proof of intentional harmful interference with a contract or business expectancy by improper or wrongful means. The banker used an improper means to obtain a confidential list of the competitor's customers to interfere with their banking with the rival bank. The bank may be liable to its rival for loss of those customers. A is incorrect because the banker used the improper means of paying a software licensee's employee for a confidential list of customers, creating liability for the lost customers. B is incorrect because the software licensor was effectually part of the scheme, through the willingness of its employee to sell the rival bank's confidential customer list. The banker who bought the list would not have liability to the licensor, which bore equal responsibility for the improper conduct. C is incorrect because there is no indication in the facts that the banker said anything false about the rival bank. The competition may have been without any disparagement. The improper conduct was in inducing the licensor's employee to sell the rival bank's confidential customer list.

168. Two nightclubs competed night after night for the same patron business, each nightclub trying to top the other with events and special offers. Each nightclub would promote its events and special offers through a variety of media including posting flyers on telephone polls and bulletin boards all over town, and leaving stacks of flyers at convenient locations. For the big New Year's Eve celebration, one nightclub paid a young man to tear down all of the advertisements its competitor had posted and to pick up and throw away all of its competitor's flyers. The nightclub had its best New Year's Eve receipts ever, and its competitor did its worst ever. When the competitor investigated and discovered the flyer issue, it consulted with local counsel. Which of the following describes the best evaluation of its rights?

A. The competitor may sue the other nightclub for interference with prospective economic advantage.
B. The competitor may seek an injunction against the other nightclub from holding further events in competition.
C. The competitor may seek an order requiring the other nightclub to publish an apology admitting its competitive wrong.
D. The competitor has no rights, the conduct of the other nightclub being competitive rather than illegal.

Answer: A. The interfering conduct need not be illegal so long as it violates generally accepted business standards. Destroying the advertising of a competitor would violate business standards. The comparative event performance indicates harm to the competitor's interest from the other nightclub's misconduct in paying a young man to destroy the advertising flyers. B is incorrect because the competitor's primary relief would be damages. It may also have a right to an injunction, but it would be to enjoin future destruction of advertising, not to enjoin competitive events. C is incorrect because courts tend not to order parties to publish apologies. That practice may potentially violate First Amendment free-speech rights. Courts will award damages and enjoin future similar misconduct. D is incorrect because the competitor has a tort claim for interference with business relations or prospective economic advantage.

Essay Question: A products company and engineering company sell dies to the same automotive-parts-supplier market. A die is a component of industrial machinery that must be finely tooled to precise manufacturer specifications and delivered timely to meet production schedules. The market for dies has grown competitive. The products company made several die sales to customers who were simultaneously considering purchasing the engineering company's dies. The engineering company's sales representatives heard from some of those customers that the products company's sales representative said that the engineering company was having tooling problems, had lost customers, and was on the verge of going out of business. **What information would you want to know from the engineering company in**

order to be able to properly evaluate its potential commercial-disparagement claim against the products company?

Answer: The question requires discerning the information necessary to evaluate an engineering company's potential business-tort claim against a competing products company that disparaged the engineering company affecting sales.

Commercial-disparagement or injurious-falsehood torts include the tort of trade disparagement. To disparage trade means to run down and harm the reputation of a person or entity in business. The elements of trade disparagement are the defendant making a false statement to harm the plaintiff's trade or business, with the defendant knowing of the falsehood or acting with reckless disregard of the falsehood, causing special damage, which the law defines as pecuniary loss.

Here, the engineering company competed with the products company for the sale of dies. The products company made die sales to customers considering buying from the engineering company. The products company may have made those sales in part by telling intentionally or reckless fabricated falsehoods about the engineering company's alleged tooling problems, lost customers, and near business failure. While the facts state that the products company salespersons in fact made those statements, the facts do not state whether or not the statements were false or the products company sales representatives knew of or were reckless as to the falsity. Thus, the engineering company would have to prove that the products company sales representatives' statements were in fact false, that the sales representatives knew of or were reckless as to the falsity, and the statements induced the buyers to purchase from the products company rather than the engineering company, causing the engineering company loss of sales as special damages. I would need to discover that information to evaluate the engineering company's claim.

In sum, I would require information on whether the products company's statements disparaging the engineering company were false and made by representatives who knew the statements to be false. Although the claim seems clearly worth investigating, one has a lot yet to learn about this claim before determining its validity.

Essay Question: A supplier supplies insulation material to a builder for use in the builder's modular-housing product. The supplier supplies the material on an open-purchase-order basis in which the supplier ships the material at the last price negotiated between the supplier and the builder, as soon as the builder's purchasing manager emails the request for product. A competitor offered an alternative insulation material to the builder, offering to undercut the supplier's price by three percent for a minimum of one year from the date of the builder's first order to the competitor. The competitor's sales agent at the same time warned the builder's purchasing manager that the supplier was having supply-line difficulties—a statement for which the agent had no basis other than an unarticulated suspicion expressed by another of the supplier's customers. **Evaluate the supplier's tortious-interference claim against the competitor.**

Answer: The question requires evaluating whether a supplier has a tortious-interference claim against a competitor who undercut the supplier's pricing but also whose agent warned of the supplier's difficulties based on only an unarticulated suspicion of another customer.

Tortious interference takes at least two forms including interference with contract and interference with business relations or interference with prospective economic advantage. A plaintiff establishes these claims by proving the defendant's intentional harmful interference with a contract or business expectancy by improper or wrongful means. The means need not necessarily be false or illegal. Improper means include violation of generally accepted business standards.

Here, the competitor sales agents would have been perfectly within the competitor's rights to offer a lower price on the competitor insulation. Price competition is a natural, healthy, and generally accepted form of business activity in a market economy. However, the competitor sales agent's warning the builder's purchasing manager that the supplier was having supply-line difficulties, when the agent had no basis other than unarticulated suspicion expressed by another of the supplier's customers, could possibly constitute an improper means of competing. We may need to know more about business practices in this field and the detail of the other customer's communication of the suspicion of supply-line difficulties. Also, the facts do not indicate whether the statement of the competitor's agent induced the builder not to deal with the supplier and instead to deal with the competitor. The supplier would need to establish both of these elements in order to have a tortious-interference claim, when the facts make neither element at all clear. The form of tortious interference, whether interference with contract or business relation, is also not clear because of the open-purchase-order dealing between the supplier and the builder. That arrangement could constitute a contract or simply a business relationship. Either, however, would do, so I would plead both theories in the alternative if investigation showed more facts supporting the supplier's claim.

   In sum, I would not recommend that the supplier proceed without additional investigation to determine the basis for the other customer's suspicion and whether the suspicion was true. The supplier could have a claim, but right now, that claim is highly uncertain.